be thrifty.

"**M**y dad's mother was always my favorite grandmother. Her husband died when my father and his four brothers were teenagers, so they had a hard time making a go of it on their Illinois farm. She was pretty grim and didn't smile a lot, but I always loved going to her home. We visited her on Sundays and she let me play "Isle of Capri" over and over again on her old Victrola. Then I would work a puzzle of the United States that I spread out across the floor. I remember a grandfather clock and a long table where we ate all our meals. She often made me onion soup, which they called onion tea back then. And when my brother Hubert was born, I got to spend the night in the big featherbed that she warmed with a hot brick."

—Marilyn Phillips, born 1929

be thrifty.

How to Live Better with Less

EDITED BY PIA CATTON AND CALIFIA SUNTREE

WORKMAN PUBLISHING • NEW YORK

Copyright © 2010 by Workman Publishing

All rights reserved. No portion of this book may be reproduced—mechanically, electronically, or by any other means, including photocopying—without written permission of the publisher.

Published simultaneously in Canada by Thomas Allen & Son, Limited.

Library of Congress Cataloging-in-Publication Data is available.

ISBN 978-0-7611-5609-3

Workman books are available at special discounts when purchased in bulk for premiums and sales promotions as well as for fund-raising or educational use. Special editions or book excerpts can also be created to specification. For details, contact the Special Sales Director at the address below.

Art direction by David Matt
Design by Julie Duquet
Illustrations by Peter Sucheski

Workman Publishing Company, Inc.
225 Varick Street
New York, NY 10014-4381
www.workman.com

Printed in China
First printing February 2010

10 9 8 7 6 5 4 3 2 1

contents

the big picture
The What, Why & How   vii

the big picture

The What, Why & How

"Cannot people realize how large an income is thrift?"
—CICERO

We're not going to pretend that thriftiness is some new invention we've come up with. Thrift is old. The Pilgrims were thrifty. Ben Franklin was thrifty. You probably have some relatives whom you consider thrifty (though you may call them something else).

What happened? For a while, thrift was all but forgotten—as neglected as an old broom at the back of the utility closet, obscured by a pallet load of paper towels. Decades of prosperity, plenty, disposable goods, easy credit, and one-click shopping made acquisition a legitimate pastime. Frugality seemed hopelessly old-fashioned.

Well, as the saying goes: Everything old is new again.

If you bought this book, or even just picked it up, you're looking for ways to save some money. Congratulations! Intention is the first step. So, how does one go about saving money? It sounds so simple: Live within your means, put some away for later, shop for your needs rather than your whims. But modern life has made it very easy to spend money that we don't have or shouldn't be spending. In some ways, it's harder *not* to spend money than it is to spend. Crazy, right? In the old days, people had to travel great distances by camel to get to the bazaar or wherever it was they went to get their goods. And what was there? Probably a handful of sheep, maybe a little pottery. Temptation wasn't really a factor. Now we don't even need to turn on our computers to buy an array of goods from every corner of the globe—we can just use our phones. Soon you'll be able to think "delicious juicy hamburger" and have one delivered right to your mouth.

In such an atmosphere, cutting back can be a challenge. But adopting a thrifty lifestyle doesn't mean you need to move to an isolated cabin and start raising your own goats. We're talking about a new thrift, a modern thrift, a thrift that takes into account all the complexities and oddities of modern life. It's a thrift with lots of twists, turns, and tricks, along with allowances for splurges and little luxuries. At its core are five simple tenets:

1. Make it or do it yourself—sometimes. Outsourcing tasks in the name of convenience is very modern. It also costs money. Sacrifice some time—within reason and to the extent that it makes sense in your life—and you'll save.

2. Choose and buy carefully. Do you really need the item? Can you get it for a better price somewhere else? Is it the right version?

3. Fix it if it ain't broke. Mend, polish, and scrub away. You'll save money and feel like MacGyver.

4. Use wisely and avoid waste. Save your vegetable scraps for stock, and cook up all the food you buy.

5. Save for the future. The flip side of living in the moment is spending for the moment. Hopefully, you're going to be around for a long time, so weigh the consequences of your present actions against the future.

How We Made This Book

To be a financial wizard, you need a good head for numbers, the ability to read spreadsheets, and a solid grasp of economics. A fancy computer and a lightning-speed Internet connection probably wouldn't hurt, either.

To be thrifty, you need good old-fashioned know-how. You'll be doing more for yourself, so you'll need to know *how*. Which is why, to make this book, we turned to a team of expert fact finders and a library of top-shelf how-to books. Whether you're cooking a chicken, planting an herb garden, or fixing your sink, you want to do things correctly—so why not ask someone who's dedicated pretty much their entire life to figuring out how to cook a chicken, plant an herb garden, or fix a sink? That's how we got from there to here. For more on our contributors and sources, see page 356.

What's in a Word?

Before we go any further, let's pull out our dictionaries and see what we can find out about this thrifty business. Though the word calls to mind the frugal use of resources and careful expenditure, its first definition in the *Oxford English Dictionary* implies a healthy dose of the good life: "the fact or condition of thriving or prospering; prosperity, success, good luck." *Thrift* can also refer generally to the rich, full growth of any plant.

Confused? It goes back to the fact that the noun *thrift* originated from the verb *thrive*. And since its earliest usage more than six hundred years ago in Middle English, *thrive* has meant "to grow

---

You're So Thrifty

A bit of trivia: In its adjectival form, *thrifty* originally meant "having success and good fortune as well as respectability." In Middle English, *thrifti* could mean "rich, healthy, or strong." It could also mean "skillful, intelligent, or of excellent quality." It was an all-around compliment. One famous usage of the word can be found in Geoffrey Chaucer's narrative poem "Troilus and Criseyde." The author praises Troilus, calling him "The thriftiest, and oon the beste knyght / That in his tyme was or myghte be." (The most admirable and very best knight / That existed then or might ever be.)

---

or to flourish, with a clear sense of prosperity." Thriving—which suggests hearty and healthy living—is a challenge and a skill. A creature can thrive physically. We can thrive in a career or in our intellectual pursuits, succeeding through ability and determination. Thriving through adversity is not merely making it through hard times, but rising to meet a challenge and growing stronger.

The noun *thrift* takes its positive implications from these origins, but in recent times it has come to refer more often to "economical management, economy; sparing use or careful expenditure of means." Indeed, as a noun, *thrift* can mean "saved resources": A *thrift institution* is another term for "bank or credit union."

THE OTHER SIDE OF THE COIN

"Thrifty" is simply chock-full of positivity. Further proof: Other words that focus on the use of resources can imply a closefisted attitude or a lack of generosity. No one, for instance, wants to be known as a *miser*. Look back far enough and you'll find that the word's history merges with *misery*, from the Latin *miser,* meaning "wretched or poor"; and *miserly* has retained some of that sense.

Cheap is also no good. It means you simply don't like paying much. Regarding goods, it connotes more than just a low price: It's a compromise in quality. No one, after all, wants to look cheap. And how eager would you be to do business with a company called Cheap Car Rental? If your only concern is holding on to your money, then that's the company for you. But if you're trying to get a good value, *thrifty* is where it's at.

> *"Most people consider thrift a fine virtue in ancestors."*
> —AMERICAN PROVERB, MID-TWENTIETH CENTURY

Your Ticket to the Good Life

The point we're making about the historical connection between the words *thrifty* and *thrive* is not academic (though we're sure the trivia delighted the word geeks among you!). The point is that the practice of thrift isn't solely about saving money; it's also about living well.

Much of the time, you'll find that the tips, recipes, and projects in this book will save you money *while improving your life.* Cutting back on impulse spending will help you control your budget. But it will also help you take more pleasure in that much-needed island getaway or the new pair of boots you do choose to invest in—and even in the old pair of boots you just polished up. Cooking thriftily will lower your shopping bills. And it may give you more time with your family, and possibly even improve your health.

What you won't find in these pages are coupon-clipping schemes so complicated they could qualify as part-time jobs. That misses the forest for the trees; couldn't your time be better spent, say, making money, or even cooking up some beans? (As you'll find out, we heartily endorse beans.) Beyond that, it's about quality of life—we heartily endorse that, too.

Will Thrift Get You to Heaven?

It's clear that thrift will benefit your wallet. But might there be eternal rewards, too? If money is "the root of all evil," is spending less of it a fundamental good? Or, if one is spending less in the moment in order to have more in the long run, might that not be considered self-serving?

It's enough to make your head spin.

Let's back up. It turns out that the New Testament evil-money passage is often quoted without its crucial introductory words: "The *love* of money is the root of all evil." The danger is not money; it's the worship of it. What's more, "A good man leaveth an inheritance to his children's children" (Proverbs 13:22). Thrift is a biblical responsibility!

A Partial Dictionary of Cheap

In the land beyond thrift lies a dizzying array of cheap, miserly, and stingy habits. Here's a partial map of the places you *don't* want to go:

H is for Hoarder. Anyone who has quietly tucked extra packets of oyster crackers into his or her pocket during a meal is a bit of a Hoarder. In hotel rooms, all bets are off. At home, open the Hoarder's cabinets at your own risk: He saves wrapping paper, tin foil, sporks, deli containers, and old Christmas cards. Anything can be reused—and usually is. Woe to those who declare a valuable item "garbage" too quickly. "You're not throwing *THAT* away, are you?!"

M is for Miser. The megalomaniacal Miser has visions of early-bird specials. Searching out anything for a discount and never one for overtipping, he believes—with a near-fanatical intensity—in the value of a dollar. The Miser doesn't haggle; he argues, with the oratorical skill of a defense attorney. He meticulously divides up the bill after dinner to be sure he was not mistakenly charged for a soda he did not order. If pressed, he will say: "It's the principle," but really, it isn't. It's the $1.50.

T is for Thriftitarian. For the Thriftitarian, saving money isn't a necessity. It's a lifestyle with access to cool subcultures: the alt-craft scene, the farm-to-table movement, and the DIY underworld of Ikea hackers. The Thriftitarian sews his or her own clothes and considers *potluck* a verb. He has co-opted the phrase "Living in a van down by the river" as an ironic mantra. Remember to always BYO at any of the Thriftitarian's gatherings and never get him a birthday gift from a big-box store. "It's not homemade? That's just not cool."

S is for Sporadic Saver. The Sporadic Saver has blissfully inconsistent spending habits. He might splurge on an executive suite at a luxury hotel, but then refuse to crack open a can of tomato juice from the minibar on the grounds that it's too expensive. For some, it's the little things that count, but for the Sporadic Saver, it's the little things that are the biggest rip-off. With this artful mix of high spending and low tolerance for markups, the Sporadic Saver maintains a sense of insouciant hedonism while still feeling fiscally responsible.

In Buddhism, attachment to material objects violates a core tenet, one of the three marks of dharma: Everything is impermanent. "Precisely because things are impermanent, we are called to treasure each precious moment as it is," says Ruben L. F. Habito, a professor of world religions at Southern Methodist University. "Because of that, we're not worried about piling up things for the future." But that *doesn't* mean that self-deprivation or the shedding of all material things is the road to virtue. The Buddha, who was born into material wealth and prestige but abandoned that life to seek enlightenment, tried denying himself basic necessities—but he discovered that going without such things as food, safety, and physical comfort was itself a distraction. The message? Beware of extremes.

A Brief History of "The Deal" | by Ruth Graham

"**F**inal sale!" "Unbeatable prices!" "Top quality merchandise at bargain-basement rates!" "Name brands for less!" "Five functions in one!" "Cheap! Cheap! Cheap!" "You just saved $54.99!" The breathless injunctions to snatch up a bargain while you still can are powerful, and they're all around us. How can you *not* jump on this deal? Won't it basically cost you more, in the long run, to pass it by? The justifications are probably all too familiar—who hasn't bought something he or she didn't need because it seemed like an unbelievable steal at the time?

There is an art to sniffing out a deal, but there's also an excess of marketing hoopla out there. And it goes way back. An entrepreneur named Richard Sears (sound familiar?) was one of the earliest pioneers of the tactic of selling cheapness. He debuted the Sears, Roebuck and Co. catalog in the 1880s, and soon it was announcing itself as the "Book of Bargains: A Money Saver for Everyone." The catalog, which included basics like saddles and clothing along with extravagances like magic lantern slide-viewing contraptions, was mailed all over America. Sears also developed a customer profit-sharing program that gave buyers gift certificates for every dollar they spent. Genius move. A customer would justify the purchase of an unneeded sewing machine with the thought that she'd save money on another purchase down the line. In this marketing ploy, Sears anticipated modern credit-card rewards programs by decades.

Other outlets promoted themselves as agents of thrift, too. The Ben Franklin chain of dime stores, which survives today, was founded in 1877 by a man who admired Franklin's frugality if not his instructions to own few things. Other five-and-tens like Woolworth's and W. T. Grants proliferated on Main Streets throughout the country during the twentieth century, carrying a huge variety of discounted dry goods. They later gave way to the slick big-box stores we know today.

Publishers also got into the game. In *Good Housekeeping* magazine, founded in 1885, the recurring character Thrifty Jane offered penny-pinching advice on canning and decorating; meanwhile, the magazine forged its reputation by promoting quality housewares, testing each advertised product in its Good Housekeeping Experiment Station. The Good Housekeeping Seal of Approval remains a standard for household quality and value. It's an unusual arrangement that means more than a simple blessing: If any product bearing the seal malfunctions within two years of purchase, the magazine (rather than the manufacturer) will replace it or refund the purchaser's money. The first installment of the Approved list appeared in 1909 and included twenty-one household appliances. By the end of the next year, almost two hundred products qualified, and the list lives on, now with hundreds of items from vacuum cleaners to shampoo. Thrift and commerce, it seemed, were convenient bedfellows.

For a bracing dose of a truly old-fashioned attitude toward spending, and a reminder of how much things have changed, we can turn to nineteenth-century magazine writer Sarah Hale. With a sternness that has gone almost extinct in the last one hundred years, she wrote with unstinting approval of the devastating 1873 depression: "[It] came just in time to put an end to an era of public and private extravagance, and to bring us back, by a sharp but salutatory discipline, to the economy and plainness of living which should distinguish the people of a republic."

A Greener Thrift, a Thriftier Green

When you go thrifty, money isn't the only thing you'll save: You'll also be going green. Reducing waste means you'll be buying less—and putting less garbage in the landfill. Buying in bulk will get you better prices—and will cut down on packaging made and thrown away. And on and on it goes.

It's no secret that modern industrialization and consumption habits have a lot to do with our current environmental fix. So it stands to reason that by returning to a more moderate way of living, you'll be doing the planet a favor. In every area, we've looked for ways to help you double the green—in your wallet, and in the world's *real* bank.

Thrift and the Long View | by Joseph Epstein

"**A**lways put something by for a rainy day." This and other proverbs, once the very catechism of good sense, came to sound like hollow platitudes in recent years, when we were lucky enough to live in an economic atmosphere of continuous prosperity. Fewer and fewer people asked how much of their income they could save for that far-off rainy day; more and more asked instead how far their credit could be extended in the present. Most unthrifty thinking.

John Maynard Keynes, the economist who advocated for deficit spending (financed through loans rather than cash) by government as a way to stimulate lagging economies, used to say that he didn't wish to hear people talk about the danger of financial schemes "in the long run," for "in the long run," he liked to add, "we all die." Yet the truth is that none of us can know with any precision just how long the long run may turn out to be. Which is why the future-minded virtue of thrift retains not only its pertinence, but also its indispensability.

In the (relatively) long run, thrift, for those who have learned to practice it, results in freedom and makes independence possible. When eliminating waste from our lives, when living within our means, when preparing ourselves for the possibility of radical reversals of fortune in an unknowable future, when behaving, in short, thriftily, we have the good feeling that we are living a well-ordered life, and that is because this is exactly what we are doing.

Thinking in the Future Tense

Thrift isn't only about budgeting. It's also a character trait. To practice it often requires deferring gratification, reckoning the consequence of one's financial actions, thinking a fair amount of the time in the future tense. Sometimes this trait is developed through sound logical thinking, sometimes it is thrust upon people through the force of historical circumstance. The generation that lived through the Great Depression of the 1930s learned it by dire necessity. Anyone who grew up with parents who went through the Depression is likely to be well acquainted with the deep distaste for waste that became part of their personal psychology. "Turn off the lights when you leave a room." "Don't leave the water running needlessly." "It's sinful to waste food." Such were among the instructions with which we all lived and which could be boiled down to a single mantra: "Squandering is immoral."

People who lived through the Depression also tended to believe that it was a cyclical event. They were fairly certain that another depression would one day occur—and that one had better be prepared for it.

On the other end of the spectrum, the father of a wealthy friend of mine used to instruct him that hearses do not come with luggage racks. By this he meant that one cannot take his wealth and possessions with him into death, so he ought to enjoy what he has earned while alive. And yet between enjoyment and profligacy a distinction surely exists—just as surely as there is a difference between spending and being a spendthrift.

> *"It is thrifty to prepare today for the wants of tomorrow."*
>
> —AESOP, "THE ANT AND THE GRASSHOPPER"

The real lowdown on all this, and on the need for reasonable thrift, comes from a man unfortunately unable to follow his own good advice: that charming small-time profligate Mr. Wilkins Micawber, in Charles Dickens's *David Copperfield*. Micawber—a character said to be partially modeled on Dickens's own father, who wound up in debtors' prison—instructs young David Copperfield: "Annual income twenty pounds, annual expenditure nineteen, nineteen six, result happiness. Annual income twenty pounds, annual expenditure twenty pounds ought and six, result misery." And so it is: Spend more than you earn, live beyond your means, and only future disaster can result.

Ask an Economist

Amity Shlaes, Bloomberg News columnist

Q Is thrift bad for the economy?

A The first thing to know is that thrift is not zero consumption—it's a different style of consumption. Thrifty people do spend discretionary funds, mostly on escapism and education—areas where you can get a bang for your buck. Movies. Reading more. Applying for a course that will give you a new skill. The difference is in reprioritizing and thinking about investing—in yourself and in your savings.

As for saving, when you put money in the bank, that money doesn't merely slumber there. It is used by banks to invest. If you're buying bonds, you're helping someone raise capital. If you buy stocks, you are investing in a business. And as soon as the regulatory environment becomes stable, those businesses venture forward and create jobs.

What About the Money?

As you may already have noticed, we've placed the chapter on money, "Thrift & Your Wallet," at the tail end of this book. That might seem a little topsy-turvy. Isn't this, after all, a book about money? Well, yes, and no. Yes, in that it's a book about saving money. No, in that it's not a book about how money works. In thriftian terms, money is simply tender. Managing your money thriftily is not a science. It is, first and foremost, a matter of lifestyle, of managing the *stuff* you buy with your money. That's why we talk about your home, your kitchen—your world—rather than what's happening on Wall Street. But you do, of course, need to tend to your bills and your overall financial health. So if you're starting from a place of credit card debt, fiscal disorder, or just plain money phobia, turn to page 337 and start there. Or go ahead and put it off until the end of the book. Just don't skip that chapter—it won't hurt, we promise.

Putting Thrift Into Action

Everyone has a friend or relative who always seems to walk away with the deals (the floor model, the best table, the sale price), who's never made a single less-than-impeccable purchase (buyer's remorse being the most painful of emotions), who somehow manages to squeeze more perks out of the toniest of vacations (grrrrr). You, too, can transform yourself into a wheeling, dealing wonder. Time to get more out of your money, whether you're working the warehouse club aisles or bargaining down the price of a jacket. First, though, you've got to make sure you really want or need that jacket.

Smarter Shopping

Consumer culture has turned many of us into professional shoppers. But how good are we? We shop with emotional fervor, but we scoop up the merchandise too fast, and we're too trusting of marketing claims and hype.

SMART SHOPPING EDICT BY BARBARA FLANAGAN

We aim to be self-sufficient by owning at least one of everything under the sun (leaf blower to espresso maker). We're obsessed with low prices and mesmerized by new "features" and "options," but we're unable to calculate value: performance over time. When the products disappoint, we toss them and start over, hoping for more exciting relationships but not really expecting our purchases to endure. Where do all of those mistakes go? Underground, incinerated, and out to sea. There has to be a better way.

What would it look like if we found pleasure and pride in living with a small and finite collection of "durable goods" (an economic term for consumer products that last longer than three years)?

Certainly we'd be able to afford better stuff—functional, lovely to look at, easy to maintain, and long-lasting. Remorse-free ownership is a beautiful thing, and in the long run, it's cheaper for us. And its benefits— decreased waste, and possibly less caustic production processes—are just plain urgent for our planet.

How do we get there? By not buying into market frenzy. By thinking before we buy, and by caring for what we have.

A Selective Spending Experiment

Let's talk about some of the invisible shopping most of us are prone to, most often in the realm of entertainment. Take subscriptions, for example. They're so convenient. One click and you're automatically a customer for years to come. The catch? It's easy to completely forget where your money is going. When was the last time you scrutinized your monthly subscriptions and canceled one? Probably never. But compare this with any recent time you went shopping. When was the last time you saw something you liked but decided not to buy it? (Good job.)

To clean house, you'll want to dramatically cut down on unneeded subscriptions on anything from movie rental plans to your cable bill. That doesn't mean you need to forego entertainment. Instead, switch to the "à la carte method" of entertainment shopping.

Here's how it works: Cancel all the discretionary subscriptions you can. Magazines, TiVo, cable, even your gym. Then, buy what you need à la carte:

- Instead of paying for a ton of channels you never watch on cable, buy only the episodes you watch for $1.99 each on iTunes.
- Buy a day pass for the gym each time you go (about $5–$10).
- Buy songs you want for $0.99 each from Amazon or iTunes.

WHY SELECTIVE SPENDING WORKS

1. You're probably overpaying now. Most of us dramatically overestimate how much value we get from subscriptions. For example, if asked how many times a week you go to the gym, chances are you'd say, "Oh . . . two or three." In fact, one 2006 study showed that gym members overestimate how much they'll use their membership by more than 70 percent. Members who chose a monthly fee of about $70 attended an average of 4.3 times per month. That comes out to more than $17 per gym visit. Financially speaking, they'd have been better off buying pay-as-you-go passes for $10 each.

2. You're forced to be conscious about your spending. It's one thing to passively look at your credit card bill and say, "Ah, yes, I remember that cable bill. Looks like a valid charge." It's quite another to spend $1.99 each time you want to buy a TV show—and when you actively think about each charge, you will reduce consumption.

3. You value what you pay for. You place a higher premium on the things you pay for out of your pocket than those that come via subscription.

Should You Buy It?

Before you add any item to your virtual or physical shopping cart, ask yourself the following questions. If you can work your way through the list without flinching, you're well on your way to making a smart purchase.

1. Do I need it?

2. Does it do what I need it to do?

3. Can I fix it myself?

4. Can I wash it in household machines or basins? Does it require professional care or fancy chemicals?

5. Does it take up lots of space, or can it be folded, deflated, or collapsed? Can it be used for double-duty?

6. Is it safe for my family, my neighbors, and all the people who helped make it?

7. Does making it, or using it, use up a lot of endangered materials—petroleum, natural gas, or ancient trees?

8. Does it improve with age? Or will it need to be tossed after a short life span?

9. After its useful life, can it be repurposed or reconstituted into something else?

10. Does it make me happy for reasons I can or can't describe?

SELECTIVE SPENDING IN ACTION

Give the program a shot for two months and see how it feels. If you don't like it, go back to your old subscriptions. But first, do the math:

1. Calculate how much you've spent over the last month on any discretionary subscriptions you have (for example, music subscriptions, movie rentals, and the gym).

2. Cancel those subscriptions and begin buying these things à la carte.

3. In exactly one month, calculate how much you spent on these items over the past month.

4. If you spent $100, try to cut it down to $90. Then $75. Don't try to change the number too fast or too radically—you want your spending to be sustainable, and you don't want to totally lose touch with what's going on in the world. But you can control exactly how many movies you rent or how many magazines you buy, because each one comes out of your pocket.

Remember, this isn't about depriving yourself. The ideal situation is that you realize you were spending $50 per month in subscriptions for stuff you didn't really want, and now you can consciously reallocate that money into something you need or love.

How to Buy in Bulk

For bargain hounds, the lure of warehouse clubs is strong—the cavernous, members-only stores sell groceries and household products in enormous sizes and at steep discounts. Their no-frills format, limited selection, rapid turnover, and reduced operating costs help them keep their prices low. Whereas supermarket and discount chains mark up wholesale prices anywhere from 20 to 40 percent, at warehouse clubs the markup on products is generally between 8 and 14 percent. Beyond bargains on food and cleaning supplies, clubs also offer good deals on jewelry, electronics, appliances, fitness and sports equipment, bedding, furniture, office supplies, toys, books, plants, garden supplies, and automotive products. They even sometimes offer cell phone plans and vacation packages, and some feature pharmacies and vision centers.

But will buying in large quantities translate into savings for you? That depends on the kinds of products you use and how much you use them.

SMART SHOPPING CHECKLIST BY BARBARA FLANAGAN; BULK BREAKDOWN BY ISABEL FORGANG

Most clubs charge a yearly membership fee. To find out if it makes sense for you to shell out the $40 to $50, take advantage of the one-day shopping pass these clubs offer. You'll pay a nonmember surcharge, but you can see just what the store has to offer and if the variety, brands, package sizes, and prices work for you. Before you go, take a quick trip to your local supermarket and make a list of the prices (both unit and package price) you pay for frequently used items. This will allow you to make valid comparisons.

Especially when it comes to dry goods, ask yourself if you have the space to store eight boxes of tissues, sixteen rolls of paper towels, and a twenty-roll package of toilet paper in order to take advantage of all those bargains. Keep in mind that when you have sixteen rolls of paper towels, you may tear through them at a faster rate *because* you have such a large supply. The more you have, the more you use. Can you switch to non-disposable items—towels for hand-drying, sponges or rags for cleaning, cloth napkins for dinnertime? And in that case, does joining a warehouse club still make sense?

Some shoppers find that, given the quantities they use, they are better off waiting for their local supermarket to have a sale, especially if they plan to stock up on the sale item or add in a manufacturer's coupon. On the other hand, shoppers with large families or who entertain frequently will almost definitely find savings in buying in bulk.

THRIFTONOMICS

Bulk Mathematics

How thrifty are warehouse clubs really? Let's get specific. In 2009, Log Cabin syrup costs $1.48 per quart at Costco. At Giant Food Stores, it was $5.32 per quart. **That's a 73 percent savings for buying in bulk.** But at Costco the syrup comes in gallon-size containers, which can be cumbersome to use when you or your kids are trying to pour syrup over pancakes. To solve the problem, decant the syrup into smaller, user-friendly containers. Store the remaining syrup in the freezer. While it won't freeze, the cold temperature will prolong the syrup's flavor.

The same goes for olive oil, another good candidate for savings at warehouse stores. A 5-liter jug of Kirkland Signature olive oil might seem overwhelming, but at only $23.32, that's 14 cents per ounce. A 51-ounce jug (not quite 2 liters) of Bertolli Classico olive oil costs $18.56 on www.amazon.com. That's 37 cents per ounce, or **164 percent more expensive than the price at the warehouse.**

Maximize the Savings

To avoid experiencing shopper's remorse on the grandest of scales, practice mindful warehouse club shopping by heeding the following tips:

Know what you really need and use. With all those titillating bargains, it's easy to run up the bills. Be aware of the extra items you place in that oversize shopping cart.

> ### Socrates on Shopping Overload
>
> Socrates was known to be frugal, and so a friend expressed surprise to find him perusing the excesses of the marketplace one day. Socrates replied, "I am always amazed to see just how many things there are that I don't need."

Store smart. Decant rice, flour, beans, and other staples into small containers to make them easily accessible. Try using a vacuum system—available at supermarkets or warehouse clubs—to prolong the shelf life of both refrigerated items and pantry staples.

Use coupons to save even more. While some clubs honor only store coupons, others accept manufacturers' coupons as well.

Join forces with like-minded friends. You can divide and freeze large packages of meat and fish for multiple future meals, but produce will spoil. Split that bag of romaine with your next-door neighbor so you don't end up storing your bargain in the trash.

Be an educated consumer. Most warehouse clubs don't have much specialized staff on hand to answer questions. So for bigger purchases like electronics, know your stuff before you shop.

Be self-sufficient. You'll likely be packing up your groceries yourself. Think of it as a free workout!

Bargain Like a Pro | by Vibhuti Patel

To get the best price on an item you want, you don't need to run all over town comparing tags. You just need to ask. Or rather, you need to practice the art of bargaining. It's a skill, but one that can be learned. And once mastered, haggling can save you money all over the world.

It happened to me recently during a business trip to Florence, Italy. Four of my colleagues headed for the outdoor leather market where, while I was browsing, the other women made their selections and quickly paid—the asking price!

I picked out two brightly colored wallets and asked the vendor, "How much for this?"

When he answered, I shook my head and started to walk away. He pulled me back with a better offer. I declined. He rattled on in rapid-fire English about the quality of his leather, and I shrugged: "I really don't need a new wallet." He asked, "Signora, how much?" I made my counteroffer. He looked horrified. I pretended to walk away. He grabbed my wrist, nodded, and wrapped up the wallets.

I paid half his asking price.

Witnessing the transaction, my companions were stunned. One asked me to negotiate a fair price for the jacket she hoped to buy. I agreed, on one condition: that my colleague keep quiet and not show real interest.

We found her jacket in a swanky boutique. I calmly asked the elegant saleswoman if she could bring down the price—by a third.

Without batting an eye, the saleswoman phoned her boss and explained, in Italian, "Two Americans are here . . ."

Bargainers' Tips and Tricks

Not a bargaining natural? No need to hang up your gloves and step out of the ring. Though some people seem to be born with the haggling gene, the art of price-point persuasion can be learned. Here's how:

- Make eye contact with and greet the seller when you approach the store or stall. Be polite.
- When you see something you like, stay cool and ask nonchalantly: "Is this your best price?"
- Bargain only when you are in the market to buy; don't bother if you know you're not interested.
- Continue to be confident and pleasant throughout the process.
- Avoid insulting the seller: Know what market prices are.
- When you really want something, leave room to backtrack.
- Buying more than one item will usually get you a reduced price.
- Try to establish good relationships with vendors over time. If you are a repeat customer who occasionally brings along friends, the prices may drop faster.

The deal was struck, Karen charged the purple jacket on her credit card, and I became a star. How did I do it?

I admit, it helps if you've grown up in Asia, where bargaining is like a mating dance—expected, even enjoyed, by both parties. My mother would imperiously feign frustration with saleswomen who came to our home in Mumbai. One toughie would routinely stomp off, only to return the following day, when both sides would resume where they had left off.

But stomping away works only when it is understood within a culture or if you are willing to give up on a deal. In fairness, you must never haggle if you don't want to buy. When you desperately want an item, leave maneuvering room so you can backtrack if necessary.

You don't have to overthink haggling. Try it anywhere. I have, even in America—when there was no recession—for the sheer joy of it. In discount stores on New York's Lower East Side, salesmen would frown at my chutzpah before lowering their "rock-bottom" prices. My favorite was a Pakistani shopkeeper. He'd welcome me, then smile in anticipation as we started our game.

Once, as I haggled over a Walkman, he came clean. "With such a small item, I have no margin," he said. "You realize, Mrs. Patel, my prices shoot up when you walk in because I know you'll beat me down." We both laughed cordially. I knew he was right but I simply could not resist. It was our shared subcontinental culture.

In Dubai, my American hostess took me to her Kashmiri rug dealer who allegedly gave a "special price" to her visiting friends. After finalizing my selections, I borrowed the shopkeeper's calculator, asked "How much?" and reminded him, "I'm buying several pieces, and I'm American now but I was born in India." He chuckled knowingly. We negotiated long and hard—Kashmiris are relentless bargainers—with the calculator shuttling between us. Incrementally, as he lowered the total, I raised my offer. We met midway. He made out a fresh bill, ripped up the original, and made me promise not to tell "the others." My host was wonderstruck.

To my continual surprise, U.S. prices often get lowered in situations where I'd never dream of haggling. I've experienced the slashing of car prices, hotel rates, and fancy foreign tours—even rents. In Virginia, a landlord lowered a reasonable rent—unasked—when I innocently inquired how much utilities normally cost; in San Francisco, a seller's market, a landlord empathized with me as the guarantor of my young daughter's lease because she was job hunting. In both cases, I had not bargained but the rents were reduced because I took the time to make a human connection. It pays to talk, to bond. And to question.

I once asked a doctor's office why I had to pay "so much" when the specialist had spent three minutes with my infant before declaring, "She needs no treatment, her wound will heal itself." The fee was promptly halved. When I got my first parking ticket, I pleaded "guilty with cause" because I was curious to see a U.S. court. The judge heard my "cause," lowered the fine from $40 to $10, and then asked, "Is that fair?" I emerged a believer in the American system: Ask and ye shall be rewarded!

Bring Back Bartering

There's bargaining, and then there's *bartering:* exchanging one commodity or service for another and skipping the money step altogether. While showing up at your hardware store with a bagful of homegrown tomatoes probably isn't going to win you any free lumber, there are plenty of work-arounds outside of the traditional realm of commerce. And you don't have to be a member of an "alternative community" (read: live on a commune) to take advantage of them.

If you don't happen to have a tomato plant or an extra goat lying around, you might be wondering how bartering applies to you. Well, you probably have at least one skill that might be desirable to someone else. Can you cook? Can you write? Can you garden? If you need shelves installed and are deathly afraid of power drills, maybe you can organize a trade with a handy friend; he helps you out with your home improvements, you give him a day's work in his garden or create copy for his website.

There are movements afoot to make such trades an organized practice. Time Banks USA (www.timebanks.org) encourages people to trade their skills and expertise with one another—building community in the process. In this bank, the currency is time. A lawyer with a neglected garden spends one hour giving legal advice to a member of the time bank; the bank gives him a one-hour credit, to be "deposited" at his convenience.

But service-bartering needn't announce itself as such, nor need it be an exact science. All it boils down to is people lending one another a helping hand. It's thrifty to use your knowledge and talents to save money. But it's also just plain kindness and good karma. Help your friends when they need you, and they'll help you.

Barter Among Friends

Befriending a stranger solely to reap the benefits of his artistic talent or special skill set is called "taking advantage." But enjoying the talents and connections of an existing acquaintance is a bonus of friendship. Just ask. Your friends will likely be flattered, and you'll be hooked up. As long as you don't abuse the system (i.e., you should offer a reciprocal gesture), everybody wins.

THE GRAPHIC DESIGNER

It's high time you had a brand, and your graphic designer pal can make that happen. Soon you'll have your own typeface, logo, and business cards for all of your personal marketing needs.

Thank-you gesture. Advertise your friend's work by including a link to his website in your promotional materials. Bring a crowd to the opening of his obscure "installation."

THE PHOTOGRAPHER

Shoots your wedding, takes flattering photos of you for your online profile. Note: Do not be demanding or attempt to direct the photo shoot.

Thank-you gesture. Fly your friend to the wedding or pick up the cost of her hotel room.

THE FASHION DESIGNER

Tailors you a chic blazer and helps you find the on-trend pants. Gets you to the best sales in town.

Thank-you gesture. Offer to write a press release or stand around your friend's studio with a clipboard, head-set, and severe expression to cultivate mystique.

THE CHEF

Demonstrates the art of leftovers, helps you ramp up your knife skills, and cooks you a sumptuous birthday dinner, sparing you all the cost and pain of going out to some overpriced tapas place where there are never enough manchego-stuffed mushroom caps to go around.

Thank-you gesture. Invite your friend over for dinner. It may be nerve-racking for you, but chefs are often so tired of cooking for others that even your clumsiest casserole will win raves.

THE MUSICIAN

Plays a gig at your home (or in your backyard), negating the need for pricey concert tickets; can write a song for your significant other that you pass off as your own; will teach you how to play the opening chords of "Louie Louie" so you can be part of the jam.

Thank-you gesture. Handle the merchandising: Make T-shirts and stickers, sell CDs, and create a specialty cocktail in honor of the band. Oh, and don't forget to be a really big fan.

The Lessons of Thrifty Millionaires

How do the rich get that way? One old-fashioned way is by saving: Putting into the bank more than comes out. That's equally true for everyday folks and world-renowned business leaders. To prove that thrift and big money can go hand in hand, here's a look at how ten big savers socked their funds away.

Secret Millionaires

When stealth savers pass on their wealth, it often comes as a surprise to their community. These five people devoted their lives to hard work, leaving money—and lessons—behind for others.

1. Work that overtime. Paul Navone worked for 50 years at glass factories in Millville, New Jersey. Over the years, working all the overtime he could get and saving most of his paycheck, he accumulated quite a nest egg. In fact, in 2007, at age 78, he gave $1 million to the local Catholic high school for a new swimming pool, and another $1 million to Cumberland County College for a new nursing education program. Not bad for someone who never made more than $11 an hour.

2. Be handy. Joe Temeczko, a Polish immigrant and former prisoner of war, lived a very frugal life in Minneapolis. He worked as an odd-job handyman, lived in a modest house, scavenged the streets for junk he could fix up and sell, and even read newspapers in the shop so he wouldn't have to buy them. After the attacks on September 11, 2001, Temeczko rewrote his will, leaving his savings to the City of New York. To the surprise of nearly everyone who knew him, those savings totaled $1.4 million. New York City used part of the bequest to fund the Daffodil Project, a living memorial to the victims of September 11.

3. Think big, live small. Even his own family was shocked when in 2003, Joseph Leek left nearly $1.8 million to an organization that provides guide dogs for the blind. Leek had lived a deeply frugal life: He wore secondhand clothes, stinted on house repairs, and watched television at a neighbor's to cap his electricity costs. He'd quietly made his fortune by investing in the stock market.

4. Live small, give big. The son of a sharecropper, James Ebbert of Quakertown, Pennsylvania, owned a lumber business. He invested his money well but lived modestly. Few people realized he had saved a substantial fortune by the time of his death, at age 90, in 2007. He left $10 million to local nonprofits, including two hospitals, two universities, three churches, two private schools, a local fire company, the local YMCA, and the Salvation Army.

5. Do what you love. Reverend Vertrue Sharp never had much income, but he saved every penny he made raising hay and cattle, preaching, and teaching. When he died in 1999, he left an estate of $2 million to various charities.

. . . and Famous Millionaires

Business innovators tend to amass impressive personal fortunes. But the smart ones don't blow it on yachts and private jets. Take a tip from this gang of five and you could have a healthy bank account, too.

1. Set an example. Sam Walton (1918–1992), the founder of Wal-Mart, was one of America's richest men. He was also famously frugal, not only in his own habits but in the mindset and practices he fostered in his employees. He bought his suits off the rack (at Wal-Mart, of course) and drove a beat-up old pickup, which he defended by saying, "Am I supposed to haul my dogs around in a Rolls-Royce?"

2. Stick to your principles. Ingvar Kamprad (born 1926) started making money at age six by buying ten-packs of matches and selling the individual books at a profit. Now, as the founder of Ikea, he is a multibillionaire, but he still knows the value of a kroner. He flies coach, drives an old Volvo, eats at bargain restaurants—and expects his employees to do the same. When an Ikea manager asked to fly first class for a meeting, Kamprad snapped, "There is no first class at Ikea."

3. Keep it simple. Warren Buffett (born 1930), one of the richest men in the world, lives in the house in Omaha, Nebraska, that he purchased in 1958 for $31,500. His wife once said of his simple tastes, "All Warren needs to be happy is a book and a sixty-watt bulb."

4. Be detail-oriented. John D. Rockefeller Sr. (1839–1937) was a self-made man who hated to waste a penny. In the early 1870s, during a visit to a Standard Oil plant, he watched a machine solder the lids on kerosene tins. He asked a worker how many drops of solder were used on each can. Upon learning that it was forty, he asked if thirty-eight drops would work instead. Thirty-eight proved unreliable, but thirty-nine worked perfectly and became standard practice at all his refineries. Recounting this story years later, Rockefeller said, "That one drop of solder saved $2,500 the first year; but the export business kept on increasing and the saving has gone steadily along, one drop on each can, and has amounted since to many hundreds of thousands of dollars."

This was a lesson he never forgot. Toward the end of his life, at his home in Florida, he was sitting in front of the fire when he asked his butler, "How long are those sticks of wood?" Upon being told they were fourteen inches long, he asked, "Do you think they would do just as well if they were cut twelve inches in length?"

5. Get real. Queen Elizabeth II (born 1926) has always paid attention to pounds and pence, but recently she has urged her family to be even more frugal (as frugal as a family that hops from one palace to another can be). She has been rewearing outfits to official events (a practice at odds with traditional court etiquette), and her husband, Prince Philip, still wears the Royal Navy uniform he wore to his wedding more than sixty years ago. The Queen insists that the lights in empty rooms in Buckingham Palace be turned off, and that any leftovers from banquets not be thrown out. Thanks to her economizing, annual expenditures have dropped from £87.3 million in 1991–1992 to £40 million in 2007–2008.

be thrifty.

inside this chapter . . .

PROJECTS

home, sweet (thrifty) home

Clean It, Fix It, Love It (Drive It)

YOUR HOME SHOULD BE YOUR CASTLE—PARTICULARLY IF YOU are the Sovereign of Savings. Staying in is guaranteed to save you money, whether your activities consist of dinner and a movie, cocktails with friends, or leisurely weekends on the couch. And whether your place is a downtown shoebox or a suburban split-level, it needs to be comfortable—for you and for your guests. The better it feels, the more time you'll spend there.

Of course there's another angle: householding can cost a bundle. And this holds true for everyone, owner and renter alike. Eventually we are all confronted with that room that needs repainting, a pile of books in need of a home, a running toilet, a leaky roof, or a dirty floor. Even the most frugal apartment-dwellers need furniture and a tasteful place to hang their hats. With some elbow grease, planning, and direction, there's much you can repair, spiff up, and maintain without hiring a pro or draining your bank account.

One of the most immediate and noticeable advantages of keeping your home in shipshape condition is a reduction in utility bills and repair costs. Well-maintained houses, and the appliances and furniture that fill them, last longer and serve you better. That also applies to the beast lurking in the garage. Saving money on your ride can be as simple as keeping the tires fully inflated—and not being afraid to lift the hood.

From cleaning and organization to upkeep, decor, and furnishing, there are loads of ways to keep a thrifty home. Find what works for you and yours, and get ready for some serious nesting.

Clean, Lean & Green

Want to save money on cleaning products? Don't just head over to the ninety-nine-cent store and load up on a slew of off-brand scrubs and sprays. If the global environmental repercussions of chemical cleaners don't seem like enough of a motivator—let's face it, sometimes organic has to take a backseat to cheap—consider your health: The fumes of corrosive cleaning products will stick around in a sealed environment, causing air pollution inside the home. The good news is that "green" cleaning products don't have to be expensive—quite the opposite. Stick with a few multitasking basics and you'll actually spend less.

Naturally Clean

I f you are looking to green your cleaning regimen but don't want to go broke in the process, baking soda and vinegar will be your new best friends; but castile soap is also a good product to know about. The typical liquid dish or laundry detergent bought from the grocery store today is made from a petroleum distillate, a toxic pollutant and nonrenewable resource. Castile is made from coconut or olive oil, both renewable resources, and is a natural and readily biodegradable alternative.

The stuff's primary selling point is that it's supremely multipurpose. It can go everywhere: in the washing machine (one quarter cup per load), in squirt bottles for hand, dish, and body washing, and in garden remedies and natural-cleaning formulas. So instead of shelling out for a cartful of various bottles of detergents, soaps, and cleaners, one product takes care of it all. (Just think how much room you'll have under the sink. . . .) Granted, castile soap is a hefty investment up front—generally $20 to $30 a gallon. But consider this: Cleaning formulas made with castile require only a few tablespoons of the stuff at a time. And it costs about half what you'd pay for an all-natural shower gel. So compared to other all-natural cleaners out there, it's a great buy.

The Essential Cleaning Toolkit

Some homeowners are notorious overcleaners. On the assumption that cleaner is better, they buy expensive, overachieving cleaning equipment designed for allergy sufferers and other sensitive people: superfiltering vacuum cleaners, sanitizing dishwashers, mite-proof mattress covers, ionic air cleaners. But most cleaning tasks can be performed with man-powered tools that work as extensions of the hands. Need convincing? Here are a few examples—some newfangled, others time-tested—of simple tools that really deliver.

THE MIRACULOUS MICROFIBER MOP

The remarkable thing about floor cleaning is that it has resisted innovation for so many millennia. You can ponder this mystery firsthand by visiting any hospital room. No matter how many supersophisticated, phenomenally costly machines surround the patient being treated with hypersanitary products and advanced pharmaceuticals, the nightly floor-cleaning ritual remains archaic: Equipped with a heavy mop made of cotton yarns and two large buckets of soapy water, a janitor enters the room, dips his mop into the first bucket, swirls the solution over the floor, rinses and wrings out his mop in the second, and repeats.

Turns out there is a better way: the microfiber mop. It can dust, wash, and polish floors more thoroughly—and antibacterially—than any mop ever made, using nothing but water.

How? It's all about the fiber. A microfiber is a very thin, synthetic fiber that's finer than one denier; that's about one hundred times thinner than a human hair. High-quality microfiber starts with Grade A yarn or better. When it's the real thing, it absorbs about seven times its weight in water, dries out two or three times faster than cotton, refuses to grow mold

---

Where to Find Castile

Castile can be found in liquid or solid form in health food stores and some supermarkets. One of the best-known brands is Dr. Bronner's, which comes in concentrated form and pretreated with herbal oils, though there are several other brands on the market (check the Internet for sources).

Hospital-Approved for Thrift & Performance

Microfiber is impressive, but will it save you money? In 1999, the University of California Davis Medical Center launched a case study with a cost-benefit analysis comparing conventional mopping to microfiber mopping. The results? The microfiber mop's slightly higher initial cost was offset by a savings of 95 percent on chemicals, 60 percent on lifetime mop costs, 20 percent on labor, and less water, too.

and mildew, sheds no lint or other allergens, holds its shape, and can be machine-washed hundreds of times.

Microfiber is made of two polymers: polyester, the most common man-made fiber, and polyamide, also known as nylon. Each fiber is composed of a star-shaped polyester core, with wedge-shaped polyamide filaments fitting into its grooves; its microscopic thinness is achieved via a dousing of chemicals during the dye-bath stage.

This complex, porous geometry helps the resulting textile collect dirt and hold water. A dense concentration of fibers—90,000 to 200,000 per square inch—creates a large surface area, essential for absorption and release. The material has abrasion on its side as well: Its sharp filaments scrape surfaces clean; used dry, they gather static electricity to attract dust.

How do you use a microfiber mop? Lightly dampen the mop pad with water, slap it on the floor, and press the Velcro-ed mop head onto the pad. Note how quickly you can mop a whole room. When the pad looks dirty, either rinse it or change to a clean pad. Let the floor air-dry or give it a glossing over with a dry pad. After cleaning, toss the pads in the washing machine or hand wash, then let air dry.

THE HUMBLE CORN BROOM

No matter the advances in technology, the corn broom is still considered irreplaceable as a serious tool of commercial cleaning. It has an uncanny ability to sweep rough surfaces as well as smooth ones, indoors or out. It doesn't just move dirt around; the fine hairs at the end of its bristles grab onto particles and move them farther up into the broom. It doesn't require much manpower; a gentle sweeping action is surprisingly efficient. As with all the best stuff, the tool improves with age: Its bristles soften, and when they finally wear out, the whole tool can be composted.

The Multitasking Microfiber Cloth

The microfiber revolution need not be confined to the floor. Try cleaning your windows with two microfiber cloths and plain water: Wet one cloth, clean one pane of glass, and polish with a dry cloth. Keep rinsing the wet cloth and keep going. The sparkling, unlinted, unstreaked glass will disprove all the contradictory advice you've gleaned about proper window washing. Branded blue chemicals, precise vinegar recipes, professional squeegees, rags, newsprint, and paper towels all become ancient history. What else can you clean with a microfiber cloth? Just about anything. A few ideas:

- Dry-dust electronic screens and other fragile equipment, along with mirrors, tabletops, and countertops.
- Clean those surfaces that the strongest chemicals just seem to smear: fingerprinted stainless steel appliances, sinks, and greasy glass cooktops, for example.
- Remove water spots, soap scum, and tub rings. No endless scrubbing, no scary foams.
- Polish accessories like eyeglasses, jewelry, purses, and shoes.
- Spot wash and dry carpet spills.
- Clean an entire car—from upholstery to control panel, washing, drying, polishing, and buffing—with nothing but water.

Light sweeping in between major cleaning can actually help to maintain floor coverings, as small dirt particles tend to scratch hardwood finishes and wear down rug fibers. And the more often that broom comes out, the less onerous that weekly or biweekly vacuuming and mopping session will be.

THE NONTOXIC TOILET BRUSH

There's nothing glamorous about a toilet brush—nor should there be. The *real* innovation is in how you use the thing.

Television commercials have taught us that we need to gear up like hazmat agents while pouring toxic potions into the dreaded bowl. Unnecessary, even in that gnarliest of places. Instead, use some distilled vinegar in a spray bottle. For light cleaning, just spray in the bowl and around the rim, and scour lightly with the toilet brush. For heavier cleaning, add a couple of cups of vinegar to the bowl and close the lid. Walk away for a couple of hours, then brush the insides of the bowl as usual.

Make Your Own Cleaning Products

If you want to try your hand at making your own cleaning products, castile soap and water can do the job alone. But there's another key ingredient. Ever notice how many commercial cleaning products feature citrus oil among their vaunted ingredients? You can get the same antibacterial effect by adding a few drops of orange or lemon essential oil to your soap, and you'll save money and packaging. Essential oils are available at most natural food markets and online, don't cost much (generally around $5 for half an ounce), and are incredibly potent—if you decide to use them, exercise restraint!

The following all-natural formulas are a great place to get started—though if you want to save yourself the labor, you can also try purging all cleaning products but for dish soap, laundry detergent, and baking soda and vinegar (see chart, page 10).

RECIPE | Pine-Fresh Floor Cleaner

If you haven't yet converted to microfiber mopping (see page 5), try this natural formula. It works just as well as commercial pine solvent cleaners, but leaves a light scent more reminiscent of a pine forest than a bucket of chemicals. You can adjust the scent to your preference by increasing or reducing the amount of essential oil used.

- 1 gallon hot water
- 2 tablespoons liquid castile soap
- 10 drops pine essential oil
- 5 drops cypress essential oil

Combine all ingredients in a large bucket. Dip a mop into the bucket and squeeze out excess liquid. Clean the floor by working in sections, using short strokes and dipping the mop as needed. Rinsing is not necessary.

FORMULAS BY KARYN SIEGEL-MAIER

RECIPE | ## Herbal Dishwashing Blend

The essential oils in this blend have antibacterial, as well as aromatherapeutic, qualities. Plus, it just smells lovely.

> Liquid castile soap
> 10 drops lavender essential oil
> 8 drops rosemary essential oil
> 4 drops eucalyptus essential oil

Fill a clean 22-ounce plastic squirt bottle with castile soap (diluted according to directions if using concentrate). Add the essential oils. Shake the bottle before each use. Add 1 to 2 tablespoons of the liquid to the dishwater and wash as usual. (*A note:* This blend is not suitable for use in dishwashers.)

RECIPE | ## Fragrant Wood Cleaner

This fragrant formula will clear away sticky grime and is safe for most finishes. But always test wood-cleaning formulas on an inconspicuous area of your furniture, like the inside of a leg or a panel underneath, before treating the entire piece. This step is a very important one, as certain wood finishes can be adversely affected by essential oils.

> ½ cup lemon juice
> 1 teaspoon liquid castile soap
> 4 drops bergamot, geranium, or sweet orange essential oil

Combine all ingredients in a small plastic spray bottle. Apply to wood and wipe clean with a damp cloth. Wipe again with a dry cloth.

The Freshest Linens

Trusty castile soap and distilled vinegar are all you need to clean and soften your linens (¼ cup soap per load and ½ cup vinegar with the rinse cycle and presto!). Throw in ½ cup of baking soda if you need a laundry booster, and a couple of drops of essential oils in the soap or vinegar if you like your towels and sheets to smell like something other than clean cotton. Do know that fabric softener (including vinegar) decreases towel absorbency. Use it only monthly on towels, if at all.

The Miracles of Baking Soda and Vinegar

Beloved by satisfied cleaners all across the land, baking soda and distilled white vinegar are the stuff of legend. Odor, germ, and bacteria removal, laundry softening, heavy-duty scrubbing—they can do it all. Buy them in bulk, and get ready to fall in love all over again.

Baking Soda: The Scrubbing, Odor-Neutralizing Wonder

Baking soda is the trade name for the chemical compound sodium bicarbonate. In baking, it's used to help foods rise. (When heated and combined with acids like buttermilk or lemon, it gives off carbon dioxide—basically, the air that puffs up your cookies.) Around the house, it absorbs grease, odors, and stains, and scours gently. But it is so versatile that you're bound to discover uses beyond those listed here. If you become a convert, check out the cyberworld of baking soda acolytes—a busy and very clean clan.

CLEANING

As a multipurpose cleanser on kitchen surfaces, cutting boards, ovens, barbecue grills, grout, bathroom surfaces, toilets, washable painted walls

To shampoo your carpet or remove pet stains

To boost liquid laundry detergent—add ½ cup soda per load

As a spot-treatment—make a paste and apply to stains before laundering

To remove water spots from wood—apply a soda solution with a damp, not wet, rag

To clean stainless steel and chrome without scratching

To degrease dishes—add to hot sudsy water or sprinkle on dishes in dishwasher

To clean and deodorize your coffeemaker—brew ¼ cup soda and 1 quart water

To clean pans with burnt bottoms—soak the pan in water and ½ cup soda overnight

HOUSEHOLD

To deice stairs and walkways

To deodorize anything—fridge, plastic food containers, litter box, trash can, laundry hamper, vacuum bags, carpet, upholstery, feet . . .

To extinguish small flare-ups on the stove—water won't put out a grease fire

To make air freshener—combine soda and scented bath salts and set out in a dish

To gently clean tarnished silverware and jewelry—place silver on a sheet of aluminum foil in a pan of hot water and soda for 10 minutes. Rinse and wipe with soft cloth.

To remove rust from metal—make a paste of soda, wipe onto rust, scrub it off with a ball of aluminum foil

To remove doggy smell—brush into your dog's fur

As a garden pesticide—see page 91

GROOMING & HEALING

To make odor eaters—fill old stockings with baking soda and keep them in stinky shoes

As deodorant—sprinkle it on straight

To soften bathwater

As mouthwash—one teaspoon per cup of water

To soak dentures

To soothe sunburn—soak in lukewarm water and soda

To alleviate heartburn—½ teaspoon soda in ½ glass of water

To relieve bug bites and bee stings—make a thick paste and apply directly

Vinegar: The Disinfecting, Squeaky-Clean Phenom

Distilled or white vinegar, which is a 5 percent acetic acid solution, kills 99 percent of bacteria, 82 percent of mold, and 80 percent of germs—but is nontoxic to humans and animals. (In fact, it's the key ingredient in pickles!) The nasties can't survive vinegar's acidity. The acids also dissolve mineral deposits and soap scum, hence the softer laundry and clean windows.

CLEANING

To clean and sanitize sinks, countertops, doorknobs, toilets—instead of bleach

To clean and prevent mold and mildew in the shower and on grout

To wash windows and glassware

To make dishes sparkle and prevent soap buildup, add ½ cup vinegar to the dishwasher's rinse cycle

To remove tough grime on the top of the fridge, or anywhere grease accumulates

To clean stone, slate, and ceramic tile floors without residue—1 cup vinegar per gallon of water

To boost floor-cleaning solutions—add 1 cup vinegar and a few drops liquid soap to 2 gallons warm water

To get rid of calcium or lime deposits on faucets and showerheads

As a fabric softener—add ¼ cup to the rinse cycle

To whiten dingy whites—soak them overnight in a pot of very hot water and 1 cup vinegar

To remove tough underarm stains on clothes—spray on before laundering

To remove salt and water stains on leather shoes

HOUSEHOLD

To kill ants and fruit flies, and keep them away

To keep cats and critters away from your yard or trash cans

To polish brass, copper, and pewter—mix equal parts salt and vinegar into a paste

To polish chrome hubcaps

To dye Easter eggs—combine 1 cup hot water, 1 tablespoon vinegar, and food coloring

As an air-freshener spray—combine vinegar with essential oil, vanilla extract, or a drop of perfume

To kill weeds, in sidewalk cracks or anywhere

GROOMING & HEALING

To soothe minor burns, sunburn, and rashes—soak a cloth in vinegar and lay it on the area

To add highlights or get rid of dandruff—rinse hair after shampooing with 1 cup vinegar in 2 cups water

As a gentle aftershave lotion

As a face toner and to clear up breakouts—combined with equal parts water

To fight stubborn athlete's foot and toenail fungus

To relieve yeast infections

Use Baking Soda and Vinegar Combined

As an Earth-friendly drain cleaner. Pour 1 cup soda then 1 cup vinegar down the drain. Rinse with boiling water.

The Handy Householder

You don't need to own a pair of paint-spattered overalls or a case full of drill bits to be handy. There are lots of small and easy fixes that are within (almost) everyone's skill set—with the right tools, instructions, and a realistic sense of your limitations. (If you aren't 100 percent sure where to turn off your water valve, for instance, it's not wise to start taking your sink apart.) But even taking on a few simple tasks will save you money—and not just on professionals' fees. For homeowners, home maintenance is especially thrifty: Whether you pay an expert or DIY, small repairs can prevent the need for larger, more expensive ones down the line and may affect your home's resale value.

"I Did It All Myself . . ." | by Suzy Ibarra

When I was a young mother, I did every sort of home repair and project you can imagine. Having left England as a single woman, I came back as a divorced mother with no support. I had to start from scratch, with no money. My sister and her husband had just bought a derelict sixteenth-century farmhouse, so my baby daughter and I moved in with them. Together, we made it habitable.

It was an old English house that hadn't been lived in for so long, plants were growing through the walls. Well, we broke through a few walls, and in doing so, we found an enormous old fireplace. Time to clean the chimney. We borrowed the brushes and became chimney sweeps for a day.

There were several windows with no glass. One day I went to the grocery store and saw that some hooligans had broken a window there. I said to the chap, "Can I have the glass?" I took it to the glass cutter, and we got two windows out of that.

Eventually, I got a job and saved up enough money for a down payment on a house. And I learned how to fix everything in that house, too. I didn't have the money to hire anyone.

When a friend of mine decided to install new carpet, she was going to throw away the old one. I said: "Right. I'll take that!" In addition to laying carpet, I put down all my own tile in the kitchen and dining room, as well as the bathroom floor and walls. It's quite easy to do, and I recommend buying a tile cutter. It's a good investment. Also in the bathroom, I built wooden boxes to hide the water pipes. With those you have to use tongue and groove: If you need to fix a leak, you have to be able to open up the wooden box and get at the pipes.

It was rare that I called a plumber. I did have a couple of overflow problems in the bathroom, but I would make a little wire piece or adapt something to fix a problem. I did only one electrical project though: I'm terrified of electricity.

The Keys to the Handy Kingdom

Being handy is a matter of following simple imperatives—a combination of common sense and practical get-down-on-your-hands-and-knees experience. With the right tools and some basic know-how, you can cut way back on those emergency repair calls and enjoy the distinct satisfaction of self-sufficiency. But follow these guidelines to ensure that your handiness doesn't become foolhardy, and expensive:

- Adopt the physician's creed: Do no harm. There's no sense in trying to take apart a bathroom faucet if you can't tell a washer from a valve seat. A botched job may seriously complicate the plumber's task and turn your attempt at thrift into a nasty surprise.
- Be realistic. Very intelligent people sometimes believe they can figure out anything, given the inclination. But electrical wiring is not logic or psychology. Learn how. Don't try to wing it.
- Make a friend at your hardware store or home supply outlet. The staff members in these places are great resources for information on which tools and materials are right for your project, and the good ones will give you tips on doing the job. If you're out to pick an expert's brain, plan your visit for a weekday. (Large discount centers can be problematic on weekends, when they may staff up with less helpful part-timers.)
- Read the directions. They may be written in pidgin, but the directions for the tool, adhesive, or replacement part can keep you out of trouble. Ditto for diagrams.
- Own a real toolbox. You need more than the few tools you stuff into your junk drawer. Get yourself a divided toolbox and start filling it with real tools. Assemble a basic toolbox like the one on page 16, and you'll be equipped to tackle just about anything that needs fixing.

HANDY KINGDOM TIPS BY ANNA JOHNSON

Ask a Home Repair Expert

Alex Bandon, editor, *This Old House*

Q How do you know when to call in a pro?

A Professionals like plumbers and electricians often have a minimum charge, maybe $300. Before calling a professional, think of how long it would take you to fix the problem. Handymen have minimums, as well. If you are going to call a handyman, have ten things for him to do.

It also depends on your skill level. Ask yourself a few questions: Do you know what you're doing? Do you have what you need? If you don't have the right tools or materials, can you access them? Not only that, do you have enough time? Know that with even a simple repair, if you run out of time and energy, you'll need to leave the project in a safe and usable state when you set it aside.

The easiest household fixes. Everyone should be able to unclog a drain or a toilet—or fix a running toilet. Fixing loose hinges, correcting a drawer that is misaligned, or patching a small hole in the wall are things you can easily do at home. Likewise, patching a hole in the wall where a nail has been removed or where a doorknob has punctured a wall is doable. And there's a lot of stuff already in your house that can be used for quick fixes. You'd be surprised how much you don't have to buy. At thisoldhouse.com, there's a gallery called "Medicine-Cabinet MacGyver" that shows the uses of dental floss, nail polish, and more.

Repairs you should never do yourself. Anything that involves a gasline. And avoid the main electricity panel—although something like installing a dimmer light switch is easy and quick. Same goes for building a door into a wall—or taking down a wall. People usually don't know where the load-bearing walls are. If you're not clear, don't even think about it.

Leave refinishing a floor to the professionals. They are really good at it, and they get the best prices on supplies. (I know exactly how it's done and what it takes, but I wouldn't do it myself.)

Overrated advice. People always recommend throwing out the highest and lowest bid on a project. Not necessarily. You have to be analytical. Sometimes the highest bid comes from the person who best knows what they're doing. Ask vendors for very detailed bids so you can really compare. They have to be able to account for their estimates.

I liken it to the nutritional information on a box of food: Maybe one item has more fat per serving—but is the serving size larger?

Also, hire a person you feel comfortable with. They're going to be in your house, and if they get on your nerves, you're going to wind up arguing.

Underrated advice. My favorite piece of advice is never to start a project on Sunday night. You will invariably be in the dark or without water on Monday morning.

Also, never pop in to the hardware store and take a guess at what you need for a project. You will definitely get it wrong and need to go back to the store again. Take the appropriate measurements. Make a detailed list.

The importance of preventative care. Prevention is observation. Observation is prevention. Twice a year, set aside a day to walk around every single part of your house. Bring a clipboard and pen and look at everything. What is looking ragged? Are trees hanging over the house? Is there a loose something in the bathroom that might indicate a leak? Those notes will turn into your to-do list for the season.

You can also prevent small problems from turning into disasters. If you notice that a door handle and lock—what's called the lock set—is loose, tighten the screws. If you keep letting the job go, you're going to get locked out—or in.

Yearly Home Maintenance Checklist

The inside of your home is only part of the battle. Keeping up with minor repairs and upkeep on your home's exterior will prevent pricier professional jobs and delay those inevitable overhauls. Here's a quick list of things that should be checked at least once a year to make sure they're working properly:

- ☐ All screens
- ☐ Air-conditioner compressor
- ☐ Air-conditioner grills and filters (seasonally)
- ☐ Basement sump pump (if you have one)
- ☐ Circuit breakers (turn them all on and off)
- ☐ Furnace filter
- ☐ Garage-door tracks
- ☐ Porch and deck
- ☐ Roof (look for leaks)
- ☐ Septic tank and surrounding area (for flooding or odor)
- ☐ Sliding-door tracks
- ☐ Vent duct of the dryer (also check the dryer exhaust a few times a year to ensure there's no lint buildup)
- ☐ Walkways and stairs
- ☐ Water heater (drain as necessary and check the relief valve)
- ☐ Weather stripping (apply in winter, remove in spring)

HOME MAINTENANCE CHECKLIST BY DAVID BOWERS

A Real Toolbox

Everyone who has a home, be it apartment share or château, needs a tool kit. Your specific needs may vary slightly—the average condo dweller can probably make do without a hacksaw—but you can't be handy without the right equipment. Invest in tools now (they should last for years), and you will save later.

Claw hammer. The universal adjusting tool, the hammer comes in several varieties, differentiated by weight and function. A claw hammer is designed to pound in and pull out nails. Get a sixteen-ounce version—a little tack hammer is not enough for many jobs.

Nails and screws. Both come in several types and sizes. Use common nails (this is a type of nail) or box nails for general use, and finishing nails for woodwork and cabinets. (Finishing nails have almost no head; the other two have fairly broad heads that stop the nail at the wood's surface.) When you need greater holding power, use screws. The head of a screw is slotted to accept a screwdriver—either a straight slot (a single groove across the diameter) or a Phillips (two grooves that form a cross in the center of the head).

Screwdrivers. Get a straight-slot and a Phillips. You probably need more than one of each: a shorter one for working in close quarters and a long-blade one for turning power. The size of the tip is also important: It should fit tightly into the grooves in the screw.

Crosscut saw. Most versatile of the several varieties of wood saw. A simple handsaw can also be used for most small projects.

Three-eighth-inch power drill. It can be cordless or plug-in, variable speed or fixed—choice depends upon budget and convenience. Drills usually come with attachments for sanding and buffing.

Carpenter's level. Used to determine if a surface (shelving, appliance, drapery rod) is level.

Adjustable wrench. Basically, a handle with jaws on the end. The lower jaw can be moved up and down to tighten the jaws over the head of a bolt or nut.

Slip-joint pliers. The jaws have only two open positions, with teeth or serrations for grabbing, holding, and turning things.

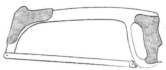

Utility knife. For cutting almost anything. A retractable blade is housed in a handle that also holds spare blades.

Metal retracting tape measure. Don't just wing it—get it right!

Hacksaw. Cuts through metal—tubing, nail heads, and the like.

Sandpaper. Comes in different grades designed to handle everything from rough surfaces to final finishing.

Toilet plunger. A rubber cup or bell at the end of a shaft that acts as a suction cup to dislodge blockages in plumbing lines.

Drain auger. For unplugging plumbing clogs. A long, flexible, metal tube with a corkscrew tip is forced through the pipe to find and dislodge the blockage.

Toilet auger. Similar to the drain auger, designed to deal with toilet blockages.

Work gloves (heavy cloth or deerskin) and **rubber gloves.** Especially if you're sanding or sawing, you need to protect yourself.

Look, Ma, No Tools!

For the following three fixes, you don't even need a tool belt. . . .

- Squeaky floor: Apply cornstarch between floorboards if the floor is squeaking. It will lubricate the boards. If this doesn't work, you may have to try nailing or screwing the board into the joist below.
- Screens: Repair very small holes in window screens by applying several layers of clear nail polish. Or mend a hole by stitching it closed with fine wire or nylon thread in a matching color.
- Removing broken light bulbs: Use a raw potato to remove a broken light bulb from its socket by first turning the switch off, then jamming the potato into the base and twisting the bulb out.

TOOL RECOMMENDATIONS BY ANNA JOHNSON; TOOL-LESS FIXES BY ERIK BRUUN

The Nine Easiest Household Fixes

Whether you're a homeowner or a renter, it's fairly likely that at some point you will be confronted with one, if not all, of the simple repairs that follow. You don't need to hire a professional to patch a crack in the wall, unclog a toilet, replace a doorknob, or spruce up the battered vinyl flooring in your kitchen. (Though you can, of course, always bribe a friend.)

PROJECT | **Patch a Crack in the Wall**

You don't have too live with those shabby, crackly walls—patch them up. But take heed if you suspect a crack may be part of a larger structural problem, or caused by a leak. Beyond your basic tools, you will need to purchase a can of spackling compound and a putty knife about an inch in width.

TOOLS: Bottle opener; putty knife; fine sandpaper

1. Scrape away any loose plaster along the crack. (Try gently running a beer bottle opener along the crack.)

2. Scoop the spackling compound onto a putty knife and run the knife over the crack.

3. Allow the compound to harden, and then apply another layer of spackling compound to the crack. Continue applying layers until the crack is completely filled.

4. When the final layer is dry, gently sand the repaired surface of the wall with fine sandpaper until it is smooth.

Bargains Aren't Always Better

Prices for repair supplies can vary significantly from store to store. In some situations, however, it's more important to deal with a knowledgeable salesperson than it is to get the lowest price. It may be cheaper to purchase the replacement parts for your leaky faucet at a large discount store, as opposed to a plumbing supply store. The trouble is that if you get midway through the project and don't know how to finish, you may not be able to count on getting help from the large discount store. The salesperson at the plumbing supply store will most likely be able to guide you to completion. So shop around for an appropriate store as you would for a doctor. It will pay off in the long run.

PROJECT | **Replace a Doorknob**

Replacing a door is definitely a job for the pros, but replacing the knob is a much more approachable task.

TOOLS: Straight-slot or Phillips screwdriver (as needed)
You may have either of the following kinds of doorknob:

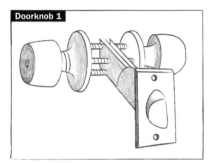

Doorknob 1

DOORKNOB 1: Mounting screws visible on the interior knob hold the mechanism in place.

Removing doorknob 1

To remove the knob, unfasten these screws and pull the interior and exterior knobs apart. You will see the latch mechanism on the inside. After unscrewing the screws in the face plate, slip the latch mechanism out.

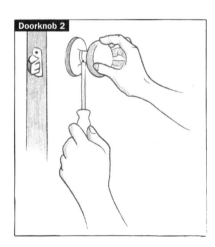

Doorknob 2

DOORKNOB 2: An internal spring catch on the stem (the narrow part of the doorknob that connects the handle to the door) of the interior knob holds the doorknob in place. You will notice a small hole or slit in the stem.

Removing doorknob 2

Push a sharp tool into the hole in the stem while pulling the interior knob off (the exterior knob should slide out as well). Unscrew the faceplate and remove the latch mechanism. *Note: Instead of a hole, some stems may have a small screw or opening for an Allen wrench.*

Replacing the knob

Once you've removed the old knob, take it with you to the hardware store to ensure that you purchase an appropriate replacement. Your new knob should feature installation insructions, but make sure that when you install the latch mechanism, the rounded edge of the latch bolt faces the door opening. (If you install it the other way, the door will not stay shut.)

PROJECT | **Fix Up Your Vinyl Flooring**

Over time, vinyl flooring can become damaged by holes, tears, and blisters. If you're installing flooring yourself, always purchase extra lengths to have on hand so you can patch it as needed; you won't be forced to replace the whole floor or settle for a mismatched checkerboard of colors. If you don't have extra flooring on hand, select a piece of flooring that closely matches the pattern of the damaged piece.

TOOLS: Metal straightedge; utility knife; putty knife (as needed); an iron (as needed); glue

Replacing a section of flooring

1. Take a pencil and draw a square around the damaged area.

2. Using a straightedge to guide you, cut along the line with a sharp utility knife. Use the section you cut out as a pattern to cut out your replacement patch.

3. If the vinyl is not glued to the subfloor, lift out the damaged section, spread glue onto the subfloor, and press the patch into place. Wipe off any excess glue that may have oozed around the edges and weight down the patch evenly for at least twenty-four hours.

If the vinyl is glued down, you can often peel it up by shoving a putty knife underneath the flooring. If that doesn't work, use the heat of an iron to weaken the glue. Place the iron on a damp cloth rather than directly on the vinyl. Lift out the vinyl and glue the patch as above.

Repairing a tear or blister

For vinyl that is torn, lift the torn section, spread new glue, and press the torn section back into place. Cover the damaged area with a weighted board for a minimum of twenty-four hours. For a blister, flatten it by cutting through its center. Then affix as you would a tear.

PROJECT | ## Weatherstrip Your Windows and Doors

You can make do with tape and plastic around leaky windows, but to prevent loss of heat in the winter, windows and doors need to be weatherstripped. It's a tiny investment of time and money, with a huge payoff in your energy bills.

TOOLS: Screwdriver (as needed); electric drill (optional)

Windows

The simplest approach is to purchase adhesive-backed foam at the hardware store. Remove the protective strip of paper from the foam and place the foam along the top of the upper window sash and the bottom of the lower window sash.

Doors

The same approach is used for sealing doors. Press the foam in place along the inside of the doorstop.

The bottom edge of the door poses a more difficult challenge. If your floor is wood or linoleum, you can easily install a door sweep: a flexible rubber attachment (kind of like a squeegee) that's anchored to a metal or vinyl strip; it should be attached to the inside of the door so the flexible portion rests flush against the floor. If you have thick carpeting or an uneven floor, ask the hardware store for a sweep that rises when the door opens and drops when the door is closed.

PROJECT | ## Clean Your Water Heater

Flush your water heater tank annually to prevent the buildup of sediment, and twice a year if you have hard water.

TOOLS: Garden hose; bucket

1. Attach a garden hose to the drain valve and place the other end of the hose in a floor drain or on pavement outdoors. Carefully open the drain valve and allow the water to drain for five minutes. Then let the water fill a bucket.

2. If the water is clear and sediment-free once it has settled, close the drain valve and remove the garden hose. If you see sediment or discolored water, repeat flushing and the bucket test until the water is clear and free of sediment.

Caution: If you have not been flushing your tank on a regular basis, don't start now. The sudden flow of accumulated sediment can cause permanent damage. If your water heater is rumbling or sizzling or the water it produces is rusty or black, there may be tank sedimentation or scale buildup. What you'll need to do is drain your tank. First, turn off the power at the circuit breaker and shut off the water supply. Drain the tank and remove the access panel to the heating elements. Remove the heating elements and soak them in vinegar, scraping off any scale.

PROJECT | Unclog a Sink

A clogged drain is such a drag; and doesn't it always seem to happen when the kitchen sink is full of dirty dishes? Fortunately, you can easily solve the problem without calling a plumber.

TOOLS: Plunger; garden hose; adjustable wrench; pipe wrench; wire coat hanger; sink auger (all tools only as needed)

Flushing the drain with a hose

First try using a plunger. If that doesn't work, try a garden hose.

1. Insert the hose into the drain and stuff a towel around and inside the drain hole to make a tight seal.

2. Have a helper turn on the water at the outside faucet while you hold the hose in the drain. That may flush out the debris and clear the pipe.

Cleaning the drain trap

If the hose method fails, you may need to clean the drain trap, the U-shape pipe under the sink. The drain trap is filled with water at all times to prevent sewer gas, rats, and other unpleasant contaminants from entering your house through the pipe. Unfortunately, the trap can clog.

1. Place a small bucket or shallow pan under the trap to catch any water that remains in the sink drain.

2. Some traps have a plug that can easily be removed for cleaning. Unfasten the plug with an adjustable wrench. If your pipe does not have a clean-out plug, remove the entire trap. Use a plumber's wrench to unfasten the two nuts that connect the trap to the drainpipe.

3. Once the plug or trap is removed, clean out the trap with your fingers or with a disassembled wire coat hanger.

4. Replace the plug or reattach the trap to the drainpipe, fastening the nuts tightly so the water does not leak but not so tightly as to damage the threads.

5. Turn on the water to test the drain and check for leaks.

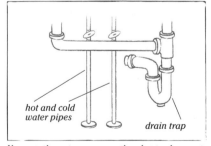

hot and cold water pipes

drain trap

Unscrew the nuts or remove the plug to clean out the drain trap.

Using a sink auger

Occasionally the clog is further down the pipe. In this case you will need to use a sink auger, also known as a plumber's snake. To assemble the auger, insert the end of the snake-like coil into the auger handle.

1. Place a bucket or shallow tray under the trap to catch any water that might remain in the drain.

2. Remove the drain trap with a plumber's wrench by unfastening the two nuts that connect the trap to the drainpipe.

3. Insert the blade of the snake into the pipe that enters the kitchen or bathroom wall. Allow the snake to run freely into the pipe. When the coil stops running into the pipe, you have reached either the blockage or a bend in the pipe.

4. Tighten the screw handle and rotate the auger handle in a clockwise direction. This moves the snake coil around the bend in the pipe or enables it to cut through the blockage.

5. Reattach the drainpipe, turn on the water, and test the drain. This process should take care of the problem.

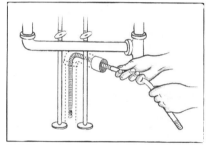

Push the auger in until you feel it hit the stoppage.

Unclog a Toilet

If your toilet becomes stopped up and overflows, first try using a plunger. If the obstruction remains, you will need to use a toilet auger or snake. Place the end of the snake into the toilet bowl. Turn the handle at the top of the hollow tube and the snake will gradually uncoil into the drain. When you reach the blockage, try to hook it and force it back into the toilet bowl by pulling up or by turning the auger handle in the opposite direction to pull in the snake. Avoid pushing the obstruction further into the trap. If at that point the blockage remains, it's time to call a plumber. The only solution left is to disassemble the toilet, which, for obvious reasons, should be left to a pro.

PROJECT | Fix a Running Toilet

Toilets that continually run between flushes waste a ton of water. What's going on inside the tank? Water level is regulated by a large floating ball connected to the shutoff valve; post-flush, water rises to refill the tank and the ball floats upward, creating downward pressure on the shutoff valve, which eventually closes. In a running toilet, the water level is too high, so water is constantly spilling into the overflow tube. What a waste!

Adjusting the water level

Most of the time, all you need to do to stop your toilet from running is to lower the water level. You do that by changing the angle of the brass arm.

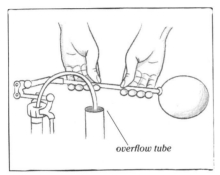

overflow tube

Fixing a running toilet may simply be a matter of adjusting the angle of the brass arm inside the tank.

1. Lift off the tank lid.

2. Manually screw the ball in a little on the connecting arm so the distance between the shutoff valve and ball is reduced.

3. If the ball is completely screwed in, gently bend the connecting arm down so the ball sits lower in the tank.

4. Flush the toilet and see how high the water rises in the tank. If it still rises above the mouth of the tube, gently bend the float arm further so the ball sits even lower.

Replacing the shutoff valve

Occasionally, toilets run because of a defective shutoff valve. Pulling up on the brass arm should close the shutoff valve; if it doesn't, you'll need to replace the old valve mechanism with a new, self-contained plastic mechanism that can be purchased at any hardware or plumbing supply store.

TOOLS: Two adjustable wrenches

1. Flush the toilet and close the water intake valve by twisting the knob.

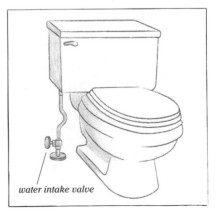

water intake valve

The water intake valve is usually located on the lower left side of the toilet.

2. Place a pan or bucket under the tank to catch any remaining water. Inside the tank, fit an adjustable wrench onto the nut that holds the old mechanism in place; use another wrench to loosen the corresponding nut under the tank. Now remove the whole mechanism.

3. To install the new mechanism, follow the instructions on the package.

4. Once your new mechanism is installed, check the water level. To increase the water level, turn the knob at the base of the regulator mechanism clockwise. To decrease the water level, turn the knob counterclockwise. Start with one turn at a time and check the water level.

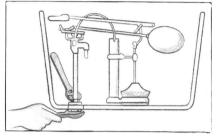

An old-school valve mechanism features a floating ball connected to a brass arm.

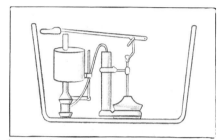

A newer, plastic valve mechanism will be more self-contained.

PROJECT | Fix a Toilet That Won't Flush

What's happening when your toilet doesn't flush completely? Unless the toilet is clogged (which you'll know because flushing will likely result in some nasty overflow), the tank is probably not filling with enough water—it's the opposite of the running-toilet problem. The solution: Raise the water level in the tank.

TOOL: Straight-slot screwdriver (as needed)

1. For toilets with a plastic mechanism, turn the knob at the base of the regulator clockwise. For older toilets with a floating ball, lengthen the distance between the ball and the shutoff valve by unscrewing the ball on the connecting arm a little. If the ball is unscrewed as far as it will go, gently bend the connecting arm upward.

2. Flush the toilet to check the new water level. You want the water in the tank to sit about ¾" from the top of the overflow tube.

3. If your toilet does not flush at all, the likely cause is that the water in the tank is leaking out as rapidly as it enters. The rubber ball or flapper that allows water to flow out of the tank and into the toilet may be creating an imperfect seal. The solution: Replace the ball or flapper.

Foundation Matters

If you're tempted to do extensive work on your house's foundation, structure, or roof, it's best to think again. Do-it-yourself projects for some parts of the home are fine, because mistakes may be cosmetic, or so obvious that you'll know they need correcting. But a well-intentioned error in more critical parts of the house can set the stage for disaster in ways that are not apparent. Improper alterations can undermine the house's structure gradually, over time, or more dramatically. Patching a crack in a basement wall may seem a simple and obvious repair job. But it may be better to let it leak than to patch it incorrectly from the inside: You could be trapping water inside the wall, leaving it no way to escape.

It is a good idea, however, to regularly examine your house for potential trouble spots. If you see something worrisome, there are things you can do to prevent or correct some problems. Here's what you should be focusing on:

Slope. Examine the ground around your house to make sure it is angled to carry water away from the foundation. Water is essential for life, but it can be the enemy of a house's structure.

Depressions. Also look for depressions that collect water in pools next to the house. If they're not too drastic, you can probably fill these yourself.

Crumbling asphalt. For asphalt roofs, bend a shingle to gauge its malleability. If the asphalt crumbles or breaks, it is a clear sign that the roof is a candidate for replacement.

Ladder Safety

Be smart about ladder placement when checking out matters on-high. A ladder should stand at enough of an angle to the wall (don't lean it against eaves or windows) to provide a solid triangular base, but not so far that it bounces when you're standing on a middle rung. The distance of the ladder from the wall should be equal to a quarter of the ladder's height.

Gutter flow. Gutters are a major protection against water damage. Not all houses have them, as it is often assumed that the roof extends far enough out to avoid problems. If you don't have gutters, observe where the water flows from the roof during a rainstorm or as snow melts. Gutters may not be necessary—but if the flow resembles a waterfall and is pounding near the foundation, it may be wise to add them.

FOUNDATION PRIMER BY ERIK BRUUN; MOLD CONTROL TIPS BY DONNA SMALLIN

To check how well your gutters are working, pour water into them to make sure it runs toward the downspout. (Also watch during a heavy rainstorm; water shouldn't be overflowing from the gutter.) If the angle of the gutter is wrong, try adjusting the hangers that hold it up. Make sure the gutter and downspout are clear of leaves and other debris. (Always clean a gutter from a ladder and not the roof.) If the downspout is clogged, use a plumber's auger or other long, flexible cable to clear it out.

Downspout direction. At its base, your gutter's downspout should direct water away from the house, not allowing it to puddle at the foundation. If necessary, use a splash pan, drain tile, or downspout extension to direct water farther into the lawn, or into drainage gullies.

Mildew. Look around the base of the house for the telltale green signs that mildew has found itself a home. Low areas on the house that are subjected to splashing rains or seeping moisture are especially susceptible. If you find mildew, clean it off with a chlorine-based cleaning mix. Once it's off, let the wood dry out, and apply a waterproof paint or other treatment.

Vines. Vines can add bucolic beauty and charm to the exterior of a house but some cling tenaciously, with tiny claws or suction cups that can damage paint and siding and are murder to remove. They may also trap dampness. If you enjoy the sight of vines, use trellises and limit yourself to the more benevolent varieties, such as honeysuckle, which are less likely to cling and tear walls beneath them.

Fend Off Mold

Mold can attack your home's structure as well as its contents (not to mention your health), and it can lead to the need for seriously expensive repairs. It usually grows in damp basements, though it can appear anywhere if the conditions are right. Here's how to keep your home mold-free:

- Be spartan. Clothing, paper, and furniture are the three biggest moisture magnets.
- Run a dehumidifier.
- In the summer months, open the basement windows.
- Avoid air-drying wet clothes in an already damp basement.
- Store firewood in a shed or garage, not in the house.
- Don't carpet the basement floor.
- To absorb musty odors left by previous mold outbreaks, set out a few small bowls of vinegar, or place a lump of dry charcoal in an open metal container.

How to Talk to the Pros

If you start a job yourself and end up needing to call in a professional repairman, you will almost certainly have to pay for the full cost of his doing the job from start to finish—so you really need to carefully weigh the limits of your expertise and time when taking on anything more than minor repairs. If you do need to call a pro for any substantial work, there are a few basic steps to follow to ensure that the job gets done properly:

Agreement in writing. To make matters as simple as possible up front, insist on a written agreement. Do not rely on a verbal understanding.

Specific concerns. The content of the agreement will depend on the nature of the repair. It should include the exact location and extent of the repair; the type, quality, color, and size of material to be used; the number of coats of paint for a painting project; an assurance that all work shall conform to local and state codes; and the pricing.

Other issues. An agreement between you and the contractor should further describe a time schedule for the job; who cleans up the mess that results from the job; the amount to which the repairman or contractor shall assume responsibility for damage to your or a neighbor's property; that any changes in the contract shall be in writing and agreed to by both parties; that you are freed from all liens that may be placed against the job for failure of the contractor or repairman to pay for materials, labor, or equipment; and a payment schedule.

Go with who you know. Select a repairman or contractor whose work you know. Inspect some of his or her previous work and ask the owners if they were satisfied with the contractor's work. If you need help, consult with an architect or other person in the business or try the Better Business Bureau.

Three bids. The variety in prices that contractors charge for work can be enormous. Some contractors will give high bids because they have so much other work that the job is only worth it to them if they are able to make a large profit. Other contractors may give a low bid because they desperately need the work. In considering bids, don't forget to factor in the quality of the contractor who submits the bid. The cheapest bid may not be the best.

Checking the job. When the job is done, inspect the project with the repairman, referring to the contract if questions arise. Sign off on the contract and make final payment after all the work has been completely corrected.

REPAIRMAN AND EFFICIENCY GUIDELINES BY ERIK BRUUN

The Energy-Efficient Home

Utility bills are a boring and expensive fact of life. Depending on where you live, you may be paying for electricity, hot water, gas, phone, Internet or any combination thereof. These things add up quickly, and more often than not, the more you're paying for your utilities, the more energy you're wasting. But you don't have to clean your clothes with a washboard in the river. Without resorting to frontier living, there are a few simple changes you can make to reduce bills and waste.

Think Big Picture

Energy usage can be reduced by altering daily household habits. But you should also approach the issue from a broader perspective by considering the following measures:

Energy audit. If you are interested in taking a serious look at specific ideas for your home, many utility companies offer low-cost or even free home-energy audits to study and define where you could be wasting energy in your house. Contact your local utility provider to find out what services are available.

Professional advice. Professional servicemen may know ways to implement energy efficiencies. Seek their advice, especially when buying a new furnace, central air-conditioning, or appliances. Frequently, energy-efficient systems cost more initially but will save you in the long run. So buy smart.

Read the labels. Read energy-efficiency labels carefully. On an energy label rated via dollars, a low number means an appliance will cost less to operate. On a label rated via efficiency, a high number means a machine will cost less to operate.

Think ahead. By planning ahead when you design, furnish, and equip your house, you can do a great deal to cut down on energy costs. Do your research regarding insulation and building materials, and consider solar panels.

Regular maintenance. Routine maintenance on heating and cooling systems and appliances will keep your energy bills down. This includes replacing filters in energy systems on a regular basis.

Applied Appliances

Obviously, the fewer appliances you have, the less it will cost you to operate them. But for those non-negotiables—like refrigeration and heat—the key is to make sure you are using the machines efficiently. If you are in the market for new appliances, look for energy- and water-saving models; but if you need to work with what you've got, follow a few simple guidelines and you will notice the savings right away (and, as a bonus, your carbon footprint will become a lot smaller):

- Defrost the fridge and freezer when ice forms, and turn the refrigerator to its lowest setting when you go out of town.
- Unplug appliances when they are not in use—most use power even when they're not turned on.
- Keep your appliances clean—vacuuming the coils on the back of the fridge every six months will make it run more efficiently. Vacuum your radiators regularly to make sure all the heat's coming through.
- Use duct tape and heavy plastic, or get fancy with weather stripping, to insulate around leaky windows, doors and air-conditioning units in winter. (See page 21 for a primer.)
- Try air-drying your clothes and dishes. Little-known fact: The clothes dryer can suck heat out of the house in winter, so don't rob Peter to pay Paul.
- Cook smart. In the kitchen, the microwave uses a lot less energy than a regular oven.

Fill the Freezer

A full freezer isn't just a sign of a thrifty home cook; it's also energy efficient. When an empty or near-empty freezer is opened, cold air rushes out and is replaced by warm air. Excess energy is expended in continually bringing the temperature back down. A full freezer holds less air, and much of the cold is concentrated in its frozen contents. If yours is empty, you may want to reconsider your cooking habits. You can also pour water into empty orange juice cartons or plastic bottles and place them in the freezer to take up space.

Electricity Smarts

If you have electric heating, you can save a bundle of money by setting your thermostat no higher than sixty-eight degrees in winter and no lower than seventy-eight in summer. Each extra degree in winter can increase your heating costs by 3 percent; in summer, each degree lower can raise cooling costs by 6 percent. You

APPLIANCE, ELECTRICITY, AND WATER-EFFICIENCY TIPS BY MELISSA KIRSCH won't notice the difference with one degree, and the change can save you hundreds of bucks a year. Also turn down the heat when you go to bed and when you're not home.

In the winter, keeping the house cooler is also better for your health. Overheating can dry you out like a slab of beef jerky. (If that's a problem for you, put a pan of water on hot radiators to get some vapor circulating.)

Choose compact fluorescent light bulbs over incandescent ones—they use a fraction of the energy and last much longer. Use the lowest-wattage bulbs possible in most rooms, saving anything higher than seventy-five watts for reading lamps and other places where you must have super-bright light. A small but illuminating secret: Lampshades with white interiors reflect more light.

Water Watchfulness

If you pay it yourself, you know that the water bill can be a significant portion of your monthly utility tab. If you pay only to heat your water, that bill is nothing to sneeze at either. Not to mention that wasting water can take a dismal toll on the environment (especially if you live in a drought-prone locale).

Fortunately, small steps can add up to big savings. Doing your laundry in cold water is an easy way to cut way down on hot water usage (and is easier on your clothes to boot). Run the dishwasher and washing machine only when you have a full load, fix leaks and running toilets promptly—a running toilet can use more than eight thousand gallons of water a year! (See how to fix one on page 24.) Little things, such as turning the water off while you're brushing your teeth, or shortening the length of your shower, save water with little inconvenience to you. Install low-flow showerheads and sink aerators to save even more.

A More Efficient Toilet

The average commode uses 5 gallons of water per flush, but fewer are actually needed. New efficient toilets use only 1.6 gallons per flush. You can reduce the amount of water in yours by lowering the water level (see page 24) or by inserting a simple water displacement device. Two possibilities include a plastic bottle filled with water or a brick covered with plastic. (You do not want the brick to erode in the water.) These devices will displace 1 or 2 quarts of water and reduce the flush accordingly. Be aware that they may also affect the flushing action.

Summer Special

Central air conditioners are complex machines, which means it's best to leave repairs to licensed service contractors. However, there are some things you can do to keep your central air-conditioning system running well:

- Keep the outdoor condensing unit clear of obstructions such as leaves and other types of debris.
- Clean the filter two or three times a cooling season. A clogged filter can cause your unit to overheat, which shuts down the system.
- Consider having your air conditioner tuned up at the beginning of each cooling season. Leaking refrigerant decreases efficiency.
- If the system won't run, check the circuit breaker box before calling the contractor.
- Use fans and open windows if the temperature outside is below 82 degrees Fahrenheit.
- Install an attic fan to blow out hot air that collects in the attic.
- Clean or replace air-conditioning filters once a month.
- Close shades and curtains to keep out the sun.
- Never set your thermostat below the desired level in order to cool a hot house more rapidly.

Efficiency by the Numbers

The average household blows through 1,000 kilowatt hours of electricity annually on appliances that are turned off but still plugged in. Items left on standby, like digital clocks, continue to use energy on peripheral functions and any item with an external transformer is pulling power constantly. Some other numbers that will (hopefully) inspire you to reexamine your habits:

- Turn off the tap while you brush your teeth or shave and save up to 5 gallons of water every day.
- How hot do you really need your hot water to be? Save 6 to 10 percent off your heating costs by lowering the temperature on your water heater from 140 degrees to 120 degrees Fahrenheit.

- Wrap your water heater in an insulation blanket to limit the loss and prevent 1,000 pounds of CO_2 emissions per year.
- If yours is anything like the average family, you'll save $150 per year on heating and air-conditioning costs by installing a programmable thermostat.

SUMMER, WINTER, AND FURNACE TIPS BY LYN HERRICK

Winter Warmer

The basic principles of efficient heating are simple: Keep warm air in, cold air out, and your heater or furnace in tip-top shape. There are a few other steps you can take to ensure a cozy winter without resorting to wearing a parka indoors:

- When the heat is on, set your thermostat as low as possible. Lower the thermostat to fifty-five degrees Fahrenheit at night. Even a few degrees' difference will lead to considerable savings. (Remember, warm clothing provides an excellent source of insulation, as does adding another blanket to your bed.)
- Keep windows next to the thermostat closed tightly so the rest of the house is not several degrees warmer than the area around the thermostat.
- Make sure your heating system is operating efficiently. If you have a furnace or heat pump, check the filter at least every other month during the winter. Clean the filter as needed and replace it when it appears to be worn out. Have a professional tune an oil-fired system once a year. Gas-fired systems and heat pumps need to be tuned only once every two years.
- If you use an electric furnace for heating, consider a heat pump. These pumps are expensive, but they can reduce your total use of electricity for both heating and cooling by 30 to 40 percent.
- Close off unoccupied rooms or rooms not currently in use. This means shutting the heat or air-conditioning vents, unless you have a heat pump. Shutting vents in this case could harm the heat pump.
- Keep your fireplace damper closed when not in use. It also helps to install a glass front to keep warm air from going up the chimney.

Respect Your Furnace Filters

Central heating and cooling systems rely on forced air to spread their benefits. The problem is that blowing air stirs up dust and dirt. The filter traps these particles so they don't gum up your appliance. A clogged filter requires that the appliance work harder, and consume more energy, so furnace filters should be replaced once a month during the winter. (They're inexpensive.) Consult your furnace manual or dealer for the location of the filter and instructions for replacing it.

Buy or Rent Thrifty

Making the decision to buy a home isn't easy. Can you afford to invest—or is it better to keep renting? There's a lot to consider. And the outcome may not necessarily be up to you. When you're looking for a loan, a low credit score (below 620) will prevent you from securing a low interest rate—and possibly even a mortgage. If you fall into this category of borrowers, renting is an opportunity to concentrate on paying off debt and building up a solid credit score.

Can You Afford to Buy?

Even if you have good credit, you'll want to put a good amount of thought into whether you're ready to buy. Renting usually comes with a lower financial burden, freeing up your extra cash for other investments or debts. It also gives you more freedom to relocate to a new city for work, or to leave the corporate world and open a scuba shack in the Bahamas. Buying makes sense for people who are willing to sink their roots—and their dollars—into something more permanent.

Perhaps an even bigger factor is the market: With all those homes available at staggeringly discounted prices, is it a good time to jump in? If you're financially stable, with access to cash for a big down payment, then the time may be right. But don't think you're in the clear just because you can squeeze out the down payment and then scrape together enough for the monthly mortgage.

Potential owners must be sure they can cover the costs without jeopardizing their future retirement savings. It's easy to anticipate costs like homeowner's insurance, property taxes, hazard insurance (such as earthquake or flood), or mortgage insurance. But don't forget about unforeseen costs. If you need a new roof or the toilet is busted, that's your responsibility.

Then there's the fact that qualifying for a mortgage now is not as simple as it was during the peak of the housing boom. Thanks to the subprime mortgage mess, long gone are the days when you could secure a home loan or buy a home by putting little or no money down. So now what? Assume you'll need a 20 percent down payment to qualify for a loan. And that's just to get in the door. Locking in a mortgage will require you to have the right ratios. Read on.

To save for a down payment and closing costs, you might have to compromise putting money toward retirement. That's okay. What's not okay is scaling back your 401(k) contributions to make a mortgage payment. The benefits of your 401(k) are the foundation of your financial future. Factoring in what you could be making in a few years time might be tempting when calculating what you can afford, but betting on tomorrow is no sure thing.

HOME ECONOMICS BY JULIANA BUNIM; INSURANCE ADVICE SUPPLIED BY KIP DIGGS OF STATE FARM INSURANCE

Running the Numbers

To determine just how much house you can afford—and secure a loan for—consider 28 and 36 as your magic ratio numbers. Your monthly mortgage payment (including principal, interest, property tax and homeowner's insurance) should not exceed **28 percent of your pretax income.** For example, if your annual salary is $50,000, your monthly mortgage payment should not exceed $1,166. That's $14,000 annually.

But that's not the only ratio mortgage lenders consider. Your total monthly debt should not exceed **36 percent of your pretax income.** This includes credit card bills, student loans, car loans, child support, medical bills, and secured loans.

That means if you make $50,000, your monthly debt obligations shouldn't exceed $1,500 (or $18,000 yearly). The lower your debt to income ratio, the more appealing you will be to the lender.

P.S. Having enough cash for a down payment and falling within the ratio of 28/36 isn't enough to ensure homeowner status. You'll also need enough to cover basic closing costs, which are estimated between **3 and 6 percent of the loan amount.** These costs can include, but are not limited to, inspections, transfer taxes, surveys, appraisals, and the lender's attorney fees. That's between $6,000 and $12,000 on a $200,000 mortgage.

Renter's Insurance

Do you need renter's insurance? If you have more items than you can afford to replace, the answer is yes. People often underestimate the amount of stuff they own.

Let's say you just graduated from college and you're living in your first apartment. All you've got is a computer, clothes, and a bed from Ikea. Not many recent grads can really afford to replace a computer. New clothes can easily run into the hundreds or thousands of dollars. And Ikea certainly isn't giving the stuff away. The average yearly cost of renter's insurance is about $200. That's less than the yearly cost of a couple of delivery pizzas each month. An agent can help you determine just how much coverage you need.

To save money on insurance, take advantage of multiline discounts. Insuring your home and car with the same carrier can cost less than insuring them separately. You may be able to bundle in other lines, like life insurance. You can reduce your renter's (or homeowner's) insurance premiums by owning a fire extinguisher. You should also consider raising your deductible, which is the portion of a loss you agree to be responsible for. A higher deductible, be it on your home or auto insurance, results in a lower premium.

Discount Decor

Decor is more than skin deep; a well-appointed home is a comfortable home, where you and yours will enjoy gathering. And the more your pad reflects your taste and personality, the better you will feel spending time there. If your place looks like a frat house—i.e., dingy paint, Grandma's old couch, and beer bottle "sculptures"—no one will be jumping at the chance to have dinner *chez vous*. That said, you needn't take out a second mortgage to live in comfort.

Don't be fooled by expensive catalogs and showrooms. Whatever your taste, from shabby chic to clean and modern, you can decorate your home thriftily and still have it look like a million bucks. And whatever its state, there are simple steps you can take to spruce things up. All you need is some ingenuity and a little DIY spirit.

Furniture on the Cheap

Remember when you first found out the price of a decent couch? That was a shock. (Or is it just us?) Quality home furnishings are expensive. If you're already stocked up with a full complement of mahogany accessories, feel free to skip ahead. For those currently setting up or fixing up a home, however, there is one surefire thrifty approach: buying (or freeloading) used furniture.

If you're impatient by nature or want to nest fast, the flea market/yard sale/Web-crawling route may not work for you. It's essentially a waiting game—wait long enough and you'll eventually find that someone nearby is giving away, or inexpensively hawking exactly what you need. But for the aesthetically inclined, the fun lies in the search.

For those in the market for a quick furniture fix, the alternative is obvious, and comes with its own set of instructions. (Hello, Ikea!) Critics will say that buying cheaply made goods isn't, in the long run, a thrifty use of money. It's a legitimate claim, as anyone who has tried to reassemble a flimsy (but nicely shaped) particle-board bookcase after a move can verify. You may wind up having to buy it again a few years down the line. . . .

But to our minds, the idea that high quality is the only true thrift isn't always practical. Sure, you can do without a fancy headboard in the master suite. But you do need, say, a place to store your books—only a hard-core ascetic would advocate stashing volumes in cardboard boxes for fifteen years until you can afford the perfect Danish shelving unit. Instant gratification isn't only for the rich!

Savvy Flea Market Shopping

If you're going the used furniture route and don't want to get tied up in the potentially time-consuming process of online bidding, get thee to a flea market. If anything, it's a nice way to spend a Saturday. But flea markets can be overwhelming—with aisles and aisles of cast-off stuff, pushy shoppers, and savvy dealers—so keep some expert tips in mind:

Be first or last. There are two schools of thought when it comes to flea market shopping. The "early bird gets the worm" approach gets you a great selection, but the "last man/woman standing" technique gets you the best deals. So if you have a specific item or need in mind, get there early. If you are more in the mood to stroll and just see what strikes your fancy, saunter in after noon and scavenge for those end-of-the-day bargains.

Recruit a friend with a truck. You'll need at least a minivan and a helping hand to cart all those great deals home; and be sure to load some rope and blankets in the back for securing your treasures. Wear super-comfortable shoes, bring a dolly or cart for transporting things, and swap your tote for a comfy backpack. Always bring a tape measure, and know your floor plan. Before you grab that steamer trunk, measure it; it's only a find if it fits. And most important, bring cash; cold, hard cash can make the difference between getting a good deal and a downright steal.

If the price is right. When you run across an item that has a no-brainer bargain price and possesses some experimental potential, sometimes it makes sense to buy it. You can paint it, distress it, transform it, and, if nothing else, write it off as research. If you aren't happy in the end, you can resell it, give it away, or donate it. The thrill of the deal, paired with a lot of imagination and elbow grease, has yielded some fantastic furnishings.

Inspect, inspect, inspect. This will cue the seller that you are interested, communicate a respect for the object, and make him or her think you are truly a discriminating buyer. Don't point out imperfections right off the bat—that's rude. When you really get down to talking price, politely pointing out any flaws will help you justify asking for a lower price.

Think Like a Decorator

You don't need to hire a designer to make aesthetic choices for you. Interior decorators aren't magicians; they have a skill they learned. And you can learn it, too. As you observe or imagine a room, let these points be your guide:

What do you see first? Every room needs a focal point or place of immediate visual interest. In an empty room, it's often obvious—a fireplace, a lovely window, or an intriguing architectural detail. If the focal point is not obvious, create one. A piece of art, an interesting piece of furniture, a beautifully painted wall, an ornate mirror, an artfully displayed collection, a bold pattern in upholstery, or a rug—all are great ways to give your room focus.

Make a statement. Go for quality in your heftier pieces, like sofas and chairs, which get more use than something like a coffee table. Keep larger, more expensive, upholstered pieces of furniture neutral, or at least in solid colors. That way you can update or change the look by simply replacing accent pillows or throws instead of doing a costly reupholstery job.

Nothing personal. Sometimes you walk into a home that's clearly been well planned and fussed over, but something is off. Next time you get that feeling, look around. You'll most likely be hard pressed to find anything—a knickknack, a sentimental collection, a quirky piece of art—that ties it intimately to its inhabitants. Homes should speak volumes about the people who live in them. Surround yourself with the things that inspire you, comfort you, and make you happy.

It's not natural. Rooms that do not have some organic element or touch of nature feel sterile and jarring. Enliven your nest by incorporating natural textures. Fresh or dried flowers, plants, a vase of twigs, a sisal rug, wooden or woven accessories—all bring a touch of the outdoors, which adds a certain vitality to any room.

Too much technology. You might be proud of your flat screen, but wires and electronic components are not decorative items. Whenever possible, camouflage the television, computer, or stereo equipment and conceal, organize, and properly attend to unsightly wires and cords. Discreetly securing the wires to the back or legs of furniture with tape will prevent them from creeping out.

Are you in the mall? "Oh, your house looks just like the catalog" is not really a compliment. Beware of homeogenizing, which can happen when you overshop at one retailer or overdo one very distinctive style of furniture or accessory.

DECORATOR TIPS BY AME MAHLER BEANLAND AND EMILY MILES TERRY; APPRAISAL ADVICE BY CAROL PRISANT AND CHRIS JUSSEL.

You are not a hag if you haggle. In a professional tone, ask the dealer, "Is this your best price?" Or you can simply make an offer of about 20 to 30 percent less. When the dealer tells you the price, a good response is, "Is there any way you would consider 'X' dollars?" You may not haggle every day, but the vendors do, and they expect it, so go ahead. (See page xxi for more advice.)

Got a Treasure on Your Hands?

Flea markets and yard sales can yield surprise treasures (*Antiques Roadshow* anyone?). If you think you are in possession of a potentially valuable object, you'll want to know how to find a good appraiser, and most particularly, an appraiser who is knowledgeable about your category of object. Some appraisers are generalists in antiques, while others have specialties such as jewelry or toys.

A formal appraisal—one in which your item or items are thoroughly described as to age, condition, and weight (for silver)—is also an inventory of your personal property. You wind up with a written, notarized document (the appraisal) accompanied by a signed statement detailing its purpose of the appraisal (estate, fair market value, or insurance—each is different) and its valuation. Naturally, appraisers charge for these services, either by the hour or with a flat fee. Ethical appraisers never base their fee on a percentage of the total appraisal. And while most appraisers are thoroughly ethical, the appraisal community itself is not regulated in any way. No license or any type of certification is required for those wishing to be appraisers, so it's a good idea to hire an appraiser who is a member of one of the well-known appraisal associations or organizations, or to contact an established auction house, which employs appraisers who work in all fields. The appraiser you hire will review the extent of the job with you, estimate his charges, and examine the objects. (Hopefully this will take place on-site; if that's impossible, the job can be done through photos, but you may wind up with a tentative and qualified evaluation.)

Start by contacting the offices of one of three national organizations: the American Society of Appraisers (www.appraisers.org), the Appraisers Association of America (www.appraisersassoc.org), and the International Society of Appraisers (www.isa-appraisers.org). These associations keep national databases of members and their specialties.

Thrift Store Flip | by Catherine Crawford

My mom has always been a bargain hunter, but one Christmas, I realized that she had nearly made it into a science. Her gifts for me that year included a beautiful crystal aurora borealis necklace and a $100 gift certificate to Powell's bookstore in Portland, Oregon, where my parents live. By some standards this is not extravagant, but it is when you come from a family with thirteen children.

Mom's previous gifts were usually much more practical—and cheap. Just the year before, we had all been given matching striped hats with pom-poms. So when I looked at my gift certificate, I did the math: Thirteen gift certificates of $100 each? That's $1,300.

Well, no. As it turns out, my mother had been spending a lot of time at the Goodwill Outlet, where Goodwill sends everything that doesn't sell in the regular stores. At the outlet, everything is peddled out of bins by the pound. To buy those gift certificates, Mom had rounded up the valuable books (first editions, even) that she had found for pennies at the outlet, selling them in exchange for store credit—which she obtained in the form of gift certificates. It took her about five months or so to generate enough credit to make that Christmas very merry.

The necklace had a similarly humble origin. It was bought with store credit at a consignment shop where Mom lugged stacks of antique linens. Over the years, she has bought bundles of lace table-cloths, pillowcases, and napkins that at first glance looked like dirty rags. No stain or wrinkle could intimidate her. No smudge would dissuade her. She learned how to turn them into exquisite linens that could be sold on consignment for shockingly high prices. It involves boiling water, bleach, Cascade, laundry detergent, the

Know Your Auctions

There are two types of auctions at which you can purchase antiques and collectibles: estate sales and consignment sales. It's not always easy to know which is which, though. In general, most estate sales are held at the home and include everything from the furniture to the contents of the kitchen cabinets. They are held to liquidate an estate so the proceeds can be disbursed to the heirs.

A consignment sale, on the other hand, usually takes place at an auction house that holds sales on a regular basis. Items from many different sources are consigned to the auction house for sale at a commission.

stove, and the washing machine. If, by the end, there is anything left of the fabric, it'll be stain free.

It's all very strategic now, but Mom's intimate knowledge of the circle of thrift evolved over time. As a young woman, she started combing through regular thrift stores and garage sales for toys and clothes to satisfy her expanding brood.

When she began living in an empty nest with just my dad, Mom had a hard time finding takers for all of her rescued, rehabilitated goods—even with thirteen kids, their spouses, and a gaggle of grandchildren. This led to the first garage sale.

Portland is home to an active community of drizzled-upon bargain lovers, and after her first sale, word spread among the regulars. Mom made more than $1,000 at the debut sale. She now has two annual garage sales and each one brings in between $1,500 and $2,500. These days, she no longer just buys what looks nice, new, durable, or charming—she knows what sells. In fact, those twice-a-year events are now mere sideshows to Mom's real bread and butter: eBay. Her eye is fine-tuned, and Mom knows exactly what she's looking for.

It took some coaxing, but once all the kids finally convinced her to invest in a computer with Internet capability, Mom was off and selling. And selling. And then selling some more. When my parents come out to visit me, my husband, and our two young daughters, the girls are lucky to get any attention from Grandma between virtual Lego transactions.

Apparently, now it's all about toys: Fisher-Price Little People, Polly Pockets, anything from the 1970s, Barbies and Barbie clothes, and especially Legos. A tiny little Lego figure called Watto (which costs about $0.02 at the outlet) sells for $30 on eBay!

Toy collectors are nothing if not passionate. Although toys bring in the most dough, Mom has sold practically everything, and usually there's a great story to go along with it. There's the "old rusty tin" that ended up in Mom's cart. She was about to throw it away when she thought she'd just check eBay to see what old tins were going for. On a whim she decided to put it up for sale because it looked like she might get $10 or so. The tin sold for more than $300. Sales have been so good that she reported $15,000 in extra income to the IRS last year.

Green It Up with Hardy Houseplants

Every home can be improved by a little greenery. Plants clean the air, calm the senses, and bring life and personality to a room. One thing they aren't, however, is cheap. And if you have a black thumb, it can get mighty expensive to keep your house in clover. Any plant will turn brown if totally ignored, but here are a few that will thrive under almost any circumstances:

Bromeliads. These exotic-looking beauties generally do better in low light or filtered sun, though the ones with gray leaves can usually tolerate more light. Keep the soil moist, and also water the plant itself according to nursery directions for the variety. Maintain by fertilizing only in spring and summer.

Grape ivy. This lovely deep green trailing plant likes to loll about in bright light. Don't soak this one: Let the dirt dry out a little in between watering and take it outside or in the tub and shower the leaves every once in a while. Maintain the soil by fertilizing regularly. For a bushier-looking plant, pinch off the tips of the vines.

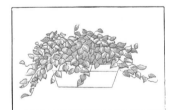

Geranium. This sun worshipper revels in the bright light of windowsills, and it spans a huge variety, both in color and foliage. (Scented geraniums have leaves with wonderful herbal fragrances like lemon, rose, and even chocolate.) Overwatering can cause deadly rot, so let the soil dry out between showers. Low maintenance is key to success with geraniums. Fertilize when you think of it; if they get pot-bound, that's okay—geraniums bloom more profusely in a smaller pot. For a fuller, bushier plant, clip off some stems.

Parlor palm, or *Chamaedorea elegans.* This classic palm grows up to four feet tall, with full, feathery fronds, and gives high-impact garden style to a room. It needs consistent watering, regular fertilizing, and good drainage but is very tolerant of low light and tight pots. It generally needs to be repotted every two or three years.

Piggyback plant, or *Tolmiea menziesii.* This happy houseplant has bright green, heart-shaped leaves. When buying, go for the smaller plant, which will adapt more easily to its new home (and will amaze you with its fast growth). As for care, piggyback plants like filtered or low light, consistently moist soil, and regular fertilizing in the spring and fall. In winter, let the top layer of soil dry out between waterings and lay off the feeding schedule.

Cost-Effective Bouquets

There's nothing like a big dramatic bouquet to raise the spirits—or complete a table setting. Of course, there is a direct correlation between cost and drama, so a big, eye-catching arrangement will set you back. But you may have the makings of a dramatic centerpiece and as many bouquets as you have vases, right outside your front door. Here are just a few ideas to get you started:

- Anything blooming in your yard: roses, spring bulbs, hydrangeas, you name it. (See page 302 for how to harvest fresh flowers.)
- Bunches of herbs: rosemary, basil, chives, and parsley will all bloom.
- The fiddleheads of sprouting ferns.
- Bunches of big, glossy leaves, such as magnolia.
- Delicate tree branches, particularly in early spring: beech, maples, gingko, fruit tree branches, whatever you've got.
- Tall flowering "weeds," such as wild fennel, sorrel, and goldenrod.
- Vegetables such as artichokes and cabbages on their stems, rainbow chard, or kale.

Little Fixes, Big Results

You don't necessarily need to buy anything new (or new to you, as the case may be) to give a room a makeover. It's amazing what a fresh coat of paint, a burst of color, and a good refinishing can do to a room and everything in it. If you like what you've got but it's looking a bit worse for wear, don't assume you need to toss it and start over; chairs, lampshades, even wood furniture can all be refreshed. This goes for flea market finds and other treasures—if the will is there, anything can be customized.

PROJECT | **Reupholster a Chair**

Between fresh paint and a new seat cover, almost any simple chair can easily be rehabbed. Look for solid construction and nice lines, and then customize. (Taking a DIY approach to puffy upholstered furniture is another thing altogether; though home-improvement television shows will tell you otherwise, for most people that is a task to outsource.)

MATERIALS: Fabric (from an old dress or skirt, or a large shirt); chairs; screwdriver; pins; staple gun

1. If you're using an old dress or shirt, lay it flat on the floor in whatever position yields the largest piece possible.

2. Unscrew the seats from the chairs using a screwdriver. Remove the old covering and use it as your template for the new one. Pin the old seat cover to the new fabric and cut out a seat cover for each chair.

3. Lay the new seat cover on a work surface wrong side up. Set the seat on it, top side down. Working one side at a time, pull the fabric onto the bottom of the seat and, using a staple gun, fasten it to the seat. Repeat on the opposite side, followed by the two remaining sides. Pay extra attention to the corners—smooth them before stapling.

4. Screw the chair seats back in place.

Paint a Hardwood Floor

Before you refinish a dinged-up hardwood floor, try painting it. Simply sand it, clean it well, and roll on a paint made for floors or porches. Seal and protect it with a few coats of polyurethane and you've got a fresh look that'll floor 'em. (Obviously, renters must check with their landlords first, and homeowners should consider the value of their floors.)

PROJECT | **Safe Stripping**

It's not what you think! So-called "safe" strippers are a good place to turn for refinishing your wooden antiques. They don't irritate your skin, their fumes aren't damaging to your health, and their contents aren't flammable or explosive—though, of course, rags and residue must be disposed of safely. Safe strippers can also be used indoors, which is ideal for apartment dwellers or for when the weather doesn't permit outdoor work.

TOOLS AND MATERIALS: Newspaper or something to catch residue; stripper; container to hold stripper; brush for application; plastic wrap; scraper; coarse and medium steel wool; coarse stripping brush; rags; soapy water; denatured alcohol, lacquer thinner, or paint thinner

1. Place the piece on newspaper to catch stripper residue, and pour some stripper into a large can or other container.

2. Apply the stripper liberally, brushing on a thick coat. Now go fishing or something. If you're removing a clear finish, such as varnish, the stripper is going to take at least an hour to work. If it's paint, you should cover the surface with a skin of plastic wrap, if possible, and go fishing somewhere far away, because the stripper will take about twelve hours to work.

3. After the stripper has had time to do its job, scrape off the loosened finish. Use coarse steel wool or a stripping pad and the stiff-bristle stripping brush to remove the residue from the nooks. Repeat this process if there's more finish to remove.

4. Scrub down the piece with rags soaked in soapy water (unless the directions on your brand of stripper advise otherwise).

5. Do one final cleanup with medium steel wool and solvent (the alcohol or thinner).

6. Let the piece dry thoroughly.

Staining Sensation

Almost anything you've stripped is going to need some staining. There are oil-based, wax-based, and water- or alcohol-based aniline stains. Alcohol-based stains are useful only when the wood has no remnant of the old finish, and their application can be a little tricky, too. Oil stains dry slowly and can be difficult to work with. Your best bet? Wax stains. They penetrate well and are easy to apply, so they're ideal for beginners.

How to apply? Just dip a disposable foam brush or a rag in the stain and apply it over the entire surface of the piece. As you work, go back and wipe off any excess before it begins to dry. Apply additional coats if you want a dark finish. After that, you're ready to topcoat with varnish or simply buff up the surface with a soft rag. In many cases, especially with oak, that's the entire process. No finish coat is needed, and you're left with a nice hand-rubbed effect.

PAINTING INSTRUCTIONS BY ANNA JOHNSON; SELECTION ADVICE BY AME MAHLER BEANLAND AND EMILY MILES TERRY

PROJECT | # Paint a Room

Freshening a paint job or changing a room's color not only provides instant satisfaction (or almost instant)—it is also far easier and less expensive than replacing furniture or carpeting, let alone hammer-and-nails renovations. And it isn't just an option for homeowners—renters can usually get permission to paint up a storm, as long as they return the place to white before they move out. One thing to know at the outset: Painting is a skill of sequence. Rush any part of the job and the whole result will suffer. It pays to be patient and mellow at every stage.

TOOLS AND MATERIALS: Two-inch brush for trim; tapered sash brush for windows (all-purpose bristles are fine); roller with a wire frame and a threaded end so you can attach an extension for doing ceilings; the best paint you can afford—to economize, use an inexpensive primer for the first coat.

Preparation

Sometimes preparing to paint is more time-consuming than painting itself. But it'll make the job easier in the long run.

1. Remove pictures, picture hooks, curtains, and brackets from walls. Remove loose paint and plaster, and patch holes.

2. Remove or cover doorknobs, electrical switch plates, and light fixtures. Plastic sandwich bags come in handy: Slip one over a doorknob and tape it into place. Cover radiators, thermostats, and woodwork with plastic sheeting or masking tape. Move furniture and rugs into the center of the room and cover with a drop cloth.

3. Wash walls to get rid of accumulated grime, grease, and mildew. Prime any wall repairs.

4. Mix your paint. If paint has been sitting for more than a week, turn the can upside down for a day or two before opening. Then, to avoid spills, pour some paint off into a separate container. Stir the remainder with a wooden paddle until it's well mixed, then gradually add back the paint you've removed and stir until well mixed.

The first coat

Work from top to bottom, starting with the ceiling, then the ceiling molding, walls, windows, and, last, the baseboards and door.

1. Paint across the width of the ceiling in squares that are roughly one yard on each side. If you're using a roller, apply paint as a series of connected W's, then fill them in by running the roller across the pattern. Start by pushing the roller away from you (a roller loaded with paint can spray when put under

pressure). Keep a rag handy—dampened with water if you're using latex paint, or paint thinner otherwise—and clean as you go.

2. Paint the ceiling molding next.

3. Then paint the wall. Start at the ceiling and paint down to the baseboard, working in sections about three feet wide. Use a brush to paint in the corners while the wall is still wet for ease in blending.

4. Windows demand their own sequence. Do sashes first. Raise the inner (bottom) sash and lower the outer (top) sash. Paint the inner sash completely, and paint the exposed surface of the outer sash. Return sashes to their proper positions, but slightly open. Paint the remainder of the outer sash, then do the frame and the sill. When these are dry, paint the inside channels (the surfaces that hold the window in place). Wipe paint drips off the glass, or razor-blade them off once the paint is dry.

5. Paint doors and baseboards last.

The second coat

If there are drips or splotches in your first coat, sand them back. The second coat is the one you have to live with, so apply it with concentration and finesse, especially when painting the baseboards. When you're done, try to get out of the house (even the least toxic paints can irritate skin and lungs). Avoid sleeping in the freshly painted room for at least twenty-four hours.

What Kind of Paint?

Quality paints are worth the investment. If you cheap out, you'll just wind up repainting much sooner than you planned and may have to do multiple coats. You have two basic choices in paints: latex, which is water-based, or oil-based. Latex paint is easy to clean up with soap and water, has less noxious fumes than oil-based paint, and is quick-drying. Oil-based paint requires solvents for cleanup, has a strong odor, and dries more slowly but also more smoothly. Experts recommend oil-based paint for applications where there is heavy use; for example, floors or cabinets that are touched frequently.

Secrets to Painting Success

The first key to painting success is one that will serve you over the long term: Know your paint. Write down the information about the paint you're using, including the brand and the specific color mix, and store it someplace safe. When it's time to touch up or paint another section in the future, you won't unintentionally come out with a two-tone room or house. When you're ready to get cracking:

Test Your Paint. Before buying huge amounts of stain or blended paints, first test the color by painting a patch in a relatively obscure corner. Display samples do not always demonstrate the subtleties of the color.

Use Good Brushes. You'll save yourself aggravation by spending a little more to buy a quality brush. The bristles of cheap brushes are not as responsive, so you may have to work harder. They also give you less control, and you'll end up with a more uneven distribution of paint on the surface. Low-quality brushes also tend to lose their bristles more readily as you paint; these are aggravating to pick out of wet paint.

And Take Good Care of Them. Before throwing out an old paintbrush with hardened paint in it, try sticking it in a pot of simmering vinegar and removing the paint with a wire brush. Rub a few drops of oil into the bristles to keep them soft.

PROJECT | **Make a Bookcase from Orphaned Drawers**

Cast-off drawers begin life again as built-in bookcases. You can build an entire bookcase all at once if you have enough drawers, or you can let it grow more organically by attaching drawers to the wall as you find them. In some cases, you may have to trim the face of a drawer so it's flush with the bottom and sides.

MATERIALS: Mismatched drawers; electric drill or screwdriver; ⅜-inch drill bit; measuring tape; ⅜-inch bolts (1¼ to 1½ inches long); corresponding washers and nuts, one 1 x 4 cut approximately 4 inches shorter than the length of the bookcase (more as needed); 1- or 1¼-inch wood screws

PAINTING SUCCESS TIPS BY ERIK BRUUN; BOOKCASE BY KATHLEEN HACKETT AND MARY ANN YOUNG

1. Lay the drawers out on the floor, open face up, and arrange them as if you were doing a puzzle, keeping the dimensions of your intended wall space in mind.

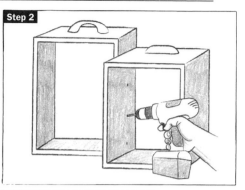

2. Using a drill with a ⅜-inch bit, drill holes in the drawers where they will be attached to each other, both horizontally and vertically, making sure you have at least 2 bolts securing every instance of overlap between drawers. (If the span of the adjoining pieces is large enough, attach one bolt at the center of the overlap and work outward in 12-inch intervals; for a smaller drawer or overlap, attach your bolts at either end of the overlap's span.)

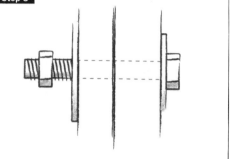

3. Fasten the drawers to one another. Slide the smaller washers onto the ⅜-inch bolts (1¼ or 1½ inches long, depending on the thickness of the wood), then thread the bolts through each hole. Slide the large washers onto the bolts, then fasten tightly with nuts.

4. To mount the finished bookcase on the wall, screw a 1 x 4 piece of pine (or any other wood you desire) into the wall studs. This step is necessary in safely securing the bookcase to the wall. (Note: If your bookcase is multitiered and will be holding lots of heavy stuff, consider fastening one 1 x 4 for each tier.)

5. Mark a spot on the wall above the 1 x 4 corresponding to the intended height of your bookcase. Measure the distance between that spot and the middle of the 1 x 4. On the inside (display side) of the bookcase, mark these measures; then, moving horizontally from the center mark, mark the inside of the bookcase at 12-inch intervals. These markings correspond to the points at which you will screw the drawers onto the 1 x 4.

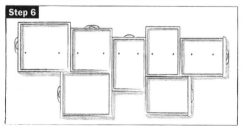

6. Have two people hold the bookcase in place and, using the electric drill and wood screws (1 or 1¼ inches long, depending on the thickness of the wood), follow the markings and fasten the unit to the 1 x 4(s).

PROJECT | ## Make a Lamp Shade

It's common to find fantastic old lamps at flea markets and yard sales whose only flaw is a dinged shade. Luckily, with a steady hand and the right materials, it's easy to create a custom paper shade yourself. (If you need to rewire the lamp, too, see how on page 54.) *A note: These directions apply to lamp-shades with circular rings.*

MATERIALS: Old (circular ring) lampshade; poster board or stiff paper; pencil; two 1-pound bag of beans (or similar weight); sharp scissors; strong glue; clothespins; razor blade

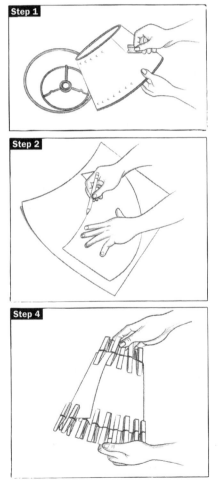

1. To remove an old fabric covering, cut and rip it off in any manner possible without bending the frame. If the frame is covered with paper, parchment, or plastic, use a gentler approach in order to preserve the old cover, which will become your new pattern. Use a razor blade to cut the trim that covers the rings. Next, carefully insert the blade under the edge of the seam that joins the ends of the covering, and work this glued seam loose. You might have to work from both the inside and the outside. At this point the entire covering should come off the frame, and you will be holding an arc-shape piece of material. Use the scissors to tidy the ragged edges.

2. Mark your pattern. If you're working from an arc, mark the new cover by laying the old pattern on a sheet of poster board or other stiff paper and tracing around it. If you don't have an arc pattern to work from and the frame is a one-piece (not two unattached rings), rub a little crayon or colored chalk on the outer edges of its rings and roll the frame on the paper.

3. Cut the marked paper, staying slightly outside the marks to allow for adjustment.

4. Starting with the top ring, attach the paper to the frame with spring-type clothespins. Continue all the way around the ring, placing the clothespins side by side. Repeat for the bottom ring. You might have to loosen pins here and there to adjust the fit as you go. The cover should fit snugly to the frame.

5. Glue the covering to the frame. To do this, remove every other clothespin from the top ring. Then, with the bottle of glue or a glue applicator (simply a bottle with a long thin nozzle), reach inside the shade and apply a bead of glue along the paper where it touches the frame.

6. Repeat this process for the bottom ring and for any inside ribs. When the glue dries, remove all the clothespins and apply glue to the spaces that were covered by the pins.

7. Using your finger or a piece of stiff paper, coat the underside of the overlapping edge (where the two ends of the arc come together) with a little glue. (Too much and

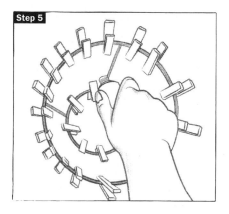

Step 5

things will get messy.) Lay the shade on its side, seam down on a clean surface, and place a bag or two of beans inside the shade, on top of the seam. The weight will press the surfaces together. Leave the beans in place until the adhesive sets and the seam is sealed.

A finishing touch

Though it's not absolutely necessary, you might want to cover the edges of the shade at the top and bottom rings. For this, you'll need ribbon that is at least 50 percent cotton; otherwise, the glue won't adhere. The type of ribbon most commonly used is a ribbed variety called grosgrain (pronounced grow-grain).

1. Measure around the shade at top and bottom, and cut two corresponding lengths of ribbon, with a little allowance for overlap.

2. Apply the glue to the ribbon and wrap the glue-covered portion over the wire, pressing it against the paper on the inside and outside of the shade.

3. Work on sections of about one and one-half inches at a time, and use a clothespin to hold the ribbon in place temporarily as you work on the next section. When you reach the end, just overlap it, glue, and clamp it into place.

PROJECT | **Install a New Lighting Fixture**

A good way to change the appearance of a room is to replace an old light fixture. An electrician will charge you an hourly rate, usually with a minimum, for a task that might take you a half hour or so. *A note:* These directions assume you are dealing with two fixtures of similar size. If that's not the case, you may need to replace the existing bracket (the support mechanism mounted in the ceiling) or even change the size of the hole in your ceiling, and the project will become more involved.

TOOLS: Straight-slot or Phillips screwdriver; wire stripper

1. Turn off the power to the light at the circuit breaker. It is not enough to turn off the wall switch. Power may remain in the white and ground wires, which can be enough to shock you.

2. Take off the bulb cover and remove the light bulb.

3. Next, unfasten any screws holding the light fixture (canopy plate) to the ceiling. The fixture should now detach from the ceiling.

4. The wires of the old fixture and the box are connected by plastic wire nuts. Remove the nuts to disconnect the old fixture.

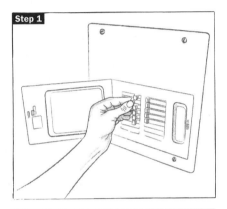

Step 1

Always Turn Off the Power

Before working on anything electrical—wiring, plugs, outlets—turn off the circuit breaker, remove the fuse for that area of the house, or turn off the main electrical switch. Always make sure the power is off by testing a receptacle on the circuit with a voltage tester or neon test light.

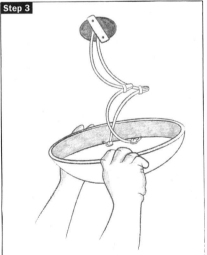

Step 3

LIGHTING INSTALLATION STEPS BY LYN HERRICK

5. There are two basic ways to attach a fixture to the ceiling. One uses screws to bolt a strap to the ceiling. The second has a stud that comes down from the center of the box and attaches to a hickey. Follow the instructions that come with your new fixture.

6. Strip ¾ of an inch off the insulation of the black, white, and ground wires of the new fixture (the ground wire is often green). Using wire strippers, cut through the insulation to the wire. Crimp down on the wire without cutting through it, then slip the coating off.

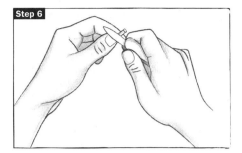

7. Raise the new fixture and connect the black, white, and ground wires to the corresponding wires in the box and fasten them together with wire nuts. Tape the wire nuts with electrical tape to make sure they stay on.

8. Secure the fixture to the support mechanism and screw the light bulb into place. Now turn on the power to see if the fixture works.

9. If so, refasten the bulb cover and the project is complete.

If the light does not come on, first test the light bulb. Next, check the wiring to make sure the connections are securely fastened and that the wires are connected black to black, white to white, and ground to ground. If you see a problem with the wiring, turn the power off at the circuit breaker before attempting to fix it. If that doesn't do the trick, it may be that the new fixture is faulty and needs to be exchanged.

PROJECT | # Rewire a Lamp

You score an amazing lamp at the flea market. You bring it home. You screw in the light bulb. . . . No dice. It's an all-too-common scenario. Don't just give up and stick the thing in your garage; rewire it, and it'll be as good as new.

TOOLS AND MATERIALS: Screwdriver; electrical cord; sharp knife or single-edge razor blade; wire stripper; socket interior; automatic plug; replacement felt; craft glue; scissors

1. Remove the harp. It's easier to take the shell off the socket if the harp is out of the way first. With the lamp unplugged, lift the two little sleeves where the harp attaches to the harp bottom. Squeeze the sides of the harp near this attachment and remove the top part.

2. Take the socket apart. Look at the socket where the shell meets the shell base. You'll see the word *press* near the switch. Push in on this with your thumb and tilt the shell away from you. The shell will come off, exposing the socket. If you're unable to loosen the shell, insert a small screwdriver at the *press* point. This will usually dislodge it.

3. Disconnect the old wire. When you remove the shell, the cardboard insulator usually remains in it. If it's still covering the socket, pull it off. Loosen the two screws that hold the lamp cord to the socket, and pull the cord out from the bottom of the lamp. You might have to take the felt off the base of the lamp to access the cord.

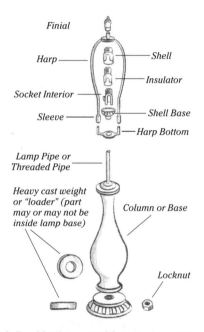

Finial

Harp

Shell

Insulator

Socket Interior

Sleeve

Shell Base

Harp Bottom

Lamp Pipe or Threaded Pipe

Heavy cast weight or "loader" (part may or may not be inside lamp base)

Column or Base

Locknut

4. Feed in the new wiring. Feed the new cord, which should be 6 to 8 feet long, through the base and up through the lamp pipe and socket shell base. Allow yourself plenty of slack at the top and tie a loose, ordinary knot in the cord several inches from the top. With a sharp knife or razor blade, slit the insulation between the two wires, just enough to start the separation. Pull the two wires apart a couple of inches, and use the wire strippers to strip about a ½ inch of insulation off each wire. Roll the wire between your thumb and index finger to twist all those little fine wires together.

REWIRING DIRECTIONS BY JAMES W. MCKENZIE

5. Match up your wires. Match the wire colors to the colors of the screws on the socket. This places the grounded side of the circuit on the threaded, outer portion of the socket—the part you could most easily touch by accident.

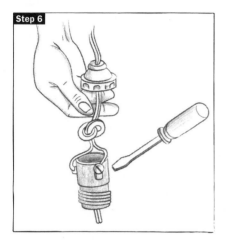

Step 6

6. Pull out the slack. Making sure there are no stray strands of wire, tighten the screws securely. Work the loose knot up as close to the bottom of the socket interior as possible, pull the slack out of the cord from the bottom, and replace the shell and insulator. You'll feel it snap into place as you push the shell into the shell base.

7. Replace the plug. If your vintage lamp comes with an old-fashioned screw-type plug, replace it with an automatic plug. To attach one, squeeze the prongs together and pull the insides out. Insert the end of the cord through the hole in the cover and, holding the prongs spread outward, force the cord as far as possible into the opening between the prongs. Squeeze the prongs together and push the mechanism back into the cover, reattaching it firmly.

8. Replace the felt. Normally, you'll destroy the felt on the bottom of a lamp when you rewire it. You can buy replacement felt from parts suppliers (even self-stick) or, for a lot less money, in small sheets at craft stores. Use a thick craft glue. Spread a coat on the base and set the lamp on top of the felt. After the glue has dried, trim the excess close to the base with sharp scissors.

Motor Skills & the Bills

One day, in a utopian future, we'll all be living in walkable cities and suburbs, trimming our carbon emissions and our waistlines. But for now, for many of us, a car is a nonnegotiable need—and a hefty expense, one that often balances rational needs with lots of emotions and intangibles. If you're in the market to buy, there are certain steps you can take to make sure your ride is suited to your budget—and to your lifestyle, too. If you already own, you'll learn how to do some simple maintenance and repairs.

At the Car Lot | by Jay Akasie

Avid autophiles may approach car lots with the zeal of warriors going into battle—but for many people, car shopping is fraught. Boil it down to a few simple principles, and it needn't be so stress-inducing. (Principles always make it better.)

Know your needs. How you will use your car should determine how much power and performance you need. A car that travels primarily to the local supermarket doesn't need especially nimble handling. The better the engine, the less precious cargo space the ride is likely to include. If you have a long and complicated weekday commute, on the other hand, "passing power" should be at the top of your list of considerations. The ability to pull ahead of or steer away from a potentially dangerous situation is derived from a powerful and agile car.

Study the safety factors. Some people say that a 1950s Buick was the safest car ever produced, by virtue of its sheer size and weight. But safety also means having the power to pass another car with ease, as well as to brake in a decent amount of time and distance. Be sure to check on what kinds of supplemental restraints (front and side airbags) are included in certain models; often the cheapest models will offer an array of airbags that rival the most expensive luxury sedans.

Test the drive. Make certain that you test-drive—and test-drive again—the models you think you'd most enjoy. Only when you hit the road will you be able to know if the match is true.

Be guided by value. Once you've made the big decision about which car to buy, you have two central questions to face. First, what's the most competitive price for the model you've selected? Second, what's the long-term implication of buying a car with a certain engine and fuel economy? To find the answer to the first, select a few models and do your research via the Web and with the indispensable buyers' reference guide, the *Kelley Blue Book.*

What with ever-changing gas prices and the environment at stake, the second question is more important than the first these days. But fuel-efficiency isn't the end-all, be-all: Within certain product lines, a car with a small, fuel-efficient engine might be less dependable and more costly to service. In general, the trade-in value of a nameplate is the best sign that a car is dependable over the long haul.

Be ready to haggle. Think of the price tag as a guideline—the dealer does, and chances are he expects to negotiate. Don't be afraid to question or refuse "dealer prep" costs that increase the sticker price. Just what exactly is an "undercarriage treatment," anyway? And the exclusive rust-proofing service? (Come on!)

Decide how to spend it. The Holy Grail of automotive financing is a 0 percent rate. Can't get any better than that! If you can't find that, look around for the lowest rate you can lock in.

A note on leasing: Obviously it's generally less frugal than buying. But there is an exception: If you use your car for business purposes (say, you drive around selling real estate), tax deductions will be simpler on a lease than on an outright purchase.

Buying New Tires (Resist the Hype!)

To get an idea of what tire buyers are up against, grab a few brochures from some local tire retail outlets. They'll give you a good sense of not only how high-tech tires are these days, but also the amount of money that goes into marketing them. Directional Tread Design! Aggressive Shoulder Tread Blocks! Tremendous Cornering Force! Can it all be true? Certainly. There are a lot of good-quality tires in the marketplace today. And there is also intense competition among tire manufacturers. As a smart consumer, you must become immune to the seduction of advertising. Your emphasis should be on "right for your car and your driving habits." It makes no sense to get hyped up about premium all-season, high-performance radial tires when you do all your driving in warm-climate suburbia.

In the Garage | by Bridget Kachur

While it's true that vehicles today can be so advanced that it's hard to fix most problems yourself, there are some basics that you can tackle on your own. You can extend your car's lifespan, preserve its resale value, and avoid costly repairs by investing a little time in maintenance.

Wash and Wax

Looking good out on the road is important to enthusiastic drivers, but some motorists think it's ridiculous to spend time and money for a spotless, gleaming car. But it's not just about looks. Proper detailing is important. To keep your car from rusting out beneath you, you must keep the exterior clean. Washing a car regularly keeps road salt, mud, and other grime from lodging in the nooks and crannies (places where rust usually first gets a foothold). Waxing isn't just for shine: It also helps prevent rust.

Follow these simple guidelines and you'll end up with a gleaming (and saleable) piece of automotive machinery:

- Wash your car only when its body is cool.
- Keep your car out of direct sunlight when you are washing, drying, or waxing it.
- Wash the wheels first, and then the car body from the top to the bottom.
- Use cold water and a commercial car-washing detergent, not dish detergent or laundry soap (they're too harsh for the paint and finish on your car).

Caution: When you are washing your car, never open the hood and spray-wash the engine. Water coming in contact with the electrical wiring will cause a short circuit, and if moisture accumulates in the air filter, your car will stall or perhaps not start at all.

Cleaning the Engine

A clean engine performs better than a dirty engine, but engine-cleaning is a messy and difficult task that's best left to professionals. There are, however, a few elements of engine upkeep you can take care of at home. Every month, use a clean, dry rag to wipe away grease, dirt, and other grime from the upper and lower radiator hoses, the air filter, the tops of the windshield-washer fluid and coolant reservoirs, the underside of the hood, and the top of the battery. Wipe down the battery last, so you don't transfer acid buildup onto other components under the hood.

STICKY SITUATIONS

Removing sticky stuff from the body of your car can be a pain. And if you end up scratching the paint in the process—argh! Here are a few grime-specific tricks to make the job simpler:

Bird droppings and tree sap. Drape a wet microfiber cloth over the area to soften it up. After about fifteen minutes, try wiping up the mess. (*Up* is the operative word—you don't want to push the droppings or sap across more of the car body than it already occupies.) You may have to do this a few times before the spot is completely cleaned up.

Deal with a Dent at Home

A slight dent may be a repair you can handle yourself. In some cases, a toilet plunger will do the trick. Moisten the edge of the rubber cup so it sticks to the car body, and hop to it. You may have to try it a few times before you get the right grip pressure. You can also use a hammer to lightly tap out the extended end of the dent from inside the car body. Cover the hammer with a rag so you don't make a new dent while trying to fix the existing one.

Bumper stickers. Turn a blow dryer to the high heat setting. Direct a flow of hot air over one end of the sticker, slowly working your way across. As the paper heats up, the adhesive will liquefy, allowing you to peel the paper from the car. If any of the adhesive remains, rub over it with a small amount of rubbing alcohol.

Decals. To remove a decal from a window in your car, use a blow dryer as directed above. If there is glue left behind, use a razor blade to scrape it away. Be careful and methodical; you don't want to scratch the window or, more important, cut yourself.

Rust, Scratches, and Dents

Repairing minor scratches and dents shouldn't be an expensive endeavor, whether you do the job yourself or bring the car to a body shop. But it's easy to botch a do-it-yourself bodywork job. Take a rust spot, for example. Unless you have a trained eye, what you think is just a small rust spot may actually be a small rust spot and a small hole. When you sand down the rust, you find the hole. Now you have to go back to the auto parts store to buy filler. When you get home, you have a lot of intensive hands-on work to do to fill in the hole, smooth down the spot, and paint over it. When all is said and done, you find that the touch-up paint that was supposed to match the color of your car doesn't. Perhaps it was the wrong paint. Perhaps the color of the paint on your car has faded. Who knows? But now you've thrown your money and your time into a futile effort that a professional could have undertaken successfully for the price of the massage you're going to need to soothe your frustration. Sometimes it simply does not pay to DIY.

Automotive Toolkit

You need a toolbox to be handy around the house, and you need one to be handy with your car, too. Even if you opt not to fix your own flat tires, you need to be ready for anything. Here's a list of car essentials. To keep everything rolling, make sure that the fluids—engine oil, brake fluid, and so on—are the types recommended for your car; check your owner's manual for details.

- Automatic transmission fluid (if your car is an automatic)
- Brake fluid (small unopened can)
- Engine oil
- Fuel additive
- Nonvolatile emergency fuel
- Power steering fluid (small unopened can)
- Premixed coolant
- Stop-leak additive for the cooling system
- Tire sealant
- WD-40
- Windshield-washer fluid
- Funnel
- Empty gas container
- Booster (jumper) cables, 16 feet (5 m), 16-gauge with sturdy clamps
- Air filter (the right size and type for your car)
- Rubber or plastic gloves
- Straight-slot and Phillips screwdrivers
- Four-arm wheel (lug) wrench
- Hammer
- Jack and jack stand
- Six wood blocks (for securing tires when you're changing a flat)
- Warning reflectors or emergency flares
- Clean rags or paper towels
- Small bottle of soda water (for removing stains)
- Rope or towing chain
- Reflective tape (to place over a broken head- or taillight)
- Duct tape (because you never know when it might come in handy)
- Oversize, bright-colored shirt (for when you must work on your car)

PROJECT | **Change the Air Filter**

In the old days, you could check the quality of an air filter by holding it up to the light. If you could see light through the filter, it was still clean enough to continue using. Filters made today, however, can be deceiving. Sometimes they're so thick that no light shines through the paper folds, even though they're quite clean. To be on the safe side, change your air filter as often as your owner's manual recommends.

TOOLS AND SUPPLIES: Straight-slot screwdriver (as necessary); new air filter (of the type recommended in your owner's manual)

1. Loosen the filter's cover. (If it's screwed down, unscrew it.) If the cover is clamped down by clips, use the head of the screwdriver to snap them open. The cover is usually attached to a large hose, so you can't remove it from the engine completely. Just wiggle it loose and carefully push it out of the way.

2. Take a good look at where and how the air filter sits. When you install the new filter, it should occupy the exact same position.

3. Using both hands, lift out the air filter.

4. Take the new air filter out of its packaging. Set it in the filter base in the appropriate position. With the tips of your fingers, push the filter down firmly all around its outer edges to make sure that it fits tightly.

5. Set the cover on the air filter. Snap on all the clips or reinsert and tighten the screws. Double-check that all clips have been reset.

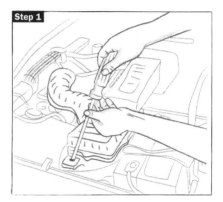

Step 1

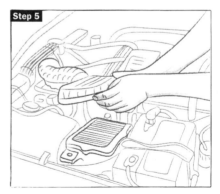

Step 5

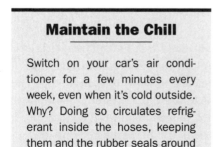

Maintain the Chill

Switch on your car's air conditioner for a few minutes every week, even when it's cold outside. Why? Doing so circulates refrigerant inside the hoses, keeping them and the rubber seals around them from drying out.

Know Your Vital Fluids

Keeping your car's fluids at the appropriate level is one of the easiest maintenance measures, and it will greatly reduce the occurrence of costly engine repairs. It doesn't take much time, either. Many fluid reservoirs have a dipstick that reaches down into them. Dipsticks make it easy to check the amount of fluid in a reservoir that is hard to reach. You simply pull out the dipstick, wipe it clean, reinsert it, then pull it out and take a reading. The only "tool" you need is a clean rag. Why can't you take a reading right when you first pull out the dipstick? As you've been driving the car around, fluid has been sloshing around in the reservoir pan, coating more of the dipstick than it rightfully should.

Automatic transmission fluid. If your car has an automatic transmission, it also has automatic transmission fluid, which you should check periodically. Park your car on level ground, leave the engine idling, and use the transmission fluid dipstick to check the level of fluid in your system.

Brake fluid. Brake fluid is held in the brake master cylinder, which is located near the back of the engine, under the windshield. For operational efficiency, the brakes need good-quality brake fluid.

Clutch fluid. If your car is a standard—that is, it has a manual transmission—you'll want to periodically check the amount of clutch fluid. The clutch fluid is housed in a master cylinder near the back of the engine, under the windshield. It often sits close to the brake master cylinder.

Coolant. Coolant is a mixture of antifreeze and water that circulates through the cooling system, carrying heat away from the engine block. If you run low on coolant, your engine is in danger of overheating.

Power steering fluid. Power steering is a system of hydraulics that makes it easier to turn the steering wheel. If you've ever driven an older car without power steering, you'll appreciate the ease that power steering brings to your driving experience, and you'll have good motivation to make sure that your car is always supplied with adequate power steering fluid. Power steering fluid usually remains good for the life of your car, but it's wise to check it periodically.

Windshield-washer fluid. Windshield-washer fluid keeps the windshield free of bugs, dust, grime, snow, ice, and other viewing obstacles. It's important to check the washer fluid reservoir frequently, because a dry washer fluid tank can turn your regular commute treacherous.

Tightening a Nut

When you tighten a lug nut, you pull the wheel in the direction of your wrench. If the next lug nut you tighten is adjacent to the first lug nut, you may inadvertently introduce a slight tilt to the wheel position; it won't straighten out when you tighten the remaining lug nuts. To prevent this, tighten lug nuts in a crisscross pattern, as shown.

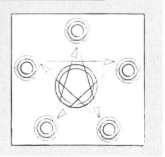

PROJECT | ## Check Tire Pressure

To check your tire pressure, take your car to a gas station with an air pump. That way, if you find that you have to add air to a tire, you can do it right there and then. Ideally, tires should be cold when you check their air pressure—it can decrease as much as one pound for every 10 degrees Fahrenheit the temperature drops. Check the air pressure in all the tires, including the spare, once a month.

TOOL: Tire pressure gauge

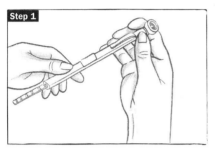
Step 1

1. Take a look at your tire pressure gauge. One end has a rounded hood containing a small point. This is the end you push into the tire valve stem. The other end has a flat or round ruler printed with numbers corresponding to air pressure in pounds per square inch (PSI) or kilopascals (kPa).

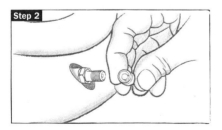
Step 2

2. Remove the cap from the valve stem of the first tire. Set the cap in a safe place—it's small and easy to misplace.

3. Push the ruler of the tire pressure gauge all the way into the gauge.

4. Press the rounded end of the tire pressure gauge against the exposed end of the valve stem. If you don't press it on securely, you'll

hear a sound as air escapes from the tire. (Don't worry—you can reinflate the tire later.) Try again. Each time you try, be sure to push the ruler back into the gauge so you'll get an accurate reading.

Step 5

5. Once you have the tire pressure gauge properly positioned on the top of the valve stem so no air is escaping, the ruler will pop out from the gauge. When this happens, remove the gauge and look at the ruler. The place where the ruler meets the end of the gauge marks the air pressure in your tire.

If the air pressure in the tire matches what's recommended in your owner's manual, put the valve cap back on.

If the air pressure in the tire exceeds the pressure that's recommended in your owner's manual, use the rounded end of the tire pressure gauge to release air from the tire. It doesn't take much time to lose a pound of air from a tire, so stop often to recheck the pressure.

If the air pressure in the tire is less than what's recommended in your owner's manual, you'll have to add more air.

PROJECT | ## Add Air to a Tire

Sure you can pay or tip extra to have a station attendant fill your tires. But if you can learn to do it yourself, why not? To add air to a tire, you'll need to visit a gas station air pump. Most are coin-operated; when you feed in the proper coins, the air starts pumping and will keep going for a while— usually long enough so you can add air to at least two or three tires, if necessary.

TOOLS: Gas station air pump; tire pressure gauge

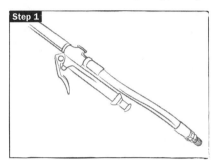

Step 1

1. Examine the end of the air pump's hose. it will have three parts: the lever, the gauge, and the feeder hose. The lever looks like a lever-type door handle. You'll pull it to start the air flow. Just above the handle is the ruler of the pressure gauge. You'll be using your own gauge, so you can ignore this. Extending from the handle just above the ruler is the short feeder hose. This is what you'll press against the valve stem to add more air to the tire.

2. Untangle the hose from the air pump and straighten out any kinks. Then drop the end of the hose next to the first tire that needs to be inflated.

3. Remove the caps from the valve stems of all the tires that need to be inflated, then start the air pump.

4. Take the end of the feeder hose and fit it directly over the tire's valve stem. As with a tire pressure gauge, if you don't fit the end of the feeder hose securely over the valve stem, you'll hear the sound of escaping air.

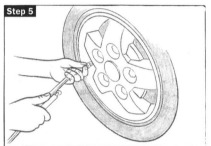

Step 5

5. Once you've managed to feed some air into the tire, stop to check the air pressure with your tire gauge.

6. Continue feeding air and checking the tire pressure until the tire is properly inflated according to the specifications in your owner's manual.

7. Don't forget to screw each cap securely back on its valve stem.

PROJECT | ## Change a Flat

A flat tire is always a major drag. And if you're not a member of AAA, it can also wind up being a major expense. But if you've got your automotive toolkit ready, you can change that flat yourself. Follow this simple procedure.

TOOLS AND SUPPLIES: Spare tire; 3 reflectors or flares; 6 pieces of wood or sizable stones; straight-slot screwdriver; lug wrench; car jack; small rag; hammer

1. Turn on your hazard lights, then set out at least three reflectors or flares. Place the first one about ten car-lengths behind your car and the others between that flare and your car. Be sure that the car is in park with the parking brake on! If you do not have reflectors or flares, prop open the hood of your car and tie a bright-colored cloth to the antenna or a traffic-side door handle.

2. Remove the spare tire and all other necessary tools and supplies from the trunk and place them nearby on the ground.

3. Secure the three tires that are not flat by wedging a block of wood or a rock in front of and behind each wheel.

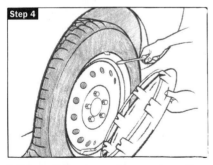
Step 4

4. Using a flathead screwdriver, pry loose the hubcap of the flat tire. Place it upside down near you.

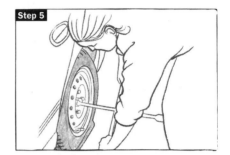
Step 5

5. Using the lug wrench, loosen the wheel lug nuts by turning them counterclockwise. Move from one lug nut to the other in a crisscross pattern (see page 63). Do not fully remove the lug nuts; just get them loose enough so you can remove them by hand once your car has been jacked up. (You'll need to apply some real muscle to that task.)

6. Position the jack under the car, following the instructions in your owner's manual. Most cars have a small notch under their frame that marks the spot where the jack should be positioned. Place the jack exactly as directed. The jack will hold the tremendous weight of your car; if it is not properly positioned, it could damage your car or give way.

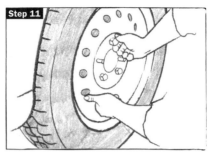

7. Using solid, even strokes on the jack, raise your car until the flat tire is suspended. Keeping your feet away from the car, wiggle the jack and its stand to make sure that it and your car are secure. Walk around your car and double-check the wood blocks or rocks. They should be firmly secured against the other three tires.

8. Remove the lug nuts by hand in a crisscross pattern and set them in the upside-down hubcap.

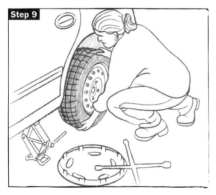

9. Crouch or sit so your chest is even with the sidewall of the tire. Using both hands, wiggle the tire loose from the bolts. Roll the tire to the rear of your car.

10. Roll the spare tire into position. Lift it up, align its notches with the bolts on the wheel rim, and wedge it into place.

11. Replace each lug nut, hand-tightening them clockwise and in a crisscross pattern. When all the lugs are hand-tightened, grab the lug wrench and tighten them further, using the same crisscross pattern. When the tire starts to rotate, you've tightened the lug nuts as much as you should.

12. Using solid, even strokes, lower the jack until all four tires are flat on the ground. Remove the jack stand.

13. Using the lug wrench, tighten the lug nuts as much as you can, using the crisscross pattern. If the lugs aren't tight, the tire will wobble. If you don't think you have the muscle for it, do your best, but stop at the next service station and have one of the mechanics tighten the lug nuts with a hydraulic wrench.

14. Hold the hubcap in place with one hand in the middle and tap around the outside of the hubcap with a rag-covered hammer. Don't pound too hard; you might dent it.

15. Put the flat tire and all the tools and supplies back inside the trunk.

inside this chapter . . .

PROJECTS

RECIPES

animal, vegetable, budget

The Well-Tended Garden & Well-Loved Pet

THE "VICTORY GARDEN" IS A THRIFT ICON—A CAN-DO RESPONSE to tightened belts and food rations. But the plain truth is that a garden can turn into a money pit faster than you can say "What's been eating my hundred-dollar rosebush?" Cultivating exotic flowers isn't exactly the thriftiest of hobbies.

Tending a vegetable garden, on the other hand, can deliver an excellent return on your investment of time and money. Still, even in that area, it's so easy to overspend: fertilizers, plants, herbicides, tools . . . suddenly you've shelled out hundreds and supermarket produce isn't looking so bad. If you shop and plant smart, though, those heirloom tomatoes and perfectly ripe melons will end up costing you pennies apiece. Indeed, the thrifty gardener has the double benefit of spending less and getting more: healthier and more bountiful crops. And hey, if growing flowers brings you joy, go for it. With a few thrift tips under your belt, you'll get more bloom for your buck.

However rewarding tending plants may be, no shrub ever brought anyone their slippers. Pets are a huge part of many people's lives—and have been since the dawn of time. But unlike his prehistoric forebears, the modern pet tends to require more than a bone tossed in its direction. That's not to say that in order to cut costs, you need to eliminate all treats and goodies. You *can* be a doting pet parent on the cheap. Your furry friends may not ask for much besides love and food, but a plush bed or customized sweater can't hurt.

A Bountiful Harvest

You don't have to have acres of land and a potting shed out back to be a gardener. Anyone with a patch of dirt, or even just a patch of sun, can enjoy the rewards of planting and harvesting. In fact, the thriftiest garden is often the most compact— intensive planting yields more veggies per dollar, and happier soil too. With a few essential tools, and a basic understanding of plants, soil, and climate, you can transform your yard into a blooming paradise (or at least get a few good tomatoes out of the deal). Just be prepared to invest some "sweat equity." As they say, green thumbs always have dirt under their nails.

How Thrifty Is My Garden? | by J.D. Roth

For people who savor its rewards, gardening is a labor of love. My wife and I have been growing our own food for more than a decade, and I've long argued that it is an excellent way to save money. But is it really? I recently decided to find out. Beginning on a January 1, my wife and I logged the time and money we spent on our food crops. We tracked everything: the cost of seeds, young plants, fertilizer, and pheromone-based pest traps; our approximate water and electricity usage; even the time we spent planting, weeding, and harvesting. And to calculate the rewards, we monitored the amount of food we harvested, as well as the cost equivalent from the local produce stand.

It wasn't a formal experiment, but we hoped that its results would help us find new ways to economize and to improve our crops in years to come.

What our analysis does not include are start-up costs. Any beginning gardener will find that this hobby isn't cheap. Besides plants and seeds, you'll need tools, fertilizers, soil amendments, watering devices, and a million other small things.

Some of these investments will last for many years, while others are annual purchases. With time—and smart choices—a kitchen garden does pay off financially. Herbs will pay for themselves quickly. Eventually, so will the berry bushes and canes, fruit trees, and fresh vegetables.

Another important note is that weather can lead to unexpected results—good or bad. A hailstorm pummeled our newly planted tomato starts in late April. Cool weather lingered into June and then returned early in autumn, shortening our prime growing season by about six weeks. The tomatoes were not happy, and our harvest was smaller than expected.

Even so, our year was quite successful. We spent $318.43 and 60 hours working on our crops. For our efforts, we harvested $586.96 worth of produce:

- $225.74 in berries (about 56 pounds)

- $294.59 in vegetables (about 167 pounds)

- $66.63 in tree fruit (about 46 pounds)

We also made use of about $20 worth of fresh herbs. For every dollar we spent on the garden, we harvested $1.91 worth of food.

I'll be honest. I was a little disappointed. Once it became clear that our garden was making a profit, I wanted the profit to be huge. It wasn't—but in my opinion a wage of $4.50 per hour (or $2.25 per person per hour) for an activity you could qualify as leisure is nothing to sneer at.

Certain economic realities cannot be changed. Even during years of normal weather, some plants are more productive than

Share the Bounty

When you buy a packet of seeds, you'll generally get more than you need. We've found that it's fun (and frugal) to split the costs with others by participating in a seed exchange. We also share equipment with friends and neighbors. Careful borrowing and lending helps keep costs down for everyone. During midsummer, we share the harvest. Our neighbor across the street lets us pick his cherries and grapes; we give him canned salsa and pickles. We trade berries with a coworker with a talent for salad greens.

Preserve the Harvest

With a little freezer space, you can prolong the pleasure of the harvest. Berries and jams are simple to freeze and then thaw during the depths of winter. (Nothing like a warm blackberry cobbler on a cold January night!) As your gardening expertise grows, learning how to pickle and can your crops (see page 175) will help to make your efforts more worthwhile.

others. For us, corn is a disinterested producer. We just don't have the space it needs to thrive. On the other hand, berries (strawberries, blueberries, blackberries, currants, raspberries, marionberries, and elderberries) love our yard, and they require little money or time. We spent about $5 on berry-related supplies, and in return we harvested $225 worth of fruit. On the other hand, we spent about $9 on our corn—and harvested $9 in corn.

The good news is that we can now use this knowledge to our advantage by focusing on plants that fare better in our climate. Next year: No more corn or potatoes. They aren't worth it for us. But after seeing how productive our fruit trees have become in just four years, we're putting in three more: a dwarf cherry and two varieties of Asian pear. Planting a fruit tree is a one-time investment that pays off big for years, and plenty of dwarf versions will fit in an average yard.

In the end, most of the benefits of our garden can't be measured in dollars and cents. To us, the garden is about value, and about our values. The garden minimizes packaging waste and fossil fuel use. We spend time outside, talking to our neighbors and building community. We love having a productive hobby we can share with others, and enjoy the challenges and triumphs that come with each year's gardening efforts. And truly, there's nothing like putting by a jar of your own salsa—made with tomatoes, peppers, and herbs that you grew in your own garden—in the summer, then opening it in the dead of winter. How do you place a price on that?

The home garden can be an excellent component of a thrifty lifestyle—and a fun way to spend time with your family. But it's important not to set your sights so high that you make gardening into more work than it needs to be. Your garden doesn't need to be perfect or magazine-beautiful. It just needs to work for you and yours.

Some people question the efficiency of using "valuable" time in the garden instead of simply paying more for organic food at the store. These skeptics point out that the "income" earned for our hours toiling in the garden is less than minimum wage. So all right. If your time is so valuable, give yourself a break. The rest of you: Pick a favorite fruit or vegetable, plant a few seeds, and join the fun.

DIY, or Call a Pro?

Deciding whether or not to tackle a gardening job yourself will depend on many things: how much strength you have, your level of knowledge, your time, and your degree of interest in taking on the project. It's never wise to take on something you can't finish, or can't do properly, because unfinished projects cost you more in the long run. The following list may help you to make the decision:

GOOD DIY PROJECTS

- Minor grading and terracing
- Correcting minor drainage issues
- Erecting unmortared masonry walls up to one foot high
- Drawing a landscape plan
- Planting a garden
- Installing a small ornamental pool
- Pruning small trees
- Building raised beds (see page 81)
- Transplanting bare-root shrubs and trees
- Planting balled and burlapped trees if the root ball is not too heavy
- Amending the soil (see page 78)
- Installing a simple aboveground irrigation system
- Sinking fence posts
- Making compost and compost bins
- Laying an informal stone walkway
- Monitoring insect populations

TASKS FOR A PRO

- Major grading and terracing
- Correcting major drainage issues
- Erecting masonry walls higher than one foot
- Making tree wells
- Felling trees
- Building a large arbor
- Pruning, spraying, and cabling large trees
- Building retaining walls
- Digging and balling a shrub or tree for transplanting
- Planting heavy balled and burlapped shrubs and trees
- Digging out large tree stumps
- Installing an underground irrigation system
- Sinking posts in very rocky or compacted soil
- Removing large stumps and boulders
- Diagnosing major disease and insect problems
- Large-scale spraying, even with low-toxicity products

DIY GUIDELINES BY BARBARA DAMROSCH

Start a Vegetable Garden

Starting a vegetable garden is exciting, but it can be a little intimidating, too. Every gardener dreams of a bumper harvest, but it's hard to know how to manage the details of planting and caring for a collection of different crops. Growing a garden doesn't have to cost a fortune in time or money, but it will if you plant beyond your resources and neglect to plan ahead. Here are some guidelines to help get you started on the right path, along with a fun veggie accessory to celebrate your newfound hobby.

The Tenets of Vegetable Gardening

Keep it simple and start small. Don't try to grow everything! Plant just a few easy-to-grow crops.

Start composting. Once you've used compost, you'll realize you can never have too much.

Mulch. To control weeds and retain soil moisture, cover garden beds with a thick layer of organic mulch.

Visit your garden often. Pull weeds as soon as you see them, add mulch where it's thin, water plants that are dry, look for signs of pests and diseases, and check for produce that's ready to harvest.

Take notes. Keep a record of the weather, what and when you planted and transplanted, when certain pests emerged, and how much you harvested.

Grow what you can't buy. Concentrate on crops that you can't find at your local supermarket or ones that offer unusual color or taste.

Plant crops you love. If you adore tomatoes or peppers, don't be shy about planting a lot of them.

Try crops your neighbors swear by. It helps to know what—and when—crops are easy to grow in your area. Along with experts at nurseries and local garden clubs, ask your neighbors for advice.

Be adventurous. Experimentation is one of the most enjoyable aspects of having a garden. Grow unusual edibles just for fun—purple-fleshed potatoes, white pumpkins, or kohlrabi, for example.

"No-Fail" Veggies The easiest crops to grow vary from region to region, but there are a few super-simple standouts. Radishes and green beans top most gardeners' "no-fail" lists. Other easy crops include cucumbers, summer squash, zucchini, garlic, leaf lettuce, snap peas, Swiss chard, and kale. Tomatoes are a bit more difficult but not by much. The newer compact hybrid tomatoes are especially easy.

Keeper-Fresh Veggie Bag

Cut down on the plastic bags with this simple cloth bag. It helps keep vegetables fresh, letting them breathe and absorbing excess moisture.

MATERIALS

- ½ yard 100 percent cotton cheesecloth, gauze, or coarse muslin, at least 21" wide
- Ruler or measuring tape, pencil
- Sewing thread, needle

1. Following the measurements and layout shown, draw a rectangle 21" wide x 15½" long. Mark ½" seam allowances along the sides and bottom. Mark two ½" hem lines along the top. Cut out the rectangle.

2. Press under ½" twice along the top edge, for the hem. Using a ⅛" seam allowance, stitch the turned inner edge.

3. Fold the bag in half, right sides together, with the side edges lined up. Using a ½" seam allowance, stitch down the side seam, pivot around the bottom corner, and stitch the bottom closed. Press the seams open and turn right-side out.

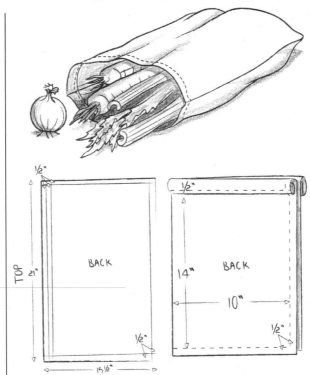

Plant a Row for the Hungry

Is your garden bursting with broccoli? Surfeited with squash? There's no such thing if you see your extra produce as a part of Plant a Row for the Hungry (www.gwaa.org/par). The program donates fresh produce to soup kitchens, homeless shelters, and other neighborhood food programs.

While a single bag of cucumbers, peas, or tomatoes may not sound like much, the yield is considerable when multiplied. To date, Plant a Row participants have donated more than 14 million pounds of herbs and vegetables. Of course, you don't have to join anything to share your harvest; just get in touch with the nearest food pantry and find out what they can use.

Know Your Soil | by Barbara Damrosch

S o much of what plants need comes from the soil. But gardeners often don't understand what good soil is or how to achieve it. They go out and buy a bag of evergreen food, or bulb food, or rose food—just as they'd buy dog food—and sprinkle it around their plants. But good soil has good structure as well as fertility, and structure is something you must work to build. Improving your soil isn't difficult to do, nor does it have to cost much, but it does require that you understand some basics.

Soils are classified according to the size of the particles of which they are composed. At one extreme is gravel, at the other is clay, with particles smaller than .005 millimeters. In between is a gradation of soils: fine gravel, coarse sand, fine sand, sandy loam, loam, silt loam, and silt. Soils with larger particles are light or sandy soils; those with small ones are heavy or clay soils. Loam is the happy medium and is considered ideal. But each type of soil has its virtues as well:

- Light soils allow water and air to move freely, so they tend to be well-drained and rich in oxygen. Light soils warm up quickly, thus stimulating early plant growth. They are also easy for plant roots to penetrate as they grow. On the negative side, water may drain through light soils too quickly, taking nutrients with it and leaving the soil dry and infertile.

Ode to Earthworms

Any gardening discussion would be incomplete without a mention of what the earthworm does for your garden as it eats its way through the soil. As organic material passes through the earthworm's body, it is ground up with the help of tiny stones in the worm's gizzard. The castings excreted by earthworms are very high in humus (and therefore perfect as a soil conditioner) as well as rich in the nutrients most easily absorbed by plants. This wiggly gardener can produce its weight in castings each day.

Earthworms also do a lot to solve the problem of soil compaction, loosening and aerating the soil as they go about their day-to-day business. Their burrows make passageways for roots, also allowing room for water.

So, the more earthworms, the better off your garden. To increase the number of earthworms, increase the amount of organic matter in your soil. Continuously add vegetable matter to encourage the earthworm population.

- Clay soils allow little space for air and water to circulate, so they are often waterlogged. This can rob plant roots of oxygen and cause the roots to rot. Because clay soils are dense, they are more difficult for roots to penetrate. (Imagine poking your fingers through sand, then through clay, and you'll sense what the same process feels like for plant roots.) Clay soils also warm up more slowly in spring. On the other hand, because they hold water and nutrients well, they are often fertile and they retain moisture in hot, dry weather.

- Different plants like different soils. Plants that need good drainage are at home in sandy soils. Plants that need the extra fertility and moisture of clay soils have strong roots that don't mind the extra push required. But the ideal soil for most plants is loam.

- What kind is yours? On a day when the soil isn't unusually dry or wet, pick up a handful and squeeze. Does it form a tight ball that doesn't come apart when tapped? Is it sticky when wet but hard and lumpy when dry? If so, it's a clay soil. If it runs through your fingers and doesn't form a ball, it's sandy. If it holds together but breaks when tapped, it's loam.

Your Soil's Chemistry

If the pH of your soil is way off, all the fertilizer in the world isn't going to do you much good. A pH test will tell you whether your soil is acidic, alkaline, or just right. The ideal pH is only slightly acidic, 6.3 to 6.8. Inexpensive test kits are available at any garden center. To get the most reliable picture of the pH, take two or more tests for each different garden area (lawn, vegetable garden, flower bed) and average the results.

Acidic soils are common in areas that receive heavy rainfall, because rain leaches out chemicals such as calcium and magnesium, that counteract acidity. If you know your soil is acidic, avoid using peat moss as organic matter—it will contribute more acidity. Well-aged manure would be a good source of organic matter because it's slightly alkaline and rich in calcium and magnesium.

Alkalinity, the opposite of acidity, is typical of extremely dry regions. If your soil is alkaline, seek out acidifying forms of organic matter: chopped oak leaves, leaf mold, ground bark, aged sawdust, peat moss, and pine or cypress bark mulch.

Feed Your Soil

No matter what your soil's structure may be, it can be improved by the addition of organic matter. How does it work? In the process of decay, formerly living things give up the substances from which they were built so that other living things can use them. What's more, in the soil, with the aid of bacteria and fungi, plant and animal matter decomposes into a substance called *humus*. Humus binds soil particles together—not densely, as with clay, but with spaces through which water and air can pass. Organic matter also moderates the soil's temperature and contains important nutritional elements for plants.

Although there are many kinds of organic soil additions to choose from, here are some of the most commonly used:

Animal manures. Thousands of years ago farmers observed that plants grew better in fields where animals pastured. Manures of farm animals are still popular soil amendments, but keep in mind that manure can be harmful to plants if it has not sufficiently decomposed. Never use any that is fresh. Well-rotted manure is odorless and looks like dark soil. Often people who raise animals have piles of it that have been sitting around for years, and they're glad to have it carted away. Or they'll sell it to you for much less than it would cost to buy it in bags. Never use manures from dogs, cats, or humans, because all of these can transmit diseases.

Plant humus. That's the term for decomposed plant matter, the most common, commercially available form of which is peat moss. It comes from plants that decomposed very slowly in boggy places. Grass clippings are a convenient (and free) source, but don't dig them into a planted garden if they've just been cut and avoid them if they are full of weed seeds (such as those of dandelions). Never use clippings from lawns unless you're sure they're herbicide- and insecticide-free. Other sources include plant debris like annuals that have finished producing or thinnings from the vegetable garden. These can be tilled directly into the soil.

Cover crops. Sometimes gardeners plant cover crops (also referred to as green manures), whose sole purpose is to provide organic matter. Rather than being harvested, these are tilled under so they can enrich the soil with nutrients. Buckwheat and winter rye are especially good at smothering weeds, and members of the pea family, such as clovers, vetches, and

SOIL AND COMPOST TIPS BY BARBARA DAMROSCH

alfalfa, are best at enriching the soil. They're especially useful in large gardens, where they eliminate the need for carting in large quantities of soil amendment.

Compost Your Waste

Another good way to add organic matter and nutrients to the soil is through composting. Compost is simply a big casserole of organic matter that you assemble yourself, usually enclosed in some sort of bin, and then leave to "cook" awhile. The cooking—or decomposing—takes place fastest when there is adequate moisture, warmth, and air. The soil's microorganisms make decomposition happen.

Composting enables you to recycle the debris from your garden, and many of the scraps from your kitchen, and put them back into growing things so that nothing is wasted. It's a handy way to deal with garden refuse and obtain a great soil amendment at the same time. Even better, it's free of charge.

HOW TO MAKE A COMPOST

Compost is made by piling layers of organic material (usually interspersed with very thin layers of soil) in a pile or stack, keeping it moistened with a hose (if rain doesn't do this for you), and letting the pile decompose. This happens very quickly at the inside of the pile, where the temperature can get as high as 160 degrees Fahrenheit, but the whole pile will eventually break down successfully if it sits long enough. Patient (or lazy) composters do just that—let it sit. Those who want their compost faster turn their piles, bringing the material on the outside to the inside with a garden fork and/ or shovel so that it, too, will have its chance at the "hot spot." Turning also fluffs up the pile, adding air that further stimulates the action. (A handy way to do this is to turn the pile into another bin right next to it.) Industrious composters turn their piles frequently, but even doing it only once, after a few months of warm weather, will bring you more quickly to the finished product: a dark, moist substance that has broken down enough so you cannot easily recognize the original ingredients.

It may take longer than you think to fill a bin. Organic materials shrink as they settle and decompose. But when you have added as much as you can, it is time to let the pile rest and do its final cooking. Hose it down if the materials seem dry, and protect your pile from dryness and excessive rain, which can leach out the nutrients.

Feeding Your Compost

What can you compost? Pretty much anything plant-based that will degrade—vegetable scraps, garden trimmings and dead leaves, shredded newspaper—the list goes on. What won't work: human, cat, and dog manure, meat and dairy products (except eggshells), grease, invasive weeds, and any plant matter that is diseased or has been treated with herbicide or pesticides. Here's a list of compostables to get you started:

- Dust from your vacuum cleaner
- Evergreen needles
- Feathers
- Garden waste (spent plants and vines, beet and carrot tops, corn stalks, and so forth)
- Grass clippings
- Hair
- Leaves
- Kitchen waste (vegetable and fruit rinds, parings, eggshells, coffee grounds and filters, tea leaves, and so on)
- Manures from herbivores (horses, cows, goats, and rabbits)
- Nutshells
- Pond weeds
- Sawdust and bark

You can buy compost activators, but the garden, yard, and kitchen provide everything you need. It's tempting to rely heavily on plentiful autumn leaves, but they tend to mat and exclude air. Also, their decomposition is largely fungal, whereas the desired action in a compost pile is largely bacteria-driven. If you have a power mower, you *can* use it to shred leaves, adding them to the pile in small amounts; but the best solution is to have a separate heap for leaves, where they can break down over the course of years, as they do on forest floors.

An Instant Compost Bin

If you have limited space or the need for only a small bin, you can compost in a garbage can. This is a great system if you are concerned about rodents or if you don't generate large quantities of compostable materials. Either galvanized metal or heavy-duty plastic cans work. Lids that don't lock will have to be secured—run a rubber tie-down strap over the top of the lid, from one can handle to the other.

Punch or drill one-quarter-inch holes in the can's bottom, sides, and lid for drainage and aeration. Set the can up on bricks or concrete blocks so it will drain properly. Now you have a compost bin.

The Wonders of Raised Beds

A raised bed is a mound of loose, well-prepared soil, six to eight inches high that will make for easier gardening and healthier crops. The beds can be permanent, with edgings of stone, blocks, timbers, or railway ties, or they can be temporary structures you re-form each time the garden is planted. Raised beds are particularly helpful if you are trying to grow vegetables in heavy soils that drain poorly. They can be used for flower gardens, but unless you are mainly in it for the bouquets than to pretty up your landscape, you are better off distributing your blooms throughout your property to maximize the visual effect.

In the long run, easy maintenance and the ability to use hand tools instead of machinery like rototillers, make raised beds a best bet for the home garden. Here are some more perks of raised beds:

- Because the beds aren't subjected to regular foot traffic, the soil always stays porous and loose and never compacts. This loose soil provides good drainage, enabling water, air, and fertilizer to penetrate easily to the roots of your plants.

- If you make permanent raised beds, the path next to each bed is never used for growing vegetables. Because it is constantly being walked on and packed down, it stays dry, clean, and relatively weed-free.

- Because the beds are segregated by the paths between them, you can take advantage of the layout to rotate the variety of vegetables you plant in each bed each year. Crop rotation maintains the soil's nutrients and discourages pests and pathogens.

- Finally, your raised-bed garden is always orderly, organized, and pleasing to the eye because it is so easy to maintain.

PROJECT | Build a Temporary Raised Bed

This raised bed doesn't require a lot of commitment, so it's a good fit for a beginning gardener.

1. Map out the area of your beds with stakes and strings. Sixteen inches is a good width, but some gardeners prefer beds 3 to 4 feet wide. Make your bed any convenient length. Walkways can be up to 20 inches wide.

Step 1

2. Using a rake, pull the soil from the walkway to the top of the bed. Stand in one walkway and draw soil toward you from the opposite walkway. Repeat on the other side.

3. Enrich the soil with compost, manure, or other organic materials. Then level the top of the bed with the back of the rake. The sides should slope at a 45-degree angle. A lip of soil around the top edge of a new bed helps reduce erosion.

From Home to Garden Shed

While you'll still need the usual complement of garden tools—a spade, a trowel, a rake, a good pair of garden shears—you can use some of the following ordinary household items in the place of many specialized accessories:

☐ Old serving utensils (but not the heirlooms!) to use as tools for digging and transplanting.

☐ An apple corer instead of a miniature dibber, to make room in the ground for tiny bulbs.

☐ Kitchen or barbecue tongs for picking up offensive things like slugs and pulling up stinging nettles.

☐ Grapefruit knives for weeding in container gardens and for transplanting seedlings.

☐ Old colanders or laundry baskets for harvesting fruits and vegetables.

☐ Heavy-duty paper clips and clothespins, to use in hundreds of ways—from sealing opened seed packets to hanging up your gardening gloves.

Plant for High-Yield Gardening

People who grow acres and acres of veggies don't worry too much about a few straggly stalks here and there. But those who have only a twenty-foot-square garden must use that small space wisely. Many factors—from spacing to weeding—have a profound effect on garden yields. Here's how to maximize returns on your sweat equity:

Space out. Vine crops such as melons, cucumbers, and pumpkins need space to roam. Certain plants are less sensitive to close spacing. Leaf crops like spinach, celery, and lettuce can grow closely together. Upright fruit-bearing plants like tomatoes have highest yields when their foliage is almost overlapping (though increasing their spacing increases fruit size).

Light or dark. Fruits such as melons and tubers like potatoes are reservoirs that hold accumulated energy gathered from sunlight by the plants' leaves. These should be placed in a spot where sunlight falls on the entire plant. Leaf crops such as lettuce and Swiss chard, on the other hand, do not need as much light. (They aren't feeding any fruit.)

Water, water, everywhere . . . To produce the best crops, plants should have uninterrupted growth—which translates to an even, constant supply of water. Under most conditions, that means about an inch per week; however, the amount a plant requires may depend on the stage of growth. A little less water while fruits are ripening, for instance, will reduce yield but improve flavor. Potatoes and onions will last longer post-harvest if the water supply is decreased just before harvest.

Weeds out. Studies show that regularly weeded fields produce six times as many tomatoes as do unweeded ones; onions, more than tenfold; carrots, more than fifteenfold. But timing is critical. Vegetables are most vulnerable to weeds from the seedling stage up until they start to bear fruit. Weed after a heavy rain; it's easier to pull weeds out of soil that is soft and damp.

HIGH-YIELD GARDENING FROM *THE BACKYARD HOMESTEAD: FROM HOME TO GARDEN SHED* BY SHARON LOVEJOY

MY THRIFT

Beans, Corn, Peas

The lean times for my family continued through World War II and into the 1950s. But having a garden helped out a lot. We canned beans, corn, peas, potatoes, pumpkins, apples, berries.

We would've saved, but we didn't have any money to save. Then again, the price of things wasn't so high: If you got a little money, you could make it go far.

—Emaline Adams, born 1917

Know Your Zone!

Let the USDA Plant Hardiness Zones Map be your guide when deciding what you plant in your garden. (If your city isn't on this sample list, enter your zip code at www.garden.org/zipzone.) Opt for plants that can withstand the coldest temperatures in your zone, or you will be digging up dead plants (and wasting garden dollars) every spring!

Zone	Lowest Average Annual Temperature	Example Cities
1	Below −50°F	Fairbanks, Alaska; Cornwallis Island, Northwest Territories (Canada)
2a	−50°F to −45°F	Nuiqsut, Alaska; Flin Flon, Manitoba (Canada)
2b	−45°F to −40°F	Unalakleet, Alaska; Pinecreek, Minnesota
3a	−40°F to −30°F	International Falls, Minnesota; St. Michael, Alaska
3b	−35°F to −30°F	Eau Claire, Wisconsin; Grand Forks, North Dakota
4a	−30°F to −25°F	Minneapolis/St. Paul, Minnesota; Great Falls, Montana
4b	−25°F to −20°F	Burlington, Vermont; Anchorage, Alaska
5a	−20°F to −15°F	Des Moines, Iowa; Denver, Colorado
5b	−15°F to −10°F	Columbia, Missouri; Chicago, Illinois
6a	−10°F to −5°F	St. Louis, Missouri; Lebanon, Pennsylvania
6b	−5°F to 0°F	New York, New York; Branson, Missouri
7a	0°F to 5°F	Oklahoma City, Oklahoma; Baltimore, Maryland
7b	5°F to 10°F	Little Rock, Arkansas; Atlanta, Georgia
8a	10°F to 15°F	Tifton, Georgia; Dallas, Texas
8b	15°F to 20°F	Austin, Texas; San Francisco, California
9a	20°F to 25°F	Phoenix, Arizona; Houston, Texas
9b	25°F to 30°F	Brownsville, Texas; Orlando, Florida
10a	30°F to 35°F	Naples, Florida; Los Angeles, California
10b	35°F to 40°F	Miami, Florida; San Diego, California
11	above 40°F	Honolulu, Hawaii; Mazatlán (Mexico)

Pick the Right Plants for Your Zone

I t's not always possible to predict whether a plant will flourish in your garden. But one widely used general indicator is the U.S. Department of Agriculture's map of winter hardiness zones (see a sample, facing page). In this map the United States and most of Canada are divided into numbered zones based on average minimum winter temperature. Plants are assigned to a zone based on how low a temperature they are able to survive. For example, a plant that is rated hardy to zone 5 is expected to survive temperatures as low as –20 degrees Fahrenheit.

Still, keep in mind that your zone might apply to your geographical area, but not to your particular yard. Your windy hill might be zone 6, while your neighbor's protected valley might be zone 7. Or, on an even smaller scale, your lawn might be zone 7 but the garden next to your house, zone 8. Before you purchase plants, try to identify these microclimates on your property so you can choose the right place to put them.

When You Buy Plants, Spend Smart

T oday plants seem to be sold everywhere—supermarkets, big-box stores, roadside stands. They often cost less in supermarkets than they do in nurseries, and it's tempting to toss a box of petunias into the cart along with the chicken and yogurt. Sometimes they'll work out fine, but it's a gamble. Plants at these stores may not have been watered regularly and may or may not be hardy in your region (and your local grocery store's staff is an unlikely source of guidance). Nevertheless, it's sometimes worth giving them a try if the price is right and they're a variety that you know. Wherever you shop, here are some things to look out for before you buy:

Yellowed leaves. A number of things can cause yellowing, all of them bad. In general, a bright green or dark green leaf color is a sign of health, but even here you can never be quite sure. Look at the seed leaves—the little pair of leaves closest to the soil, which were the first to emerge. If these are a healthy green, the plant had a good start and has been cared for since.

Wilted leaves. A good watering might perk up the plants. Might. But you don't know if they've been neglected so often that they're permanently weakened.

Tall, spindly plants. Whether you're buying annuals, perennials, or shrubs, you generally want compact, bushy plants with many stems. Taller is usually not better and often indicates that the plant suffered from lack of light during growth, was not pinched or pruned enough, or has been growing in a pot for too long.

Plants in bloom. Many nurseries display these most prominently, because blooming plants lure the most buyers. But you want to let the plants do their growing in your garden, not in nursery pots.

Signs of bugs or disease. Look for insect bodies, stickiness, oddly distorted leaves or crowns, blackened areas, mushy or rotten places, spots, blotches, streaks, holes, or jagged bites taken out of the leaves. The plants have been weakened by the problem, and if you bring an infested plant home, the insect or disease may spread to other plants in your garden.

Weeds in the pots. Weeds rob a plant of water and food and show neglect by the nursery.

Roots crawling out of the pot's bottom. These pot-bound plants are often starved, and may contain girdling roots that have wound their way around the pot and can strangle the main root years later. They may well respond to good care, but loosen the root systems before you plant them.

Plants with small, underdeveloped root systems. These plants will come out of the pot if you pull only slightly. Look for a plant that seems more rooted-in. Damaged or rotted roots indicate weakened plants.

Nicks, scars, or cracks in trunks and stems. These may have weakened the plant, and can be an entry point for disease. They also point toward general neglect.

Balled plants where the ball is dry or damaged. Balled-and-burlapped trees and shrubs must be kept watered and handled very carefully. If the ball of earth is broken up so it feels like a bag of loose soil when you tip it, do not buy the plant. The roots will surely have suffered and are a bad bet for transplanting.

The No-Buy Solution | by Barbara Damrosch

Buying some of your plants at nurseries is probably inevitable (use the tips on page 85 to make sure you get the most for your dollar), but also consider growing plants from seeds, which cost far less than already-sprouted plants, or from leaf and stem cuttings, which cost nothing (other than the start-up cost of that first plant). And there may be a sentimental factor, as well: Take a cutting from a loved one's garden, and you'll have a growing, tangible reminder of that person for years to come.

PROJECT | Grow a Plant from a Stem Cutting

It seems miraculous: You cut off a part of a plant and get a whole new one. But in fact, growing from stem and leaf cuttings is easy. If you already have some plants you like, don't buy more; just clone the ones you have. If you covet thy neighbor's shrubbery, ask nicely if you might snip a little stem. (Just don't raid their garden under cover of night. That never ends well.)

The night before you take the cutting, water the plant so the stems and leaves will have plenty of moisture in them. Have your potting mix ready in a clean container before you take the cuttings. The mix can be comprised of sand, perlite, vermiculite, peat moss, or a combination thereof; it's easiest to use a commercially prepared sterilized soilless mix.

TOOLS AND MATERIALS: Potting mix; shallow clay pot or small plastic flat with drainage holes; sharp knife or razor blade; rooting compound (optional); pencil

1. Select a stem that has several sets of leaves on it and snip off a cutting four to six inches long. Make the cut at a slant, just below a node (the point where a leaf joins the stem). Remove the leaves from that node. You can remove the next set, too, but there should be at least one set of leaves left on the cutting.

Step 1

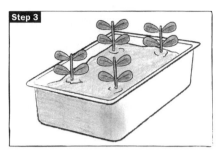

2. It's not required, but you'll give the rooting process an extra boost if you dip the end of the cutting in a rooting compound—a white powder containing rooting hormones, available at stores that sell plant supplies.

3. Make a hole in the potting mix with a pencil. It should be an inch or two deep, depending on the length of the cutting. Stick the cutting in so the end is at the bottom of the hole. Firm the mix lightly around the cutting and water it gently but thoroughly.

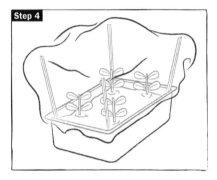

4. Cover your container to keep the air inside humid, and wait for the cutting to root. Put the container in a plastic bag or spread plastic wrap over it, supporting the wrap with sticks so it doesn't touch the plant. Or put the flat or pot in a large transparent plastic box. While it is rooting, the cutting should have plenty of light but not direct sun, and it should be kept at a temperature of 65 to 75 degrees.

5. Check regularly to make sure that the cutting doesn't dry out. The plastic should look moist or foggy. Water as needed, or let air in if it looks too sodden in there or if you see mold. Cuttings of plants with fuzzy leaves will prefer drier air in which their soil is moist but their leaves are dry.

6. Your cutting should root in two to five weeks. It will stand up in a perky way with good color and even fresh new growth, but if you're not sure, tug on it ever so slightly. If it resists, it has rooted.

7. Dig up the roots very gently using a spoon or fork, and place the plant in a small pot using a similar potting mix or one with a larger percentage of soil. Don't fertilize the cuttings at all until about a month after they root—the roots aren't ready for it yet.

PROJECT | **Grow a Plant from a Leaf Cutting**

For plants with fleshy stems, such as gloxinia, African violets, strepto-carpus, rex and Rieger begonias, peperomia, jade plant, and sedum, leaf cuttings are an excellent way to propagate. Some plants, such as jade, gera-niums, and Christmas cactus, are so easy to root from leaves that all you need to do is stick the bottom end of the leaf into the ground. It may take a bit longer to get full-size plants with this method than with stem cuttings, but since each leaf makes several plants you'll have more of them.

TOOLS AND MATERIALS: Potting mix; shallow clay pot or small plastic flat with drainage holes; sharp knife or razor blade; pencil

1. Using a razor blade to make a slanted cut, detach a few healthy young leaves from the mother plant, leaving one or two inches of stem attached.

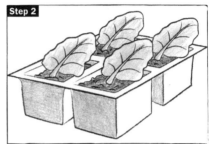

2. Insert the stems in a moistened soilless rooting mix so that they lie almost flat on the soil surface, and lightly firm the medium around the stems. Keep the soil and air moist, as with stem cuttings.

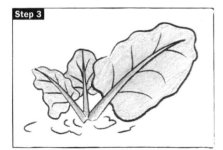

3. Wait for new little plantlets to form.

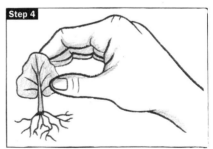

4. When the plantlets have developed root systems, transplant them to individual pots.

Keep the Pests Away, Naturally

Like a well-stocked pantry for a cook, a good "medicine cabinet" will save a gardener time and money, especially when it comes to pest control. Luckily, this arsenal doesn't have to involve heavy weaponry: You may already have many of the necessary ingredients for safe and natural deterrence at home. Store them in a handy location—out of reach of both children and pets. (Note that liquid soap is the basis of many garden potions. It helps ingredients blend together; and is also a surfactant, or wetting agent, which means it assures uniform coverage of leaf surfaces or insect bodies.)

The Well-Stocked Garden Pantry

- Aspirin (uncoated)—dissolved in water, fights mildew, black spot, and more.
- Boric acid or borax—wipes out ants, roaches, and more.
- Canola oil—use to smother insects and as a surfactant.
- Castor oil—repels moles.
- Chili powder—pesticide and repellent.
- Cinnamon powder—antifungal and anti-ant.
- Corn gluten meal—inhibits germination of weeds.
- Epson salts—provides a quick shot of magnesium to promote growth of flowers and foliage.
- Essential oils (mixed with water)—pest buster.
- Fermented salmon—thwarts deer, chipmunks, and other critters, and is rich in nutrients.
- Fish emulsion and kelp—organic fertilizers that promote healthy soil and plants.

- Flour (not self-rising)—for sprinkling on plants plagued by grasshoppers.
- Honey—a lure for ants.
- Rubbing alcohol (70 percent solution)—desiccates insects.
- Molasses (blackstrap or horticultural grade)—jump-starts microbial action, feeds beneficial insects, and attracts harmful insects to traps.
- Petroleum jelly (or mentholated rub)—a slick barrier to apply to trunks and stems.
- Liquid castile soap—available in health food stores, a base for many garden potions. (See recipe.)
- Tabasco sauce—pesticide and repellent. (See recipe.)
- Vegetable or mineral oil—destroys insect pests and can be used as a barrier.
- Vinegar (apple cider or white)—fights fungus, kills weeds, and destroys pests.

Three More to Keep on Hand

Not all homemade concoctions work in every situation. However, some simple solutions really do work—as well as or better than chemicals, at less of a cost to the environment and bank account. *A note:* Always test homemade sprays on a small portion of the plant before going to town; to prevent sunburned leaves, apply sprays early in the morning.

Garlic. Proven to kill and repel whiteflies, aphids, beetles, and other insects. Combine about 4 ounces garlic extract and a few drops of soap. Blend and then dilute with water in a spray bottle (about 90 percent water), and bugs beware! (You can also blend an entire head of garlic with 2 cups of water, strain, and add to 1 gallon of water.)

Baking soda. Proven to control powdery mildew and prevent its spread. (What can't it do?) Combine 1 tablespoon baking soda, 1 to 2 teaspoons soap, and 1 to 2 teaspoons vegetable oil, and add to 1 gallon of water. Spray on at the first signs of mildew.

Beer. The most effective way to control slugs without poison. Slugs can't resist the brew, fall into the trap, and drown (drunkenly, perhaps!). Make sure that the top of your trap (a bowl or deep saucer) is level with the ground.

Pepper the Pests

Treat cucumber beetles, leaf hoppers, aphids—you name the pest—with a peppery spray made with Tabasco sauce. You can also use Tabasco to dissuade raccoons and rabbits from nibbling tender shoots.

½ cup apple cider vinegar
1 teaspoon Tabasco sauce
(or other hot chili sauce)
⅛ teaspoon liquid soap

Combine ingredients in a jar, shake well, and decant into a spray bottle. Apply to both tops and bottoms of leaves. Reapply after a rain.

Cabbage S.O.S.

For the cabbage family, powdered cayenne pepper works to repel everything from cucumber beetles and spittlebugs to leaf hoppers and cabbage loopers. And there's scientific authority behind this treatment: Entomologist Dr. Geoff Zehnder of Auburn University credits cayenne pepper with protecting cabbages better than any standard chemical insecticide.

2 tablespoons cayenne
6 drops liquid soap
1 gallon water

Combine ingredients, let sit overnight, and stir thoroughly. Spray weekly to protect all members of the cabbage family, including broccoli, cauliflower, kale, and Brussels sprouts, from destructive critters.

Bambi Be Gone

Deer eating up your veggies? Poke a hole with a needle and fishing line through tiny hotel soap bars (wrappers on, and the smellier the better) and hang several on each bush or tree. Each bar of soap will keep deer away up to a distance of about 3 feet.

PROJECT | ## Grow a Plant from Seed

Allow a few plants to reach their full maturity, harvest the seeds, and you won't have to buy seeds the following spring. Now there's a bargain! Here are some pointers:

- Most seeds can be stored for at least a year and still germinate, as long as the storage conditions are right. Try to keep seeds consistently cold, or at least cool; fluctuating temperatures can be fatal. The refrigerator is an ideal place to store most seeds.

- Seeds begin to germinate when they absorb water, so unwanted moisture in storage translates to the death of seeds. Always dry seeds thoroughly before placing them in storage containers. Make sure the containers themselves have no trace of moisture inside and that no moisture can enter them.

- You can store seeds in a variety of containers: screw-top glass jars; paper envelopes, labeled and sealed inside glass jars; film canisters; prescription medicine bottles; and tins with metal lids. The container shouldn't be airtight (lack of air will suffocate seeds), but you should be able to close it securely.

The Case for Growing from Seeds

In today's busy world, many of us look for the easiest and quickest ways to achieve a goal. Buying plants at the nursery is fast and simple. Why bother starting your own plants from seed? For several reasons.

Growing your own plants from seed is more economical, a particularly important consideration if you have a large garden. If you get in the habit of gathering and saving seeds from the plants you already grow, you'll be able to grow free plants for years to come. You may want to try new plants from faraway places—or perhaps an heirloom favorite—but it's not always possible to find these varieties in nurseries. There's also the fact that some plants do well only when grown from seed. These include some annuals, like California poppy, sunflower, sweet pea, and nasturtium, and vegetables such as beets, carrots, radishes, and peas. And as an added bonus, for the youngest gardeners, seedlings can offer a thrillingly visual introduction to the wonders of vegetal creation.

THE CASE FOR SEEDS FROM *COUNTRY WISDOM & KNOW-HOW*

Collecting Your Seeds

Observe your plants carefully and note when and how they disperse their seeds. This will give you a good sense of when to collect seeds from each plant. The seeds are usually visible at the end of a branch or stalk of a mature plant.

How to collect seeds depend on the type of plant you are working with. Some seeds can be removed from their pods by hand. With others, the entire plant must be cut down and threshed (beaten to loosen the seeds). Many seeds can simply be shaken free of their pods into a container.

Once you've collected and cleaned your seeds of debris (either by hand or in a sifter), spread them out indoors to dry for a week or so. (The exception: Seeds with beards or tufts should not be given this extra drying time.)

Storing Your Seeds

Once your seeds are ready for storage, clean and thoroughly dry old plastic or glass jars and lids. Gather a stack of four unfolded facial tissues. Into the center of the tissues, scoop two tablespoons of powdered milk (a safe, natural desiccant) from a newly opened container. Fold the stack into a flat packet and tape closed.

Pour your seeds into a clean envelope, seal, and label with the date and seed variety. Tuck it into a jar with the pouch of powdered milk and close. Store in the refrigerator and replace the milk packet after six months.

One way to get your cuttings to release their seeds is by placing them upside down in a paper bag. Tie the bag shut and poke a few small holes throughout for air. Set aside until seeds are released.

Clean seeds of excess debris, either picking them over by hand or rattling them about a bit in a sifter.

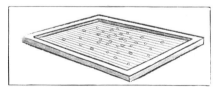

Spread seeds out to dry indoors on a clean window-screen or other flat surface that's surrounded by a ridged lip. (You don't want your seeds rolling away.)

GROWING, COLLECTING, AND PLANTING SEEDS FROM *THE BACKYARD HOMESTEAD*; STORING YOUR SEEDS BY SHARON LOVEJOY

Planting Your Seeds

When the time comes to plant your seeds—i.e., frost is no longer a threat and it's the right sowing time for your given vegetable—all you generally have to do is punch little holes in rows where you want the plants to grow (making sure to space them out according to the size of the mature plant), drop a couple of seeds into the holes, cover them lightly with soil, and keep them moist. The process itself is simple, but here are workarounds for common planting problems:

- If the soil is dry on planting day, wet the rows with a sprinkler after planting is complete.
- Keep the soil slightly moist until the seedlings emerge. Once the seeds germinate, don't let them dry out.
- After a rain or watering, a clay soil may become so hard that young seedlings can't burst through. Here's how to beat crusty soil: Drag a garden rake carefully over the seedbed with just enough force to break up the crust. The tines should penetrate only about one-quarter inch of the soil. You may have to water hard-packed seedbeds before loosening the soil.

PROJECT | ## Protect Your Seedbeds

Birds are welcome guests in any garden—unless you've just planted a bunch of irresistible seeds. Luckily, it's easy to keep birds out (unlike, say, rabbits). The simple fix is a tent of small-mesh chicken wire.

TOOLS AND MATERIALS: Chicken wire; gloves; shears; bricks or rocks

1. Use the type of wire that's 4 feet wide. Wearing gloves, cut it to a length equal to that of your planting bed, plus 2 feet—an extra foot for each end. If you have long rows, cut several pieces of chicken wire and overlap them.

2. Fold the wire in half lengthwise, creasing it so it stands up in a triangle. Fold up a 6-inch-wide flap on each long side, and crease that fold as well. Bend the folded flaps back down so they stick out at right angles, like feet, and place them flat on the ground, centering the top of the tent over the planted area.

3. Anchor the flaps with bricks or rocks. (The ends of the tunnel are open, but birds seldom walk in to get at the goodies; they tend to avoid spots where aerial takeoff isn't instant.) That's it—just don't forget to remove the tent before it bends the young plants.

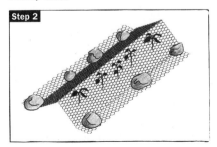
Step 2

Gardening for the Gardenless

No yard? Don't despair—anyone with a speck of outdoor space can easily plant and enjoy a container garden. Whether you have a tiny balcony, a patch of concrete, or just a windowsill, you have what it takes to grow flowers, herbs, and even vegetables! Here are some tips for various types of outdoor space:

Balcony. Most balconies are rectangles with two short and two long ends, with one of the long sides usually abutting the wall of the building (which does a good job of blocking any sun), so plants get full sunlight only about 25 percent of the day, when the sun is directly facing them. (See Know Your Zone!, page 84, for tips on choosing plants for your particular microclimate.) Make sure you know how much vertical space you have to work with before planting something tall, or be prepared to pinch and prune. If your only outdoor space is a fire escape, you may be tempted to put a few containers there. But before you do, check the fire department regulations. You must not block firefighters' access, and in some communities that means nothing on the fire escape.

Patio. In most cases, the sun hits three or sometimes all four sides of a patio as it moves across the sky, so sun orientation is less of a concern than it is with a balcony. If your patio is made of concrete, you'll need to watch for reflected heat in summertime.

Rooftop. Anyone who lives in a tall building and is able to develop a rooftop garden is fortunate indeed. You'll be blessed with sun from all sides; but there are some problems you should be aware of. One is the curse of high winds. Walking on some roofs damages them and causes leaks below, so weight can also be an issue. The heat reflection in summertime can be fierce. Plus you have to get water up there. However, many city-dwellers are happy to deal with those challenges in exchange for a garden!

Stoops and steps. If you're planting right outside your front door, make sure you leave room for humans to pass—look for a container that is tall rather than wide, with a small footprint. Fill containers with sweet-smelling plants to welcome your visitors. If you're concerned about theft, here's how to lock down your greenery: Before you fill the container, lay a short, fat dowel or length of pipe across its bottom; thread a chain or metal cable

GARDENING AND CONTAINERS FOR THE GARDENLESS BY ROSE MARIE NICHOLS MCGEE AND MAGGIE STUCKEY up through the drainage hole, then slip the dowel through a link of the chain. Lock the other end of the chain to something solid, like a drainpipe or handrail.

Window box. Fastened onto an exterior wall underneath a window, window boxes have some of the same sun orientation challenges as balconies, but to a lesser degree—usually they're out of the way of the roof's shadow. Because window boxes have so much surface area in relation to their depth, it's difficult to keep them moist. Be sure you know how to get water to them—if you can't reach a window box from the ground, make sure the window opens!

Hanging container. Baskets brimming with cherry tomatoes or nasturtiums add a bright splash to patios, balconies, or porches. Remember that a large container filled with soil and plants can be surprisingly heavy; choose your location carefully, and make sure your hook or bracket is strong enough and secured firmly.

Creative Containers

A sneaky expense of container gardening is the pots—they aren't cheap. So look for used ones or search thrift shops and yard sales for items that were never meant to hold plants, but nevertheless do so very nicely. Some ideas:

☐ A very large wooden salad bowl with drainage holes drilled in the bottom makes a handsome planter for salad greens, which have shallow roots.

☐ An old metal washtub drilled with drainage holes can accommodate a small herb garden.

☐ A large commercial mop bucket made of galvanized zinc becomes a sturdy all-purpose planter.

☐ Large decorative food tins can hold fanciful arrangements—especially if their design is printed directly on the metal, rather than on a paper label.

☐ Large old toys like a dump truck with missing wheels, a child's wheelbarrow, or a toy wagon make delightful receptacles for a child's garden.

☐ Straw baskets in all shapes and sizes, with handles for hanging, are sweet holders for diminutive flower gardens. (Add a liner first.)

Invite the Birds, Enhance Your Garden

A garden doesn't feel complete without birds—and they can do wonders for pest management. (Some will even pollinate your plants, free of charge!) By planning and developing your backyard as an inviting natural habitat with diverse native food plants, sheltering shrubs and trees, a water source, and nesting sites, you will encourage birds to stick around, not just eat and run. You will end up with a lively garden and spend less on pesticides—well, maybe not quantifiably so, but you'll be helping along your area's native fauna. Here's how to transform your yard into a habitat:

1. Plant as many native species as possible—plants which by virtue of their indigenous nature are best suited to your region.

2. Control pests by natural means—that is, let nature take its course by encouraging beneficial insects (which are often killed when pesticides are used), bats, and, of course, insect-eating birds to take up residence in your neighborhood.

3. Reduce the size of your lawn, which will cut down on mowing (thereby reducing air and noise pollution) and fertilizing. These large expanses of clipped green grass are unproductive spaces that could be filled with plants beneficial to wildlife.

PROJECT | Pinecone Bird Feeder

If you aren't the carpenter type, you can easily make a bird feeder that will win you many feathered friends.

MATERIALS: Strong twine; large, open pinecones; aluminum foil; cookie sheet; vegetable shortening or peanut butter; birdseed (or oats, sunflower seeds, or millet)

1. If needed, dry the pinecones. Preheat the oven to 175°F. (The lower the temperature setting at which the pinecones dry, the less brittle they will be.)

2. Spread the pinecones on a foil-lined cookie sheet and place in the oven. After approximately 1 to 2 hours, the pinecones will have opened and will be dried. Allow to cool before handling.

3. Tie a length of twine to one end of your pinecone for hanging.

4. Coat the pinecones with the shortening or peanut butter, making sure to fill the petal openings. Cover with birdseed, oats, sunflower seeds, or millet, or a combination of each.

5. Suspend from tree branches around the yard.

Become a "Kitchen Gardener"

We've all come home to discover neglected onions and potatoes turning into plants in the pantry. Usually, that's when they get tossed. But what if you gave them some soil and let them do their thing? You'd end up with a charming, and free, houseplant! Here are a few ideas for transforming veggies into greenery—on purpose.

Grow a Beet Plant from a Beet

{LOW LIGHT}

Beet plants have stunning dark green foliage with thick red stems. The leaves reach a length of 6 to 8 inches.

Buy firm, fresh beets with tiny new leaves sprouting at the top. Select a soup bowl or serving dish and fill it two-thirds full with moist potting soil. Remove all the foliage from the beets, being careful not to nick their flesh. Place the beets on top of the soil, pressing them in gently and leaving them two-thirds exposed. Fill in around the beets with more moist soil, and water well.

Within five days, leaves and stems emerge from the tops of the beets.

Grow a Lentil Plant from a Half-Dozen Lentils

{BRIGHT SUN}

A lentil plant will grow to about a foot tall, with delicate gray-green leaves and small bluish flowers.

Fill a 4-inch pot two-thirds full with moist potting soil. Place a half-dozen lentils on the soil and cover with one-quarter of an inch of soil. Place the pot in a brightly lit window and keep the soil moist. Seeds sprout within a few days. The plant will last a few months.

Grow a Ginger Plant from a Nubbin of Ginger

{INDIRECT SUNLIGHT}

What you know as the flavoring in your chicken dish is actually an underground stem, called a *rhizome,* whose buds grow into stems and narrow leaves. The white flowers are delightfully fragrant—each stem holds as many as fifteen blooms.

Select a shallow, wide pot large enough to accommodate the ginger. Fill three-quarters of the pot with moist potting soil and lay the ginger on top of the soil. Keep the soil moist and put the pot in a place that is brightly lit but not sunny.

The ginger plant grows quickly—in six weeks it can be as tall as 3 feet. A healthy plant should sprout for several months.

BEET, LENTIL, AND GINGER PLANTING INSTRUCTIONS BY DEBORAH PETERSON AND MILLICENT SELSAM

Grow Some Garlic from an Old Clove

It's possible to grow a nice little head of garlic by taking a clove you have sitting around in the kitchen and sticking it in the ground this fall. You don't even have to peel it. Come spring, the chances are good that your little clove will have become a whole head. (Your chances are even better if the garlic is organic—supermarket garlic is sprayed with a chemical that inhibits sprouting.)

When to plant. In most growing zones, the advice to would-be garlic growers is to plant in fall, before the first frost. Then, after three or four days of watering, apply a layer of mulch to protect the garlic through the winter.

How to plant. Professional garlic growers refer to cloves of garlic as *garlic seed*. You can purchase garlic seed of very high quality meant specifically for gardening; if you're planting with store-bought garlic, use only the large cloves from the outside of good-size heads. If you are planting in a cold climate, plant the cloves 2 to 4 inches below the soil line. Otherwise, plant them about 1 inch deep. In either case, the cloves should be placed pointed-end up. They should be set at 3- to 5-inch intervals, with at least 18 inches between rows.

Be patient. Garlic sprouts very quickly—sometimes in as little as three days. However, it has a long way to go before each clove becomes a new head.

Make a Garlic Braid

Braiding garlic heads is probably the best way to preserve your garlic and keep it on hand throughout the year. The braids also make truly sensational presents—as long as you're sure the recipient is a garlic lover!

Begin weaving the braids as soon as you pull the heads from the ground, so the stems will still be pliable. Start with three fat heads of the garlic. Braid their leaves together, then start adding other heads (as when French-braiding hair). For braids you plan to give away, weave the heads so closely together that the leaves don't show. Otherwise, a little space between the heads will make it easier to remove them one at a time as needed.

When you've done as many heads as you want, braid the last of the leaves and tie off with raffia or twine, forming a loop for hanging. Hang the finished braids where they'll get the benefit of a lot of air circulation.

PROJECT | **Tin Can Bird Feeder**

In just a few steps, you can turn an empty coffee can into a sturdy, and thrifty, bird feeder.

TOOLS AND MATERIALS: Crosscut saw or handsaw; drill with ½" drill bit and 1¼" paddle bit; screwdriver; one ¾" x 6" x 19" board; one 1-pound coffee can; one ½" x 15" dowel; one 4" T-strap hinge and screws; three 1½" screws or 6d nails

1. From the ¾" board, cut pieces as illustrated.

2. Glue and nail or screw the *back* and the *bottom* sections of wood together.

3. With a can opener, remove the underside of the coffee can. Center the can on the *bottom* of the wood, and draw a circle around it. Remove and, with the paddle bit, drill into the wood, making three evenly spaced holes ⅜" deep (they should not penetrate all the way through) and centered on the line that marks the outside of the can. (The half of the shallow circle outside the can becomes a tray from which the birds will feast.)

4. Between the holes for seeds, drill three ½" holes through the *bottom* for the dowels, just inside the can's outline.

5. Cut the dowels to length and insert. Place the can over the dowels; it should fit snugly.

6. Place the *roof* on top of the *back* of the structure and mount the hinge, screwing the rectangular leaf into the *roof* and the strap into the *back*. To fill the feeder, open the roof and fill the tin can with seeds. Mount the feeder atop a wooden post by screwing up through the bottom of the can.

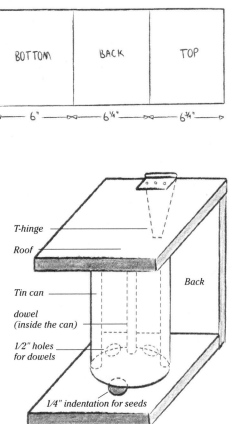

6"

BOTTOM | BACK | TOP

⟵ 6" ⟶ ⟵ 6¼" ⟶ ⟵ 6¾" ⟶

T-hinge

Roof

Tin can

dowel
(inside the can)

1/2" holes
for dowels

Back

1/4" indentation for seeds

TIN CAN BIRD FEEDER FROM *COUNTRY WISDOM & KNOW-HOW*

Furry Family Members

If you're looking for ways to reduce your expenses, adding a new pet to your household is not exactly a step in the right direction. If you decide to buy a purebred animal, it may be expensive. There are food costs and potential health care costs, too. But let's face it—when those two little eyes look up at you, your money is well spent. With a wagging tail, a soft purr, a happy tweet, even a dash across the aquarium, pets provide companionship, laughter, and calm. When you're down, they can boost your spirits. And they always make a night at home a happy prospect. Expensive? Maybe. But animal lovers will find that with a little effort, you can reduce the costs—and maximize the joy.

The Case for Mutts

Purebred dogs are the designer labels of the pet world—you buy them because you like how they look and behave, and you know roughly what you'll be getting. Mutts, on the other hand, are the plain brown wrapper of dogdom. They are the generic brand, a no-name animal, the unbreed. And every thrifty would-be pet owner should consider the mutt.

Some things to consider: Adopting a mutt will cost you hundreds or even thousands less than buying a purebred. Every mutt is one of a kind, and in these days of mass-produced merchandise, being unique is a priceless commodity. Mutts are not perfect, and that's their appeal—you won't find a snaggletooth in a well-bred dog. But mutts are often healthier than purebreds, because they have not been inbred. They tend to live longer. Think of rescuing a mutt as a form of recycling. It feels good to give someone a second chance.

For Working Parents

If you don't have time to walk your dog as much as you'd like, investigate the possibility of time-sharing your pooch with someone who loves dogs but doesn't live with one. You may have a retired neighbor who would love to take a stroll with a canine companion in the middle of the day, or know a kid who could visit after school and do homework while your dog enjoys some company.

MUTTS BY JULIA SZABO; WORKING MOMS AND DADS BY ARDEN MOORE

Thrifty Dogs by Breed

Should you decide to buy or adopt a purebred dog, keep in mind that some are more high-maintenance than others. By definition, purebred dogs come from a more limited gene pool than the average mixed-breed. Sometimes efforts to achieve a certain coat color or body type inadvertently pass along undesirable traits at the same time. That doesn't mean all purebred dogs have congenital defects, or that no mixed-breed dogs do—mutts can get have dysplasia and bad knees, too. But the following breeds have been determined to be thrifty or not based on a veterinary cost index. The index ranks a breed's likely veterinary expenses over the dog's lifetime, based on the disorders that are more common in that breed and how expensive they are to treat.

$ HEALTHY HOUNDS

The following breeds can be expected to cost you routine veterinary expenses, such as vaccinations, heartworm prevention, and dental care:

- American Eskimo Dog
- Anatolian Shepherd Dog
- Bedlington Terrier
- Briard
- Brittany
- Brussels Griffon
- Canaan Dog
- Flat-Coated Retriever
- Fox Terrier
- German Wirehaired Pointer
- Greyhound or Italian Greyhound
- Ibizan Hound
- Irish Terrier
- Jack Russell Terrier
- Japanese Chin
- Komondor
- Manchester Terrier
- Norwich Terrier
- Pharoah Hound
- Portuguese Water Dog
- Puli
- Saluki
- Sealyham Terrier
- Staffordshire Bull Terrier
- Swiss Mountain Dog
- Tibetan Terrier
- Welsh Terrier

$$$ PRICEY POOCHES

The following breeds are more likely to incur expenses for two or more significant medical problems:

- Akita
- Basset Hound
- Beagle
- Bernese Mountain Dog
- Boston Terrier
- Chihuahua
- Chow
- Cocker Spaniel
- Dachshund
- Dalmatian
- Doberman Pinscher
- German Shepherd
- Golden Retriever
- Great Dane
- Irish Setter
- Irish Wolfhound
- Keeshond
- Labrador Retriever
- Malamute
- Maltese
- Newfoundland
- Old English Sheepdog
- Pekingese
- Pointer
- Pomeranian
- Poodle
- Pug
- Saint Bernard
- Samoyed
- Schnauzer
- Shar-Pei
- Shetland Sheepdog
- Siberian Husky
- Springer Spaniel
- Vizsla
- Weimaraner
- Welsh Corgi
- Yorkshire Terrier
- West Highland White Terrier

Ask a Veterinarian

Bernadine Cruz, Laguna Hills Animal Hospital, Laguna Hills, California

Q When should I take my pet to the vet?

A If you notice a dramatic change in your pet's appetite, weight, water consumption, or behavior, you should consider making an appointment. Let's say you have a snake who's usually a good eater, but now you offer him a mouse and he's not interested—he just looks at it and seems to say, "I'll eat it later." That's an indication that something's not right.

How to prepare for a checkup. Know your pet. Keep a health diary. Small changes in your pet's behavior will give your veterinarian more information during an examination.

How to economize on pet food without sacrificing pet health. Some people buy cheap pet food because the premium brands seem too expensive. But the high-quality foods are more nutritious and more digestible, so pets need to eat less of it. One way to economize is to buy in bulk or download coupons from manufacturers' websites.

If you're tempted to make homemade food for your pet, understand that it is very difficult to meet the nutritional needs of dogs and cats. They are not little people. They need certain amino acids and proteins.

Pet insurance? Too often, I see people make life and death decisions based on money, so I strongly recommend pet insurance. You can compare policies online, but ask your vet which policy he or she recommends, because you'll be using the policy with that vet. Some policies can be used only at a particular hospital, others you can use anywhere in the world.

Preventive care. Ask your vet or technician to show you how to clean ears, trim nails, and brush teeth. Keep your pet up to date on his or her vaccines and buy heartworm medication; even indoor pets can get heartworm disease. Good flea and tick control is also very important. Bathe a dog or cat only from the neck down. Water in an animal's ears can cause an infection.

Senior pets should have wellness exams twice a year. Your older pet may look healthy but have underlying issues. Say a cat is losing weight, acting very energetic, and drinking more water. The owner may think everything is fine, but if I hear an abnormal heartbeat, I'll know the cat has an overactive thyroid.

Why Cats Have Condos

You can extend the life of your cat by keeping her indoors. Indoor cats live an average of twelve to eighteen years, while outdoor cats live an average of five to six years. The risk factors include vehicles, coyotes and other cat-hunting predators, and Mother Nature's weather extremes.

WHY CATS HAVE CONDOS BY ARDEN MOORE

Protecting Mr. Bigglesworth for Life

Many vets recommend pet health insurance—it can lighten the financial burden of pet ownership and allow you to focus on what's best for your pet rather than how much you have in your bank account. But is a monthly premium a thrifty investment for you? To figure that out, calculate how much you spent on different categories of veterinary care over the past year and think about what kinds of medical treatment your pet is most likely to need in the next year or two. Then compare the costs and coverage associated with a few different plans, talk to your vet, and, if it looks worthwhile, select a policy that makes the most sense for you. Health insurance policies vary widely in coverage and cost so keep the following in mind:

- If you're getting a puppy or kitten, look for a policy that covers vaccinations, spaying or neutering, deworming, and identification microchips, as well as injuries and illnesses.
- If you spend a lot on prescription medications, look for a policy that covers all or part of that cost. Many policies do not.
- If you have an older pet, look for a policy that covers routine dental cleaning, prescription medications, and diagnostic tests such as blood work, EKGs, and X-rays.
- If your pet has a chronic or recurring condition, look for a policy that covers preexisting problems. Many don't cover hereditary or congenital defects. Others will cover preexisting problems only if the pet has not needed treatment in at least six months. If your pet's breed is predisposed to an inherited health problem—such as hip dysplasia in dogs—find out whether it's covered.
- If you favor alternative treatments, look for a policy that covers acupuncture, chiropractic work, and holistic medicine.

The Power of Petting

Scientists report that when people pet their cats and dogs, they experience an increase in theta waves, a brain wave pattern that shows a reduction in feelings of anxiety. Just a few minutes of petting releases positive biochemicals, those feel-good hormones such as dopamine, oxytocin, and serotonin. At the same time, levels of fight-or-flight biochemicals are reduced. Research shows that the good feelings work both ways, meaning that your pet benefits as well.

INSURANCE BY BETSY BREVITZ; THE POWER OF PETTING BY ARDEN MOORE

Feeding for Thrift and Health

Tempted by those pricey people-style dog dinners they're always hawking on TV? Don't be fooled by the magic of marketing and technology! The meaty chunks or slices are probably soy (textured vegetable protein) pressed into meat shapes. There's nothing wrong with feeding a dog soy protein, but if you think you're feeding him roast beef, you're mistaken. The gravy? It's mostly water and salt. The peas and carrots? They're adding more visual appeal to you than they are nutritional value to your dog. If meat and vegetables are what you're looking for in a canned dog food, choose a variety that's named for the meat only (just "Beef") and add a variety of cooked vegetables from your own refrigerator. (Limit fresh food to 25 percent of your dog's intake, and steer clear of tomatoes, garlic, onion, and any veggies your particular pooch doesn't happen to tolerate—you'll find out what they are soon enough.)

RECIPE | Heavenly Kitty Hash

When you feel like spoiling your kitty a little, swap out her regular food with a serving of Heavenly Hash every now and again.

> 1 cup water
> ⅓ cup uncooked brown rice
> 2 teaspoons vegetable oil
> ⅔ cup lean ground turkey
> 2 tablespoons chopped liver

1. In a medium saucepan, bring the water to a boil. Stir in the rice and oil and reduce the heat to low. Allow the mixture to simmer for 20 minutes, covered.

2. Add the ground turkey and chopped liver. Stir frequently and simmer for 20 more minutes.

A Cheap Treat

If you aren't into cooking for your pet, roll bits of canned food into little balls rather than relying on purchased commercial treats. You can also cut lean, cooked meats into itty-bitty pieces (no bigger than the size of the nail on your little finger).

RECIPE | **Leaping Liver!**

Making your own pet food may raise nutritional concerns and generate plenty of debate. But you *can* make the occasional treat, rather than buying them at the store. Here's a quick recipe for a simple cookie that your dog will love. It may briefly stink up your kitchen, but the good news is that you can make a batch and store it in the freezer for as long as three months.

> **1 pound sliced beef liver**
> **(save the juice)**
> **¼ cup water**
> **1 small box corn muffin mix**

1. Preheat the oven to 350°F. Spray an 8½ x 11-inch baking pan with cooking spray.

2. Grind the liver in a food processor one slice at a time. Add a little water with each slice so you end up with a liquid.

3. Thoroughly combine the muffin mix and the liver liquid in a large bowl.

4. Pour the liver mix into the prepared pan.

5. Bake until the middle springs back at your touch, 20 to 25 minutes.

6. Cool and cut into small cubes. (Organ meat, while good for your dog, is too rich to give in large amounts.)

Where's the Beef?

Pet food labels are tricky, so get to know the U.S. Food and Drug Administration's dog-food naming rules:

- To be called Beef for Dogs, a food must contain at least 70 percent beef by weight.
- Something called Dog Food with Beef needs to contain only 3 percent beef by weight.
- Something called Beef Flavor Dog Food must include only a detectable beef flavor.

The message? The simpler the name, the more meat you're getting.

The Home Groomer

If your dog requires a fancy haircut or special handling, a groomer may be a necessity. But you can avoid that expense, or at least cut it way back, by primping your pooch yourself. Besides the occasional whisker trim, a bath is normally all a dog needs. There's no hard and fast rule for how often to bathe your dog. But when he gets dirty or begins to develop that doggy smell, it's time for a bath!

HOME GROOMING BY PAULA KEPHART

To give your dog a bath, you'll need castile soap or dog shampoo, mineral or olive oil, cotton balls, a washcloth, and a large towel. If you live in an area where fleas and ticks are a problem, use a flea-and-tick shampoo. If your dog's skin or hair tends to be dry, you might also need a conditioner. Never use human shampoo on a dog—hair care products for humans sting the eyes and are formulated for different a different type of hair.

1. Put your puppy in a tub or basin of lukewarm water. (If you're bathing your dog outdoors, you can use a children's wading pool.) Don't start scrubbing right away—give your pet a chance to get used to the water.

2. Dip two cotton balls in a little mineral or olive oil and place one in each of your dog's ears. This will keep water from entering the ear canal.

3. Pour water from the tub over the dog's back and shoulders until he is thoroughly wet. Don't splash water over the dog—he may become frightened—and don't pour water over his head.

4. Use your hand to scoop up a bit of water to wet your dog's face. Be sure not to get any in your dog's eyes or nose.

5. Drizzle a line of shampoo down the dog's spine, from between the ears to the base of the tail. Rub this in well, adding more water

to create a better lather if necessary. Go easy on the pressure at first.

6. Gently clean your dog's ears and face with the washcloth.

7. Drizzle some shampoo onto the washcloth and use it to scrub the feet, the chest, and under the tail.

8. Pour water over the dog to rinse. Run your fingers through the coat to make sure all the shampoo is rinsed out.

9. If your dog has dry skin or brittle hair, apply a conditioner, following the directions on the bottle. Rinse if necessary.

10. Help your dog out of the bath and use the towel to dry his coat. Remove the cotton balls from his ears.

11. Once he is dry, brush your dog's hair. Brushing after bathing will stimulate the skin and distribute the natural oils.

Fleas-Flee Dog Rub

Fleas, ticks, and other skin parasites are the bane of all pet owners. You should brush your dog (or cat) regularly, keeping an eye out for the pesky pests. To banish fleas, you'll have to use a chemical flea-killer—ask your vet for a recommendation. Then, keep them away with this natural—and aromatic—potion.

Slice 12 lemons in half and put them in a 1-gallon jar filled with water. Place this jar in the hot sun for a week, until the lemons begin to turn moldy; then strain and rebottle. (Or boil the lemons, remove from heat, allow to steep overnight, then strain.) Stored in the refrigerator, this infusion will last for several weeks. Rub this mixture onto your pet daily.

DOG RUB FROM *COUNTRY WISDOM & KNOW-HOW*

Win the Battle Against Cat Hair

An occasional trip to a professional groomer may be necessary, but you can keep cat hair under control with consistent upkeep. Here's how:

- Use two-sided tape to attach plastic self-grooming combs along the lower corner of a wall. Your cat will enjoy rubbing against the plastic bristles for a self-administered back scratch any time he desires.
- Dampen your hand, then run it gently against the direction of your cat's coat. This technique removes dead hair better than combing and also promotes hair growth.
- Choose a grooming time when your cat is relaxed and feeling receptive to attention. If possible, set aside five minutes a day.

Remove Pet Accidents from Carpets

The unfortunate truth for pet owners is that dog and cat "accidents" aren't always accidental—if Fido and Kitty are marking their territory, woe to the antique Persian rug that stands in their path. Here's how to save your rug, and your relationship with your fluffy friend:

- Use a white towel to blot the damp area as soon as possible.
- Apply a solution of one-quarter teaspoon of dishwashing liquid and one cup of warm water with a white towel. Avoid overwetting. Absorb moisture with paper towels, rinse with warm water, and repeat as long as there is a transfer to the towels.
- Next, apply a solution of one cup white vinegar and two cups water with a white towel and blot dry. Stand on the towel to promote absorbance.
- Secure a half-inch layer of paper towels on the area with a heavy object. When thoroughly wetted, replace. Continue to replace until towels no longer absorb moisture.
- Try using an all-natural enzyme-based cleaning product as an alternative method. The enzymes actually digest the stain- and odor-causing proteins in the pet urine.
- Do not use ammonia or other cleaning chemicals with strong odors on the stained spot, as they do not effectively cover the odor and may encourage your pet to reinforce its urine scent mark.
- To discourage a pet from resoiling a previously soiled area, lay a sheet of foil on the spot for a week or two. It will be unappealing for your pet.

BATTLE AGAINST CAT HAIR BY ARDEN MOORE; CARPET-CLEANING TIPS BY DONNA SMALLIN

Pet Toys for Less

Pet toys are a multibillion-dollar industry. But pets don't have expensive taste: an empty paper bag is a cat's idea of bliss, and dogs just want something to chew on or chase. Still, we must keep our furry friends entertained, so here are a few ideas on how to cut corners:

- Keep your dog's playthings stashed in a small toy chest or a pretty basket. Bring out a few at a time to keep your dog occupied but not overwhelmed by the selection. By rotating toys so your dog doesn't tire of them, you can renew her excitement. (Wow! I thought that toy squirrel was lost for good!) This tactic also saves you money at the pet supply store. Everyone wins!

- Put a teaspoon of uncooked rice in an empty plastic film canister or medicine bottle and seal the cap with tape to prevent it from being pulled off. Roll it to your kitten when he is in a playful mood. The sound will probably prove irresistible, and your kitten will quickly begin batting around the toy.

- Create homemade cat toys by filling a knotted piece of fabric or an old cotton sock with dried catnip. When the catnip loses its zip, refill the toy with a fresh helping. Just make sure there are no stray strings for kitty to swallow.

PROJECT | Ultra-Simple Homemade Cat Bed

When topped with fleece and set in a warm, sunny location, this bed will quickly become a cat magnet. Best of all, it's easy to launder—just remove the fleece blanket and throw it in the washing machine. (If you suffer the misfortune of a flea infestation, you can wash the bed as well.)

MATERIALS: Old pillowcase; rags, old towels, and worn-out T-shirts; needle and thread

1. Stuff an old pillowcase with layers of rags, worn-out towels, or old T-shirts. Use enough filling to make the bed at least an inch thick and wide enough to fit the cat comfortably.

2. Sew the open end of the pillowcase, again adjusting for size, and add a few stitches around the edges to secure the stuffing, so it won't bunch up when washed.

3. Arrange the cat bed in the area you've selected. Drape a small fleece blanket or baby blanket over the bed and tuck in the corners to secure it.

PROJECT | **A Scratching Post**

Unfortunately, just about anything that stands upright in the house is apt to become a scratching post for an untrained kitten or cat. Most cats, however, will learn to use a scratching post instead of the couch or table legs if you provide them with one—and any scratching post costs less than a reupholstery job. For the DIY cat lover, scratching posts are easy to make and will outlast store-bought posts. Most carpet supply stores have remnants free for the asking.

MATERIALS: A thick piece of plywood at least 24" square; an 18" length of 4" x 4" lumber; two sturdy angle irons with screws to fit them; piece of carpet remnant (same size as plywood); sandpaper; soft marking pencil; small power drill; screwdriver; contact glue; contact cement; heavy hemp rope

1. Sand the edges of the plywood to remove all splinters.

2. Mark the center of the plywood with the pencil and place the 18-inch length of 4 x 4-inch lumber upright on it.

3. Mark the placement of screw holes on both the 4 x 4 and the board, using the angle irons at opposite sides of the dowel.

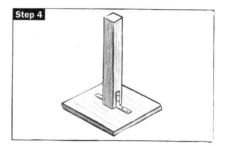

Step 4

4. Drill small holes to start the screws and screw the angle irons tightly in place.

5. Cover the board with carpet, gluing it firmly in place.

6. Apply contact cement to the dowel, beginning at the bottom and working a small area at a time.

7. Begin wrapping the dowel tightly with heavy hemp rope, pushing each spiral close to the previous one and adding more glue to the post as you work upward.

8. Finish the top with a tight single knot and nail it in place, so the knot is on the top of the post. Cut the rope a few inches above the knot and unravel the end to make a stiff, brushlike tassel for the cat to swat at.

Paw It Forward

If your beloved pal is a former pound puppy or kitty, occasionally buy an extra bag of treats, a toy, or a bed and donate these items to the animal shelter from which you adopted him. Most shelters maintain lists of the supplies they need. It's a great way to help other animals in need of loving homes and to remind yourself of how glad you are to have rescued yours.

PAW IT FORWARD BY ARDEN MOORE

PROJECT | ## An Instant Dog Sweater

Don't trash that old baggy sweater! Instead, turn it into a quick and adorable dog vest. You can give it extra flair, if you wish, by embroidering your pooch's name on the back. Alternatively, if you see a suitable sweater at a yard sale or thrift store, snap it up. Choose a sweater with sleeves that suit the size of your dog. A good-size Labrador might fit into the sleeve of a men's large, say, and a cocker spaniel into a ladies' medium. (Old and baggy is key here; tight sleeves won't work.)

MATERIALS: Scissors; sweater; if decorating, yarn, embroidery needle (big enough to accommodate yarn), chalk

1. Using a sharp pair of scissors, detach one sleeve from the sweater by cutting along the seam where the sleeve is joined to the bodice.

2. Hold the sleeve up to your dog, with the wrist opening near his or her neck and the armpit opening stretching to just in front of the hind legs. Eyeball where the front legs need to slide through, keeping in mind that to make a turtleneck, you'll need a bit of extra length on the wrist end to fold back. Cut holes in the sweater for your dog's front legs.

3. Try the sweater on your dog and trim the length in the back to fit your pooch.

Personalize Your Dog's Sweater

1. Using chalk, write your pet's name where you want it to appear on the sweater.

2. Thread the yarn through the needle and tie a knot in one end of the yarn. Bring the needle up from the wrong side of the sweater to the right side at the beginning of the first letter.

3. Hold down the yarn on the sweater's surface with the end of your thumb about ¼ inch away from where the yarn came up, following the chalk line. Insert the needle back in the hole the yarn came up through, forming a loop. Pull the yarn fairly taut, still holding a loop down with your thumb. Bring the needle back up at the point where your thumb is, catching the loop.

4. Continue stitching this way to form a chain that follows the chalk line you've drawn. Finish your chain stitch with a simple knot.

inside this chapter . . .

RECIPES

food & the thrifty cook

Making the Most of Every Morsel

As grandmothers the world over love to remind their kin, everybody's got to eat; and most of us want to enjoy it. Unlike the cable bill, food isn't something you can just cut out of your budget—thank goodness!—so the issue becomes, how to eat well while saving some money.

All the advice out there usually boils down to a few essential principles: Cook at home, limit your purchases of pre-made convenience foods, and avoid wasting the food you bring home. Yes, there is some comparison shopping involved. Yes, there is meal-planning. And yes, yes, yes, there are plenty of delectable treats!

No matter the size of your budget or family, you'll see the difference in your bank account, and possibly your waistline, too, if you stick to a home-cooking regimen. Whether you're just starting to make your lunch or you're ready to pickle the cucumbers you grew in your backyard, you'll find plenty of culinary inspiration, as well as guidance on how to maximize your thrift in shopping for and preparing your food. The one commitment you have to be ready to make at the outset? Own your kitchen. You are now the captain of your own personal restaurant. (Feel free to delegate to shipmates as needed.)

Ask a Chef

Nicole Marino, former chef, Savoy, New York

Q How can I be thriftier in the kitchen?

A The profit margins in the restaurant business are infamously tight, so people who work in professional kitchens know they'd better not be seen wasting anything. The frugal home cook may not be inclined to buy a whole pig, butcher it, cure some hams and bacon, and grind up the scraps for sausage, but certain practices *can* carry over.

Save everything. Pack your freezer. Always have one ziplock bag for vegetable scraps. When it's full, make stock (maybe with some leftover bones or meat trimmings) and freeze in small portions. (See page 140 for directions.) Use the stock to add flavor to sauces, stews, and braises, or to make soup. Make soup or tomato sauce in double batches and freeze the leftovers, and you'll always have a super-easy meal on hand. Make pesto from fresh herbs, then freeze the sauce—another quick way to add flavor to a dish. Cut up leftover bread, toast it in the oven, grind it into breadcrumbs, then toss it in yet another freezer bag. Use your homemade breadcrumbs to top vegetables and pasta dishes, to bread fish or chicken, or to thicken a soup.

Leftovers that don't freeze well can be used up in other ways. Fry extra potatoes for breakfast. Stir-fry leftover rice with veggies, egg, and soy sauce. Toss excess pasta into soup, along with the rinds from hard cheeses, which add richness and flavor. Meat bones can be added to a pot of beans.

Of course, the savings start with your purchases. A typical restaurant kitchen has a good supply of staples on hand and receives deliveries of perishables (meats, dairy, seafood, produce) a few times a week. This is a good guideline for a home cook: Stock up on staples, so you've always got some options in your pantry, but don't overbuy perishables; it's no fun throwing away wilted vegetables or turned milk. Wash and prep your vegetables right when you get home, then store them correctly so they last, and try to use them quickly. It's also important to be creative with what you have. See what's in the pantry and freezer. If you have a recipe you want to try, but you don't have exactly the right ingredients, improvise a bit rather than buying more stuff.

A Note on Soup & Thrift

When you're starting your thrift journey, you will inevitably be told again and again: Make soup! It's good advice. Soup costs little and goes a long way. But you can't eat it every day, nor do you have to. There are many other thrifty meals to be made—casseroles, quiches, and roasted meats, to name a few. And if you need some backup, remember the antisoup words of legendary interior designer Elsie De Wolfe: "You can't build a meal on a lake."

The Thriftiest Ingredients

Those celebrity TV chefs certainly look like they're having a good time, with their duck Bolognese sauce and their 15-cheese ravioli. "You, too, can make this at home," they assure you. But what they don't mention is the cost of all those fancy ingredients. There's nothing wrong with splurging on special occasions, but everyday cooking isn't thrifty if your recipes depend on truckloads of delicate gourmet greens, a pinch of spice you'll use only once, and a dollop of cream that's bound to go bad before you use it again.

Healthy, delicious meals can be created with simple ingredients and techniques. To prove it, we've taken a look at the four old-school food groups (grains, meats, produce, and dairy), focusing on low-cost items that serve multiple roles (beans and chicken, for instance).

You may notice omissions. Store-bought lettuce, for instance, didn't make the cut: Unless you're a daily salad-eater, lettuce often wilts before it gets used up. Hardier leafy greens last longer and can be used in a number of different ways.

Every home cook will have a different opinion about which ingredients are essential, and anyone on a restricted diet will have to address individual needs. But the ingredients on our list were chosen for their ability to multitask and hold up in the pantry, fridge, or freezer.

Thrifty Grains, Beans & Legumes

- Dried Beans
- Rice
- Pasta
- Cornmeal
- Flour

Dried beans score high points on the thrift meter: They're inexpensive and can be stored for up to a year. Which is why they're so widely used around the world—whether cooked into soups and chili, pureed into hummus, or eaten whole in burritos and salads. As a cheap source of protein, they pair well with rice and pasta, two starches that are also inexpensive and versatile. Cornmeal comes in handy for polenta, corn bread, and as a coating for fried foods. And flour does it all: bread, pasta, cookies, and treats of all sorts.

The Case for Dried Beans

Yes, canned beans are cheap, and when time is at a premium, they come in handy, but dried beans win in matters of taste. A from-the-can white bean salad or slow-cooked chili will wind up mushy and mealy; but with home-cooked beans, you control the cooking time, so you can opt for a firmer texture. And dried beans are absolutely the cheapest way to go: A 1-pound bag generally costs less than $1. That one bag yields more than 6 cups of cooked beans and broth. A 15.5-ounce can of beans, at the same price, gives you 1 to 2 cups.

The only things necessary to cook dried beans successfully are water and patience. The dried beans that take the least time to cook are lentils (legumes, really, but for our purposes let's call them beans)—30 to 40 minutes because you don't have to soak them first. For other beans, the minimum time is about 3 hours, using the quick-soak method and keeping them slightly firm. (A slow cooker comes in handy.)

If you're freezing beans, you'll get a better result if you cook them to a fairly firm texture so they don't get too soft upon reheating. We like to freeze ours in batches in quart-size ziplock plastic freezer bags. Lay them flat to freeze and they'll defrost faster. Be sure to include some of the broth when you are packaging the beans for freezing—it will help ward off freezer burn, and you can drain it off later if your recipe doesn't call for it.

RECIPE | Beans from Scratch

There's really nothing to it, but just to prove that there's no magic involved, here are instructions for plain cooked beans, using both the 1-hour quick soak and the traditional overnight method.

`Makes about 6 cups`

1 pound dried beans

1. Pour the beans into a colander and rinse under cool water, running your fingers through the beans to find and rinse away any clumps of dirt.

2. For a quick soak, place the beans in a Dutch oven or soup pot and add water to cover by 2 inches. Place pot over high heat, cover, and bring to a boil. Then remove the pot from the heat and let the beans soak for 1 hour.

For an overnight soak, place the beans in a Dutch oven or soup pot. Cover the beans with water by 2 inches and cover pot. Let the beans soak for 8 to 12 hours.

BEAN EXPLAINER, CHART, AND SOUP RECIPE BY BEVERLY MILLS & ALICIA ROSS

Cooking Your Beans Right

There are many kinds of beans out there. Not sure how long to cook them? This handy chart has you covered. All figures are based on a dry quantity of 1 pound. The figures in the water column refer to the cooking water only, not cooking water plus soaking water. But the amount of water you use depends on how old your dried beans are. The older the bean, the drier it is and the more water it takes to tenderize it. Check the beans frequently to make sure they are covered in water during simmering. Add water as necessary.

Bean Type	Soak	Water	Cooking Time	Yield
Black beans	Yes	about 6 cups	1½ hours	6½ cups beans and broth
Black-eyed peas	Yes	about 6 cups	2 hours	7 cups beans and broth
Chickpeas	Yes	about 7 cups	2½ hours	7 to 8 cups beans and broth
Lentils	Not required	5 cups	30 to 40 minutes	6 cups beans and broth
Pinto beans	Yes	about 6 cups	2 hours	7 cups beans and broth
Red beans	Yes	about 6½ cups	2¼ hours	7 cups beans and broth

3. Drain the beans, discarding the soaking water. Return the beans to the pot and add 6 cups water. Place the pot over high heat, cover, and bring to a boil. Uncover, reduce the heat to low, and simmer the beans until they reach the desired tenderness (see above for cooking times). Add more water if necessary to keep beans covered during cooking time.

4. Remove the beans from the heat and set aside to cool or to use in a recipe. The beans can be covered and refrigerated for up to 4 days or frozen in 1-cup batches for up to a month.

Lower Your Overall Food Costs

O ne can save only so much money on food, given the fact that eating and good nutrition are basic human requirements. It also doesn't make economic sense to sacrifice your health by eating cheap junk foods: Medical bills are way more costly than decent food. While there are some rules you'll need to follow if you want to save, it's not rocket science. Here's a quick overview of basic, time-tested, money-saving techniques:

The Tenets of the Thrifty Cook

- **Avoid restaurants.**
- **Set a realistic grocery budget** (the easy part), and stick to it (the somewhat hard part).
- If self-discipline is a challenge, **pay with cash.** For most people, it's tougher to part with the real thing.
- **Eat more food that's economical** but still nutritionally sound (think beans, grains, and tougher cuts of meat that tenderize after slow cooking). Eat less food that's expensive (think seafood and steak). Eliminate costly foods that have little or no nutritional value (think soda and dessert).
- **Look beyond the supermarket.** Consider farmers' markets and CSAs (see page 172) for produce, ethnic food shops for spices and pantry staples, and club warehouse stores for your bulk needs (see page xix).
- **Make foods from scratch,** particularly convenience items (see page 165).
- **Grow your own vegetables and herbs.** One or two tomato plants can pay

big dividends without gargantuan efforts. Growing a few favorite herbs in a pot can spare you the waste of a too-big bunch from the supermarket (see page 156).

- Finally, **how much you can save depends on how much you already spend.** Or put another way, it depends on how thrifty you already are. If your weekly grocery cart is normally brimming with fully cooked entrées, filet mignon, and peaches out of season, your cost savings can be immediate and huge. But if you're already buying store brands and economy sizes, and eating beans twice a week, it may be a challenge—though not an impossibility—to trim a lot more.
- **Stop throwing food away.** Cook up what you buy, and eat your leftovers. (We're all guilty of this anti-thrift offense, and stopping is easier said than done; see page 154 for tips on how to rise to the challenge.)

For Cheap Eats and Health, Embrace "Peasant Food"

All too often, eating cheap means eating badly. It's the greasiest slice of pizza that costs only $2. A hot dog and a soda for lunch will set you back maybe $4. But historically, the most inexpensive foods were simple to gather, easy to cook, and healthful. It's only in recent decades that the cheapest foods were processed and industrially produced, leading to an epidemic of obesity.

The good news is that eating well and reducing your food bill are not mutually exclusive. One easy way to do both is to take a look at the foods that have helped people get by on a shoestring. Many Eastern European cuisines rely on turnips and other root vegetables for soups. A winter turnip soup, for example, can be made by tossing a few pork bones and cubed turnips into a pot, adding enough water to cover, and simmering. Ginger, scallions, salt, and a dash of white pepper add flavor to a very simple dish. Most cultures around the world use some form of dried beans, which are commonly priced at less than a dollar a pound and are packed with vitamins. Just soak, cook, and serve with rice, pasta, or potatoes.

And keep in mind that many deprivation foods have turned chic. Polenta mixed with expensive creamy cheese may be on the menu at fine restaurants, but it's still just cornmeal. A friend of mine used to cringe when her Italian grandmother stooped down to collect the dandelion leaves that sprouted between the cracks of the sidewalks; now that she sees them for sale in gourmet grocery stores, she knows better.

Seven Simple Rules for Thrifty Grocery Shopping

1 Never shop when you're hungry. Everything looks good then, and you stop thinking about saving money or eating well. You're also likely to arrive at the checkout with a half-eaten box of Ho Hos.

2 Buy fish and fruits when they're in season locally.

3 Don't assume that just because a food is advertised, its price is the lowest. Compare prices, bargain hunt, enjoy the thrill of the chase.

4 Buy generic when you can't distinguish any difference from national brands. All milk has to meet government standards, so there's no reason to pay extra—unless you are buying organic or from a local dairy.

5 Watch as groceries are scanned or check your receipt—that two-for-$5 special often rings up as $3.99 per.

6 Coupons can be deceptive—25¢ off a premium brand can still result in a price that's higher than that of a generic version. You may also be tempted to buy items you never knew you wanted (and actually don't want) simply because you have a coupon.

7 Always make a list and don't deviate from it. Lists also prevent repeat visits for forgotten items.

CHEW ON THIS

Waste not, want not. Every year the average U.S. household throws away at least 470 pounds of food, according to research by the University of Arizona's Garbage Project. That equals 14 percent of the food that's brought into a family's home. Stop the insanity!

RECIPE | # Bean & Pasta Soup (aka "Pasta e Fagioli")

This Italian pasta and bean soup makes for a hearty, and extremely economical, meal. If you have leftover (cooked) turkey or chicken on hand, throw it in. Just add the meat in Step 3 and cook until heated through.

Serves 6

- 2 teaspoons olive oil
- 1 large onion
- 2 medium-size carrots
- 1 clove fresh garlic, minced
- 3 cans (about 14 ounces each) vegetable or chicken broth, or 6 cups homemade (see page 140)
- 2 cans (14½ ounces each) Italian-style stewed or diced tomatoes
- 1 teaspoon dried Italian seasoning
- 1 cup elbow macaroni
- 1 can (15 ounces) red kidney beans, or 1½ cups homemade, defrosted if frozen
- 1 can (15 ounces) white beans, such as navy beans, or 1½ cups homemade, defrosted if frozen
- ¼ teaspoon black pepper, or to taste
- ⅓ cup shredded or grated parmesan cheese, or to taste

1. Heat the oil in a 4½-quart Dutch oven or soup pot over medium heat. Peel and coarsely chop the onion, adding it to the pot as you chop. Cook, stirring from time to time, while peeling and slicing the carrots into ¼-inch-thick rounds. Add the carrots to the pot and cook, stirring frequently, until they begin to soften, about 3 minutes.

2. Add the garlic, broth, tomatoes with their juice, and Italian seasoning to the pot. Cover, raise the heat to high, and bring the soup to a boil.

3. When the broth comes to a boil, add the macaroni and cook, uncovered, at a rolling boil for 7 minutes. Meanwhile, rinse and drain the beans.

4. Add the beans and bring the soup back to a boil. Continue to cook until the macaroni is tender, about 3 minutes more. Season the soup with black pepper and serve, sprinkling the parmesan cheese on top.

RECIPE | ## Cornmeal & Water (aka "Polenta")

Sometimes, slow cooking is all it takes to elevate an ordinary ingredient to the sublime. You *could* buy quick-cooking polenta (essentially, partially pre-cooked cornmeal), but the taste and texture are no match; and as you won't be able to bake with the quick stuff, you'll get more out of a regular box of cornmeal. You can throw in toppings (cheese, sautéed mushrooms, wilted greens) to your heart's content, but even plain polenta makes for a satisfying side dish. P.S. The constant stirring everyone so dreads is not really necessary after the first phase of cooking.

Serves 4

> 4 cups water
> 1 teaspoon salt
> 1 cup cornmeal
> Milk, butter, salt, and pepper to taste

1. In a heavy saucepan, bring water and salt to a boil and gradually whisk in cornmeal.

2. Continue to whisk until the water returns to a boil and the polenta begins to thicken, then turn the flame to low. Simmer, stirring every 10 minutes or so, until the polenta is thick and pulls away from the side of the pan, about 40 minutes. (If the mixture seems to be getting too thick, stir in a splash of milk; repeat as necessary.)

3. Remove pan from heat and keep covered until serving. Season with milk, butter, salt, and pepper to taste.

RECIPE | ## Johnnycakes

As you'll see, if you follow our advice, you'll have every ingredient for these johnny-cakes in your fridge and cupboard at all times. The simple cornmeal pancakes have a very long history—the first johnnycake recipe appeared in print in 1739. (The Founding Mothers are always good for a thrifty recipe or two.) They have the texture of fluffy pancakes, with an extra nudge of corn in the flavor.

Makes about 8 johnnycakes

½ cup flour

1 cup cornmeal

2 teaspoons sugar

1 teaspoon salt

1 egg, lightly beaten

1 cup hot milk

1 tablespoon butter

1. Mix the dry ingredients, then stir in the remaining ingredients.

2. Drop the batter by spoonfuls onto a hot, greased griddle or skillet and fry to golden brown on both sides. Repeat until all the batter is used.

3. Serve with butter and syrup or fruit.

Why You Need Flour

At some point in life, you will be invited to a meal and asked to bring dessert. There's no shame in buying the treats, but if you turn up with something you baked in your own oven, you will always be greeted with an extra smile.

Baking is a skill that requires exact measurements and attention to detail. Which means it's a love-it or hate-it activity. Even haters should learn to prepare at least one dessert, be it cookies or cake, pastry or strudel. Make it well, and turn it into your signature.

Should you extend your baking skills to bread, you may find yourself turning into a convert—the ability to bake good bread is one of the most rewarding and money-saving skills a home cook can develop.

Even committed nonbakers need flour; it's an essential thickening ingredient in some sauces and gravy and central to panfrying breaded chicken or fish. And homemade pasta depends on it. Basically, full kitchen ownership practically requires that you buy flour and use it.

RICE PUDDING RECIPE BY BEVERLY MILLS & ALICIA ROSS

RECIPE | ## Yesterday's Rice, Today's Rice Pudding

What better way to use that leftover cup of cooked rice than in a delicious, old-fashioned rice pudding? You can add spices, nuts, and dried fruits, but this is the classic version—raisins optional.

Serves 6

Butter for the pan
1 cup cooked medium- or long-grain rice
½ cup raisins (optional)
3 large eggs
½ cup sugar
2 cups whole or 2% milk
1 teaspoon vanilla extract
½ teaspoon ground cinnamon

1. Preheat the oven to 325°F. Lightly butter an 8-inch-square glass baking dish. Set it aside.

2. Combine the rice and raisins (if desired) in a 2-quart or larger saucepan, add 1 cup water, and heat over medium heat until the rice is rehydrated, about 10 minutes. Drain, if necessary, and set aside.

3. Meanwhile, whisk the eggs, sugar, milk, vanilla, and cinnamon together in a medium-size bowl. Add the drained plumped rice and raisins to the mixture. Stir well and pour into the prepared baking dish.

4. Bake the pudding, uncovered, until the center is almost set and a knife inserted within 1 inch of the side of the dish comes out clean, about 45 minutes. Serve warm, at room temperature, or chilled.

Let's Call Pasta a "Good Carb"

Pasta has been through some hard times over the past couple of decades. It's the food that makes us fat, cry the carb-haters. It's supposed to be a side dish, counter the more European-minded. The truth falls somewhere in between: everything in moderation. From a thrift-conscious perspective, a box of dried pasta guarantees that you'll always have the basis for a meal. Toss pasta with the bare minimum of ingredients—olive oil, cheese, tomato, or even an egg—and you've got dinner. Add some protein and a vegetable, and you've got a balanced meal.

Commercial brands of dried pasta are easy on the wallet: Most start at less than $2 for a pound. Fresh pastas can cost twice as much, around $4 a pound—so if you want fresh and are willing to put in a little time, it may be worth learning to make your own.

Pasta can be made from just flour, salt, and water, but adding an egg and olive oil gives the dough more substance. The costs of the ingredients are minimal: a dozen eggs start at around $2.15, and 2 pounds of flour costs about $1.80 (less if you're buying in bulk), and you'll be using much less than that. The equipment may set you back a bit: Pasta machines with a hand crank start at about $30. And of course, the time factor. But with a little bit of practice, you'll be able to roll out a pound of pasta in an hour.

Is pasta making thrifty? It depends. If you're not particular about texture, then the dried versions will do just fine. But if you're going to pay for fresh in stores or restaurants, your wallet will thank you for making your own. If you come to enjoy the process, you can make fresh pasta as a gift. (Pasta making can also be a fun project in which to involve children.)

MY THRIFT

Eleven Eggs and Flour

I grew up in a large family, and during the hard times, we learned how to make homemade noodles. My grandpa would bring one egg for everyone: 11 eggs and some flour. There were so many, we had noodles drying everywhere.

—Noreen, born early 1920s

RECIPE | # Fresh Pasta from Scratch

Fresh pasta cooks in just 1 or 2 minutes. Don't boil the noodles too long and let all your hard work turn to mush!

Pasta dough can be kneaded, rolled out, and sliced by hand, but it *is* easier to work it through a pasta machine—essentially, a set of rollers through which the dough is rolled on successively thinner settings. At the end, it's almost translucent. Handmade pasta will be slightly thicker. Make the dough by following Step 1, then divide it into palm-size portions. With a floured rolling pin, roll out one portion until it is about as thin as a coin. With a sharp knife, slice into pappardelle-size strips about ¾-inch wide, or (for an easier option) cut into wide sheets for lasagna.

Makes about 1 lb.

> 3 cups flour
> 4 large eggs
> 1 tablespoon olive oil
> 1½ tablespoons cold water

1. Combine flour, eggs, olive oil, and water in a food processor. Process for about 30 seconds, until the mixture has the consistency of coarse sand.

2. Pour the mixture out onto a floured board and knead it with the heel of your hand until it comes together. Divide the dough into three or four manageable pieces.

3. Set the pasta machine on its thickest setting and roll the dough pieces through the machine one at a time.

4. Fold the dough in half over itself once or twice and roll it out again.

5. Repeat this process until the dough is smooth, doesn't tear, and has the texture of suede. Set the rollers on the machine to progressively thinner settings, rolling the dough through the machine once at each setting.

6. Cut the dough into the desired width by machine or by hand.

A note: To keep fresh pasta from sticking to itself, sprinkle it liberally with coarse semolina flour while tossing or coiling (shake off before cooking). Refrigerate if you're going to use within the week, or freeze. You can also dry the pasta slightly, making it less sticky, by hanging it over rope or the back of a chair. If you dry it completely, it will keep for months in an airtight container.

PASTA-MAKING DIRECTIONS BY JAMES PETERSON

How to Bake Bread

Good bread is not only thrifty, it's miraculous. Just a few humble ingredients transform, almost on their own, into the staff of life. No question, it's cheaper to make bread than buy it. A 2-pound package of flour can cost as little as $1.80 (and will make about four small loaves), while loaves of bread start at $2.50 and can cost as much as $5 or more. But it's also a matter of quality—for freshness, homemade can't be beat.

The same essential techniques are used to make most yeast breads: proofing, kneading, rising, shaping, and baking. Once you are familiar with these steps, you are ready to tackle almost any bread recipe.

Proofing. The proofing step has two functions: it gets the yeast off and running, and it's the best way to be sure that the yeast is active. To proof, stir the yeast into a little lukewarm (95°F–110°F) water, along with a bit of sugar or other sweetener, and let it sit for 5 minutes or until foamy. If you don't see any signs of life after 5 minutes, the yeast is dead. Toss it out and start over with a new supply.

Kneading. The kneading process combines ingredients and gives your bread texture. Traditional kneading is done on a floured board, with floured hands. Form the dough into a pancake shape. Using the heels of your hands, push the dough away from you. Then fold it over and rotate it a quarter turn. Keep doing this, adding more flour to the board and your hands as necessary, until the dough is elastic and has lost its stickiness.

Many bread bakers prefer to "knead" their dough in a food processor, pulsing on and off until a nice dough is formed, then giving the dough a final turn or two on a floured board. If you have a heavy-duty mixer with a dough hook, you can knead using the mixer.

Rising. After the dough has been kneaded, place it in a bowl greased with 1 tablespoon of oil and turn it around until it's greased on all sides. Cover. (A clean dish towel, plastic wrap, or foil works well.) Let it sit in a warm place (ideally between 80°F and 85°F) until it has doubled in size. This will usually take about an hour. If your kitchen isn't warm, placing the bowl of dough into a gas oven with a pilot light works well. You can achieve the same effect inside a cold electric oven by placing a pan of boiling water on the bottom rack, under the bowl of dough.

Punching down. Bang your fist into the center of the risen dough! Turn the dough over and punch again, then fold it a bit; continue folding and punching until the dough is thoroughly deflated.

BREAD-BAKING AND RECIPE FROM *COUNTRY WISDOM & KNOW-HOW*

Shaping. Flatten the dough into a rectangle. The length of the rectangle's shorter end should be equal to the length of the loaf you want or of the pan you're using. Flattening the dough with a rolling pin is a good idea, because it will get rid of any air pockets in the dough. Roll up the dough tightly from the short end, then pinch the ends and tuck them under. For a round loaf, flatten the dough into a square, then tuck the edges under.

Baking. Breads can bake directly on baking sheets sprinkled with a little cornmeal, or in pans, right on the oven's racks. The classic way to find out if a loaf has baked long enough is to carefully remove it from the pan and rap it with your knuckles. If the bread sounds hollow, it's done. If you don't hear a hollow sound when you rap on the loaf, put it back in the oven for a few minutes more. (You don't need to return it to its baking pan.)

Finishing. It's a nice touch to rub the top of a baked, warm loaf with a little soft butter or some milk to give it an appealing shine. (Another technique is to brush the top of an unbaked loaf with an egg wash consisting of an egg yolk beaten with 2 tablespoons of water.) When the bread is thoroughly cool, put it into a paper or plastic bag and store it at room temperature. Or freeze it. (If you want the bread sliced, it's best to do this before you freeze it.)

Shape the Dough

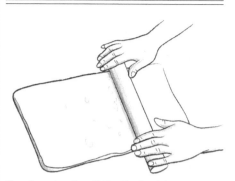

On a floured surface, flatten the dough into a rectangle.

Roll up the dough tightly.

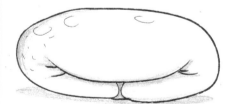

Pinch the ends of your log and tuck them under.

RECIPE | "Artisanal" Quality Multigrain Bread

Here's a basic recipe for a fresh home-baked loaf. Make a three-grain bread, a five-grain one, or whatever you like. If you decide to experiment, keep a written record of what you use and how it works out so you can replicate your favorite combinations.

Makes 2 small loaves

1 package active dry yeast

2 cups lukewarm (95°F–110°F) water (or use milk for half of this)

2 tablespoons honey or sugar

1½ cups (total) any combination of: cornmeal, barley flour (or pearl barley, soaked or parboiled), raw oats, millet, triticale, quinoa, rice flour, soaked or sprouted wheat berries, or a mixed-grain cereal

1 tablespoon salt

2 cups whole-wheat flour

3 cups all-purpose flour

1. In a large bowl, proof the yeast in the warm water with the sweetener.

2. Stir in the combination of grains and the salt, then the whole-wheat flour and 2 cups of the white flour.

3. Turn the dough out onto a floured surface and knead in the rest of the white flour.

4. Let the dough rise in a greased bowl, covered, until doubled in size.

5. Punch down the dough. Shape into two loaves and place in two greased 8½ x 4½-inch pans. Let rise until doubled again.

6. Preheat the oven to 350°F.

7. Bake for about 1 hour.

RECIPE | # Cheaper-than-Delivery Pizza

Just say no to phoning it in. People of all ages love pizza and can join in the fun of preparation. Feel free to make lots of dough, as the extra will keep well in the freezer. It's great to be able to grab a frozen hunk of dough, thaw and roll it, and create toppings from whatever you have in the pantry or fridge.

Makes two 12-inch pizzas or four 8-inch pizzas or ten 4-inch pizzas

1 tablespoon active dry yeast
1 cup lukewarm (95°F–110°F) water
1 teaspoon sugar
½ teaspoon salt
2 tablespoons olive oil
2 cups all-purpose flour
½ cup whole-wheat flour
1 tablespoon cornmeal
Toppings of your choice

Pizza Toppings

- Plain canned tomato sauce
- Dried oregano, dried or fresh chopped basil
- Pesto
- Red pepper flakes
- Grated mozzarella, or a combination of cheeses
- Chopped steamed broccoli
- Thinly sliced onion
- Sliced fresh tomatoes
- Sliced mushrooms
- Pepperoni
- Sausage
- Grilled chicken

1. To make the dough, dissolve the yeast in the warm water in a large bowl. Stir in the sugar, salt, oil, and flours. Stir the dough vigorously with a wooden spoon for 20 strokes.

2. Scrape the dough onto a floured counter and knead it until smooth.

3. Let the dough rest for 5 minutes before rolling it out. This is an important step because it allows the dough to relax, making it easier to roll.

4. For two pizzas, divide the dough in half; roll each half into a 12-inch circle on a floured surface. Lift the dough onto a pizza pan or baking sheet sprinkled with 1 tablespoon cornmeal.

5. Preheat the oven to 475°F.

6. Spread your favorite toppings on the waiting pizza dough. Bake for 10 to 20 minutes, depending on the size, or until the dough is lightly browned and the cheese is melted. Serve hot.

PIZZA RECIPE BY DEEDEE STOVEL AND PAM WAKEFIELD

The Thrifty Meat & Fish Corner

- Beef and Pork Roasts
- Ground Meats
- Sliced Deli Meats

- Whole Chicken
- Canned Tuna
- Local Fish

Learn how to cook the less expensive cuts, and meat can be economical. With beef and pork, a thrifty approach means using larger cuts and the tougher portions of the animal. But ground meats can also be low cost and versatile. A chicken should be bought whole; it can be roasted or braised, sliced up for parts (do it yourself—see page 135—or ask your butcher to do it for you). Canned tuna stores well and is more versatile than you may think. But the catch of the day at a local fish market may be the tastiest deal of all.

THRIFTONOMICS

A Case for the Brown-bag Lunch

"Oh, it's just a sandwich!" When it comes to the weekday lunch rush, it's easy enough to think of your convenient dash to the deli or pizza place as a negligible expense. After all, you're not sitting down to a three-course meal! But deep down, you know it's no good for your wallet. Perhaps you just need a little convincing.

Everyone's got different lunch preferences, but let's start with the old standard: a turkey sandwich. Packing a no-cook lunch costs approximately $3.75. Here's the breakdown: A 20-ounce loaf of ordinary, grocery-store-staple whole-grain bread costs about $3.29. There are about 20 slices in a loaf, so that means two slices of bread for your brown bagged sandwich cost about $0.30. Add 3 ounces of sliced turkey breast (cost is $1.21, assuming turkey is $6.49/pound), lettuce ($0.05, assuming $1.00 a head), tomato ($0.10, $0.49 per tomato), and an ounce of Swiss cheese ($0.50). That sandwich costs $2.61. Throw in a soda (average cost of a can from a 12-pack: $0.32), an apple ($0.60), and some pretzels ($0.22 an ounce) for an entire meal for $3.75.

Compare that to an $8 jaunt to the deli. Even if you bring your lunch just twice a week (not so hard!), you'll save around $8.50 a week. Sounds like small change, but over the course of a year that's $442 in savings. Brown bagging it might not sound glamorous, but how do you like the sound of an airline ticket to a tropical sandy beach? That's what $442 could buy you. It could also pay your cell phone bill for the entire year, or take a chunk out of your car insurance payments.

RECIPE | ## Shepherd's Pie

Stretch the meat, stretch the dollar by using an equal ratio of meat and potatoes. This traditional British dish was originally made with lamb or mutton—hence its name—but beef has since become the preferred meat.

Serves 6 to 8

FOR MASHED POTATO LAYER

3 pounds russet potatoes, peeled and cut into 1½-inch chunks
½ cup vegetable oil or butter (or a combination)
2 large onions (1¼ pounds total), chopped

FOR MEAT LAYER

3 slices white bread
1 large onion, finely chopped
3 pounds ground beef
2 large eggs, beaten
3 cloves garlic, crushed

2 teaspoons kosher (coarse) salt
Freshly ground black pepper to taste

1. Prepare the mashed potato layer: Place the potatoes in a large pot, add water to cover, lightly salt it, and bring to a boil. Reduce the heat and gently boil the potatoes until tender, 20 to 30 minutes. Drain and mash the potatoes.

2. Meanwhile, heat the oil and/or butter in a very large skillet over medium-low heat. Add the onions and cook slowly, stirring occasionally, until very soft and golden, 30 to 40 minutes.

3. Strain the onions, reserving the oil/butter. Puree the strained onions in a blender, and combine the puree with the mashed potatoes. Add about 2 teaspoons salt, and the pepper, and set aside. Preheat the oven to 350°F.

4. Prepare the meat layer: Place the bread in a shallow bowl, add water to cover, and soak for 1 to 2 minutes. Then drain the bread, and using your hands, squeeze out the excess water. Crumble the bread into bits in a large bowl. Add the onion, ground beef, eggs, garlic, salt, and pepper, and mix together.

5. Spread about one third of the mashed potato mixture over the bottom of a 13 x 9-inch baking pan. Pat the meat mixture evenly over the potatoes, then cover it with the remaining mashed potatoes. Jab all over with a fork. Brush lightly with the reserved oil/butter, and bake until the meat is cooked through and the potatoes are golden brown, about 1¼ hours. Cut into squares and serve hot.

Know Your Thrifty Cuts of Beef

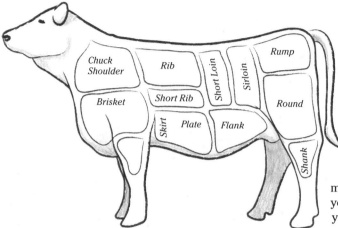

Chuck
Shoulder

Rib

Short Loin

Sirloin

Rump

Brisket

Short Rib

Skirt

Plate

Flank

Round

Shank

Sure, chicken's cheap, but that doesn't mean you have to become a pollotarian (yes, that's a real term) to be thrifty. The best meats for your money are those big, flavorful cuts that are tough unless treated with a gentle touch— like a long, slow braise. Give the following cuts of meat a chance and you (and your wallet!) will be glad you did.

Chuck comes from the shoulder and neck of the cow. The term *cold shoulder* comes from a custom in medieval French châteaux wherein guests who outstayed their welcome would be served a cold shoulder of beef (the chuck!) or pork as a sign to get out—but a nice pot roast is sure to entice your dinner guests to stick around. Slightly fatty and tough, the chuck is the tenderest of the cheap cuts and is often used for ground beef. Because of its fat content, it benefits from being cooked for a long time on low heat. Bring out its rich flavor by braising, stewing, or roasting. *Other names: pot roast, chuck eye steak, blade roast, cross rib roast*

The ribs of the cow are cut up into a few different sections, the three most popular being the short rib or "flanken" (from the underside of the cow), the back rib or spare rib (from the back of the cow), and chuck "ribs" (a boneless cut that is often prepared as short ribs). Ribs are inexpensive in part because you are paying for a lot of bone, and of course because they aren't dainty and quick-cooking. But grilled or braised (think Korean-style grilled short ribs or French *pot-au-feu*), it doesn't get much better than ribs!

The round is cut from the back of the cow, just below the rump. A much leaner cut than chuck, it also benefits from a slow, moist method of cooking; here, the lack of fat means the meat can easily dry out. This is the classic cut for such delicacies as sauerbraten and beef *braciole*. *Other names: top round roast, rump roast*

Brisket comes from the breast section beneath the ribs of the cow. It is just about the toughest cut of meat out there, but it's a great choice if you have enough time to barbecue or braise it properly—and a sandwich with the delicious leftovers makes a cheap lunch. You'll find it at your butcher either cut flat or to a point. (Cut to the point, it has a little more flavor due to the fatty layer or *deckle* that is left on.)

The flank and skirt sections are on the underside of the cow. There was a time when these cuts were considered good for nothing but ground meat. But all these cuts need is the right marinade and a good grilling, and they're as tender as any tenderloin! Upscale restaurants have caught on to the secret, which has jacked up prices slightly for this cut, but it's still comparable to and less expensive than the loin cuts. *Other names: hanger steak*

Know Your Thrifty Cuts of Pork

On the whole, pork is cheaper than beef, with some cuts being cheaper than others. Again, the delectability of the finished product all depends on finessing the cooking time and temperature to tenderize tougher cuts and keep lean ones moist. Traditionally, pork cuts get pricier as you work your way toward the tail, hence the expression "living high on the hog." Fortunately, you can live low on the hog and not cast pearls before swine. Or something like that.

Shoulder butt is the section of the pig below the neck at the shoulder. A barbecue mainstay for *carnitas* or pulled pork (see page 296), it is fatty enough to stay moist during the long, slow cooking time. *Other names: Boston butt, pork blade steak, Boston roast, pork butt roast*

Picnic shoulder is the lower half of the shoulder and arm. It's even cheaper and fattier than the shoulder butt, and when smoked is known as a picnic ham. This meat is often ground for sausage and slow-roasted to make Cuban *puerco asado*.

The hock is cut from the ankle joint or lower leg of the pig (not to be confused with the foot). The hock is usually mostly skin and gristle, which means it's great for adding flavor to vegetables and stews (particularly if smoked).

Spare ribs are the ribs most people think of when they think "barbecued ribs," but there are actually three rib cuts. Baby back ribs come from the back and are the tenderest but most expensive. Rib tips (or riblets), from the underside of the pig, are less expensive but so small you have to buy lots to make a meal. Spare ribs, which are cut from the side of the pig, are meaty, half the price of baby backs, and just right for a barbecue.

Pork belly or side is one of the least expensive cuts of pork. It freezes easily and is mostly fat. (It's the source of most bacon.) The cut has long been a staple of Asian cuisines, and has recently made a splash at some very fancy restaurants. Marinated, braised, and grilled to a crispy finish, home-cooked pork bellies are a gourmet treat for a fraction of the price.

The loin produces the leanest pork, and what are generally the most expensive cuts (such as the tenderloin, which is almost fat-free). But in the loin you'll also find pork chops, which cook quickly and are as delicious as lamb chops, at less than half the price! *Other names: pork tenderloin, pork center loin chop, pork sirloin roast*

Ham shanks are often cured and used to make prosciutto and other thinly sliced cuts. This meat will vary in price depending on how it's prepared, but a whole cured ham shank is generally less expensive than a ham made from the butt. *Other names: city ham, country ham, fresh ham*

RECIPE | # Cook a Chicken

A whole chicken is a gift that keeps on giving. Roasted or braised, as in this recipe, it handily feeds a family of four. The carcass can be used for chicken stock (page 141) or a curative chicken soup. You can also fry the livers for a treat, if you're so inclined. (And if fried chicken livers aren't to your taste, your cat or dog is guaranteed to love them.) Pound for pound, in most grocery stores whole chickens cost a fraction of those packages of precarved parts. All in all, an ideal ingredient for the thrifty kitchen.

Serves 4

> 3 medium-size carrots
> 2 medium-size ribs celery
> 2 large onions
> 4 medium-size potatoes
> 2 teaspoons seasoning salt, such as Lawry's
> 1 whole chicken (about 3½ pounds), defrosted if frozen

1. Preheat the oven to 350°F.

2. Peel the carrots and cut them into 1-inch pieces. Place the carrots in a 4½-quart or larger Dutch oven or slow cooker. Cut the celery into 1-inch pieces and add them to the pot. Peel the onions and potatoes, quarter them, and add them to the pot. Sprinkle 1 teaspoon of the seasoning salt evenly over the vegetables.

3. Remove the neck and any giblets that may be packaged in the cavity of the chicken. (Reserve them for use in gravy or discard them.) Place the chicken, breast side up, in the pot on top of the vegetables. Rearrange the vegetables, if necessary, so the pot lid can close tightly. Sprinkle the remaining 1 teaspoon seasoning salt evenly over the chicken. Pour ½ cup water into the pot alongside the chicken (taking care not to pour it over the chicken) and cover the pot.

4. Bake the chicken until an instant-read meat thermometer registers 180°F when inserted into a thigh (do not touch the bone), about 1½ hours, or 7 to 8 hours in a slow cooker on low.

CHICKEN RECIPE AND CARVING INSTRUCTIONS BY BEVERLY MILLS & ALICIA ROSS

PROJECT | ## Carve a Chicken

Don't be intimated by the prospect of carving a chicken (cooked or raw). You don't need a power tool or a culinary school degree. The best tool is a pair of kitchen shears (or other sturdy utility scissors). Here's how to go about it:

1. Place the chicken, breast side down, on a large cutting board or plate.

2. Starting at the tailbone, use the kitchen shears to cut straight along both sides of the backbone to the neck. (The backbone is about an inch wide, and the connecting bones on either side of it are very thin.) Remove and set the backbone aside to make stock or soup (or discard it).

3. Turn the chicken over. Use the scissors to cut straight between both halves of the breast. The breast is held together mostly by cartilage, which is easy to cut. There is one bony spot, which you can cut around with the shears; or which you can cut through with a sharp knife.

4. Next, separate the leg portion (thigh and drumstick together) from each breast half by lifting the drumstick away from the breast. It will be easy to spot where the skin lifts away from the meat between the thigh and the breast. While still lifting up on the drumstick, cut along the skin with the scissors, following the contour of the thigh. You will be cutting more or less in a semicircle, and as you cut, the thigh will continue to lift away from the breast. (If you wish to serve the wings and drumsticks separately, use a sharp knife to cut them off at the joint.)

5. If you are carving a cooked chicken, add any juices released while cutting to the pan juices to make gravy, or pour the juices over the carved chicken. If you are cutting up a raw chicken, wash your hands, the shears, and the cutting board thoroughly with hot, soapy water. Don't let the chicken come in contact with anything you will be eating raw.

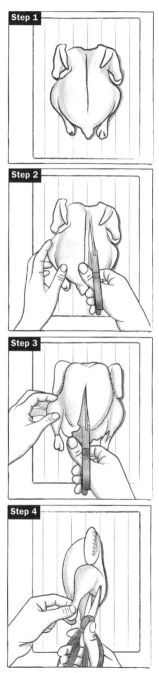

A Hunter's Manifesto | by Steven Rinella

Are hunters thrifty? As a hunter myself, I know it's a complicated question. An equivalent would be to ask a parallel question: Are cars thrifty? In both cases, there is a spectrum of answers. You can be the hunting equivalent of a Hummer, burning up extravagant amounts of resources for limited gains. Or you can be the hunting equivalent of a Prius, maximizing those same resources for output and sustainability.

I've been both kinds of hunter, the Hummer and the Prius. My Hummer days began when I was just a kid. Back then, I had every intention of becoming a modern-day hunter and gatherer. I read every book that I could find about the early pioneers and mountain men of the American West. I looked forward to becoming a penniless and miserly hermit living alone in a remote wilderness cabin. I'd have my own smokehouse and a cobweb-choked root cellar, where I would preserve my hard-earned food for the miserable and frozen winters that I'd joyfully endure.

In real life, my early subsistence-hunting ambitions were thwarted by the complexities of living in a proper house with my parents. My mom was very pragmatic. She conducted weekly shopping trips with an eye toward routine and efficiency, and she wasn't a big fan of mealtime complications or surprises. She treated the critters that I brought home from the swamps and woods as being outside of her regimented program. My ducks, rabbits, and squirrels were often improperly cleaned and packaged by my young hands, and then sequestered in a back corner of the basement chest freezer.

Once the meat was in there, my mom figured that it was effectively transferred to my dad's culinary jurisdiction. After all, he was the one who had introduced me to hunting. The problem with this system was that my dad figured that my mom should do the cooking. On the rare occasion that he was inspired or coerced to prepare a meal, he would dig out a package from the freezer and go to the garage to scorch the best morsels in an industrial-size deep fryer that he bought at a restaurant foreclosure auction. The result of this system was that a great deal more game went into that freezer than ever came out in edible condition.

In short, it wasn't too thrifty.

Fast-forward to my college days in Michigan's remote Upper Peninsula. I was finally granted my dream of being a penniless miser in a frozen and desperate home. I loved it. My relationship to the tangible results of hunting underwent a fundamental transformation. I no longer viewed fresh venison and rabbit as hypothetical meals belonging to an indeterminate future. I couldn't afford to. Rather, fresh game was meant for today's lunch and dinner, and hopefully tomorrow's as well. During my first semester away, a period of four months, my two roommates and I consumed four deer that were culled from a historically abundant local herd. We ate them right down to the hearts and livers.

My transformation from a sporting hunter to a food-based hunter forced me to rethink my entire relationship to the bounties of the natural world. I began to view wildlife as a valuable resource that needed to be handled with care and respect. I developed both a conservation and culinary ethic that incorporates an exhaustive and frugal use of all parts of any animal I harvest.

> ### MY THRIFT
>
> ### It Was Meat
>
> During the Great Depression, we ate squirrels and rabbits and even groundhogs, all of which had to be boiled well before they were browned and roasted. Preparing a groundhog was not easy. It took a special process to make sure the meat was safe to eat and that its "wild" flavor was removed. You had to scrub it first, then boil it in water, and then put some baking soda in the water, then rinse it off again. Then sometimes you'd scrub it and boil it again, but usually after one time you were ready to brown it and stick it in the oven. It was meat, and we ate it.
>
> —Valetta Barraclough, born 1918

I'm not nearly as broke nowadays, but as a hunter, my love of frugality extends beyond any fluctuations in my specific needs. I make a series of well-planned hunting trips every fall and winter. For me, these double as vacations. But instead of coming home from vacation with a hangover and an empty wallet, I come home with enough organically produced, free-range, sustainable game meat to feed myself and my wife throughout the year.

We eat a lot of fairly normal things, like burgers, steaks, and roasts made from caribou and deer. And, because I don't let anything go to waste, we also eat a lot of not-so-normal stuff. I make cured sausages, pemmican (dried ground meat and fat), and jerky from lower quality cuts of meat. I render lard from black bears and duck fat from wild mallards. I pickle big jars of pheasant gizzards. I use the jowls of wild boars for head cheese and squabs for pâté. I eat the marrow from elk bones. I preserve jars of hasenpfeffer stew made from local squirrels and confit made from Canada geese. It's a Prius-like existence, and I'm enjoying every mile.

Fish Fillets, Three Ways

The wonders of air transportation make it possible for stores all over the country to sell fresh fish of high quality. But prices will vary according to season, availability, and location, so when possible, eat local and let the fishmonger be your guide to value. If you're concerned about mercury in fish, the Food and Drug Administration's Center for Food Safety and Applied Nutrition maintains a website with plenty of information on this subject: www.cfsan.fda.gov.

Novice cooks tend to be intimidated by the prospect of preparing fish, but in fact it's supremely easy—and by buying fillets, you'll sidestep any complicated carving or scaling, along with fishy-kitchen cleanup. Fillets also cook in minutes (how many depends on the thickness and oiliness of the fish), so they make for a quick weeknight dinner. And as fun, festive dinner-party fare, inexpensive white fish fillets can be grilled or panfried for fish tacos.

The following instructions work for pretty much any fish fillet. Try something on sale, in season, or a trusty standby like salmon.

Five Things to Do with a Can of Tuna

Don't be spooked by visions of endless mystery casseroles. A cupboard-full of tuna needn't be a recipe for a permanent fifties time warp. There are plenty of delicious (and fresh-tasting) dishes to be made with this old-timey thrifty standby. And canned tuna is a low-cost source of lean protein.

1. Combine with white beans, fresh herbs, onion, olive oil, and lemon juice for a hearty salad.
2. Layer with onion, sliced hardboiled egg, raw veggies, and olive oil and vinegar on fresh, crusty bread for a *pain bagnat*. Wrap tightly and allow flavors to meld before serving.
3. Sautée with oil, garlic, red pepper flakes, capers or olives, and fresh parsley for a quick pasta sauce.
4. Serve with radishes, olives, tomatoes, and boiled potatoes and green beans for a *salade Niçoise*. (Forget the vinegar in your dressing. Niçoise salads taste best when drizzled with a mixture of lemon juice, olive oil, and Dijon mustard.)
5. Toss with pasta, Cheddar, and milk for a fortified mac 'n' cheese.

Poached. Place your fillets skin side down in a skillet large enough to hold them without crowding (you may need to use a couple of pans), sprinkle them with salt and pepper, and pour in enough liquid to come about halfway up the sides of the fillets. The best poaching liquid is equal parts white wine and water, but water with some lemon slices will work in a pinch. Throw in some herbs and spices (e.g., parsley, thyme, and shallots; or cilantro, garlic, and ginger for an Asian twist); cover the skillet tightly and simmer over low heat until the fillets are opaque in the center (somewhere in the 5-minute range). Remove from heat and let stand about 5 minutes before serving so the fish doesn't fall apart.

Panfried. You'll never go back to frozen fish sticks again! Make sure you get skinless fillets for this treatment. (Frozen is okay for frying.) Rinse your fillets and dry them slightly. Dredge both sides of the fillets in a shallow dish of seasoned flour and/or cornmeal (use salt, pepper, cayenne, garlic salt, you name it) and fry them in a skillet preheated with a teaspoon of hot oil. If you want an extra crunchy crust, dip the fish in beaten egg white before dredging.

Grilled. Probably the easiest way to prepare fish, and perhaps the tastiest too—if you are lucky enough to own a grill. Grilling fish really is as easy as sticking it on a hot grate and cooking it until it's done (opaque and flaky), turning it once. For most fillets, this should take about 3 minutes per side. A few things to keep in mind: Make sure the grill is clean and well-oiled or the fish will definitely stick. The fish should be oiled (or marinated) for the same reason. And avoid thin or delicate fillets—they can't take the heat.

Budget Fish

There are many reasons some fish might be cheaper than others. Fish can be marked down because it's been overly plentiful as a catch—fishermen have caught too many of one type. Or it may be a type that's bony and hard to fillet (like porgy) or on the lighter, less oily, or mild side (any type of whitefish). Don't let those factors discourage you. A fish that doesn't lend itself to neat fillets can be cooked whole or shredded, and a fish with a lighter flavor is a perfect foil to strong sauces and spices. Here are a few types of fish you can usually spot for less:

- Bass
- Catfish
- Char
- Cod
- Grouper
- Haddock
- Perch
- Porgy
- Snapper
- Sole
- Tilapia

For the Love of Broth

Making your own broth is the essence of thrift: It prevents waste, cuts out an unnecessary expense, and encourages home cooking. If you've ever cut up a vegetable or two, you know there are some pieces that wind up as waste: asparagus stems, leftover celery, and perhaps onion or carrot ends. But these discarded bits are still loaded with flavor and nutrients. A similar principle applies to chicken. A few more reasons to go homemade:

- **Fewer cans, fewer boxes.** Why buy something packaged when there is a low-effort alternative that does not require the creation, transportation, and removal of garbage?
- **No more lurking liquid.** You're cooking a dish and the recipe calls for one-half cup of broth. You buy the can, use what you need, and store the remaining contents in the refrigerator for a month. Maybe you come up with a way of using it, but more likely it winds up getting tossed.
- **You make the call.** You get to decide what goes in and what is kept out of your broth.

Vegetable Broth

Makes 10 cups of broth

1. Collect rinsed and relatively dry vegetable trimmings in a 1-gallon-size, ziplock plastic bag in the refrigerator or freezer. Most anything goes, but pass on broccoli, cabbage, cauliflower, leafy greens, and Brussels sprouts, which don't taste good when cooked for so long.

2. When you've filled approximately three-quarters of a gallon bag, you've got enough veggies to make your broth.

3. Place the trimmings in a 4½-quart Dutch oven or soup pot and cover them with water. The exact amount of water doesn't matter. Some vegetables will float, so just press them down to make sure there's enough water to cover. Bring the water to a boil over high heat, reduce the heat to low, and simmer, covered, about 1½ hours. Check periodically, and add more water if necessary.

4. When cooked, ladle the liquid through a strainer and discard the solids.

5. Freeze or refrigerate in 1- or 2-cup batches in airtight, hard plastic containers. Covered and refrigerated, the stock will keep for up to 3 days; covered and frozen, for up to 2 months. Thaw overnight in the refrigerator, or defrost in the microwave.

Stock Versus Broth

Stock and broth are interchangeable in soups and stews, but not necessarily in sauces. Stock is typically made with meat and bones of chicken or beef. The bones yield gelatin, which adds richness, but, more important, will serve as a thickener when used in reduction sauces. Broth does not include bones, but can include meat.

STOCK RECIPES BY BEVERLY MILLS & ALICIA ROSS; FLAVORING IDEAS BY VICTORIA WISE

Chicken Stock

Makes 12 cups of stock

1. Place the chicken parts in a 4½-quart soup pot. Pour enough cold tap water over the chicken to cover it (about 10½ cups).

2. Next, add 1 peeled onion cut in half; 2 medium-size carrots cut in half (no need to peel them); and a rib or two of celery cut in half (and any saved vegetable trimmings). Cover the pot. Bring the water to a boil over high heat, then lower the heat and simmer, covered, for 1½ to 2 hours. Check the stock from time to time, adding more water, if necessary, and spooning off any foam that collects on top.

3. When the stock has cooked, transfer the chicken pieces to a bowl to cool. (The meat can be removed from the bones for later use.) Discard the vegetables. Cool the stock a little and ladle it through a strainer.

4. After the stock has been refrigerated for several hours, skim off any fat from the surface.

5. Freeze or refrigerate in 1- or 2-cup batches in airtight, hard plastic containers. Covered and refrigerated, the stock will keep for up to 2 days; covered and frozen, for up to 2 months. Thaw frozen stock overnight in the refrigerator, or defrost it in the microwave.

Around the World

When it comes time to use your vegetable broth, you can add extra ingredients to match the cuisine you are preparing:

Latin American: chili pepper, fresh or dried
Japanese: daikon, kelp, shiitake mushrooms, ginger, bean sprouts
Pacific Rim: lemongrass, coconut milk, galanga (a relative of ginger)
Russian: parsnip, parsley root, cabbage
Indian: cumin seeds, coriander seeds, cardamom pods

How Do You Make Yours?

There are multiple ways to go about making a chicken stock, each of which takes about 5 minutes of prep time:

1. If you've just roasted and served a whole chicken (or parts on the bone), the carcass can be tossed in a large pot with water and boiled with vegetables.

2. If you're poaching a bird (for a chicken salad, say), add vegetables to the water. Remove the chicken when it has cooked and is ready to use for your intended purpose. Remove the meat and toss the bones back into the stock. The remaining liquid may need more time to reduce and gain flavor, but you won't have wasted a thing.

3. If the grocer discounts chicken parts, snap them up for stock. You can make the 12-cup stock recipe with one 2½-pound chicken, 12 to 15 wings, 8 thighs, or 8 drumsticks. It goes without saying: Don't throw away the cooked meat when you're done—much of its flavor will have gone into the broth, but it can still be added to well-seasoned casseroles, soups, salads, or stews. If you buy whole chickens with necks, freeze the necks and collect them to add to the stockpot.

The Thriftiest Fruits & Vegetables

- Onion
- Garlic
- Celery
- Root Vegetables (Carrots, Potatoes, Parsnips)

- Hardy Greens (Kale, Bok Choy)
- Canned Tomatoes
- Lemons
- Apples

Root vegetables are the workhorses of the kitchen: They can be roasted, boiled, mashed, pureed, sautéed, or stored in a cool, dry place for weeks. Chop equal portions of onion, carrot, and celery and you've got what French

---

Peak Produce

These days, you can get pretty much any fruit or vegetable you want, any time you want it, at the supermarket—but it most likely had to travel a very long way to get there. Convenient, but that out-of-season produce costs more. The best way to make sure you are getting the best prices, and the freshest fare, is to check out your local farmers' markets. This chart will give you a general sense of what to buy when, though of course harvest schedules depend on geography (in February, California doesn't much resemble Massachusetts).

SPRING	SUMMER	FALL	WINTER
Asparagus	Apricots	Apples	Beets
Blackberries	Blueberries	Broccoli	Cabbage
Leeks	Cherries	Brussels sprouts	Carrots
Lettuces	Corn	Cauliflower	Citrus
New potatoes	Eggplant	Collards	Daikon
Radishes	Green beans	Grapes	Onions
Rhubarb	Herbs	Kale	Rutabagas
Scallions	Melons	Pears	Turnips
Shell peas	Peaches	Persimmons	Winter squash
Spinach	Peppers	Pumpkins	
Strawberries	Plums	Winter squash	
	Summer squash	Yams	
	Tomatoes		
	Zucchini		

chefs call mirepoix, *a flavorful and aromatic foundation for soups, stews, and sauces. Add some garlic and you've got the beginnings of a stir-fry. Apples move easily from snack to baking ingredient to applesauce. Lemons brighten the flavor of almost any dish. And with a can of tomatoes on hand, your pasta will never be lonely again.*

Slice an Onion More Efficiently

To develop your kitchen skills, practice slicing and mincing onions and shallots the way the pros do. Why does it matter? Because the texture of the onion is key to the texture of your dish, and the better your knife skills, the shorter your prep time. Plus, looks do count—why do you think chefs spend all that time on their presentation?

For best effect, the key is to slice your onion or shallot in three directions, leaving the whole attached to the base so your final slices result in a fine mince.

1. Notice that the layers of the vegetable attach at one end. Keep this end, called the root end, intact.

2. Holding the knife with the blade horizontal to the cutting board, slice the vegetable into the thinnest possible layers, from the end opposite the root toward the root—getting as close to the root as possible without cutting through it.

3. Next, with the knife in the normal upright position, slice the onion from the tip to just before the root, so the onion is now sliced in two directions.

4. Switch directions, slicing the vegetable crosswise, and it will fall apart into tiny bits. Chop off and discard the root end.

The Juiciest Lemons

The juiciest lemons and limes have the thinnest skins. To get the most juice from your citrus, microwave the fruits on high for thirty seconds, then let stand for a few minutes before cutting or squeezing.

ONION CHOPPING EXPERTISE FROM JAMES PETERSON; LEMON TIPS BY MELISSA KIRSCH

Make Your Own Garlic Paste

You don't need a garlic press, a mortar and pestle, or any other specialized implement to mash garlic to a paste. Here are three tricks that achieve an equally fine result:

1. The French grandmother's fork method: Press the tines of a fork against a cutting board. Rub a peeled garlic clove back and forth over the tines to make a quick paste.

2. Thinly slice a peeled garlic clove and sprinkle with salt. With a sideways scraping motion, mash the salted slices with the side of a large knife. The salt provides the friction to create a fine puree.

3. Holding the handle of a large chef's knife, turn the knife upside down, with the sharp side up. Use the flat, dull back of the blade to crush the peeled garlic clove to a rough puree.

RECIPE | Pantry Potage (aka "Greek Lemon Soup")

Check out the ingredients—this is thrifty simplicity at its most elegant. The orzo (a tiny, rice-size pasta) and broth in this traditional Greek soup can be prepared in advance and the eggs added at the last minute.

Serves 8

> 5 cups chicken broth (see page 141)
> 3 cups plus 2 tablespoons water
> ½ cup orzo
> 4 large egg whites
> 2 large egg yolks
> Juice of 2 lemons

1. Bring the broth and 3 cups water to a boil in a large saucepan. Add the orzo and cook over medium heat for 7 to 10 minutes, until the pasta is tender but not soggy.

2. Beat the egg whites with the remaining 2 tablespoons water in a large bowl until soft peaks form.

3. Beat the egg yolks with the lemon juice in a small bowl. Fold into the egg whites.

4. Add some of the hot broth to the egg mixture and stir gently to warm the mixture. Add all of the egg mixture to the hot broth and simmer, stirring constantly, until the soup thickens slightly. Serve at once.

RECIPE | ## Can't-Believe-It-Came-Out-of-a-Can Tomato Soup

Tomato soup, particularly served alongside a grilled cheese sandwich, is comfort food at its finest—and this one tastes positively luxurious, especially given the fact that the tomatoes are canned. If you like yours creamy, stir in a dollop of sour cream right before serving. If you aren't a fan of dill, just leave it out.

Serves 8

2 tablespoons unsalted butter

2 tablespoons extra-virgin olive oil

2 cups diced onions

1 tablespoon finely minced garlic

½ teaspoon ground allspice

6 tablespoons chopped fresh dill leaves

Salt and freshly ground black pepper to taste

6 cups chicken or vegetable broth (page 140)

2 cans (28 ounces each) peeled plum tomatoes, drained and chopped

1 teaspoon sugar

1. Melt the butter in the olive oil in a heavy pot over low heat. Add the onions and cook, stirring occasionally, until softened, about 10 minutes. Add the garlic and cook, stirring, for 3 minutes. Sprinkle the allspice over the onion mixture and cook for 1 minute longer.

2. Add 4 tablespoons of the dill, season with salt and pepper, and continue to cook over low heat, stirring, for 5 minutes. Add the broth, tomatoes, and sugar. Bring to a boil, then reduce the heat to medium-low, and simmer, partially covered, for 20 minutes. Remove from the heat and let cool slightly.

3. Puree the soup, in batches, in a blender or food processor. Return the soup to the pot and stir in the remaining 2 tablespoons dill. Taste, and correct the seasonings if necessary.

4. Serve hot, or let cool; then refrigerate for 4 to 6 hours to serve cold.

Ode to Canned Tomatoes

Fresh tomatoes aren't in season very long—hence the ubiquity (and necessity) of canned tomatoes. For a quick sauce, break up whole tomatoes with a wooden spoon, pour them over sautéed garlic and onions, and simmer for 15 minutes. Canned tomatoes can also be added to more complicated sauces, vegetable soups, chili, and even pot roasts. They can even be turned into a quick salsa: just mix with chopped onion, jalapeño, parsley, canned corn, or anything else you like.

TOMATO SOUP RECIPE BY SHEILA LUKINS

RECIPE | ## Simply Elegant Roasted Parsnips

This old-fashioned, nearly forgotten root vegetable is lovely when roasted and slightly caramelized. Parsnips look like pale carrots, but their flavor is a heady cross between butternut squash and chestnuts. *Note:* This roasting technique can be applied to any hardy vegetable—beets, carrots, potatoes, peeled winter squash—for a simple and delicious cold-weather side dish.

> Parsnips
> Olive oil
> Salt and pepper

1. Preheat the oven to 375°F.

2. Peel the parsnips and quarter them lengthwise. With a paring knife, remove the central core (even small parsnips have a hard core). If the parsnips are small, just trim the ends; if larger, cut them into 3-inch lengths.

3. Season well with salt and pepper and toss with the olive oil, then place the parsnips in an earthenware dish or roasting pan. Bake for 30 to 40 minutes, until they are fork-tender and lightly browned. They can be cooked in advance and reheated.

RECIPE | ## Stick 'Em In the Oven Apples

You can make roasted apples with all manner of add-ons, including nuts, cream, dried fruits, or spices. But this simplest version yields concentrated, caramelized juices and the purest apple flavor.

> Baking apples
> Apple juice or cognac
> Sugar

1. Preheat the oven to 375°F.

2. Employing a twisting motion with a paring knife, remove the stem from each apple in a conical shape. Reserve the stems. Carefully scoop out the apple cores with a melon baller or small sturdy spoon, leaving ½ inch or so of flesh at the bottom of each apple.

3. Put the apples in a glass or earthenware baking dish. Fill each apple with sugar, then add a splash of juice or cognac to each one. Replace the stems and sprinkle sugar generously over the tops.

4. Bake the apples on the top shelf of the oven for 45 minutes to an hour, until the skins burst. Serve at room temperature, making sure to spoon the juices over each portion. Serve alone or drizzled with cream.

BAKED APPLE AND ROASTED PARSNIPS RECIPES BY DAVID TANIS

The Thrifty Dairy

- Eggs
- Parmesan Cheese
- Butter
- Milk (fresh or powdered)

With eggs in the kitchen, you can make countless meals, from elegant omelets to hearty fried egg sandwiches to traditional egg salad, and a variety of desserts, such as custards and meringues. Milk can be used in baked goods and added to coffee, but it is also a central ingredient to homemade cheese and yogurt. Parmesan cheese stores well for months and adds a strong flavor punch to a wide variety of foods. And butter, well—it makes everything better.

Buying and Storing Eggs

To set an eternal question to rest: There is no difference in taste or nutritional value between white and brown eggs. The color of an egg's shell is determined by the breed of hen that laid it.

Freshness, however, does affect taste, so always buy the freshest eggs available. Eggs are best used within one week of purchase, but will last up to three weeks in the refrigerator. (Keep them in their carton to seal them off from refrigerator odors.)

A simple test will tell whether an egg is still fresh: Place it in a small bowl of water. A fresh egg will stay on its side; an older egg will stand straight up and float. Eggshells are porous to air, but if so much air has permeated the shell that it has made the egg buoyant, it's a clear sign that the egg has been sitting around too long and should be thrown away. Old eggs will not necessarily spoil or cause food-borne illness, but they may dry up, lose flavor, or develop unpleasant odors.

Need Milk?

Devoted cereal eaters and parents of milk-age children aside, many of us exhibit only the occasional need for milk—a splash in our coffee, a smidge in our tea. If that's the case for you, consider whether you might be able to switch to a cheaper option: dehydrated milk. Not the sweet condensed liquid you'll find in a can, but the powdered stuff that most often comes in a box. It doesn't spoil, and its uses are varied—from kitchen to garden to bath. Of course, cereal eaters can use it as intended—reconstituted with water—but some will find the taste disagreeable. In coffee and in various recipes, however, you almost can't tell the difference.

RECIPE | # French-Chef-Quality Omelets

Perfect for any time of day, the omelet can be jazzed up with meat, vegetables, and cheese, or simply garnished with a little salt. Don't be put off by all those difficult techniques. Anyone can make a decent omelet. But here's a helpful tip: The omelet will not set correctly if there are too many eggs in the pan; too few and it will cook too quickly. So it is always better to make more omelets than to overload the pan with too many eggs.

Serves 1

> 3 large eggs
> 1 teaspoon butter

1. Prepare a filling (if desired) and set aside.

2. Gently beat the eggs with a whisk in a medium bowl.

3. Put a small frying pan on high heat and let it get hot, about 30 seconds. Spread the butter around the pan. When the butter stops sizzling, pour the eggs in all at once. Let the bottom set, about 15 seconds.

4. Slip a spatula about a third of the way under one side of the omelet. Lift up that edge and tilt the pan toward it so the loose, uncooked egg on top runs toward the area of open pan. Continue until there is no more loose egg on top.

5. Quickly spread the filling (if using) down the middle of the eggs. Fold the thicker side of the omelet over the filling or fold in half if no filling is used.

6. Take the pan to the serving plate and use the spatula to nudge the omelet onto the plate.

7. Wipe the pan clean with a cloth or paper towel and start again, if need be.

Anything Goes— In an Omelet

Fillings for omelets can be anything you like—and anything sitting around in the refrigerator that needs to be used up. Here are just a few classic combinations, although each ingredient could be used alone.

- Parmesan cheese and parsley
- Spinach and feta cheese
- Tomatoes and basil
- Cheddar cheese and broccoli
- Sautéed onions and mushrooms
- Ham and Swiss cheese
- Sausage and sweet red peppers

OMELET RECIPE BY BOB SLOAN

What Kind of Butter, What Kind of Cheese?

Does every kitchen really need butter? Should it be salted or not? And when is it better to use oil? It all depends on how you cook—and what your doctor says about cholesterol.

You can certainly get by without butter, but it's called for in many recipes—for both baked goods and savory dishes. To answer the question of salted or not: Bakers and serious cooks tend to prefer unsalted because it allows for greater control of the amount of salt in a recipe.

As for cheese, the answer—to us at least—is clear: If you must have only one cheese, let it be parmesan. Toss it with pasta, use its rind to flavor soups, serve it with crackers, drizzle it with balsamic alongside a sliced pear . . . It's not just delicious, it's versatile.

If you use it regularly, you'll want to ensure that it stays fresh. Always slice off only as much as you're going to use at one time. Then moisten a piece of cheesecloth or other cloth—even a paper towel will do—and wrap it around what's left. Then, wrap the cheesecloth-wrapped cheese in aluminum foil (foil is not completely airtight and won't suffocate the cheese). Store it in the vegetable compartment of the refrigerator. Don't worry about surface mold. Merely scrape it away, and don't buy quite so much cheese next time.

What to Do with Leftover Cheese

Never discard little leftover bits and pieces of cheese lurking in your refrigerator. The tag ends of Brie, Cheddar, farmer cheese, chèvre, Roquefort, mozzarella, and scores of other cheeses can be quickly transformed into a tasty mixture that the thrifty French call *fromage fort* ("strong cheese"). Seasoned with fresh garlic and a few splashes of wine, it makes an assertively flavored topping for toast or thick slices of crusty country bread and tastes best when briefly melted under the broiler.

To make *fromage fort,* gather together 1 pound of leftover cheese (3 kinds is enough, 6 or 7 will be even better). Trim off any hard rinds, mold, or very dried out parts from the surface. Toss 3 or 4 peeled cloves of garlic into a food processor and process for several seconds until coarsely chopped. Add the cheese to the garlic along with ½ cup dry white wine and at least 1 teaspoon of freshly ground black pepper. Process until the mixture becomes soft and creamy, about 30 seconds. Transfer the mixture to a crock or bowl. Cover tightly with plastic wrap and refrigerate for up to one week.

RECIPE | # Fancy-Pants Parmesan Cheese Puffs

Cheese puffs (the French call them *gougères*) are popular as hors d'oeuvres in fine restaurants and at elegant parties. And soon, at your house. They are easy to make and require no fancy ingredients (supermarket-quality parm will do), though they are sure to impress your friends and family. You can make them with other cheeses, too—Gruyère is more traditional. Try them alongside classic tomato soup (see page 145) for a comforting feast. Eat the puffs right away, though, because they don't make good leftovers . . . not that there will be any of those!

Makes about 40 pieces

> 7 tablespoons unsalted butter
> 1¼ cups all-purpose flour
> 3 whole large eggs
> 3 large egg whites
> 1 cup (about 4 ounces) finely grated parmesan cheese
> Freshly ground black pepper
> Pinch of salt (preferably kosher)

1. Cut the butter into slices and put in a saucepan with 1 cup water. Bring to a simmer.

2. When all the butter has melted, add the flour and stir over medium heat until the dough pulls away from the side of the pan. Dump the dough into a mixing bowl.

3. Work in the whole eggs, one by one, with a wooden spoon, and then add the egg whites. Continue mixing until when you make a deep groove in the dough it closes in on itself.

4. Work in the grated cheese. Season with freshly ground black pepper and a pinch of salt.

5. Preheat the oven to 450°F.

6. Onto a baking sheet, pipe the cheese puffs into small mounds of about 1½ tablespoons each, leaving a couple of inches between them. *(If you don't have a pastry bag, just cut the corner off of a ziplock plastic bag, fill it with dough, and squeeze out the cheese balls.)* Bake until puffed and golden brown, about 10 minutes. Turn the oven down to 300°F and bake for 15 minutes more.

GOUGÈRES RECIPE BY JAMES PETERSON

In the Dairy Kitchen

If you love cultured dairy products with a handmade "artisanal" quality, you can have them for no more than the price of the cheapest yogurt, butter, and cheese. And you'll have the satisfaction of knowing the artisan: you! Cheese and butter recipes are often surprisingly easy and quick. The only indispensable, must-have tool for dairy-making is an instant-read thermometer.

RECIPE | ## Mozzarella in Minutes

Instead of springing for the handmade stuff, try hand-making it yourself. You can make all kinds of cheese at home, but the stretching and kneading of mozzarella is probably the most fun. To track down rennet and citric acid, look in grocery and health food stores or online.

Makes about 1 pound

> ½ rennet tablet
> ¼ cup cool bottled water (chlorine-free)
> 1 gallon whole milk (not "ultra pasteurized")
> 2 teaspoons citric acid
> Salt (optional)

1. In a small bowl, crush the rennet into the water and stir to dissolve. Pour the milk into a non-reactive (not aluminum or cast iron) pot and place the pot over medium heat. Sprinkle the citric acid over the milk and stir to combine. Heat the milk to 88°F. (The milk will curdle.)

2. Add the rennet solution to the milk and heat, stirring every few minutes, until it reaches 105°F. Turn off the heat. Large curds will appear and begin to separate from the whey (the clear, greenish liquid they are floating in).

3. With a slotted spoon or mesh strainer, scoop the curds into a large glass bowl. If they're too liquid to handle, let them set in the whey for a few more minutes. Press the curds gently with your hand and pour as much whey as possible back into the pot. Microwave the curds on high for 1 minute, then drain off the excess whey. With a spoon, shape the curds into a ball and let cool. Microwave two more times for 35 seconds each, and continue to siphon off the whey and work the cheese into a ball. In the meantime, salt the whey and place it over medium heat until it reaches 175°F. (If you don't have a microwave, use a slotted spoon or strainer to dunk the curds into the heated whey for a few seconds in between kneadings.)

4. When the cheese is cool enough to handle, knead it like bread dough until it is smooth and pliable. If you like, you can sprinkle 1 to 2 teaspoons salt into the cheese while kneading it. If the cheese is difficult to stretch and breaks easily, dip it into the hot whey for a few seconds and keep kneading and stretching.

5. When the cheese is smooth, shiny, and taffy-like (this takes just a few minutes), it is ready to eat. Shape it into balls and eat it immediately or cool it in ice water and refrigerate, covered.

RECIPE | ## Amazing Homemade Yogurt

Freshly made yogurt really does taste better than store-bought. You don't need a yogurt maker (though such a machine is expedient and often comes with containers). The one indispensable tool, again, is the instant-read thermometer.

Makes 1 quart

4 cups fresh whole milk
⅓ cup powdered milk (optional, as a thickener, if using low-fat or skim milk)
2 tablespoons plain yogurt (with "live cultures")

1. Slowly heat the milk in a saucepan over low-medium heat.

2. Add the powdered milk, if using. (It makes a thicker yogurt.)

3. When the milk is between 180°F and 190°F on an instant-read thermometer, remove the saucepan from heat. Cool it to 115°F–120°F.

4. Mix a small amount of milk in with the starter yogurt and then stir the mixture back in with the rest of the milk.

5. You are now ready to put your yogurt in an electric yogurt machine, if you have one, or pour it into a slightly warm quart jar and put it in the oven with the heat off but the lightbulb on. You can also wrap the jar in several towels and keep it in a warm place. The yogurt will take about 4 hours to set.

6. Once it sets, put it in the fridge to firm up. The yogurt is ready to eat once it's thoroughly chilled.

THRIFTONOMICS

The Yogurt Equation

The health benefits of yogurt-eating are attractive, but the cost benefits of making your own are staggering.

At the store, a half-gallon of milk costs $1.70 to $2.00. That half-gallon makes 32 ounces of yogurt. A 6-ounce container of yogurt costs $0.69 to $1.99. Which means that by making your own, you'll get five times the yogurt. Five yogurts for the price of one!

RECIPE | ## Classic Vanilla Ice Cream

Go ahead and treat yourself. This simple, fast recipe can be made as rich or as low-calorie as you desire. Variations are infinite. If making "still-frozen" ice cream without an ice-cream maker (see box), these quantities will fill 2 shallow pans.

Makes 1½ quarts

> 1 quart heavy or light cream or half-and-half
> or 2 cups each heavy and light cream (see Note)
> 1 cup sugar or ⅓ cup honey
> 1 tablespoon pure vanilla extract

1. Scald the cream by slowly heating it in a saucepan until it reaches just below the boiling point. Small bubbles will begin to appear around the edges. Stir for several minutes, then remove from heat.

2. Stir in the sweetener. Pour into a bowl, cover, and refrigerate.

3. When the cream is completely chilled, stir in the vanilla. Pour into your ice-cream maker and follow its freezing directions.

A note: If dairy allergy is a concern, substitute soy milk for the cream, and skip the scalding step. Combine soy milk, sweetener, flavoring, and ¼ cup vegetable oil and chill and process as directed.

No Ice-Cream Maker?

If you don't own an ice-cream maker, you can still make delectable frozen desserts, and with minimal effort. The ice cream will be "still-frozen" (as opposed to "churned"), and it's a snap. Here's how it works:

1. Prepare the ice-cream mixture per the recipe you're using, and pour into shallow trays such as cake pans.

2. Place the pans in the freezer at the coldest setting for 30 minutes to 1 hour, or until the mixture is mushy but not solid.

3. Scrape the mixture into a chilled bowl and beat it with an electric mixer on high speed until it becomes smooth.

4. Return the mixture to the tray and the freezer. When almost frozen solid, repeat the beating process. Add flavorings like chopped nuts, fruits, or liqueur, if desired.

5. Return mixture to the tray and cover with plastic wrap to prevent ice crystals from forming on top of the cream. Place in the freezer until solid.

ICE CREAM INSTRUCTIONS FROM *COUNTRY WISDOM & KNOW-HOW*

Avoid Waste by Using Up Every Last Bit

A heel of bread here, a nubbin of celery there . . . The culprits—items that go bad before they're used up—tend to be repeat offenders. Learn how to handle them and you'll achieve total leftover dominance (an essential hallmark of the thrifty home cook).

Upcycling Your Leftovers and Odds and Ends

- **Soups, stews, and other "mixed-up" dishes.** Leftovers may dry out as solids soak up liquid over time. Resuscitate them and change the flavor by adding a different liquid— clam juice instead of tomato juice, for example. You can bolster the dish by adding a fresh ingredient and a new herb. Or you can puree it so its texture goes from chunky to smooth.

- **Casseroles such as rice pilafs and baked bean dishes.** Add stock, toss in an additional ingredient, and serve as hot soup.

- **Stir-fries.** Refry with a new ingredient; add salad dressing and eat chilled or at room temperature; or mince, thin with a sauce, and toss over a bowl of pasta, lentils, or grains.

- **Poultry, veal, pork, and fish.** With leaner flesh, it's best not to reheat— you don't want it to dry out. Small amounts of leftovers can be chopped and gently warmed in soups, stews, or pasta dishes where texture won't matter as much. Use them cold in salads or as sandwich stuffers. (Be sure to use leftover seafood within a day.)

- **Red meats like beef and lamb.** Especially when cooked plain, these are a bit easier to reheat because they are fattier and thus juicier. Chop into pieces and reheat in soups, stews, casseroles, and stir-fried dishes; use in salads and sandwiches—both hot and cold; or mince into burrito or taco fillings.

- **And don't forget celery!** The world is full of recipes calling for three ribs of celery. Embrace the rest of the stalk: Chop and mix into green salads; slice into matchstick sizes for a snack; serve with hard cheeses; use in vegetable broth (page 140); make cream of celery soup; chop and toss with carrots, garbanzo beans, scallions, and olive oil for a quick salad; as a side dish, braise in the oven with parmesan cheese, salt, pepper, and two tablespoons of vegetable stock or water.

Leftovers Can Heal a Neighborhood

"**G**rowing up during the Great Depression taught me not to waste a thing. When my husband and I started our family, more than 60 years ago, I would never have dreamt of throwing out food. All week I saved leftovers and on Saturday morning everything went into a pot of soup. That was the meal every single Saturday lunch. It became known as Saturday Soup.

My kids remember that soup having any number of ingredients, including all kinds of meat, like beef tongue, heart, and liver. I'd always throw in some barley to stretch it. Another staple on the Saturday Soup table was cheese and crackers.

My husband and I had eight kids, and over the years, we did well for ourselves. I became a doctor, and he had a successful insurance business. But we never forgot the importance of being thrifty. We washed plastic baggies and cutlery for repeated use. We continued garage sale hunting. Saturday Soup remained an important part of our family life.

It really wasn't what we ate, but that we ate it with each other—and everyone and anyone was welcome to join us. The neighborhood kids all wanted to join the meal. The kitchen table seated twelve, and when one person was finished with their meal, another took his or her place.

Even when my children grew up and started their own families, they automatically came each week for Saturday Soup. There was no organizing or invitation. It was assumed everyone came and spent time together as a family.

My husband, Andy, volunteered at the local state mental hospital and would often invite patients. About thirty years ago there was a psychiatric patient named Walter who was blind and deaf, and he just loved babies. We would put a baby in his arms and everyone loved watching his face light up. To this day some of my children still get together with their grown children and grandchildren weekly."

—*GWEN TRUDEAU, 86*

Pita Chips

You will find endless possibilities for these simple chips, which are a great substitute for greasy potato chips and a thrifty use of stale pita.

Pitas, cut in half crosswise and then split open
Butter or olive oil, at room temperature
Garlic salt
Dried parsley

1. Preheat the oven to 350°F.

2. Spread each pita lightly with butter or olive oil and transfer to a baking sheet. Sprinkle them lightly with garlic salt and parsley.

3. Bake the pitas for about 15 minutes or until browned, watching carefully so they don't burn.

4. Cool the pitas completely on the baking sheet and then break apart into tortilla chip–size pieces; store in an airtight container for up to 5 days.

The Thrifty Pantry

- Sugar
- Salt
- Peppercorns
- Olive Oil
- Vegetable Oil

- Vinegar
- The herbs, spices, and condiments you use most
- Tea and/or Coffee

We've all got our favorite herbs and spices, but some ingredients are basics. For many, sugar starts off the day in tea or coffee (and, yes, you should be making your coffee at home—see page 164 if you need convincing). It's also a key ingredient in treats of all kinds. Salt, pepper, oil, and vinegar are also non-negotiables. As for condiments, many can be made at home—and they'll most likely taste better that way. A few recipes will get you started, but if you're curious, head to the store and take a look at the labels on items like specialty dips, taco seasoning, and cocktail sauce. You might be surprised to learn that you have all the necessary ingredients at home.

The Gardenless Herb Garden

You don't need a country home with acreage to grow your own herbs. All you need is a window that gets at least five to six hours of sun a day. In fact, if the only outdoor space you have is shaded, herbs are actually better off indoors, in a sunny window. Herbs grown indoors need plenty of water and an occasional feeding. A little extra humidity not only helps their growth but keeps the foliage succulent and tasty. If the air in your dwelling is dry, place the pots in a tray filled with stones and keep the tray filled with water just up to the bottom of the pots; this keeps moisture in the air. Except for rosemary, which appreciates it, don't mist herbs—it encourages fungus. But all herbs do like to be rinsed off in the sink from time to time.

Though almost any herb is worth trying indoors, you'll find that some do better than others. Rosemary is a clear winner; it even blooms indoors in wintertime! Sage may be sparse indoors but even a few of those fresh leaves for soups or pasta will make it earn its keep. With the less successful herbs like basil, keep the plants for as long as they're healthy. Once they succumb to whiteflies or the indoor blues, just bid them farewell. For more on container gardening and gardening in general, see chapter 2.

HERB GROWING ADVICE BY BARBARA DAMROSCH

The Herb & Spice Dilemma

Your spice cabinet can easily become the most expensive investment in your kitchen. And spices don't have to be exotic or the selection extensive for the prices to start adding up. To add insult to injury, spices don't stay fresh forever. (Many books and magazines will tell you that spices should be replaced every six months, but most spices continue to add flavor and body for a year or more, provided they're stored on a relatively cool, dark shelf.)

Shelf life aside, spices and dried herbs present some special challenges for the budget-minded cook. Let's say you get the urge to try your hand at Indian cooking. Based on an unscientific survey of several cookbooks, most recipes require between six and ten herbs and spices. If you want to experiment with just one dish and you have to buy turmeric, cumin, mustard seeds, garam masala, saffron threads, and whole cardamom pods, your investment in spices alone can top $25. This same situation comes into play with many other ethnic cuisines. What's the thrifty cook to do?

- Whenever possible, buy premixed spice blends. It may seem more "chef-like" to buy spices separately, but you're cooking for your own kitchen, which doesn't have a financier behind it. One jar of Italian seasoning combines a balanced blend of marjoram, thyme, rosemary, savory, sage, oregano, and basil. It's a bargain if you consider what each separate jar would cost.

- Find a store that sells spices in bulk. If you tend to use a ton of thyme, buy that up and you'll get a better deal; conversely there's no need to pay $4.50 for a jar of turmeric when you need only a pinch! Many upscale specialty markets and some ethnic markets sell spices in bulk, as do some larger supermarkets.

- If you know you can't use a whole jar of a spice, shop with a friend and split the bottle (and the cost).

- The more of a spice you buy, the less it costs per ounce. For example, warehouse clubs sell 20-ounce containers of chili powder for only a little more than it costs to buy a 2½-ounce bottle in the supermarket.

- If a recipe calls for a number of spices and you have all of them except one, just omit it. If a dish is full of flavor, you'll probably never notice that it's missing ¼ teaspoon of cardamom.

- Keep all red spices—cayenne pepper, chili powder, paprika, and red pepper flakes—in the refrigerator or freezer to prolong freshness.

SPICE TIPS BY BEVERLY MILLS & ALICIA ROSS

DRYING TIPS BY ROSE MARIE NICHOLS MCGEE & MAGGIE STUCKEY; MICROWAVE-DRYING BY VICTORIA WISE

PROJECT | ## Dry Your Herbs, Avoid Waste

You have more fresh herbs than you know what to do with. What to do with the surplus? What gardeners and cooks have done for thousands of years: Dry them, and store them for use later on. The process of drying is simple—you can do just fine by tossing a few cuttings on a paper towel and leaving them there to dry until you remember to check on them—but it helps to keep a few things in mind.

1. Unless the leaves are spattered with mud, herb sprigs need only the lightest rinsing (as long as you haven't used any toxic sprays on your plants, in which case you shouldn't be eating your herbs).

2. Find a spot indoors that is warm and dry and has good air circulation. A spot near the ceiling is always a bit warmer than the rest of the room. A great spot is on top of the refrigerator.

3. To dry just a small amount, lay the sprigs out flat on a paper towel or paper plate. For larger quantities, bundle the sprigs with twine and hang them upside down.

4. Leave everything undisturbed until the herb is dry, which will take anywhere from a few days for small leaves to a couple of weeks for larger ones. It's counterproductive to leave them longer than that; all they'll do is collect dust.

In the Microwave

If you're jumpy or just don't want herbs hanging around your house, there's an even quicker way to dry your excess bounty: Zap them in the microwave. First, rinse the sprigs or branches. Spin dry and lay them on a large microwave plate. Microwave on medium for about 3 minutes, until they look crinkled. Let stand for 5 minutes. Strip off the leaves, transfer to an airtight jar, and store in the cupboard. Freshly dried herbs will keep longer than store-bought dried herbs, up to one year if tightly closed.

5. Strip the leaves from the stems. If the leaves are large (as with some basils), you can either leave them whole, in which case they retain their flavor better, or crumble them, in which case they take up less storage space.

6. Store away from heat and direct sunlight in a glass container with a tight-fitting lid; avoid plastic, which often imparts a hint of "eau de plastic" to whatever it contains.

7. Label the jars. All little dried green things look alike, and even though you think you'll remember which herb is which, chances are you won't.

PROJECT | ## The Green Freeze Method

Herbs that have been frozen taste fresher than dried herbs, but only for the first four months or so after freezing. After that, flavor declines rapidly, so freezing should be thought of as an adjunct to drying, not a substitute for it. Note that chives don't freeze or dry well. Use them fresh or substitute scallions.

Method 1

To freeze lemon verbena, lovage, marjoram, mint, oregano, parsley, sage, or tarragon, use whole leaves (discard stems). To freeze dill, fennel, or thyme, use tender sprigs. Basil discolors when it is frozen, so if you want it to stay bright green, dip branches in boiling water, just for a second or two, then remove, discard stems, and gently dry the leaves.

Whatever you're freezing should be completely dry. Spread the herb out in a single layer on a cookie sheet and place the sheet in the freezer. As soon as the herbs are frozen, usually in no more than an hour or two, pack them in heavy plastic freezer bags and put the bags in freezer-safe containers for storage.

Method 2

To freeze cilantro or chervil, which tend to fade rapidly when frozen whole, combine 1 tightly packed cup of chopped herb with ⅓ to ½ cup of water in a blender or processor, and process until you have a coarse puree. Freeze in ice-cube trays.

As soon as they're frozen, pack the cubes in plastic freezer bags in glass jars. Use the cubes as you would the herb (1 standard-size cube equals about 2 tablespoons freshly chopped), remembering you will be adding liquid as well.

HERB-FREEZING TIPS FROM *1,000 GARDENING Q&AS*

Where the Flavor Really Is

Want more flavor in everything you cook? Start by using whole peppercorns. Buying and grinding whole peppercorns will intensify the flavor of the food you cook far more than sprinkling pulverized powder over it. (Pepper loses much of its flavor pretty soon after it's ground.) If you don't have a pepper mill, you can crush the peppercorns with a mortar and pestle or a coffee grinder. (Just be sure to clean it thoroughly.)

An Oily Tutorial

Most home kitchens need only extra-virgin olive oil and a neutral cooking oil. But with the myriad choices available, a little knowledge is helpful. When selecting an olive oil, try to find one that balances quality and quantity at a price that fits your budget. The oil should have plenty of flavor, yet not cost so much that it becomes too precious to use in large quantities. The ideal olive oil enhances salads and sautés and is priced low enough to use by the cupful, say for a marinade. Don't spend $35 for one liter of artisanal oil if you plan to pour it all over your roast. The flavor will be lost once the meat cooks.

When it comes to selecting a cooking oil, there are specifics to consider. Canola oil has a neutral flavor and some health benefits (a low quantity of saturated fat and high quantity of monounsaturated fat), but it cannot be used for deep-frying. For that you need corn oil, which functions well at high temperatures. Vegetable oil, though, can be used for a variety of purposes—light frying and baking, as well as making your Southern fried chicken nice and crispy. A few other oil-related tips to keep in mind:

- The less processed and adulterated your oil, the more healthful and better tasting it will be. Commercially processed vegetable oils are often extracted with chemical solvents and treated with additives. If possible, buy oils that are "cold-pressed."

- Since they are volatile—their flavor can dissipate at room temperature—nut and seed oils should be stored in the refrigerator.

- Extra-virgin olive oils don't tolerate high heat—they smoke and their flavor dissipates—so reserve them for flavoring and for cooking at moderate temperatures. Also note that their cost can vary widely, but high cost does not always indicate great oil.

- For extra flavor, you can infuse decent supermarket olive oil with olives. Half-fill a glass jar with green and black unpitted olives and then fill the jar with olive oil. When the oil's gone, eat the olives and start over. You don't want to do this in larger batches because the olives will get mushy if they sit for more than a week.

- Use flavorless vegetable oils such as grape seed or canola when you don't want an assertive flavor. (You can also use grape seed oil as a beauty treatment—see page 249.)

- Both grape seed and peanut oils have a very high smoke point. This makes them excellent candidates for high-temperature cooking, such as searing meats in a hot skillet.

OIL KNOW-HOW FROM SALLY SCHNEIDER

RECIPE | ## Homemade Mayonnaise

Save money, *and* eat better. When it comes to mayo, you'll have a hard time going back to commercial once you've tried the real thing. The flavor is fresh and light, without the cloying sweetness (or weird additives) you find in the jarred stuff. Add fresh herbs, garlic, or other seasonings to make instant sauces and dips that are both classy and cheap.

Makes 3 cups

> 2 large egg yolks
> 1 whole large egg
> 1 tablespoon Dijon mustard
> Pinch of salt
> Freshly ground black pepper, to taste
> 2 to 4 tablespoons fresh lemon juice
> 2 cups vegetable oil or olive oil

1. Combine the egg yolks, whole egg, mustard, salt, black pepper, and 2 tablespoons of the lemon juice in a food processor; process for 1 minute. (Or whisk until blended and bright yellow.)

2. With the motor running, add the oil through the feed tube in a slow, steady stream. (Or gradually whisk in half the oil, a few drops at a time, and then the remaining oil in a steady stream. You will need to whisk continuously for about 10 minutes.) When the mayonnaise is thoroughly blended, turn off the processor and scrape down the sides of the bowl. Taste the mayonnaise and correct the seasonings if necessary; if you are using vegetable oil, you will probably need to add the remaining 2 tablespoons lemon juice.

3. Scrape the mayonnaise into a container, cover, and refrigerate (it will keep for 5 days).

A note: Since you are eating raw eggs, make sure they are very fresh and, ideally, organic. Never serve raw eggs to pregnant women, infants, or anyone with a weakened immune system.

HOMEMADE MAYONNAISE BY JULEE ROSSO & SHEILA LUKINS

RECIPE | # Raspberry Jam Vinaigrette

All a salad really needs is a sprinkle of oil and vinegar. But sometimes your greens want a little more razzle-dazzle. There's no need to spend money on bottled dressings, which are loaded with calories, preservatives, and artificial flavorings. Just whip up your own with ingredients you have on hand.

Makes about 1½ cups

3 tablespoons seedless all-fruit raspberry jam
⅓ cup red wine vinegar or cider vinegar
¼ teaspoon salt
¼ teaspoon black pepper
1 cup vegetable oil

Put the jam in a 2-cup glass measuring cup and microwave, uncovered, on high power until the jam just melts, about 15 seconds, or melt in a small pan over low heat. Remove the container from the microwave and add the vinegar, salt, and black pepper. Whisk until well combined. Slowly add the oil in a thin stream, whisking constantly until it is thoroughly blended. Serve at once or cover and refrigerate until ready to serve.

RECIPE | # Pseudo-Caesar Dressing

Traditional Caesar dressings can contain anchovies and raw egg, but in this modified version, the creamy spiciness of Dijon mustard stands in.

Makes about ¾ cup

1 lemon
2 tablespoons red wine vinegar
2 tablespoons Dijon mustard
¼ teaspoon black pepper
2 cloves fresh garlic
½ cup extra-virgin olive oil

1. Cut the lemon in half and squeeze the juice from both halves through a strainer into a 2-cup or larger bowl. Add the vinegar, mustard, and black pepper. Peel and finely mince the garlic cloves and add them to the bowl. Whisk until well combined.

2. Drizzle the oil into the bowl in a thin stream, whisking constantly until all the oil is added and the dressing is slightly thick. Use the dressing immediately or cover and refrigerate for up to 3 days. (Whisk the dressing to recombine, if necessary.)

RECIPE | **Quick-Pickled Carrots**

Proof that carrots don't have to be a snooze, this crisp and lively Mexican condiment is a wonderful specimen in the category of "refrigerator pickles"—quickly brined vegetables that don't involve canning and should be eaten within days of preparation. (See page 175 for information on other types of pickling and canning.)

Use as little or as much red pepper or sliced jalapeño as you like, and remember, the seeds are where much of a pepper's bite comes from. These pickles go well alongside any Mexican dishes and will spice up an ordinary salad or sandwich as well.

Makes 6 servings

1 pound carrots, peeled and sliced
3 cloves garlic, thickly sliced
Vegetable oil
1½ cups white vinegar (or 1 cup vinegar and ½ cup lemon juice)
½ tablespoon salt
1½ cups water
Pinch of crushed red pepper or sliced jalapeño (to taste)

Sauté the carrots and garlic briefly in a splash of oil. Add the remaining ingredients and simmer for 10 minutes. Cool completely. Place the carrots in a glass container or jar and refrigerate overnight.

White Vinegar

Pure white vinegar has hundreds of household uses. (See page 11 for a few.) In the kitchen, it can be used in place of fancy varieties of vinegar—though it should be used sparingly as its flavor is highly acidic. If you're working with simple raw ingredients, the choice of vinegar may have more bearing on the recipe; but especially when cooking, the difference may be negligible—experiment and see. If a recipe calls for a dry wine, in many cases you can substitute a small splash of vinegar instead.

Sugar, Sweet & Simple

Especially these days, the grocery-store baking-supply aisle is packed with an incredible array of sugar options. Most are relatively cheap, so the choice is up to you. Some tips to make your thrift a little sweeter:

- Though there's nothing inherently unthrifty about brown sugar, its moisture tends to evaporate in the cupboard, causing it to cake up into a rock-hard block—and that means brown sugar in your trash can. The solution: Keep it in the fridge, where it will retain its moisture and its delectably chewy texture.

- If you don't have brown sugar but need it for a recipe, you don't have to run out and buy it. Make your own by simply mixing granulated white sugar with molasses. (Of course, that assumes that you have molasses on hand—but maybe you do!)

- If you're in the market for pure cane sugar, get thee to a Latin market, where you'll avoid the "all-natural" markup.

THRIFTONOMICS

A Big Mug of Savings

Everyone loves to talk about how much money we'd all save if we cut out those lattes. Odds are you've already downgraded your coffeehouse habit from espresso-based drinks to more frugal cups of regular coffee. But how much can you save by making it at home?

At the coffee shop: If you drink black coffee five days a week, at a cost of about $1.75 per cup, you're spending $474.25 a year for your caffeinated convenience.

At home: That same cup of black coffee only costs about (drumroll) 17 cents. That's just $46.07 a year!

The math: Our tabulation assumes that you've used 3 ounces of coffee grounds to make an 8 ounce cup of goodness. High-quality beans cost about $8 per pound, with one pound giving you about 48 servings of brew. What about the equipment? Well yes, there is an initial investment—but you don't need a highfalutin coffeemaker to make a good brew. A plastic coffee filter cone is about $3, and dead easy to operate. You line it with a paper filter, plop it on your mug, spoon in your grounds, and pour in the boiling water. Tada! The $3 filter cone can be used every day, and the cost of filters adds up to $0.03 a cup (480 for $12 = $0.03 per cup). That brings your coffee brewing total up to $68.30 per year, if you want to get technical about it.

The verdict: Make coffee at home and save more than $400!

CAFFEINATED THRIFTONOMICS BY JULIANA BUNIM

Too Busy to Cook?

It's an unfortunate trap. You "can't" cook because you're too busy working to make ends meet, but because you don't cook, you overspend on your food budget. Even worse, the less often you cook, the more ill-prepared you are to do so at a moment's notice. So the cycle perpetuates itself. What to do? Grocery stores are packed with products designed to make your life easier—everything from sliced mushrooms to shredded cheese. But convenience can be costly. (It all boils down to the familiar choice between time and money.) Prepared items *are* worth it if they make the difference between cooking at home and going out, or paying more for prepared meals. But there are gentle ways to work a little more DIY into your routine.

DIY Convenience Foods | by Beverly Mills & Alicia Ross

I f those presliced mushrooms make it possible for you to make a pot of mushroom soup (page 167), then they are a thrifty buy. But when you have a free half hour or so, try to get in the habit of making your own convenience items. All you need is a sharp knife (or a food processor) and some ziplock plastic storage bags (or refrigerator storage containers). Here are some easy-to-make starter items:

"Baby" carrots. You're not going to get the cute shape, but you can make a small carrot stick that will taste exactly the same and have the same snackability factor. Peel the carrots and trim away the ends. Cut the carrots in half lengthwise and cut the pieces into sticks. Store the pieces in a ziplock plastic bag in the vegetable bin for up to a week.

Celery sticks. Rinse and dry the celery ribs. Cut them in half (or thirds) lengthwise. Cut into "sticks" of any length you prefer. Store the pieces in a ziplock plastic bag in the vegetable bin for up to a week.

Sliced mushrooms. Cut away any tough stems. If the mushrooms are dirty, use a soft brush or a paper towel to brush away the dirt. If you rinse the mushrooms, they'll need to be used within a day. Slice the mushrooms and wrap the slices in a paper towel. (Mushrooms that touch plastic don't store as long.) Place the towel-wrapped package in a ziplock plastic bag. Store in the vegetable bin for three to four days.

Shredded cabbage. Cut the cabbage into quarters and discard the tough core. Using a long, sharp knife, cut the cabbage into thin shreds. Store the shreds in a gallon-size ziplock plastic bag in the vegetable bin for up to four days.

Chopped onions. Peel the onions and chop them. Refrigerate in a ziplock plastic bag or container with airtight lid. Store them in the vegetable bin for up to four days. Chopped onions can also be frozen in a ziplock freezer bag for up to a month. (Lay the bag flat until the contents are frozen so the onions won't freeze in a clump.)

> ## Double the Green
>
> Glass food-storage containers are healthier than plastic ones, but that doesn't mean you need to buy something specific for the job. Just reuse jars from peanut butter, mayonnaise, jam, and other food items. If you happen to have plastic takeout containers at home, you should try to find a use for those, too, though preferably for nonfood items. (They're great for sorting and storing hardware or craft supplies.) If you just won't give up on disposable sandwich or freezer bags, consider extending their life span by washing and drying them out between uses.

Shredded cheese. Use a food processor, if you have one, to shred hard cheeses. (Soft and semi-soft cheeses like mozzarella must be grated by hand.) Store the shreds in a ziplock plastic bag in the refrigerator (up to one week) or freezer (up to one month). Sometimes very large bags (2 pounds or more) of pre-shredded cheese at the supermarket are cheaper than whole cheeses, so compare costs.

Pre-cooked surplus. You're making extra-large portions of beans and rice and freezing what you don't immediately use in small batches, right?

RECIPE | **Creamy Mushroom Soup**

If you pre-slice your mushrooms and onion (or let the grocery store do it for you), this hearty main dish soup will take just minutes to prepare.

Serves 4

> 3 tablespoons butter
> 1 package or 6 ounces presliced portobello mushrooms
> 1 package or 8 ounces presliced fresh button mushrooms
> ½ cup chopped onion
> 2 tablespoons dry sherry or white wine, optional
> 1 can (14¾ ounces) chicken stock (or homemade, see page 141)
> 3 tablespoons cornstarch
> 3 tablespoons water
> 2 cups milk or half-and-half
> Dash of hot pepper sauce, or to taste
> Salt and black pepper to taste

1. Melt the butter in a 4½-quart Dutch oven or soup pot over medium-low heat. Meanwhile, chop the portobello mushrooms into bite-size pieces. Add them to the pot with the button mushrooms. Cook until the mushrooms have released their liquid, about 4 minutes, stirring from time to time. Add the onion and sherry (if using) and cook for 1 minute to evaporate the alcohol.

2. Add the chicken stock, cover the pot, raise the heat to high, and bring the soup to a boil. Reduce the heat to low and simmer for 3 minutes more to develop the flavor.

3. Meanwhile, combine the cornstarch and water in a small, lidded container. Shake well until the lumps disappear, then set aside.

4. After the soup has simmered, raise the heat to medium-high, add the milk, and stir. Shake the cornstarch mixture again and add it to the pot, stirring. Cook until the soup is thickened, 3 to 4 minutes, stirring from time to time. Season with hot pepper sauce, salt, and pepper and serve.

Addicted to Takeout?

I f you live in an urban or suburban area, there are probably countless places that serve or deliver cheap, fast takeout food. And if you're juggling a busy schedule, chances are you avail yourself of their services at least a couple of times a week.

For many, "home cooking" has come to mean transferring pad thai noodles from a Styrofoam container onto a plate. Takeout can be a way of life—especially for young adults and working parents. The reasons are convenience and time: Takeout means you don't have to shop for groceries, and you don't have to spend time cooking and cleaning up. You don't even have to spend time thinking about what to feed yourself or your family.

But convenience comes at a price. Spending $8 on dinner may seem economical, but that one dish is worth a fraction of the cost in ingredients, and the price tag translates to hundreds or even thousands of dollars per year in extra spending. Takeout generates mountains of packaging and disposable containers, and the food is usually higher in fat, calories, and sodium content than just about anything homemade. You also miss out on the therapeutic quality of cooking: Even boiling water for pasta forces you to slow down and concentrate on something other than whatever is eating up the rest of your time.

If you are determined to spend less money, start with a time-out on takeout. Don't go cold turkey—there's no need to feel deprived, and you are far less likely to stick with your plan if you do. Start by determining to nix, say, one takeout meal per week. If you just can't give up the kung pao chicken, there's an easy way to get your fix *and* become a more confident cook in the process: Make it yourself.

Believe it or not, stir-fries, curries, and pizza are easily within the reach of even beginner cooks. The key is to plan ahead and stock your pantry and freezer with the right ingredients for your favorite takeout meals. If your favorite dish is beyond the scope of a normal home kitchen, chances are it shouldn't be eaten too often anyway. (Yeah, "Bloomin' Onion," it's personal!) Before you make your weekly trip to the grocery store, take a minute to check your "takeout supply" to make sure you have everything in stock. An occasional trip to an ethnic market may be in order, but it will be worthwhile because you'll find far better deals on a variety of foods than you would at the supermarket.

Turn Takeout Into Make-In

Here's how to get started on "make-in" dinners. With a little practice, you may well end up tossing that takeout menu collection!

Think about which dishes you eat most often. Look up recipes for the foods you tend to order. Start simple by focusing on books that emphasize fast and easy dishes. Look for websites that offer advice or user comments.

Stock your kitchen with the necessary ingredients. Need fish sauce? Coconut milk? Track down these specialty pantry items, and buy enough so you have them on hand when you need them.

Make the freezer your friend. If bite-size pieces of beef or broccoli florets are key ingredients in your favorite foods, slice a good-size quantity and tuck them away in small freezer bags so they're ready to go.

Consider the rice cooker. If you are a fan of Asian or Indian food, a rice cooker is a solid investment for as little as $20. It will ensure perfect grains at practically zero effort.

Consider the slow cooker. Cooking a hot meal after a long, hard day at work can be a drag. Wouldn't it be nice to have it waiting for you when you get home? That's what the slow cooker is all about. Put the raw food in before you leave for work, plug it in, then go earn your bacon. When you return at the end of your workday, you'll be met with a delicious pot roast. If you're committed to eating at home more often, this is one contraption worth considering.

Know your dough. For a quick home-made pizza, try using a prebaked pizza shell. If you prefer to work with frozen dough (the results will taste fresher), buy it in the grocery aisle or ask your local pizza shop if they'll sell some. Set it out before you leave for work in the morning, and when you come home, it will be ready to roll. Preheat the oven. Top with sauce and mozzarella, and you can have a fresh pizza in minutes. Add whatever toppings you have on hand.

RECIPE | Homemade (Secretly Healthy) Fried Rice

At about a dollar per serving, this Chinese dinner beats takeout by a mile. It's also low in fat and full of fresh vegetables.

Serves 4

Salt
1⅓ cups long-grain rice or 4 cups cooked
3 tablespoons vegetable oil
2 large eggs
1 large onion (for about 1 cup chopped)
1 large green, yellow, or red bell pepper (for about 1½ cups chopped)
8 ounces button mushrooms
3 cloves fresh garlic, minced, or 1 tablespoon bottled minced garlic
¼ cup apple juice or dry sherry
3 tablespoons soy sauce, plus more for serving (optional)
1 to 2 bunches scallions (for about ¾ cup chopped)
1 can (8 ounces) chopped or sliced water chestnuts, drained (optional)
1 cup frozen green peas
1½ tablespoons toasted sesame oil

1. Bring 2⅔ cups lightly salted water to a boil in a covered medium-size saucepan over high heat. Add the rice, stir, and reduce the heat to low. Cover the pan and simmer until the rice is tender, about 20 minutes.

2. Meanwhile, heat 1 tablespoon of oil in an extra-deep 12-inch skillet over medium heat. Beat the eggs lightly, pour them into the skillet, and cook without stirring (as you would an omelet) until they are almost dry, 2 to 3 minutes.

3. While the eggs cook, peel and coarsely chop the onion and set it aside. When the eggs are ready, transfer them to a plate and set aside. (Do not wash the skillet.)

4. Heat the remaining oil in the same skillet used for the eggs over medium heat. Add the onion and cook, stirring occasionally, until it just begins to soften, 2 to 3 minutes.

5. Meanwhile, stem, seed, and cut the bell pepper into bite-size pieces and add them to the skillet. Rinse, pat dry, and coarsely chop the mushrooms, discarding any tough stems. Add the mushrooms and garlic to the skillet. Cook, stirring, for 2 minutes.

SINGLE-COOK ADVICE AND FRIED-RICE RECIPE BY BEVERLY MILLS & ALICIA ROSS

6. Add the apple juice or sherry, soy sauce, and cooked rice. Stir occasionally while you slice the scallions, using the white and enough of the tender green tops to make ¾ cup. Add them to the skillet and stir well.

7. Drain the water chestnuts (if using) and add them to the skillet. Add the peas and sesame oil. Cut the eggs into thin strips, add them to the pan, and stir. Stir-fry to heat the water chestnuts and peas and to mix in the sesame oil, 1 minute. Serve at once, passing extra soy sauce at the table, if desired.

Shopping & the Single Cook

The single cook may be able to eat whatever he likes, whenever and wherever he likes, but he does face some particular challenges. No stranger to the browning, unused head of cauliflower, he must exercise special caution in order to avoid waste (especially when it comes to produce) and to find appropriate portion sizes. For the single cook, a family of four's meal plus leftovers would translate to eight identical meals—and a very angry palate! A few handy workarounds should help keep the excess and doldrums in check:

- The fresh meat, seafood, deli, produce, and bakery departments are perfect places to buy the exact amount you need without paying any more per pound than if you were buying for a family of six.
- When food sold by the pound is packaged in containers larger than you need, ask the department manager if he can divide a package. Stores are usually happy to help you buy only what you need.
- Many stores sell cartons that contain just six eggs. If you don't see any on display, ask the manager to cut a carton in half.
- The bulk foods section of the store also allows you to buy small quantities. If you can't eat a whole box of cereal or a whole can of nuts before they go stale, buy only the amount you need from the bulk bins. (You'll be able to get more variety this way, too.)
- Invest in storage containers to keep leftovers fresh. If you're going to freeze your leftovers, be sure to use bags or containers made especially for the freezer so your food won't get freezer burn (see page 174 for tips on how best to store on ice).

Can, Pickle, Freeze

It bears repeating that one of the central tenets of thrifty cooking is avoiding waste. But you can't stick everything in the fridge and pray you'll get to it before it spoils. (Haven't you noticed that most of the time, you don't?) A little boning up on what to keep and how will go a long way toward taking your leftovers from blah to bam.

Taking the CSA Challenge | by Peggy Burns

A few months after we moved to a French-speaking neighborhood of Montreal, my husband and I received a flyer offering us a *"panier de légumes biologique."* As we slowly translated the brochure, with the help of an online dictionary, we learned that by joining the local CSA, we could receive a basket of organic vegetables every week, for twenty weeks from June through November. It would cost us $25 (Canadian) for a basket with enough produce to feed two people. The pick-up point was only a block away at the local health food store, where, ironically, the organic produce was priced way too high for our budget. The farm was called Jardins d'Ambroisie. How could I say no?

We've been enrolled in the CSA for three years now, and the first year was definitely the hardest, the most wasteful, and the most expensive. Even though we already ate very little processed food and even less fast food, I didn't know how to adapt my cooking to the seasons, as opposed to what looked good in the supermarket. While I thought I was healthy, I honestly had no idea which vegetables and fruits were in season when. I did all of my shopping at grocery stores where the food is shipped in from all over the world. In a globalized food economy, seasons don't really exist.

So when the baskets started arriving during the first year, we were caught off guard by the bounty. Having been a vegetarian for ten years already, I was astonished to learn about foods I didn't know existed, like Jerusalem artichokes and fiddlehead ferns. Every week, we would frantically search for recipes. Whole heads of lettuce, melons, and zucchini would go to waste because we didn't want to eat the things every day (and didn't know enough recipes to mix things up). With the mountains of root vegetables that came our way in October and November, we didn't make nearly as many soups as we could have.

That first year I added to my waste by robotically shopping for bananas or oranges. That's what I always ate for breakfast, and I wasn't ready to switch to fresh local strawberries—even though I had a basket waiting for me at home.

The next summer, however, was a transformation both in budget and mind. With a better understanding of when foods were in season, we were armed with recipes for the bonanza of vegetables that came our way. We made salads, salsas, and casseroles. We ate vegetables fresh, grilled, baked, and every other way you can. We realized that we will never love Jerusalem artichokes and rutabaga, but we also learned to put them in the box for trades, where more often than not we'll find ourselves in a conversation with a neighbor about how to prepare the offending item. (Or what not to do!)

Overall, we found ourselves rarely shopping. As a result, we had much more time to enjoy summer and, most important, we had more money in the bank. We probably saved as much as $200 a month—even though the price of the basket increased to $34.

In addition to the savings, we started to really enjoy the pleasures of eating locally grown food. It's nice to know that Japanese mibuna leaves

Know Your CSAs

Community Supported Agriculture (CSA) began 30 years ago in Japan when a group of women recognized that more and more of their food was being imported. They organized a group that bought directly from a farmer, inaugurating the system that came to be known as CSA. The Japanese word for a CSA is *teikei,* which means "putting the farmer's face on food."

Most CSAs begin with a farmer and sometimes a core group of members, who draw up a budget that includes all farm production costs, including salaries and overhead, for one year's operation. The total cost is divided by the number of families the farm will provide for, and that determines the cost of one share of the harvest. Each week, shareholders go to the farm or to a pickup site to collect their produce, with one share's worth enough to feed a family of four for a week. Most CSAs offer half shares, as well, and make arrangements for installment payments. The benefits *and* the risks of the harvest are shared by the farmer and the members.

grow wonderfully here in Quebec. We visited the farm and showed our kids where the food comes from, which leads me to one of the best aspects of the basket. Every week, we take our kids in the station wagon to get the basket, and if there are fresh blueberries or strawberries, they are almost gone by the time we get home—and the culprits have very messy faces.

There is one downfall to the basket of vegetables: It makes the other thirty weeks of the year, which is the grueling winter in Montreal, all that much harder to bear. But that's why the top item on my to-do list is a food-related one: Learn how to pickle and can.

Freezing Tips

Freezing is the easiest way to store meats and many vegetables and fruits. A full freezer will not only enable you to cook at home at a moment's notice, it will also allow you to enjoy great produce year-round—no matter what pallid fare happens to be available at the supermarket. (There's also the added bonus that filling your freezer is energy-efficient.) What to freeze? Tomatoes, green beans, peas, corn kernels, parsnips, berries, persimmons, and peach halves all freeze beautifully. Just keep in mind that freezer preserving is essentially a short-term method. Fruits, vegetables, even meats become "freezer burned" and lose flavor within a few months. That aside, if you decide to "put by" in the freezer, follow these tips:

- Glass jars are subject to cracking in extreme cold and also take up far too much space in the freezer. Instead, use plastic containers or freezer bags to package ingredients.
- Whether you are using plastic containers or freezer bags, make sure the ingredients you are freezing are completely cool before packaging them.
- If using plastic containers, leave an inch of headspace to account for expansion. If you pack the ingredients to the top, the container will either burst or pop its lid, and the contents will become freezer burned.
- If using freezer bags, zipper bags are the way to go, especially for anything that has any liquid, such as berries or tomatoes. You can fill them, squeeze out the air, zip them up, set them in the freezer, and walk away until they're stiff. Then you can stack them to make more shelf space for the next round.

Can This? Can Do!

Got an abundance of cucumber? The time-honored thrifty solution is to learn to can and pickle. Canning—sealing ingredients into a sterile environment—keeps flavors bright and concentrated. With the boiling-water–bath method of canning, jars are packed with acidic or blanched foods. The jars are then submerged in boiling water until every particle of food reaches a temperature high enough to kill the molds, yeasts, and bacteria that cause food to spoil. The method also drives out any air in the jar and in the food itself, creating a vacuum that seals the jar's rubber-coated lid.

Every fruit and vegetable is handled slightly differently depending on its acidity and how much sugar and water it contains, so don't try to improvise. As in baking, it is best to follow recipes carefully (at least until you have them memorized). We've included three delicious boiling-water–bath canning recipes—a fruit preserve, a relish, and a pickle—but you can find hundreds more online. Check out the recipes in the U.S. Department of Agriculture's "Complete Guide to Home Canning," which is available at www.usda.gov, or on the Ball canning jar website, www.freshpreserving.com.

Pickling 411

Pickling preserves food with vinegar and/or salt, which kill the bacteria that cause food to rot. Uncanned pickled vegetables must be kept in the fridge and eaten within a few weeks. (Pickles that are shelf-stable have been pickled and then canned.)

An important safety note: Only food that is precooked or naturally acidic should be canned in a boiling-water bath. *Clostridium botulinum,* the bacterium that causes botulism, exists in the soil and is always on fresh foods, though not in dangerous quantities. In a vacuum-packed, nonacidic environment, it can grow to a potentially fatal level. Low-acid foods such as meats, seafood, and fresh vegetables other than tomatoes should be preserved with the pressure canner method (not discussed here but worth graduating to after gaining experience with the boiling-water–bath method). Among the highly acidic foods suitable for canning using the boiling-water–bath method are: pickles, relishes, salsas, tomato sauce, chutneys with vinegar, most fruits, and sweetened spreads such as jams, jellies, butters, and preserves.

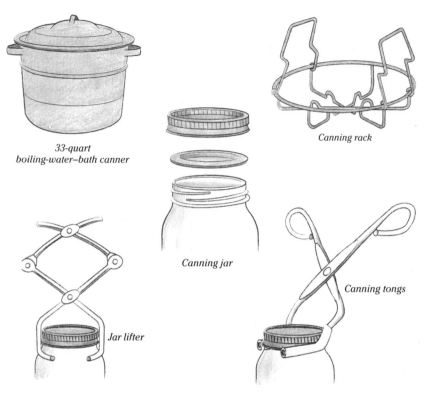

33-quart
boiling-water–bath canner

Canning rack

Canning jar

Canning tongs

Jar lifter

Equipment

- A 21- or 33-quart boiling-water–bath canner with a lid and a jar rack. The better ones are made of stainless steel, aluminum, or porcelain-covered steel. But any large pot with a lid can be substituted as long as it is at least 4 inches taller than the jars (deep enough to allow 2 inches of water to cover the jars plus 2 inches of "boiling room").
- A wire rack for the bottom of the pot to hold jars away from the direct heat and from each other to prevent cracking. In lieu of a jar rack, you can go the really old-fashioned route and position kitchen towels between the jars to prevent breakage during the canning process.
- A pair of home-canning tongs or a jar lifter to remove the hot jars from the boiling-water–bath canner
- Jars and lids
- A timer
- A large supply of clean dish or tea towels

PROJECT | Part I: Sterilizing and Filling the Jars

The first part of canning involves prepping the food and sterilizing the canning jars. Here's how.

1. Clean the food and, if needed, cut it into pieces of uniform size. Prepare as directed by recipe.

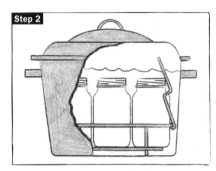
Step 2

2. Sterilize the clean canning jars by filling them with hot (not boiling) water and lowering them onto a rack placed in a water-filled pot. Make sure there's at least 1 inch of water above the rims of the jars. Bring the water to a boil and boil for 10 minutes. Keep jars hot.

3. Remove a jar and immediately fill it with food. If you are using the raw-pack method, pack it tightly. If you've opted for the hot-pack method, fill the warm jar loosely.

4. Add very hot water, syrup, or juice, according to the recipe, to the jar until it covers the food. Allow for proper headspace.

5. Remove air bubbles by inserting a nonmetallic utensil into the jars and firmly pressing the food.

6. Using a clean towel, carefully wipe the jar rim clean to allow a good seal to form.

7. Apply the jar lid and secure it with the screw ring.

8. Repeat steps 3, 4, and 5 until all jars are filled. Reserve the water used to sterilize the jars for the canning process.

PROJECT | Part II: The Boiling-Water Bath

The steps below are based on the canning recommendations made by the U.S. Department of Agriculture—in other words, this is how to can food safely.

1. After packing the jars and fitting them with lids and screw rings, fill the canner (or pot) halfway with water (or use half the water reserved from sterilizing jars) and heat it to 140°F for raw food or to 180°F for cooked food.

2. You may either put the empty rack in the canner and then load the jars onto the rack with a jar lifter, or you can place the packed jars on the canner rack first and then, using the handles, lower the rack into the hot water.

Step 2

Step 3

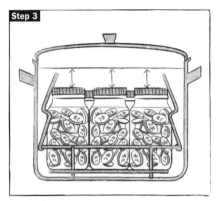

Step 8

3. The water level should be at least 2 inches above the lids of the jars. Add more hot water, if necessary.

4. Heat the water to a full boil.

5. Once the water is rapidly boiling, set a timer for the number of minutes specified in your recipe. Cover with the lid and reduce the heat enough to keep the water at a gentle boil. Be sure to adjust as needed for altitude.

6. Check the canner to make sure the water level is still 2 inches above the jars, and add boiling water, if necessary.

7. When the specified time has elapsed, turn off the heat and remove the lid, keeping your face away from the hot steam.

8. Place a folded towel on the counter near the canner. Use a jar lifter to remove the jars, placing them on the towel. Keep them at least 1 inch apart to allow air to circulate.

9. Allow jars to cool at room temperature for 12 hours. Don't be concerned if you hear an occasional snap; it's the sound of a lid sealing.

10. When the jars are cool, test the seal of each by pressing on the center of each jar's lid. Any lids that spring back rather than remaining concave have not been properly sealed. These jars should be stored in the refrigerator and used first.

11. Jars that have sealed properly can be stored in a cool, dry, dark place for up to one year. Clearly label the jars with contents and date.

RECIPE | ## Old-Fashioned Peach Preserves

The essence of summer. Try these preserves on ice cream or in homemade yogurt (page 152). The mystery ingredient: Ascorbic acid, commonly known as vitamin C, prevents browning. Upping the amount of lemon juice will work, but not quite as well.

Makes 7 pints

EQUIPMENT
> Boiling-water–bath canner
> seven 1-pint jars

INGREDIENTS
> 1 quart water
> ½ teaspoon ascorbic acid (crystals, powder, or crushed tablets)
> 3½ pounds (about 7 large) ripe peaches, peeled, pitted, and chopped
> 5 cups sugar
> ¼ cup fresh lemon juice
> ¾ teaspoon pure almond extract (optional)

1. Prepare an acid bath by pouring the water into a medium-size bowl and adding the ascorbic acid.

2. Dip the peaches in the acid bath; drain well. Combine the fruit, sugar, and lemon juice in a heavy 6- to 8-quart saucepan. Stir over medium heat to dissolve the sugar.

3. Boil slowly, stirring constantly, until the mixture thickens, the fruit is translucent, and a cooking thermometer registers 220°F.

4. Stir in the almond extract, if using.

5. Remove from the heat and skim off the foam, if there is any, with a metal spoon. Ladle into sterile jars, allowing ¼ inch of headspace. Cap and seal.

6. Process for 10 minutes in a boiling-water–bath canner.

RECIPE | ## Corn-Zucchini Salsa

Serve this salsa with tortilla chips or try it atop grilled chicken breasts or fish. It's got just the right amount of bite.

Makes 2 pints

EQUIPMENT
Boiling-water–bath canner
two 1-pint jars

INGREDIENTS
3 medium zucchini, cleaned, trimmed, and diced
1½ teaspoons salt
2 ears yellow corn, husked, silk removed
4 tablespoons olive oil
2 large tomatoes, seeded and chopped
1 cup fresh lime juice (8 medium limes)
½ cup apple cider vinegar
2 jalapeño peppers, seeded and minced (wear rubber gloves)
¼ cup finely chopped scallions with tops
3 cloves garlic, minced
¼ teaspoon freshly ground black pepper

1. Toss the zucchini with the salt and "sweat" them for 3 minutes in a nonreactive colander. Rinse and dry on paper towels.

2. Coat the corn with 2 teaspoons of the oil and roast on a cookie sheet in a 400°F oven for 30 to 40 minutes. Cool. Cut off the kernels and scrape the cobs.

3. Combine the zucchini, corn, remaining oil, tomatoes, lime juice, vinegar, jalapeños, scallions, garlic, and pepper in a heavy saucepan. Bring to a boil and cook for 2 to 3 minutes.

4. Ladle into hot, sterile jars. Cap and seal.

5. Process in a boiling-water–bath canner for 15 minutes.

RECIPE | # Bread & Butter Pickles

These classic sweet-and-sours are a delicious addition to any appetizer spread. They're also great with falafel, tuna salad sandwiches, and hamburgers.

Makes 7 pints

EQUIPMENT

Boiling-water–bath canner
seven 1-pint jars

INGREDIENTS

6 pounds (about 4 quarts) medium-size cucumbers, scrubbed and sliced ⅛-inch thick

1½ cups (about 1 pound) peeled and sliced small white onions

2 cloves garlic

⅓ cup salt

several trays of ice cubes

4½ cups sugar

2 tablespoons yellow mustard seeds

1½ teaspoons celery seeds

1½ teaspoons ground turmeric

3 cups distilled white vinegar

A Warning List for Spoiled Canned Food

Food safety is important, so toss the item in question if you see any of the following:

1. The jar has mold on it, food has leaked out during storage, or the inside of the lid is moldy.
2. The food in the jar is completely and very darkly discolored. (Uniform light gray or brown discoloration may be caused by minerals in the water, in which case the food is safe to eat.)
3. The food looks shriveled, spongy, slimy, or cloudy.
4. The liquid in the jar is not static and seems to bubble.
5. The jar's contents "shoot" out when the lid is opened.
6. The food has an "off" odor.

1. In a large mixing bowl, combine the cucumbers, onions, and garlic. Add the salt and mix thoroughly. Cover with ice cubes. Let stand for 3 hours.

2. Rinse well, then thoroughly drain the mixture, and remove the garlic cloves.

3. Combine the sugar, mustard seeds, celery seeds, turmeric, and vinegar in an 8-quart saucepan and bring to a boil over high heat. Add the drained cucumber mixture and cook for 5 minutes.

4. Pour the mixture into sterile jars, leaving ½ inch of headspace. Cap and seal.

5. Process for 10 minutes in a boiling-water–bath canner.

PEACH PRESERVES, CORN-ZUCCHINI SALSA, AND BREAD & BUTTER PICKLE RECIPES BY CAROL W. COSTENBADER

inside this chapter . . .

GAMES

CRAFTS

the family that saves together

The Rules, the Scoop & Some Good Old-Fashioned Fun

In a perfect world, children would be born with a sense of thrift: They'd be delighted with what they're given, they'd routinely offer to help with chores, and they'd gracefully pay their way through college. Dream on. Until that magical day comes, parents will have to do the teaching.

From a child's point of view, the benefits of thrift can be difficult to grasp: If we can eat out one night a week, why not every night? While an explanation of finances may not do the trick, the good news is that by practicing thrift, you'll be imparting it to your kids. It's a virtue that children learn by watching, as well as by helping out in the simplest of ways.

The costs of raising a child are considerable, true, but there are ways to save money without sacrificing your offspring's happiness or development. In fact, quite the opposite—who says the children of millionaires have more fun? (They certainly wind up with entertaining problems!) There are challenges. Spendthrift influences abound, and time travel or the worldwide confiscation of cell phones and video games are not options. But with some attention, you can orchestrate a simpler, less wasteful, and, yes, happier life for your family.

The New Parent Corner

Many things disappear from your life, and your budget, once you've had a baby: long dinners out with bottles of wine, movies, novels, concerts . . . You do, however, discover many new ways to spend your money, and most of them—from onesies to teething rings to humidifiers—are designed to be almost as irresistible as your tot.

The baby-products market preys on parental insecurities: Are you doing absolutely everything you can to ensure that your child is safe, healthy, rested, well fed, entertained, and as smart and cute as (or smarter and cuter than) the kid next door?

We must breathe deeply and remember that the human race thrived for many thousands of years before the advent of visually stimulating black-and-white abstract sea creature crib mobiles.

A Better Registry

Babies make people happy, and one way friends and family members express that happiness is by buying (or making) gifts. Doing some homework and setting up a well-thought-out baby registry (or just putting out the word about what you want) can help you make the most of the goodwill. Here is a step-by-step plan:

1. Canvass like-minded friends to learn what they consider necessities, and what's just nice to have. Use our guidelines (page 328) as a starting point.

2. Determine what you might inherit or borrow from friends or family. Weigh what you think you'd be willing to have secondhand, and what you'd prefer to buy new.

3. Research online and in stores, and seek recommendations and reviews from friends and family to zero in on specific brands and models.

4. Instead of registering at one store, consider posting your wish list on a website such as myregistry.com, kaboodle.com, or alternativegiftregistry .org, which allow you to include items from different stores.

The Rules for New Parents

Gifts and hand-me-downs aside, there's no getting around the fact that you'll be doing *some* shopping in the name of baby preparedness. The rule of thumb? Don't think—or shop—too far down the road. Babies' rapid growth renders their stuff obsolete frighteningly fast. Plus, every child is different, and you never really know what you need until you need it. Some things just won't work for your baby (the swing that he hates), or for you (the carrier that tweaks your back). Stock your home with items that will get you through the first couple of months, and then step back to reassess—but understand that sometimes you just have to throw money at a problem. (Wets through six brands of diapers! Sleeps only when being jiggled! Gnaws on her crib rail like a beaver!), and it's best to make peace with that. Still, there are ways to buy smarter:

- Know the gender of your baby? Resist the temptation to over-dose on pink or blue stuff so that items can work for a sibling.
- Keep the tags on everything until the very last minute, in case you need to return.
- Try to resell any unused items you can't return, as well as gently used items that baby has outgrown. (Unless you want to hang onto the items for a potential second child.)
- For both selling and buying, join an online community or neighbor-hood-based parenting group, and keep up with their classifieds online or via an email list. EBay and Craigslist are good, too, but a "hyperlocal" network makes transferring the goods quicker and easier.
- Remember that consignment stores and swap meets—online or in the real world—are great sources for all things baby.
- For secondhand items that could be unsafe—cribs, high chairs, car seats, bouncy chairs—borrowing or buying from a source you trust can provide peace of mind. Another (icky) reason to buy from a trusted source: bedbugs. Bedbugs can be transmitted on furniture, clothing, and belong-ings; can live for up to eighteen months without a host; and are becoming a bigger problem all the time. They don't carry disease, but what comfort is that?
- Register or, if a friend inquires, ask for gift cards from diapers .com or big-box stores to cover expenses for basics like diapers and wipes and for things that you'll need as baby grows.
- Approach big-box baby super-stores with extreme caution and an ironclad list, or avoid altogether—especially if you are hormonal, exhausted, or both.

Diaper Dilemma

To go cloth or not to go cloth? For new parents, it's often a fraught question. When weighing diaper pros and cons, you should do some cost research, because prices for cloth diapers (and laundry, whether you do it or decide to outsource it) and store-bought diapers can vary significantly. In general, cloth diapers are less expensive than disposables. One estimate puts the overall cost of disposables, from birth to potty training, at more than $1,500; the startup cost of cloth diapers is somewhere around $100 (though costs escalate significantly if you outsource the laundering). But cloth diapers have other plusses to recommend them: Obviously, they create less waste, and some research indicates that children reared in cloth diapers can be toilet trained earlier, which means the laundering costs will factor in over a shorter period of time.

Laundering diapers at home may be the thriftiest option, but it requires time—and a tolerance for unpleasant odors. Some first-time parents may prefer to use disposables and wait to embark on the cloth-diaper journey until the second child. Be prepared to try a few different approaches until you find the formula that works best for you and your baby. Do some research online, where you'll find thriving communities of cloth-diapering devotees, or ask an experienced friend or relative to show you the ropes. There are a lot of options on the disposable to semi-disposable continuum—prefolds, pocket diapers, all-in-ones—and experienced parents know lots of tricks. If you want to pursue cloth diapers, a new(ish) and less labor-intensive diaper gives you the best of both worlds: The gDiaper (www.gdiapers.com) features cotton covers with flushable inserts.

Baby's toiletry kit doesn't stop at diapers. It includes powder, wipes, and special baby soaps and lotions. Those delicate creatures deserve (and require) special care and pampering! While these aren't big-ticket items, in the spirit of every-little-bit counts, here's a way to cut corners without sacrificing on pampering (no brand-name pun intended).

Bath Toys

Bath time toys should be free! Why spend on ducklings when you can simply recycle plastic drink bottles and cups and old watering cans? Measuring caps from liquid laundry detergent make for adequately floatable flotsam, and never underestimate the fun you can have with a plain old washcloth.

PROJECT | **Make Your Own Baby Wipes**

Don't fritter away your dollars on wet paper towels. And what are they soaking in anyway? Make your own baby wipes and rest easy.

1. Cut a roll of heavy-duty paper towels in half with a sharp knife to get two miniature rolls.

2. Remove the cardboard center from the inside of one half and place the paper towels in an empty wipe box or plastic container. (Save the other half for your next batch.)

3. Mix together 1½ cups water,

1½ tablespoons baby oil, and 1½ tablespoons baby shampoo.

4. Pour the mixture over the paper towels. Turn the towels over to make sure the mixture gets on both sides, close the wipe box, and shake it a bit.

5. Wait 10 minutes for the liquid to be completely absorbed before using.

Cloth Diaper Cheat-Sheet

If you decide to go the cloth and DIY laundering route, be prepared to spent lots of quality time with your washing machine. Here are some simple tips for sparkling diapers:

• Prewash diapers with laundry soap in cold water on the presoak cycle to remove soiling without setting stains. Then wash a second time in hot water with a cold-water rinse.

• Fragrance-free soap is recommended for laundering baby items; that means castile is a good bet. See page 4 for a refresher on its uses.

• Add ½ cup of baking soda to the wash to whiten and soften diapers. (Added bonus: When you add baking soda, you can use less soap.)

• You can use small amounts of bleach occasionally to sanitize and whiten, but regular use will weaken the fabric.

• Fabric softener will reduce the diapers' absorbency, so use it only occasionally.

• An alternative to fabric softener is white vinegar; use ½ cup in the rinse cycle. Wash diaper covers separately, as vinegar will reduce their waterproofing. Always follow the instructions on the care label for diaper covers.

• Put the diapers in the dryer on the high heat setting for 60 minutes or until they're completely dry. Machine drying helps sterilize the diapers. Or dry diapers in direct sunlight, which also sterilizes them.

• Once you're done, run an empty wash cycle with bleach or vinegar to disinfect your washing machine before you launder the next load.

DIAPER CHEAT-SHEET BY DONNA SMALLIN; DIY WIPES BY ABBY PECORIELLO

Baby's Personal Chef

In the beginning, feeding your child is relatively easy. Baby gets almost all of his nutrients from breast milk or formula. A mere four to six months later, he's ready for more. But how does a parent determine what and how much a baby wants or needs to eat? In desperation, most parents reach for the familiar jars of prepared baby foods from the supermarket; others spend hours in the kitchen, slavishly trying to prepare perfectly balanced meals made especially for baby. Relax. You don't need to go to such extremes.

From the day your child begins to eat solid foods, his meals can be much the same as yours. If your own diet is not what it could or should be, this is the perfect time to lay down a new set of rules for everyone in the household. When you prepare vegetables for yourself, set aside a few spoonfuls to puree for baby. Save some leftover breakfast oatmeal to warm up for a snack later in the day. With almost no extra work on your part, your child will have the advantages gained from eating freshly prepared foods. And you won't have to fork over gigantic sums of money for mountains of teeny jars.

THRIFTONOMICS

Mashed-up Carrots, Grocery v. DIY

If you're having trouble seeing the upside to mashing veggies, take a look at the numbers. For brevity's sake, let's say your baby eats two servings of pureed vegetables per day. For brevity's sake again, let's imagine baby eats only one vegetable: carrots. A 4-ounce jar of pureed organic carrots costs $0.99. The average price of a one-pound bunch of organic carrots is $1.54, which yields four servings of mashed carrots at a per-serving price of $0.39. Applied over the course of six months, the homemade to store-bought comparison yields a savings of $219.

Even if you're not ready to turn your kitchen into a baby-food factory, you can save money by making baby food as an extension of your own meal preparation. You'll be saving a little here, a little there, and while it may not be revolutionary, think of the packaging you're not using. And mash away.

Store-bought	Homemade
$0.99/jar	$0.39/serving
$1.98/day	$0.78/day
$361.35/half-year	$142.35/half-year
SAVINGS = $219	

BABY FOOD TIPS BY RENA COYLE; THRIFTONOMICS BOX BY JESSICA ASHER; CLOTHING TIPS BY KELLY BARE

Baby Food Cheat-Sheet

Cooking for an infant is different than cooking for adults. Baby palates are finicky and undeveloped, and there are some things they can't tolerate. For best success, keep the following points in mind:

- Until your baby is accustomed to eating, his or her food must be strained and almost liquid.
- Begin introducing new foods mixed with the familiar taste of formula or breast milk.
- When preparing a dish for the entire family, set aside the baby's portion before seasoning.
- Introduce one new food at a time and check for allergic reactions.
- Freeze any just-cooked-and-pureed foods as soon as possible. Whether you freeze in cubes or sealed jars, mark the packages with contents and dates.
- Adapt favorite recipes for baby by exchanging sugar with fruit juice concentrate or natural sweeteners. Hold off on the salt.
- Your baby's first foods must be softened by cooking. Later, soft fruits and vegetables, such as pears, peaches, and cucumbers, can be pureed raw. A child of eight or nine months can eat many foods uncooked and with minimal pureeing.

Baby's Personal Stylist

Parents-to-be will need a basic supply of onesies, bibs, and tiny socks before baby comes. But again, you won't know how big your baby is going to be upon arrival or how fast she will grow, so be careful not to overdo it. Many newborns fit into "newborn" sizes for only a week or two, if even that long. Err up in size rather than down, and remember that it's just fine if your baby's clothes are a bit roomy. (The exception is sleepwear, which should be snug-fitting and flame-retardant.) More tips:

- Especially if babies in your family run tall, outfits and sleepers without feet will last longer. Pants and skirts should have elastic or adjustable waists.
- Overalls work well for babies of all sizes: Their length is adjustable and their girth is accommodating of chubbier babies.
- Babies don't need any shoes until they begin to walk on potentially dangerous surfaces; even then they should wear only soft-soled shoes. Rigid soles may impede healthy foot growth and development.

Raising Thrifty Kids

"Thrift . . . needs to be urged in order to counteract abundant opportunities from the lollipop cart to the wiles of the securities salesmen." (*Journal of the National Education Association of the United States,* 1922)

As part of a post–World War I, nationwide movement toward thrift, schools across the United States heeded the call for thrift education. The curricula covered basic economics, and good citizenship—which one attained through careful spending and saving. Parent-teacher groups joined in, even helping to create school savings banks complete with young tellers and "officers."

Formal programs in thrift education, along with those school savings banks, have by and large gone the way of sewing classes and the slide rule—and the "abundant opportunities" have extended far beyond the lollipop carts of the 1920s. Today's children are exposed to upwards of 3,000 marketing messages a day. More than any previous generation, they've been inculcated with the value of *spending.* It's time to take thrift education home.

Laying the Groundwork | by Jane Hammerslough

Before parents set up their thrifty homeschooling programs, they should examine their own assumptions. From long-ago feelings of deprivation or plenitude to current desires to have your children live "better," few issues are as emotionally complex as those surrounding money.

Ask yourself what feelings about spending, saving, and budgeting *you* are bringing to the table. How do your own background and childhood experiences influence your attitudes and behavior? And what do you wish to repeat—or change—when imparting values to your own children? What mistakes have you made? What have you done correctly? How do your approaches to saving and spending compare with those of your spouse? Before broaching the issue with children, take some time to consider how you feel, share ideas with your spouse, and think of ways you might lead by example.

One way to go about things is to aim for "transparency" in matters of family finance. A business that encourages participation by sharing information with employees might serve as a model. While specific numbers might confuse young children, they can certainly be introduced to the concepts of comparing and making choices. It is unnecessary to share every detail of one's stock portfolio or tax return, but it is important to explain some key concepts: fixed expenses, variable expenses, and discretionary income, though you don't have to use those terms. When children enter preschool, it is time to discuss the differences between needs and wants. Older, school-age children and teens can benefit from hearing about budget specifics, such as the cost of the monthly gas or electric bill. (If a child knows the difference that, say, closing windows or wearing a sweater can make in heating bills, he may actually comply!) Elicit ideas on budget-trimming as a family so kids feel they're part of the decision-making process. Draw children into discussions about choices in saving, investing, and charitable giving.

Kids don't instinctually grasp the concept of delayed gratification, so make it a point to look for applicable teaching moments: Skip the baseball cap now and you may be able to get those sneakers you want later; spend the last of your allowance on those comic books and you may regret it when something comes up at the end of the week. While watching movies and television, talk about characters' decisions to spend or save—or question the level of reality involved. Any shopping trip is rife with opportunities to talk about money and budgeting, from the concept of saving for a toy you really want to the notion that designer brands are intrinsically desirable. Pose specific questions about specific products—what does your teen expect to get out of that expensive pair of jeans?

Outside the realm of shopping, make thrift fun by coming up with creative ways to "make do," whether that's planning a road trip, collaborating on holiday greeting cards, or cooking together. It'll save you money and simultaneously promote problem-solving. Fixing a toy or shining an old pair of shoes helps kids develop basic skills, along with resourcefulness, ingenuity, and a sense of accomplishment.

MY THRIFT

The Important Stuff

My sister and I shared a sturdy little safe where we saved money from our paper route. We didn't have much, but we were motivated to save because our mother drilled into us that we should save for our futures, for college. We were always breaking into that safe for little things, but we did learn to save for the important stuff.

—MariCecile Streitburger, 43

Using Allowances for Good | by Cynthia Copeland

Should you give your kids an allowance? Yes, if you use it as a teaching tool. Give your child a consistent "income" and the right context, and he can learn to budget, spend wisely, prioritize, and distinguish between needs and wants. Having (or not having) money in the bank—or shoebox or pocket—quickly teaches a child that there is a limit to what he can buy. With practice, he can also learn how to save for something expensive, using patience and discipline to reach his goal.

A structured allowance plan does entail some work for parents: It takes commitment and may become a new source of friction between you and your child as the lessons take hold. But the easier option—doling out cash on a by-request basis—results in children knowing mainly how to beg and plead, rather than spend.

If you feel you can't afford to pay out an allowance, know that the goal is not to spend extra money on your offspring. What goes into your child's pocket should essentially be what you are already spending on movie tickets, comic books, or small treats. The difference is, he gets to make the decisions (within reason) about how to allocate the money. In fact, most parents realize a savings: Without an allowance system, it's easy to lose track of how much money is dispensed day to day.

Cash for Chores?

Despite the fact that about two-thirds of parents pay their children for chores, experts don't recommend the practice.

Ode to the Piggy Bank

Saving is one of the best ways to learn the value of a dollar. And what's cuter than a pink, chubby piggy bank for stashing those pennies and dimes? According to one theory, the origin of piggy banks has much to do with thrift. The image may be an allusion to the need for foresight and planning: The farmer spends money on feed to fatten his pig, then recoups the cost when the pig is sold for slaughter. Another explanation: In the fifteenth century, household jars made from a type of clay—called "pygg" in Middle English—were used to store money. By the 1700s, the shape (and spelling) had evolved to "pig."

No matter what shape the bank— pig, elephant, log cabin, or faux ATM—its owner will doubtless grow into an adult with memories of saving up for a very special purchase.

While an allowance teaches financial management, chores teach kids about their responsibilities within the family. There's a certain amount of work everyone must do *for free* as a member of Team Family—and every child needs to learn that lesson in order to grow into a functional and self-sufficient adult. Linking an allowance to chores will make dishwashing and room-cleaning seem like choices: If a child doesn't need money this week, she may decide not to do her chores. Or if she finds another source of income, like mowing lawns or babysitting, she may opt out of household duties.

Expert recommendations aside, some parents won't feel comfortable giving a no-strings-attached allowance. If you do decide that the allowance will be dependent on chores, you can choose to pay per task, or you can spell out the weekly requirement in detail. Be sure to establish a clear understanding of consequences for unfinished chores: Will the payment be reduced? Will it be eliminated that week? How many reminders are given before the consequence is enforced? No matter what you choose, be consistent with your plan and make your expectations clear. For more on making chores happen (and minimizing the whining), see box, page 194.

As a hybrid solution, you can keep a list of special household jobs that kids can do for extra money: painting, washing windows, or helping with a major spring cleaning of the house or garage. The lesson there is about applying oneself: When saving for something special, hard work makes the goal a reality sooner.

When to Start

When children are old enough to notice the price tags on the items they want, it's time to consider an allowance. Some financial experts say that as soon as a child is old enough to ask for something in a store, he is old enough to learn fiscal responsibility; but that can be as early as age three or four. When you feel that your little one is capable of making choices and

Chore Cheat-Sheet

Studies show that fifty years ago, nearly all children helped maintain the house—free of charge! Beyond teaching your child important life skills like time management and cooperation, assigned chores can help strengthen self-esteem. Some things to keep in mind:

- Too many chores will overwhelm young children. At a family meeting, involve the entire family in choosing both the chores and the appropriate consequences for doing, or not doing, them.

- Help your children keep track of chores with visual aids that use words, pictures, or stickers to record tasks completed.

- Be honest with your child, and admit that not everything we have to do is always fun. Emphasize how happy and proud you feel after completing a difficult task.

- Don't forget to teach the child how to do the chore properly. Young children will not automatically know. Break down the chore into manageable steps.

- Focus on giving a few simple directions at a time. Young children have trouble remembering more than three steps at once.

- Give them the right tools. Kids get a kick out of using their very own kid-size equipment whenever possible.

- Consider your child's size and stage of development when organizing your household, and make things easily accessible for him.

- Set goals and deadlines.

- Take the time to praise a job well done. Make your praise specific, focusing on exactly what the child did well, to help build his internal motivation to repeat those steps.

- Many children cooperate better when everyone is working together at the same time—they find working as a group easier and more fun.

- Appreciate how powerful routine can be; establish a weekly "clean-up" time. Once the routine is in place, it takes the place of constant reminders (aka nagging!).

- Be consistent; when you decide on a chore, let your child know that she is expected to do it every time. Inconsistency diminishes the importance of the chore in the child's mind.

- Respect your child's ability by resisting the temptation to "do it for him." This may take a lot of patience, but the result—a more confident, capable child—is well worth it!

- Acknowledge and praise your child's effort rather than criticizing the quality of his work. Strive for completion, not perfection.

CHORE CHEAT-SHEET BY GAIL REICHLIN AND CAROLINE WINKLER

understanding the idea of limited resources, then he is ready. The advantage of starting early is that younger children may be more receptive and responsive, whereas middle-schoolers spend less time with parents and are not as likely to listen to their financial advice.

How Much, How Often?

In deciding how often to dole out the cash and how much to give, the factors to consider include: your child's age, your family values and budget, what the allowance is expected to cover, and patterns in the community (also known as "what my best friend gets").

Surveys suggest that most parents pay a weekly allowance of between 50 cents and a dollar for every year of the child's age, meaning that a 10-year-old would be given between $5 and $10 a week. A Nickelodeon/ Yankelovich Youth Monitor survey found that six- to eight-year-olds receive

The Rules for Parents

An allowance will help instill financial responsibility in children, but the parent is the most important piece of the puzzle. If talking about money makes you uncomfortable, you're going to have to work through those feelings—your advice and involvement are essential. The key point to cover at the outset is the value of designating some money for spending, some for savings, and some for sharing, as in a charity or religious donation. But you'll need to engage in an ongoing dialogue to help your child learn to manage her money.

There's a fine line between teaching and micromanaging. Once you give an allowance, let your child handle the money, even if you know that the $20 toy won't last twenty minutes before it breaks. Mistakes—losing money, lending money, overspending—will happen, but mistakes are opportunities for learning.

When a problem does arise, it's time to get involved, to explain the problem and find a solution. But after presenting some options and offering reassurance, bow out. If you replace lost money or offer additional money when the allowance is gone, valuable lessons are lost. Let the consequences do the teaching.

One rule should be set in stone: Don't use allowance to try to modify a child's behavior. Offering extra money for good behavior or top grades (or withholding money because of bad behavior) confuses the matter. If a child's behavior necessitates action, revoke privileges such as television or social activities. For a job well done, offer praise, a hug, or something that is special within your family.

about $5 a week, nine- to eleven-year-olds pocket around $7, and twelve- to seventeen-year-olds are given about $17 every week. If that sounds like a lot of money, consider the fact that American teens spend between $150 and $160 billion a year on purchases, with just over a third of that coming from allowances.

Whatever you decide to pay, don't be surprised when the subject of a raise comes up. Have a system in place: You can offer to review the amount on every birthday or at the start of a new school year.

As for distribution, a weekly allowance is standard, but some parents switch to monthly pay during the teen years. You might decide to give your child his allowance on the day that you get paid. Set a good example by paying on time.

For teens, you might also offer a special, twice-yearly clothing allowance. But if you strike that deal, don't supplement it if they spend so much on brand-name shoes that they don't have enough for new T-shirts. That's the tough but necessary lesson. (And how tough is it really?)

MY THRIFT

Pay You for Living Here?

When I was a teenager I had a job that earned $1.98 for 12 hours of work. I gave my mother all my money so she could buy food with it.

At home, all the kids pitched in with the chores. We took pride in our roles around the house. All the kids knew their parents needed their help, and we felt good because we were needed.

As for the modern notion of an allowance, well, my mother wouldn't have known what an allowance was. She would have looked at me like I was crazy! She would have said: "You mean you want me to pay you for living here?"

—Agnes Watt, born 1928

The Credit Card Dilemma

For many parents, talking to children about credit is a bit like talking to them about sex: uncomfortable to say the least. But it's not a discussion you can put off. Lenders are marketing credit cards to younger and younger children in an effort to instill brand loyalty at an early age. The board game Life now allows players to use pretend Visa cards. "Cool Shoppin' Barbie" makes her purchases with MasterCard and AmEx. If parents don't teach children about credit, the marketers will.

You may not want your children to have credit cards at all, but eventually these young spenders will get their hands on plastic—and they need to understand what owning a credit card entails. A good time to broach the

Allowance Cheat-Sheet

When talking about money, be conscious of your delivery. Saving won't sound like an appealing concept if you make it too abstract; try presenting it as postponed or delayed spending. In addition, consider some other allowance advice:

- Have your tiny titan keep a journal. She can create a spending plan that includes a list of needs versus wants. Your child should also have a detailed list of everything she is responsible for purchasing to avoid confusion and misunderstandings.

- Many banks offer children's savings accounts. Deposits can be as small as a dollar or two at a time with no minimum necessary and no fees. The official bankbook, in which the child can track his or her savings, is a rewarding part of the learning process.

- Although parents should refrain from telling a child what to buy, house rules should apply to allowance purchases. In other words, if your teen is not permitted to buy M-rated video games, an allowance doesn't change that rule.

- Your teen might benefit from learning to use a prepaid debit card that he can track online. You can deposit his allowance each week onto a special card, such as MasterCard's "Allow Card." Your child will be able to withdraw money from an ATM and buy items online.

topic is when credit card offers are mailed to the minors in the house. The offers are so tempting and seem so . . . adult—as are the consequences of the cards' misuse. To stave off disaster, use your own credit card statement to explain minimum payments, interest rates, card fees, and what happens when you exceed a credit limit or pay late. Talk about credit scores and how they impact a person's ability to get a loan for a car or a house. Together, do the math and figure out how much a charged item ultimately costs if only the minimum amount is paid off each month. (For a guideline, see page 349.)

Should you get a credit card for your preteen or teenager? If your child is mature enough (and if you have the energy to exercise appropriate supervision), the use of a card can teach valuable life lessons.

To assess whether your child is ready, first see how she does managing a checking account. Help your child open one and teach her how to deposit and withdraw money, and balance the account. Give her other financial responsibilities too—keeping track of her cell phone minutes and texts and paying that bill each month. Then, even if she handles these tasks well, you might want to start by giving her a prepaid credit card (available in stores like Wal-Mart) and seeing whether she blows through the money in a week or carefully plans her spending and keeps track of the account balance. When your teen has demonstrated that she can practice solid money management skills, consider getting her a credit card with a small line of credit. The card should be used for predetermined situations, such as emergencies or when it's problematic to use cash or a check.

When the bills come, sit down with your teen to go over the statement together. Kids must understand that it's not wise to charge more than they can repay in full at the end of the month. And as always, leading by positive example is the best way to teach: If you use your plastic sparingly and pay off your balance in a timely fashion, you are demonstrating the proper way to use credit.

Possible Bumps in the Road

What does an allowance pay for, and what still falls under the parent's purview? To determine what it should cover, add up what you currently give your kids to pay for the things they request. Listen to their needs. Then, together, come up with a list of what items they will be expected to buy out of their allowance. Be specific: When you say movies, does that include rentals? Does "music" mean iTunes downloads as well as CDs? How about birthday gifts for friends? What about the fees for events like that school-sponsored whitewater-rafting trip? The more detailed the list, the less room for misunderstanding.

The other question that's likely to come up concerns advances. Letting kids borrow against an allowance is not an easy decision: You don't want to encourage them to spend beyond their means, and yet we've all been faced with the occasional necessary and unexpected expense. When it comes up, make it part of the broader financial education. Write out and sign an IOU agreement with a date the money is to be paid back; some parents may even want to add a small interest payment.

Don't be discouraged by a few false starts; you may have to try a few different arrangements before you find the one that works best for your family. Stay flexible and be willing to restart the process after you've assessed the shortcomings of the previous plan. Your efforts will pay off when your kids leave home with a solid financial education.

Dealing with the "Gimmes"

"I need it!" "All the other kids have one!" "Why not?" And the clincher: "But you have one!" Sound familiar? Every parent knows that when a kid wants something, he'll morph into a master negotiator. Your debating skills may be bolstered by a superior grasp of logic, but your child has unlimited time, energy, and determination on his side. The answer may seem simple (just say no), but the reality is more complex. If your kids have grown up in a culture of plenty, the shift to thrift may be a shock; expect to wage an ongoing battle for some time. The good news is that if you model good old-fashioned virtues ("Waste not, want not"), you can make an impression on your children—no matter their age. Of course, virtue doesn't win arguments, so keep the following tips in mind:

- Emphasize how hard you work to earn your money, and let your child know you must make decisions about how to spend it. Tell your child that the amount of money you have is limited, and that even grown-ups can't get everything they want.
- Make a wish list for each member of your family and display it. Point out that in your family, "needs"—like food and warm clothes—will be taken care of quickly, but "wants"—like a new car, vacations, and toys—may take some time.
- Encourage your child to explore making rather than buying.
- Consider how you celebrate your child's birthday. Think about paring down birthdays to just the family and a few friends. Children who are routinely treated to clowns, pony rides, and magicians may take elaborate celebrations for granted.

- Instead of springing for the latest toy, consider a special family outing to celebrate a birthday.
- Involve your child in thanking people for their thoughtfulness and gifts. When sending thank-you cards, have your child dictate a message, color a simple picture, or put the stamps on the envelope.
- Let your child know that it's polite to express appreciation for presents, even if they aren't exactly what she had in mind.
- Help your child understand that different families have different amounts of money and set different priorities. It's helpful for children to learn early on that comparing themselves to "the Joneses" is not worthwhile.
- Make a conscious effort to model delayed gratification.
- Have patience—developing an appreciative attitude is a process that takes time.

GIMMES BY GAIL REICHLIN AND CAROLINE WINKLER

The Toll on Your Wallet

There's no getting around it: Children are expensive. Many of the costs—child care, clothes, education, and more—are inevitable. But what about cell phones, credit cards, and the jeans of the week? In a perfect world, your child would want only what is useful. Thrift Edens notwithstanding, there *are* ways to cut costs on all the big-ticket items. First, some parents will have to get over associations between spending and love. When it comes to children, you certainly can't buy love—or good behavior, or future happiness, or an easy adolescence. . . . You get the picture.

The Child Care Issue

As working families know, it's a challenge to reduce the costs of child care without sacrificing quality. Ranked as the average family's second highest expense, child care consumes about 9 percent of a family's monthly income (and the cost is rising at double the rate of inflation). But parents have come up with all sorts of creative resolutions to the day-care dilemma, from bartering with babysitters to "share care."

Corporate benefits. When evaluating day care options, start with what your employer has to offer. Some companies offer on-site facilities for a minimal cost. Smaller companies might team up to support a consortium child care center (a facility close to several workplaces) or work out discount plans with area day-care providers. Others offer child care tuition to allow employees to pay for home day care.

Nearly all employers offer a child-care flexible spending account (FSA): the plan devised by the Internal Revenue Service allows parents to set aside up to $5,000 annually from their paychecks to use tax-free for expenses related to day care. (Also remember to take advantage of the Child and Dependent Care Credit on your income taxes—$3,000 for one child and $6,000 for two in 2008—though how much you can claim is affected by how much money you deposit into your FSA.)

If none of these programs are available or helpful to you, see if your supervisor is willing to consider job sharing, flextime, or telecommuting, and have your spouse do the same. The cost of child care can be reduced

CHILD CARE OPTIONS BY CYNTHIA COPELAND

significantly by cutting back on the number of hours a week that outside coverage is needed. Although you will give up some couple time, it can work as a short-term arrangement when children are very young.

Public school and university offerings. When it comes to child care bargains, don't overlook the education system. Some public high schools and universities have preschool programs that train students in child care. The cost is minimal and the student-to-toddler ratio is often one-to-one.

College-age caregivers. Do you live near a college or university? Education majors make terrific caregivers; class schedules often leave them with entire days free (and clearly they are interested in kids). You may even find someone who's willing to be a live-in nanny in exchange for room, board, and a small stipend.

Nanny sharing. Budget-conscious families unwilling to sacrifice home-based care for their children often opt to share nannies—sometimes called "share care." Sharing might mean alternating days or weeks with another family, or it could mean having one nanny watch the children of two families simultaneously. Regional parenting websites connect interested families, and local agencies match families and manage the fees and legal issues.

Babysitting co-ops. You've probably discovered that a little friendly exchange among peers is a great way to find free, trustworthy caregivers—other parents. A babysitting co-op or exchange network operates in much the same way as informal swapping, with greater flexibility and more options. Co-op members earn points or coupons every time they babysit for another family's children, and they can spend the points at their convenience. Most co-ops are for part-time care, but some are full-time systems, involving more complex rules and regulations and perhaps even a board of directors to handle the issues that can arise.

Bartering. As the practice of bartering grows more common, there's no reason to think it can't extend to child care. What would you be willing to trade? Use of your second car on the weekends? Even traditional day care centers might be open to the idea of an exchange. Do you have items to donate to the center? Can you offer up a few Saturdays to help build a new playground?

Chat with other parents in your community for inspiration and ideas, or for more information about local resources, check out the nonprofit website www.childcareaware.org.

Save on School Lunches

When it comes to saving money, packing a school lunch would seem to be a no-brainer. Brown bagging *has* to be cheaper, right? Not necessarily. With all the high-priced, overpackaged, snackable, and squirtable kid-targeted lunch foods on the market, the tab can quickly rise. Fear not. Here are some kid-tested tricks for packing economical school lunches that will be the envy of the cafeteria.

Cheap Lunch 101

- Create a budget target, and do the math. First, determine what you think is a reasonable per-day amount to spend on a school lunch. Use the shelf labels in the supermarket to help you compute the per-unit cost of prepackaged foods and snacks. Figure out how much meat, cheese, fruit, bread, and peanut butter you'll use in a given week, then divide the total by five to see what each day's lunch costs. You may be surprised at what a deal the cafeteria lunch turns out to be!

- Invest in an insulated thermos. Single-serving thermos containers are perfect for keeping soup and leftovers hot and yogurt, Jell-O, and fruit salad cold.

- Ask for feedback about what your kids are and aren't eating in lunches packed from home. (Don't nag, or you won't get the truth!) There's no reason to send apples at 50 to 60 cents each if they're just getting thrown in the trash.

- It's a fact that kids love small cups and tubes of foods like yogurt and applesauce, but these cute little packages are the most expensive way to buy food. Fortunately, small, reusable plastic snack cups are readily available, and if you scoop the applesauce from a large jar into your own snack cup, the savings are huge. Same goes for fruit such as peaches, pineapple, and raisins.

- Look for reusable drink cups that don't leak and are sold with a built-in straw. You can decant juice from a large bottle into the cute cup for an individual serving that costs just pennies.

- If you need to send plastic spoons and forks to school, buy heavy-duty utensils and ask your kids not to throw them away. Heavy plastic utensils go through the dishwasher without peril and can then be reused. (You could send stainless steel, but common sense tells you a spoon will get lost every now and then.)

LUNCH TIPS BY BEVERLY MILLS AND ALICIA ROSS; RECIPES BY KATHLEEN CANNATA HANNA

Having It Your Way at the Brown-Bag Café

Children and teens aren't the only ones who should bring a packed lunch—adults save money that way, too. (See page 130 for a breakdown of how much.) But who has time to pack individual lunches tailored to each family member's taste preferences? In this build-a-lunch model, he who hates olives can simply leave them out.

Make-Your-Own Turkey Wrap

The ingredients below make for a great combination, but there are no limits on what can be rolled up inside a tortilla, and wraps are supremely portable, to boot. Let each lunch-eater select his own fillings, and everyone's happy.

Makes 4 wraps

4 (10-inch) flour tortillas
¼ cup mayonnaise
2 teaspoons horseradish
12 ounces smoked turkey, thinly sliced
4 large romaine lettuce leaves, washed and dried

1. Combine the mayonnaise and horseradish in a small bowl.

2. Spread a thin layer of the mayonnaise mixture on each tortilla and divide the turkey and lettuce evenly among the tortillas. Roll the tortilla tightly around the filling and wrap in foil or plastic wrap.

3. Serve immediately, refrigerate, or pack in a cooler until ready to eat.

Make-Your-Own Pasta Salad

This pasta-salad recipe functions like a deli counter, a blank slate that will please the vegetarian and salami-lover alike. Just prepare the pasta, present the ingredient options, and let everyone go to town.

Serves 4 to 6

Salt
1 pound short pasta, such as corkscrews or farfalle
Italian, Caesar, or Greek salad dressing

1. Bring salted water to a boil for the pasta.

2. Meanwhile, choose desired ingredients and toss gently in individual-size to-go containers.

3. Cook the pasta in the boiling water until al dente. Drain and rinse briefly under cool water; drain well. Add to the individual containers with chosen ingredients; drizzle with enough dressing to coat everything well.

4. Serve warm or chilled.

POSSIBLE TOPPINGS

Marinated artichoke hearts, drained and quartered
Roasted red peppers, drained and sliced
Thinly sliced salami
Thinly sliced deli ham
Canned tuna in vegetable oil, drained and flaked
Thinly sliced red onion
Chopped tomato
Broccoli florets
Pitted green or black olives
Cubed provolone cheese
Grated Parmesan cheese

The Closet Jungle

Between growth spurts and wear and tear, kids cycle through their clothes faster than you can say, "But we just got you that!" That's why the magic words when it comes to children's clothes are *secondhand, off-season,* and *mend, mend, mend.*

Every parent faces the same issue, which happily means that there is always a steady stream of supply and demand: parents trying to clear space in their closets and parents looking for reasonably priced or free hand-me-downs. Take advantage of your circle of friends and family, and check classified ads or auction websites for gently worn stuff.

If you have the space, keep your older children's clothes for younger siblings. To alleviate the childhood condition known as cast-off angst, make a game out of it: When will younger sister be big enough to fit into big sister's clothes? Buy new clothes for younger siblings and secondhand for older children from time to time in order to balance the equation.

When shopping for new children's clothes, abandon the notions of quality and longevity you'd apply in shopping for yourself; since you're not looking for items that will last forever, after a certain point it doesn't really pay to seek out quality. If you establish a strong enough value system at home, your kids *will* survive the pain of not having had the just-so pair of jeans or the of-the-moment ironic T-shirt. Be on the lookout for bargains and off-brand merchandise. If you see something drastically reduced in a size that's too big, go ahead and buy it—it will fit in no time. A couple of times a year, supplement the basics with an item that's "on trend" to ensure that your kid isn't kicked off the island. (Let's face it, children can be brutal.)

Of course, from time to time you'll want or need or give in to the pressure to spring for clothing items that aren't thrifty in the least. As in every other area, occasional lapses are to be expected—and enjoyed. The point of saving, after all, is to be ready for that rainy day (or that fancy birthday party, prom, or—gasp!—first date).

Fancy Footwear

Clothing can be handed down and reused, but shoes are tough to repurpose; most parents prefer to buy them new to ensure proper support and for hygienic reasons. This expense will continue to come up at every age, every year. Active children and teens wear out sneakers quickly, but children of any age grow out of shoes faster than you can believe. And tastes change quickly: There's always a cooler pair to be had. (On that score, it's best to be a little bit firm and replace as needed—not necessarily as wanted.) It may be tempting to buy cheap athletic shoes, but they wear out fast and may cause problems in the joints or feet. Footwear for special occasions or extracurricular activities (from sports to ballet) may be handed down depending on use: If your son quit football after three practices, pass on those cleats.

Nine Money-Saving Clothing Strategies

1. If a child turns crabby about wearing hand-me-downs from a bossy older sibling, try getting clothes from a revered older (and not quite as familiar) cousin instead.

2. Have separate clothes for school and play. Save the name brands for school and have kids change into play clothes when they come home.

3. Wait for sales—but know your stores. Don't wait so long that all the winter coats are gone!

4. Find thrift stores near tony communities, and learn when the new merchandise is put out.

5. Volunteer at a community rummage sale. You'll probably get first pick.

6. If you have both boys and girls, buy gender-neutral clothes when possible.

7. Save pricey, name-brand merchandise for birthdays and holidays.

8. Children's tastes in cartoon characters change quickly. If you treat them to a novelty T-shirt, spend as little as possible on it.

9. All kids leave things behind, so know that you will have to replace items due to loss. Console yourself with the knowledge that you didn't overspend in the first place.

MY THRIFT

I Set It All Aside

I used to hoard money in a beautiful white ceramic piggy bank my mother had given me. I was obsessive about saving. Between the ages of nine and fourteen, I never touched that piggy bank: I sold my lunch tickets, returned gifts, took my tiny allowance of $5 a week, and set it all aside. Around age fifteen, my vintage clothing habit kicked in and I did start to spend what I had saved. But even then I was frugal. I hated the feeling of not having money. My parents had grown up poor and were always stressing financial independence. I'm still a huge saver, and I love balancing the books for my art gallery.

—Risa Needleman, 27

The Teen Years

If you thought parenting a newborn was demanding, wait till the marketing messages start to take hold of your teenager. Teens are like money pits into which you will be asked to deposit all your income—disposable and otherwise. How you choose to handle this stage depends on your style of parenting, but be prepared for some money-related battling. Three particular areas to be aware of:

- Credit cards. They can be used for teaching and for emergencies (see page 196), but don't be surprised if the charges don't exactly correspond to life-threatening situations. Keep a close eye on the statements and act swiftly when spending gets out of hand.

- Cell phones and Internet usage. Tweens and teens have a lot to talk about—on the phone and via text messages and e-mails. They also have an insatiable desire for music. With so many devices that allow fast access to both friends and new tunes, parents must watch how those charges are racking up. Choosing the right phone and texting plan will help, as will vigilance. The same goes for Internet shopping: Those small charges, a buck here and a buck there, will add up quickly. Watchfulness is key, as is a sense of shared responsibility.

- Vehicles and gas. Finally your little angel will be able to drive herself to band practice. But what happens when she leaves with a half tank of gas and returns with the car on empty? Expect this to be an area of negotiation (not to mention constant worry). Set out clear rules and expectations. If an extra car is not in your budget, introduce your teen to the idea of saving for one well before her sixteenth birthday. Money saved from an after-school job or extra chores can go into a special account. Keep the goal in sight by pricing cars together and establishing the connection between wages and savings: How many hours in the pizza shop does it take to buy a new car versus a used car? How much will insurance cost and will more work hours be needed? And what about the cost of gas?

The College Prep Conundrum

Financing your child's college education (or part of it) is likely to be one of the biggest expenses you'll face as a parent, but the buck certainly doesn't stop there. Anxious parenting and increased competition have conspired to extend the college application process, and its concomitant costs, into a years-long endeavor that begins as early as preschool.

How many hours of music class will guarantee that your baby grows to love Mozart? What sports will help Junior get into the best college? What volunteer work will make her look compassionate enough? The anxiety and efforts are understandable; especially in challenging job markets, parents feel compelled to do anything they can to protect their children's futures. But if every activity is geared toward the holy grail of college admission, the value of the activities themselves is lost. And from an economic standpoint, you may wind up spending a lot of money on expensive classes that don't stick.

There is another way, and (surprise!) it involves a do-it-yourself mentality. Before you outsource your children's activities to experts, do what you can to create a stimulating environment at home. Watch for signs of interest, or lack thereof, and let natural inclinations blossom.

Make the arts a regular part of your life. After all, if you rarely listen to classical music yourself, why would you expect your child to care about it? Go to concerts as a family. At home, make listening active: Sit quietly together or make up dances to up-tempo pieces. If your child can pluck out songs on the piano, she may have a natural talent. If dancing takes over, follow that path. Same goes for the visual arts: Start by encouraging arts and crafts and visiting local museums.

Get your children involved in sports or in physical activity of some kind—for that "well-rounded" bit, sure, but also for their health. Play catch in the backyard, explore the options at your local community center, join some teams. (And look into getting gently used equipment.)

Volunteer with your children, and start early. Children learn by example. If you make it a family affair, the notion will become practice— and you won't have to drag your grumpy teen through the motions in a last-minute college-app frenzy.

Ask a College Counselor

Bill McClintick, President, National Association for College Admission Counseling

Q When it comes to the cost of college, what's a thrifty parent to do?

A If you can afford to foot the bill for college, you will give your children a great gift: They'll enter adulthood debt-free. They'll get to keep their earnings, and—best-case scenario—they can start saving early. If you can share the responsibility of college costs, look at it this way: You will help your children understand the value of their education, and they may be less likely to waste the opportunity if a portion of the cost is coming out of their own pocket. Starting out with a $20,000 debt is not an insurmountable setback, given that they have 10 years to pay it back.

Why not let the kids pay? Some parents say, "I paid my way through school. You can, too." Well, it was different when tuition was, say, $2,000 or $3,000 for a state school. What eighteen-year-old is going to make $15,000 a year delivering pizza as a part-time job?

How to save. Every year, make sure you are setting something aside each month to take the sting out later. It could be $50, $100, or $250. Just tuck away whatever you can. There are savings assumptions built into the financial aid formulas. Be sure you look at a variety of options before selecting a savings tool. If the stock market is tanking, maybe bonds are safer. There is some wisdom in finding a balance between 529 plans, Coverdell accounts, and bonds. (See box.)

Saving for Education

Be prepared to do some serious research when it comes to saving money for your children's college education; each method of saving has its own benefits, tax structure, and impact on the financial aid formula. The 529 plans (named after Section 529 of the Internal Revenue Code) are offered by states and come in two forms: Prepaid tuition plans that give you a guarantee on the price of future tuition at in-state public colleges; and college savings plans that do not guarantee the cost of tuition, but offer more growth potential. Coverdell accounts are educational trusts that can be used only for the designated beneficiary. Savings bonds issued by the government (EE and I bonds) offer a low-risk investment and protection against inflation. For comprehensive information on applying for financial aid and saving for college, visit finaid.org, a public-service website.

Financial aid. There are two financial aid formulas. The first is the federal methodology, and you apply for that by filling out a Free Application for Federal Student Aid (FAFSA). It will tell you what your child is eligible for and the amount you will be expected to contribute—the Expected Family Contribution (EFC)—based on what you have in the bank (your income and assets but not the value of your home). Check every few years to see if there have been shifts. As your income and assets change, so will your EFC.

Public institutions rely on the FAFSA formulation almost exclusively. Many private colleges will require an additional form, the College Scholarship Service (CSS) Profile. This is a supplement to the FAFSA, and it digs much deeper into your financial situation.

What you're saving for. Financial advisers may scare you into thinking that you have to pay for the full price of college. What you want to be saving for is the EFC figure. Let's say a college costs $40,000 a year, and your estimated family contribution is $15,000 per year. You don't need to set your savings goals at four years of $40,000 tuition. In fact, you'd be foolish to do so. If you earmark that money for education, it will be factored into your ability to pay. Save for the $15,000 figure.

Student debt. Students have ten years to repay federal student loans at very low interest rates. It's not unreasonable, and education is a good investment. The problem comes when kids start going beyond that timeline or are looking at debt burdens of $30,000 to $40,000 or more. And when they're not coming from federal programs, the loans have higher interest rates and shorter paybacks.

Consider geography. Many great schools work hard to keep their price tags down. Colleges in New England tend to price themselves higher than colleges in the South or Midwest. It's based on what the market will bear. If you're looking to save money, consider geography.

What About the SAT?

SAT prep does give test-takers an advantage, but you don't have to spring for an expensive prep course; there are low-cost and free resources out there. Some options:

- The booklet "Taking the SAT Reasoning Test," published by the College Board (the organization that administers the test) should be available at no cost from a guidance counselor.
- Take advantage of the SAT and College Board services. Students who take the SAT more than once can sign up for a service that helps them learn from their first test. It costs about $24, but it pinpoints specific areas of weakness.
- Several SAT schools offer less expensive online versions of their courses. Investigate these sites before signing your teen up for a class or tutoring service: The Princeton Review's website (www.review.com); Kaplan's website (www.kaptest.com); the website PrepMe (www.prepme.com).

Fun Games, Cool Crafts

Games help pass the time on rainy days and long car trips, but they're also an essential part of a child's learning process. They encourage sportsmanship, quick thinking, and creative problem solving. They're just plain fun. And of course, they can often be played with nothing more than a slip of paper and a pen, the contents of your kitchen cupboard, or a simple deck of cards. Let's bring back game-playing!

Recycling Bin Games

O nce virtuous, the act of recycling has become a dutiful part of refuse disposal. Up the ante and the thrift factor by turning the contents of your bin into kid-friendly props. What can you make, or do, with pieces of junk mail? Old coffee tins? Before the big green trucks come pick them up, those and other widgets could be headed for a trip through the fun-cycle.

GAME | Turn a Cardboard Box Into a Family Playhouse

Start with one giant appliance box, or cut all the end flaps off two big boxes and tape them together with wide packing or duct tape to make one giant playhouse. Draw a door and cut it on the top and right sides only, so that it is still attached along the left edge and can be opened and closed. Cut windows. Tape shoeboxes under each window to create window boxes. On a sunny day, take the project outdoors and use washable paint to decorate the exterior of the house. Draw flowers where the window boxes are attached or add plastic flowers inside the window boxes.

Hang or tape your child's drawings on the inside to add some original artwork. Add an assortment of children's books for cozy reading. A medium cardboard box turned upside down becomes a stove on which to cook the family meals. Use markers to draw the knobs and burners on the stove. Bring in a few pots, pans, and bowls so your child can stock the kitchen with utensils. Gather up a few cushions or pillows to create the living room.

And that's a playhouse. It'll take a few hours to create, with parent and child working together, but it will lead to many more hours of fun for your child and her playmates. Cost? Nada.

CARDBOARD HOUSE AND GAMES BY BOBBI CONNER

GAME | # Name Your Groceries

This is a fast-action game using alphabet cards, perfect for younger kids just learning to spell.

Ages: 6 to 10; Players: 3 to 4

MATERIALS: 23 blank index cards or once-used printer-paper, cut into squares; marker; a die

To prepare: Write one letter of the alphabet on each index card, except for the letters *V, X, Y,* and *Z.* Shuffle the cards and place the deck facedown on the floor. The children sit in a circle with the die and alphabet cards in the center.

To play: One player draws an alphabet card from the deck and rolls the die. The number he rolls determines the number of grocery store items, beginning with the letter on the alphabet card, he must think of. If, for example, the child draws the letter *B* and rolls the number 4, he must quickly call out four items found in a grocery store starting with the letter *B*—beans, bananas, bread, and beets.

This game is fun to play without keeping score, or you can give each player one point for every item called out (the higher the number rolled, the better the chance of winning the game).

GAME | # Junior Bowling

Save a bunch of small plastic soda bottles and put them to good use in this mini-bowling game. Your preschooler will be ready for the (bumper) lanes in no time. If you want, you can even buy a team bowling shirt from the local thrift store to make the game feel official. Added bonus: The bottles make a really satisfying "plop" when they go over.

Ages: 3 to 5; Players: 1

MATERIALS: Small plastic water or soda bottles with screw tops; playground ball or tennis ball (depending on child's ability and challenge level)

To prepare: Partially fill the plastic bottles with water. (The more water, the harder the bowling pins will be to topple. For the youngest children, fill the bottles a third full.) Screw the caps back on tightly. Line up the bowling pins on a hard floor surface in a *V* formation.

To play: Your child stands several feet back from the bowling pins and rolls the ball toward the pins to see how many can be knocked down.

P.S.: Putting the pins back up can be part of the fun, too.

Create a Family Game Night

One first-rate way to cut your entertainment costs and incorporate more family playtime into your schedules is to create a family night. Put it on your calendar, once a month or once a week, and try to make a commitment, even during the teen years. What you do together will change as the children move through each stage of their development, but the main ingredients remain the same—fun, play, and time together!

Charades

If you're playing with an older crowd (ages seven and up), try a traditional game of charades, with a mix of different categories. Write book or movie titles, famous people (fictional characters, musicians, actors, politicians), song titles, or quotations on slips of paper. Each player takes a slip and acts out, without speaking, whatever's written on it. Indicate the category by pantomiming opening a book (book title), cranking an old-fashioned movie camera (movie title), putting hands on your hips (person), making air quotes with your fingers (quotation), and so on.

As clues, you may hold up a number of fingers to indicate the number of words in the particular title; and then to indicate which word you're acting out. Lay a number of fingers on your forearm to indicate the number of syllables in a particular word; tug on your earlobe to indicate that the word "sounds like" another word or action; and touch a finger to the tip of your nose if one of the players has guessed correctly. Rules often vary from family to family, so make sure everyone is on the same page before starting the first round. For older children and adults, time each acting session for about three minutes. For large groups, split the group into two competing teams.

Getting the Kids on Board

You're not going to get very far if snacks aren't involved. Start with some easy foods like pizza or sandwiches eaten picnic-style on a blanket on the floor, or decide to have breakfast for dinner.

Set aside two hours for the event, and select a variety of games. (Nearly everyone will get tired after ninety minutes of playing one board game.) Create a personalized game night to suit your family's style, interests, ages, and individual personalities.

GAMES AND INSTRUCTIONS BY BOBBI CONNER

Celebrity

This family classic goes by many different names, including Who Am I?, Hollywood Minute, and, oddly, Mies van der Rohe.

Start by cutting or tearing many small slips of paper. Ask everyone in the group to write the names of famous people on the slips of paper (one name per slip), fold the pieces of paper in half, and drop them into the bowl. The names may include cartoon characters, family friends that everyone knows—even family pets are fair game!

The group is split into two teams. The team that goes first chooses one person to be the "celebrity." The celebrity draws names from the bowl one at a time and gives clues in the first person as to his new identity. For example, if the first slip of paper carries the name of George Washington, the player might say, "I was the first president of the United States" or "I chopped down a cherry tree." After a teammates guesses correctly, the player sets the slip of paper aside and draws another one. The celebrity's goal is to get his teammates to correctly guess as many identities as possible in one minute.

After one minute, the celebrity's team counts all the correct guesses, and one point is awarded for each correct guess. Then play goes to the other team. Play continues between the two teams until each person has had the role of "celebrity" an equal number of times.

Family Mobile

You probably don't have a family crest, but every family is entitled to its own mobile. It makes a lovely keepsake and puts to good use some of those excess photos you have lying around.

MATERIALS:

Scissors (for adult or supervised use only); several sheets of construction paper or poster board in assorted colors; photos of individual family members and pets; nontoxic white glue; nontoxic markers; single-hole punch; string or yarn; wire coat hanger

1. Cut out hearts from construction paper, one for each member of the family. Vary the colors and sizes, but make sure each heart is large enough to contain a photograph.

2. Cut out heart-shaped pictures of each member of the family from the photographs.

3. Glue one photo to each paper heart, then decorate or label with markers.

4. Punch single holes in the center of the hearts. Thread various lengths of yarn through the holes and tie knots.

5. Tie the hearts to a wire clothes hanger at varying lengths.

Card Game Spectacular

Teach a child to play cards and you'll open up a world of enjoyment. Card games encourage sharp math skills and careful strategy. They reward patience and sportsmanship. They can be played at any age and any social setting—from playground to dorm room to Granddaddy's porch. And best of all: A deck of cards costs about $2.

GAME | Old Maid

The object of this game is for players to get rid of all their cards by making pairs. The player left with the Queen of Spades is the Old Maid.

Players: 3 to 6

Dealer: Find the four queens in the deck of cards. Take out the Queen of Spades and put it back in the deck. Set the other three queens to one side—you won't need them for this game. Shuffle the cards.

Deal out all the cards, one at a time, face down. Some players will end up with more cards than others.

Players: Look at your cards—without letting anyone else see what you have. Any pairs (matching numbers or matching face cards) you find go back on the table, facedown. If you have three cards with the same number, one stays in your hands. If you have four cards—two pairs—all four can go down.

Player on dealer's left: You go first. Make a fan of your cards and hold them out, facedown, to the player on your left.

Next player: Pick a card from the fan. If the card makes a pair with one you already have,

put the new pair facedown on the table. If not, the card goes into your hand. Now fan out your cards for the player sitting to your left, so he or she can select a card and continue the round.

Play goes around in a circle, with players choosing cards and putting down pairs, until everyone has run out of cards. Everyone, that is, except the person holding the Old Maid—the Queen of Spades.

Everyone shouts "Old Maid!" and the game is over. The Old Maid deals the next round.

GAME | # Spit

The object of this fast-paced game is to get rid of all your cards. Aces are both low and high in this game. *A note:* There are more competitive versions of this game out there, but this slightly simplified iteration may prevent Spit-induced hysteria while still increasing the heart rate.

Players: 2

Both players select a card from the deck. Whoever has the higher card deals.

Dealer: Shuffle the cards. Deal them all out, facedown and one at a time. Each player should have a stack of 26 facedown cards.

Each Player: Lay out fifteen cards as follows:

Step 1: From left to right, line up a row that starts with one card faceup and four cards facedown.

Step 2: On top of the second card from left, place one card faceup, then three cards facedown on the next three cards in a row.

Step 3: On top of the third card from left, place one card faceup, then two cards facedown on top of the next two cards in the row.

Step 4: On top of the fourth card from the left, place one card faceup, then one card facedown on last card in the row.

Step 5: On top of the last card in the row, place one card faceup.

Stack the rest of the cards, facedown, at the far left of the row. This is your "Spit" pile.

Dealer: When both players are ready, shout "Spit!"

Each Player: Take the top card from your Spit pile and put it faceup between the two setups, next to your opponent's. As quickly as possible, play cards in sequence, up or down, from your faceup rows onto either of the Spit piles.

As you play a faceup card in a row, turn the next facedown card over; if you play a faceup card with nothing under it, move another faceup card into the empty slot and turn over the card it was covering.

When both of you are "stopped"—you can't play any more cards—shout "Spit!" again and put another card from the Spit pile into the center.

If neither of you can play any cards onto the cards just played, shout "Spit!" again and put out another card.

If your Spit pile runs out, take your pile from the center (leaving the top card), turn it over, and continue playing.

Shout "Out!" when you have played all the cards from your faceup row. You have won the round. Take the smaller of the two piles from the center.

Loser: Take the larger of the two piles from the center.

Both Players: Combine your piles and shuffle them well.

Both Players: Lay out another ten cards in the same pattern.

Play as before.

The first player to get rid of all her cards is the winner.

INSTRUCTIONS BY GAIL MACCOLL

GAME | ## Concentration

The object of this card game for those who don't fancy themselves card players is to collect as many cards as possible by making pairs.

Players: 2 to 4

Use a large flat area, such as a big table or the floor. Shuffle the cards well.

Lay the cards out, facedown, in a large rectangle. Make sure the cards do not touch each other.

Decide who will go first. The youngest, perhaps, or by alphabetical order of first names.

First player: Turn over any two cards, being careful not to disturb the nearby cards.

If the turned-over cards are the same number or letter—two sixes, for instance— pick them up and put them beside you. Then turn over two more cards.

If the cards don't match, turn them back over in the same position they were in. Your turn is finished.

Next Player: Turn over another card. If it matches the number or letter of a card you've already seen, try to remember where you saw that one and turn it over.

If you make a match, pick up the two cards and put them beside you. If not, turn the cards back over.

Players: Take turns, turning over cards and trying to make pairs. A turn lasts as long as a player can make pairs. When all the cards have been picked up, the game is over. The player with the most pairs is the winner.

Kitchen Cupboard Games

Whether they are in elementary school or high school, budding scientists get a kick out of mixing together your trusty baking soda and vinegar— here, relieved from their workaday duties and promoted to center stage. These experiments are classics that cost little and deliver maximum fun.

GAME | ## Backyard Vesuvius

This chemical reaction isn't dangerous, but it is very, very messy—which is probably why it's been a favorite with kids for decades. It goes without saying that this is an outdoor experiment, so make sure you do it on a dry (low humidity) day. If your kids are feeling really resourceful, they can add some to-scale model houses at the base of their volcano.

the family that saves together **217**

MATERIALS: 3-foot-square plywood sheet; empty 1-liter bottle (glass or plastic); modeling clay or papier-mâché (enough to form a "volcanic cone" about 13 inches across at its base; see page 221 for papier-mâché instructions); 1 tablespoon baking soda; 2 teaspoons dishwashing detergent; red or yellow food coloring; ¼ cup vinegar

1. Put the empty bottle in the middle of the plywood sheet. It will be the center of the volcano.

2. Build the volcano around this bottle, using either modeling clay or papier-mâché.

3. Work on and decorate the volcano while it is still soft, carving out gullies and ravines to conduct and collect the lava flows.

4. Make sure the finished volcano has enough time to dry (this can take up to 3 days).

5. Add the baking soda, dishwashing detergent, and a squirt of food coloring to the empty bottle.

6. Measure out the vinegar and pour it into the bottle.

7. Stand back as the forces of nature take over!

Daydreaming Is Free

Your child looks like he's swinging happily on the swing set. But he may also be dreaming up all sorts of good ideas—creating new lyrics for a song, inventing a story about a fantasy character, or wondering about shapes in the clouds overhead. All this thinking, wondering, inventing, and creating is a powerful part of play. Children need time for daydreaming in their daily routines. Here are some outdoor play activities that provide opportunities to dream, invent, and create:

• Set up a tent and have a "campout" for a few hours.
• Build a fort, hideout, or lean-to with cardboard boxes.
• Draw designs (or a maze) on the sidewalk with chalk.
• Create roadways and a village in the sandbox.
• Skip stones across a pond or a lake.
• Have a spontaneous nature scavenger hunt outside.
• Use binoculars to watch birds and squirrels in the trees.
• Write letters and words in the sand at the beach.
• Sketch or draw in a peaceful place outside.
• Invent a fantasy team of your favorite baseball players.
• Gaze at the stars from the deck or backyard.
• Invent an obstacle course or a miniature-golf course.
• Look for a four-leaf clover.

DAYDREAMING PLAY BY BOBBI CONNER

GAME | The Sandwich-Bag Bomb

Kids—and many grown-ups—may think of acids and bases as harmful chemicals that white-coated scientists keep locked away. This experiment is a simple way to show that a kitchen cupboard has these chemical "agents" in abundance. Vinegar and baking soda react dramatically and quickly, producing carbon dioxide in equal portions as a result. The carbon dioxide soon fills the bag and then, after straining at the bag's seams, pops it with a bang. With just a little outlay in time and equipment, you can get "more bang for your buck," as they say.

MATERIALS: A ziplock sandwich bag; paper towel; 1½ tablespoons baking soda; ½ cup vinegar; ¼ cup warm water

1. This experiment will work only if your sandwich bag has no holes. Test it by half-filling it with water, zipping it shut, and turning it upside down over the sink.

2. If no water leaks out, you're fine. Empty the test water.

3. Tear a sheet of paper towel into a square measuring about 6" x 6".

4. Pour the baking soda onto the center of the paper towel, then fold the towel into an "envelope" with the powder inside it.

5. Pour the vinegar and warm water into the bag.

6. Carefully but quickly add the paper towel "envelope" to the bag and seal it.

7. Shake the bag a little, then put it on the ground and stand back.

8. The bag will inflate and then pop with a satisfying bang.

GAME | Frankenstein's Hand

Just as with the sandwich bag, here the gas increases the air pressure inside a glove. As more gas is produced, the pressure increases, gently inflating the glove. You can add a little ketchup at the bottom to up the gore factor. This experiment is a perfect activity for Halloween parties.

MATERIALS: 3 tablespoons vinegar; drinking glass; 2 teaspoons baking soda; rubber glove

1. Pour the vinegar into the glass.

2. Add the baking soda to the inside of the glove. Hold the glove by its wrist and shake the powder into the fingers. Add a little ketchup if you like.

3. Carefully attach the glove to the top of the glass so there's no gap.

4. Pull the glove upright by its fingertips and shake gently, allowing the baking soda to drop into the glass.

5. Stand back and watch as Frankenstein's hand comes alive.

Arts & Crafts | by Bobbi Conner

When kids craft, they discover that they can make things themselves, that not everything has to be purchased from a store. Unlike high-energy physical games or amped-up, competitive games, crafts tend to settle kids into a place of quiet concentration. So enjoy a rare opportunity for simple, focused activity.

RECIPE | Homemade Play Dough

Why purchase play dough when it's so easy to mix up a batch right at the kitchen counter whenever your child runs out?

MATERIALS: 1 cup flour; 1 cup water; ¼ cup salt; 1 tablespoon vegetable oil; 2 teaspoons cream of tartar; 1 to 2 teaspoons food coloring

Combine all the ingredients in a saucepan and mix well. Stir the ingredients over low to medium heat for about 5 minutes. When the mixture forms a ball, remove from the heat. Turn the ball of goop onto a cookie sheet and let it cool. Once cool enough to handle, add food coloring and knead with your hands for several minutes until the dough becomes smooth. Store in an airtight plastic container.

Note: *Play dough is trouble if it gets ground into the carpet, so it's worth creating an easy-cleanup play dough place. The kitchen table or breakfast counter works well. Another option is a yard sale coffee table reserved especially for messy crafting.*

Other smooth surfaces that are just right: giant rimless cookie sheets; lids from large plastic storage tubs; vinyl place mats or oilcloth tablecloths (that allow you to shake the dough crumbs into the trash); a large plastic cutting board (used exclusively for play dough!).

RECIPE | Homemade Finger Paint

Using ordinary kitchen ingredients you most likely have on hand, you can easily make an assortment of inexpensive finger paints.

MATERIALS: 2 tablespoons sugar; ⅓ cup cornstarch; 2 cups cold water; ¼ cup clear dishwashing detergent; serving spoon; food coloring; small yogurt containers with lids

1. Combine the sugar and cornstarch in a small saucepan. Add the water and stir until all the lumps dissolve. Cook over very low heat, stirring constantly.

2. Continue to cook and stir until the mixture becomes clear and thick like gelatin. Remove from the heat and cool to room temperature.

3. Add the dishwashing detergent.

4. Spoon a small quantity into each container and add a few drops of food coloring to create the desired color. **Safety Alert:** *Because these paints contain a generous amount of dish detergent, they are not appropriate for toddlers or other children who put things in their mouths.*

CRAFT | **Put that Finger Paint to Use**

Sometimes *art* means "permission to make a mess"! (Don't worry, it's a snap to clean up.)

MATERIALS: Newspaper; washable, nontoxic finger paints (see 219); paper (shiny finger painting paper or plain drawing paper) or a cookie sheet

Put newspapers down on the floor or a table for easy cleanup. Give your child finger paints to spread around on finger painting paper. For short-lived, messy painting fun, have your child use finger paints on a cookie sheet at the kitchen table.

CRAFT | **Pop-Up Greeting Card**

This three-dimensional pop-up card looks wiggly and animated, and kids love the element of surprise.

MATERIALS: Construction paper; scissors (for adult or supervised use only); colored pencils, markers, or crayons; glitter; nontoxic white glue; clear tape; envelopes

1. Your child folds a piece of construction paper in half or into quarters to make a greeting card, using colored pencils, markers, or crayons to decorate the front of the card. She decides what the "pop-up" shape should be and outlines it in pencil on another sheet of construction paper. (Possible shapes might include a heart, birthday cake, present, the words "I Love You" or "Celebrate," and so forth.)

2. Your child cuts out the image, following the outline, and then cuts a few ½" x 5" construction paper strips.

3. Next, she folds each strip accordion-style (folding the end of a strip over ½ inch, then under ½ inch, over and under, to create a series of folds).

4. To support the pop-up shape, your child attaches one end of the accordion strip to the back of the pop-up shape with small pieces of clear tape; the other end of the accordion strip is taped to the inside of the card. Your child can test out the mechanism by pressing the pop-up image down to make sure it pops up when released. (The length of the paper strips may need to be adjusted, depending on the size of the pop-up shape. If the strips are too long, the pop-up shape may droop; too short, and it may not "pop" enough.)

CRAFT | **Papier-Mâché Bowl**

There is something indescribably fun about getting your hands in slippery papier-mâché goop. It's messy, and takes days to dry. And that's part of the appeal.

MATERIALS: Papier-mâché goop (see recipe); newspaper or recycled vinyl tablecloth; newsprint paper; scissors; medium balloon; felt-tip marker; large plastic margarine tub or bowl; duct tape; cookie sheet; safety pin; washable paint or nontoxic poster paint; paintbrush

1. Make the goop. Cover your kitchen table with newspapers (or set a table up outside). Place the goop on the table.

2. Tear or cut newsprint pages into strips about 1" wide and 6" long. (It's best to tear a large quantity of these strips before proceeding to the messy part of this project.)

3. Blow up the balloon and tie the end. Use the marker to draw a "stop line" all the way around the balloon, about halfway up from the bottom. (You'll be using the balloon as a mold for the bowl, and your child will be lining up newsprint strips along this marker.)

4. Place the knotted end of the inflated balloon inside the margarine tub and secure the bottom of the balloon to the tub with strips of duct tape. Place the margarine tub (with balloon attached) on the cookie sheet to catch any drips while you work and while the project dries.

5. Dip a newsprint strip into the bowl of goop, making sure it is completely covered. Pull the strip out, holding it over the goop bowl, and smooth off any excess goop by sliding your index and middle fingers down the length of the paper strip. Place this strip around the balloon.

6. Add more strips until you've completely covered the balloon up to the stop line. Now begin to layer, applying four layers of strips. Use your hands to smooth out each strip so that it doesn't have bumps or lumps. Don't go crazy here—the finished bowl's handmade texture will add to its beauty.

7. Allow the bowl three or four days to dry completely (drying time may vary depending on your climate and humidity level). Once the newspaper is dry, pop the balloon with the safety pin and decorate the bowl with paints.

Note: *You may use newspaper instead of newsprint paper, in which case you'll need to prep it with a layer of white paint before you begin to decorate in earnest.*

Supervise all balloon play to prevent children younger than eight years old from choking on uninflated balloons or balloon pieces. This is a decorative bowl and is not intended for holding food of any kind.

Papier-Mâché Goop

2 cups cold water
½ cup flour
2 cups water
4 tablespoons sugar

Stir cold water and flour together in a bowl, blending well to dissolve lumps. Pour 2 cups of water into a saucepan and bring to a boil. Add the cold water and flour mixture, stirring constantly, and bring to a boil. Remove from heat and stir in the sugar. Let mixture cool to room temperature.

GAME | **Fortune Teller**

This classic game guarantees hours of fun. All of your child's friends will want their very own fortune tellers, so be ready to churn some out.

MATERIALS: Computer paper; pen; scissors

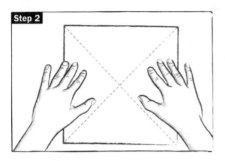

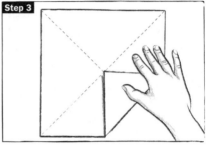

1. Cut an 8½ x 8½-inch square from a sheet of computer paper and lay it flat on the table.

2. Fold one corner to the opposite corner, making a diagonal crease. Open the paper

and fold it diagonally in the other direction. Make a crease, then open the paper.

3. Fold each of the four corners into the center.

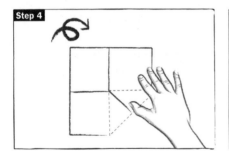

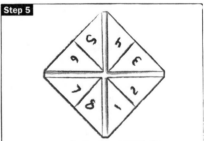

4. Flip the paper over, and fold the new corners into the center.

5. Write a number from one to eight in each of the small triangles on the sides of the paper.

Step 6

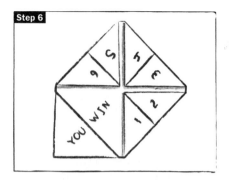

Step 7

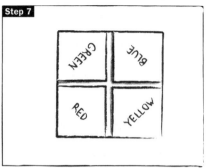

6. Open each of the numbered flaps and write eight different messages inside. Close the flaps.

7. Flip over the folded paper and write the name of a different color on each of the four squares.

8. Fold the fortune teller in half so the four colors are facing out.

9. Position the thumb and index finger of each hand under each of the four flaps, finessing the folds a bit so the fingers are inside each of the points.

Into the Crystal Ball

Forget the worn-out fortune teller messages of yesteryear. Here are some themes to spark imaginative, kid-friendly messages:

- Surprises or discoveries you will make
- Wacky jobs you might have as an adult
- Fabulous travels and adventures
- Silly outfits you will wear
- Sports you will master
- Outrageous outer-space beings you will encounter
- Type of vehicle you will drive
- Gizmos you will invent
- Fantastic dwellings you will live in

Step 9

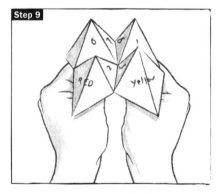

10. Your child holds her fortune teller with the color flaps showing. She asks her friend to pick a color. If the color is blue, your child flaps her fingers back and forth one time for each letter in the word: b-l-u-e (four times). Then she asks her friend to select one of the numbers on the four flaps that are showing. She moves her fingers back and forth as she counts out the number. At last her friend selects one of the numbers showing, and that flap is lifted to reveal her fortune.

inside this chapter . . .

PROJECTS

RECIPES

EXERCISES

taking care of you

Mind, Body, Spirit, Wallet

YOU CAN'T PUT A PRICE TAG ON HEALTH. ILLNESS, HOWEVER, HAS a hefty price indeed—in medical bills, but also in lost work time and higher insurance premiums, among other hidden costs. So getting and staying healthy is probably the single thriftiest lifestyle choice you can make, and fortunately you don't have to spend much to do it. Investing in yourself can be as simple as walking more or learning to meditate. No fancy gym or guru required.

Of course, you've got to look your best to feel your best. Low cholesterol and spotless arteries do not a fashion plate make—and even the style-averse need to look presentable at least some of the time! The good news on that front is that thrift and quality often go hand in hand—you just have to shop, and primp, strategically. Rather than going into debt for trendy, disposable fashions you can't launder yourself, invest your cash in a few well-made classics that will outlive fleeting styles. Learn to maintain your wardrobe properly, and it will keep you looking sharp for years.

The finishing touches—good haircuts, makeup, face creams, and beauty potions—may not be strictly speaking *necessary,* but who wants to stick to a regime of soap and water? Slathering on a face mask and taking a scented bath can erase a week's worth of stress. Your beauty rituals need not be sacrificed in the name of thrift. In fact, you probably already have the fixings for all manner of highfalutin spa products and skin-care remedies in your kitchen. If you're feeling confident, you might even tackle the at-home haircut; but you can always spring for the salon with all the money you'll have saved on dry cleaning.

Saving on Style

If you've become accustomed to spending—or to overspending—on your clothes, breaking the habit may be as hard as quitting smoking. But the thrifty thing to do isn't necessarily to start cutting your own patterns. A more approachable first step is to declare an end to impulse buying and to start planning your purchases. That means saving for high-quality items and eliminating the disposable clothing and redundant splurges. Disciplined spending takes effort, but the reward is sweet: a classic wardrobe that, properly maintained, can serve you well for years. Indeed, choosing quality over quantity is the time-tested European approach that separates the elegant from the merely trendy.

Secrets of a (Thrifty) Fashionista | by Genevieve Roth

My father taught me one basic rule about finance: If you can eat it, wear it, or listen to it, pay cash. I never had trouble following his advice in the food or music departments: I can repurpose leftovers and borrow records. But clothing is another story.

After college, I moved to New York and took a job at a glossy men's magazine. All of a sudden my jeans and cowboy boots—they had seemed so chic during my senior year—were woefully inadequate beside the uptown tastes of my colleagues. I was a girl without an iron in a dry-clean-only world. I needed help.

It wasn't taste I lacked, but funds. And I was unwilling to drown myself in debt for cooler work clothes. At first, I battled this dilemma the way many young women do: I held out for January discounts and stood in line at

SHOPPING ADDICTION CURE AND SAVINGS STRATEGIES BY MELISSA KIRSCH sample sales. Then I discovered eBay. If you learn how to work the system, you can pay rock-bottom prices for high-end merchandise. These are the rules that have transformed my closet and kept the creditors away:

Shop first, eBay later. EBay is not a department store. If you expect it to have everything you want, when you want it, in exactly your color and size, you will be disappointed. So don't "shop" on eBay. Shop in the same places you've always shopped, but when you find something you like, don't buy it. Instead, write down as many details as possible: the brand, the size, the color and, if you can find it, the style number. Many higher-end brands give their garments names, so be sure to make note of that, too. A typical note of mine would say: "I want the Diane Von Furstenberg 'Mula' dress in a size four in eggplant. Charcoal looks good, too." When you get home, pop the details into eBay and see what comes up. Sometimes, especially with big brand names, you score right away. Other times, it'll take a few weeks. Which is why the next step is important.

Set aside your online shopping time. Be warned: EBay has made addicts out of stronger women than me. To avoid getting sucked into a black hole, set aside a time every week to check for your list of items. If they are there, fantastic. Make a bid. If not, wait until the next week.

Check out the seller. All kinds of people—retailers, chronic over-shoppers, fashion editors—sell things on eBay. Before you make a purchase, make sure you can answer the following questions:

- What is the seller's rating? I don't buy from a seller with a rating below 99 percent.
- Where is the seller located? Shipping costs are an area where many eBay sellers make extra money. I try not to buy items coming from foreign countries (unless I'm desperate for them) or with clearly inflated shipping costs.

Help for Shopping Addicts

If you walk into a store and fall hopelessly in love with something, say to yourself: Ten minutes ago, I did not know that this irresistible watch/ red leather tote/cashmere sweater existed, and I was relatively happy. I can walk out of this store and pretend I never walked in. I know it will be possible for me to still live a full life without the red bag because I was doing just that before I saw it.

Try it. Usually, by the time you get home you'll have forgotten all about the item in question.

- Does the description of the item match the photos? Quite a few eBay sellers will pull photographs off of the Internet to illustrate their listings. To make sure you know what you're getting, read the fine print. Is the item you're interested in "NWT" (new, with tags) or is it previously worn? I tend to buy almost all of my clothing new, but it's fine to buy pre-worn items online if you feel comfortable with the way they've been maintained. (If I do buy something used, I send the seller a list of questions about its condition. One I always ask is: Has it been stored in a smoker's house?)

- What is the return policy? Occasionally, the things you buy on eBay won't work for you. The item may turn out to have been a bad choice. The item may not be all it was advertised to be. It's important to know where you stand in terms of returns in either scenario.

Make the bid. If you're satisfied with the answers you receive, make the bid—but be careful. It's easy to get caught up in the excitement of bidding and accidentally overspend. Avoid that trap by using a sniping program. "Sniping" describes the art of waiting until the last minute to place a bid. There are many websites that allow buyers to "snipe" an item without actually being online at the time of purchase. (I use bidslammer.com.) You enter the maximum amount of money you're willing to spend; the computer program places the bid for you; and when the auction is over, you are informed of the outcome via e-mail.

Once I understood how eBay worked, I started to get familiar with the brands that fit me well and the sizes and colors that worked for me. Now, I can hit the site without going to the department stores first, as long as I have a general idea of what I am looking for (work dresses, cocktail dresses, and so forth). If things come in not exactly right, that's okay. I just take them to my tailor (with whom I have developed a very good relationship as a result of all of this), return them, or, worst case scenario, turn around and resell them on eBay myself.

MY THRIFT

You Didn't Know When You Were Going to Get Another

When you got a new dress, you were careful with it because you didn't know when you were going to get another one. We didn't have much, but we made the best of what we had.

—Valetta Barraclough, born 1918

Five Ways to Save on Clothing

1. Spend more on clothes for daytime wear than on your out-on-the-town getups. You can get away with a lot under veil of night, but the cold light of day is unkind to sequined polyester tube tops.

2. Shop off-season for the best bargains. Winter coats in April, bathing suits in early fall. The end of the season is when you find the massive sales and the ridiculous markdowns, because no one's thinking *cashmere scarf* when it's 90 degrees out. Except you.

3. Save your receipts to take advantage of price adjustment policies—most chain stores have them. If you buy a sweater for $80 and the store marks it down to $35 the following week, you can march back and get $45 back if it's within the adjustment window (usually anywhere from two weeks to a month).

4. Read tags. If you can't wash or iron the clothing yourself, it's probably not worth it.

5. Try to shop less at the mall. Unless it's Super-Duper Sale Time, you can probably find most things for less money on the Web. Since you don't get the benefit of a dressing room when shopping online, be sure to check the site's return policy so you can send stuff back if it doesn't fit (or you hate it).

Five Ways to Build a Better Wardrobe

1. Make your choices based on fabric and material. When in doubt, go natural, not man-made. Even a poorly cut shirt will look better if it is made of cotton rather than acrylic. Don't be afraid of silk: It can be hand-washed and always looks better than imitations like shiny polyester.

2. Buy the basics in neutral colors. A black, gray, or camel sweater will give you many more uses than the same sweater in purple, red, or orange.

3. Never buy an "it bag." What makes vintage handbags so attractive? Their mix of classic design and patina from use. But a one-season must-have inherently lacks the first and can never acquire the second.

4. Take care of your stuff. Hang your clothes on the proper hangers. Keep your shoes in boxes or bags. Spend some time cleaning and protecting your leather goods. If clothes or shoes need mending or fixes, don't procrastinate.

5. Acquire new clothes strategically. It's not enough for an item to be in your size and favorite color. Is it within your budget? Do you need it? Where will you wear it? Does it work with other pieces in your wardrobe?

A Few Good Suits | by Jay Akasie

Walk into any reputable men's store to buy a suit, and you're going to spend at least $800 for a no-frills, off-the-rack ensemble. But why buy nothing special when for the same price, you can get much more?

What many gents don't realize is that for about the same price as a standard suit, you can have one that's made-to-measure. The fit will be superior, and you'll get to choose from more fabrics than are typically found in a store's inventory. After having done it both ways, I can say that made-to-measure feels better, looks better, and gives you more bang for the buck.

Make no mistake: I'm not suggesting you commission a "bespoke" suit. These are the suits that made London's Savile Row famous, and they start at about $4,000. But of course, you get what you pay for: A man known as a "cutter" takes several precise measurements of your body and transfers them onto brown paper, which is used as a pattern for the fabric the expert tailors will then stitch by hand. (The word *bespoke* is derived from the era when a City of London banker would go to Savile Row for his suit and chose a bolt of cloth. That bolt had "been spoken" for.) With made-to-measure suits, also known as custom-made suits, a tailor takes several measurements and then tweaks one of his existing patterns to address your physique, putting the whole suit together using a sewing machine.

My first made-to-measure suits were from a tailor named R. M. Rock. Although he's based in Hong Kong, he makes the rounds of northeastern cities for fittings. His business strategy is a sound one: He's been an institution at Harvard Business School for decades, and he's growing in popularity at Columbia Business School. Second-year students often wear his suits to job interviews. Graduates stick with him throughout their careers and tell their colleagues about him, as well.

He comes to New York, where I live, about four times a year and sets up at a Midtown hotel room. Within a month, you'll receive your suits in a package from his shop in Hong Kong. Other custom tailors make it even easier by coming to your office for a fitting.

One thing a good tailor will do every time you visit him is to measure you, particularly around the waist. "Men don't like to think they've gained weight, but invariably they do," Mr. Rock said.

Purchasing a made-to-measure suit may not have all the fanfare and tradition of the bespoke route. But there are pleasures in getting to know your tailor and having some say in the outcome. One of the best aspects of the suit, for me, was that the tailor made sure the arms of my suit weren't too long. Too many men wear suits with arms that cover a good part of their hands. With your arms hanging straight by your side, a suit should extend down to the lower part of your wrist so a half-inch of the shirt underneath can be seen.

A good tailor will also take some time to help you select fabrics. In my case, Mr. Rock brings hundreds of books of fabrics and asks me where I will be wearing the suit—so he can suggest the right fabric.

Some things to keep in mind, regardless of where your suit comes from: If you travel frequently for business, you don't want to arrive from the airport looking like a wrinkled mess; certain fabrics rebound better after a couple of hours in an airplane seat. And though gray flannel or tweed look great, they tend to be impractical for most men, as they're heavy for a day in a warm office. A light- or middle-weight fabric can be worn in three out of four seasons.

A thrifty guideline is to stock your wardrobe with just a few suits in four basic colors (solid blue, solid gray, plus blue and gray pinstripe) and each in a durable middleweight fabric. Any shade of gray is a better choice than black, which as a suit color tends to cycle through a serious spectrum of acceptability. Dark gray is acceptable at funerals; for black-tie events, you should probably be wearing a tuxedo.

If that sounds like a recipe for a dullard's wardrobe, keep accessories in mind: It's far more economical to combine a small number of suits with an array of shirts and neckties of varied and interesting patterns than it is to buy lots of suits in lots of patterns and colors.

How a Suit Should Fit

Whether you're buying custom-made or off-the-rack, look for the following signs of fit in quality menswear (or have your suit altered to fit):

- Trouser hems that break over a third of the length of the shoe in front and brush the top of the heel in the back.
- A jacket collar that lies evenly at the back and sides of the neck.
- A shirt collar with space for one finger between the collar and the skin of the neck.
- Jacket shoulders that don't extend too far beyond the natural shoulder line (if they do, the jacket is too big), and that fit smoothly over the shoulder blades in back.
- A jacket sleeve that leaves a half-inch of shirt cuff visible when your arms are down by your side.
- A back vent (if there is one) that doesn't pull open, a sign that the jacket is too tight.

Hello, Chanel! | **by Bernadette Serton**

People who see me breezing around town in my Chanel suit—an off-white tweed number with black trim—probably think I have serious money. Or that I married into money. But in fact, I just happen to have a Chanel suit. Better yet, it is exactly the one I wanted, and I didn't go into debt for it.

In 2006, my boyfriend and I decided to marry, and to save money, we agreed to elope. I was willing to give up the pageantry of a wedding, but a woman's need for finery will not be denied: I wanted to wear a Chanel suit on my wedding day. No matter how many times the calculator said I could not afford to dress like Jackie O., the dream would not die. Chanel represented to me the pinnacle of taste and classic style. It called to mind Audrey Hepburn and Princess Diana. I wanted be able to look back in ten or twenty years and think: "That was a beautiful choice, and I would do the same again."

At age thirty-three, I had never owned an item of clothing I didn't find on an Ann Taylor or Banana Republic clearance rack. I was proudly making my own way in Manhattan, paying off my credit card debt, and contributing to my 401(k) retirement plan. But I wanted one really good suit to start off my new life. And I didn't want to spend a year searching consignment stores for a used one; vintage has never been my thing. A new Chanel would cost as much as a mid-priced wedding dress, I reasoned, but the virtue of the suit would be that I could wear it on other special occasions. The question was: How could I swing a $4,800 suit on a book editor's salary without handing my freshly minted husband a huge credit card bill?

After a quick review of my assets, I saw an answer: my car. My beloved Volkswagen convertible was thirteen years old. I had purchased it when I was fresh out of college and had moved to the suburbs of Washington, D.C. I always referred to it as the "Barbie Dream Car." It was not the right car for my new life, I concluded. I wanted to be a grown-up. We wanted a family. And babies shouldn't ride in convertibles, right?

I sold the car of my youth to pay for the Chanel of my future. In the end, the $1,600 I got for it covered only the less expensive half of the suit: the skirt.

I could have bought the suit at one of the exclusive Chanel stores in Manhattan, but I had good reason to go to Bloomingdale's. My Aunt Jane, whom I invited to join me, had collected a wad of Bloomingdale's coupons, as had her friends. With these in hand, rock-bottom prices would be ours to have. We were gaming the system.

Or so we thought. I have never been more embarrassed to present coupons. It felt like trying to buy beluga caviar with food stamps. And as it happened, the coupons didn't apply to designer goods anyway. I wondered if one could receive a discount for humiliating oneself, but the gentleman attending to us couldn't have been nicer. He seemed like a regular guy who also lived on a budget. And after witnessing our coupon debacle, he gave me a comparable discount of $100, something I wouldn't have guessed he could do.

Then he asked, "Do you want to save 10 percent on today's purchase by opening your own Bloomindale's charge account?" Oh, yes. *"I do,"* I said, as I had practiced. That saved $480.

And finally, did I prefer to pick up the suit once it was fitted, or have it delivered? Shipping the purchase to New Jersey or Connecticut meant Bloomingdale's wouldn't collect the 8.25 percent sales tax. I glanced lovingly at Aunt Jane (who lives in New Jersey) and saved $400 more.

In the fairy-tale-come-true end, I cut about $1,000 off the price of a Chanel suit by wielding coupons that turned out to be no good, opening a charge account I'd never use again (see box), and bringing along my aunt.

Of course, I'm quite pleased that the suit I wore on my wedding day still fits me. But it gives me true and lasting satisfaction in other ways: I will wear it forever—and for just as long, my friends will be telling me how clever I was.

What's the Deal with Department Store Cards?

It seems like you can get a dedicated credit card from pretty much any store at which you drop cash regularly these days. They lure you in with the immediate 10 percent off your purchase today just for signing up. Okay, that's a good deal if you're spending a lot of money. So if you absolutely must, get the card, take the discount, go home delighted with your purchases and the money you've saved, and then *pay that card off*. Before the plastic even comes in the mail, call, write, e-mail, pay it off. Then cancel the card. Store credit cards impose some of the highest finance charges of all credit cards out there. Read that fine print, those Terms and Conditions. We're talking a 20 percent annual percentage rate (APR) or higher, with severe penalties for late payment.

Ultimately, the best move is to resist the temptation and steer clear of the cards in the first place.

The Thrifty Wardrobe Basics

Invest in the best quality basics you can afford, and it will pay off in durability, elegance, and fit. As with so many things in life, the key to thrifty chic is to establish a solid foundation, over which you can layer on accessories and touches of flash. The following staples will never go out of style (unlike those couture parachute pants).

A MEN'S WARDROBE

Navy blazer. Just like you wore when you were twelve. It never goes out of style.

Camel topcoat. One word: dashing.

Gray wool suit. Two buttons or three, no closet is complete without one of these.

Cashmere or Merino V-neck sweater. A four-season classic that should be part of any layering plan.

Brown wingtips. Worn by everybody from Winston Churchill to the guy who does your taxes.

Canvas sneakers. They won't do much for you at the gym, but they make a retro statement.

Dark jeans. You need at least one pair without holes or paint stains.

A few silk ties, a knit tie. Silk ties are needed for work and semiformal occasions, but for more casual affairs, a knit tie—à la Alex P. Keaton—is both preppy and hip.

"Expensive" khakis. A good pair may cost $100, but they'll last.

White cotton dress shirt. As versatile as a Swiss army knife.

A BASIC WOMEN'S WARDROBE

White button-down shirt. It doesn't have to be expensive—just crisp and clean.

Flattering pair of jeans. Find a cut that looks good on your body and forget the trends.

Little black dress. It goes anywhere, from the office to a black-tie function.

Skirt suit. It's a three-in-one: wear the jacket with jeans, the skirt with a sweater, and the suit all together.

Black pants. Slimming and versatile, they're good for work and play.

Lightweight wool sweater. An extra layer comes in handy on spring days and when you travel.

Black pumps. Buy ones that fit well and wear them with everything.

Colorful flats. A bright dash of color adds personality to the basics.

Trench coat. Elegant and flattering in any weather.

Leather handbag. Spend what you can on a timeless, quality bag you love—and make it your statement.

Why Shoes Should Be Good

When it comes to shoes, you may think you're outsmarting the system by reaching for a pair of bargain-basement clompers and scoffing at the three magic words that have come to signify quality—*Made in Italy*. There is certainly a time and a place for cheap shoes (Hello, bridesmaids!), but in general it's worth investing in quality. In the long run, "cheap" shoes don't cost less. Spend a bit more and you'll be able to wear the things for years—well-made shoes hold up over time and can be repaired over and over.

If you're going to invest, you want to make sure you get what you pay for. There are lots of trendy shoes, many made by top fashion names, that will wear out quickly. As with all things, knowledge spells the difference. Italy has a top reputation for shoes because of superior construction and high-quality materials. But there are ways that brands can trick a consumer into thinking that a shoe is Italian made when in fact it is not. "Italian-made shoes say 'Made in Italy,'" says Beth Whiffen, the owner of a boutique shoe store in Santa Monica, California. "If you see something like, 'Sole made in Italy,' then the rest of the shoe may have been made somewhere else."

Caring for Your Shoes

If your local cobbler is a little surly, consider things from his perspective: You might be surly, too, if you spent your day fixing problems that could easily have been prevented. Shoes, like cars and relationships, require constant maintenance to perform at their best. And that's where your cobbler's practiced hands and hard-won wisdom come into play. Fernando Costano has been repairing shoes for nearly three decades at a small New York shop called Brooklyn Heights Shoe Master. Here is some of his wisdom on extending the life of your shoes:

- "The first thing you need to do is get your shoes shined and conditioned once a week," says Fernando. (Obviously, you can do this yourself, although Fernando doesn't mention that.) He recommends a

Leather Care

Rather than buy an expensive little bottle of shoe leather cleaner, buy a larger bottle of leather upholstery cleaner and use it on all your leather belongings. Even better, make your own leather conditioner by mixing one part white vinegar with two parts linseed oil in a jar.

SHOE QUALITY AND COBBLER TIPS BY PETER HYMAN; CARE ADVICE BY JEAN COOPER

cream-based leather conditioner to keep your shoes soft and to prevent cracking (wax products can cause the leather to dry out over time). He also recommends applying a waterproof coating when you first buy the shoes, especially for suede or other specialty materials like cordovan.

■ Have a rubber dancer's sole put on the bottom of each shoe. This extends the life of the sole while also providing extra cushioning and protecting the tip of the shoe. Rubber heel tops are also a beneficial addition, adding both protection and a level of comfort.

■ "When you're not wearing your shoes, it's a good idea to put shoe trees in them, to keep the shape," says Fernando. Shoes should be stored in a dark place because sunlight can discolor or fade leather.

Five Ways to Extend the Life of a Shoe

If the shoe fits, take good care of it. Dancer's soles and old-fashioned buffing aside, here are five preventative and reparative measures you can take to prolong the life of your footwear:

1. If your shoes get soaked or muddied, wipe them clean while they are still wet and apply a coating of matching shoe polish to the damp uppers. Then stuff the shoes firmly with newspaper, pushing it compactly into the toes with the handle of a wooden spoon. This blocks the shoes into shape, and the paper will absorb some of the dampness.

2. The only shoes that cannot be dyed successfully are made of smooth plastic or nonporous synthetic materials. Most other shoes can be dyed to extend their life and freshen their appearance.

3. Canvas, denim, and satin shoes can be protected against stains. While they are still new, spray them with a fabric protector.

4. Use a matching permanent marker to touch up scuff marks on scratched or worn heels.

5. To store out-of-season shoes and boots, polish or clean them as usual, making sure they are dry before you put them away. Vinyl footwear can be stored in plastic bags, but leather and suede shoes should be wrapped in soft cloth or tissue paper. (Leather will dry out if it is stored in plastic.) Ideally, shoes should be blocked with paper or shoe trees; stuff the shafts of boots with paper.

Caring for Your Clothes

Little known and highly economical fact: In many cases, the words "Dry Clean Only" can be dismissed. If a garment is made of multiple fabrics or a fabric blend (cotton/poly), it should be dry-cleaned. Garments that are 100 percent silk, linen, cotton, or wool (including cashmere) can be hand washed or tossed in the delicate cycle of your machine. Just use cold water and a gentle detergent; for smaller delicate items, look for one of those mesh laundry bags made for lingerie. Dry on a flat rack and steam press if necessary.

Of course, the easiest way to reduce your dry cleaning bills is to start at the top, by purchasing clothes that can be washed by hand or in the machine. But the decisions aren't always obvious. Let's say you're shopping and you find a T-shirt in some fancy silk blend. It's marked down from a ridiculously stratospheric price to $35. "Why, $35 for a silk T-shirt, that's not bad at all!" you think to yourself, bargain hunter that you are. Wait. Check the tag. The "affordable" T-shirt that requires dry cleaning is not an affordable shirt. This is not to say you should not own fine garments that require dry cleaning. It is only to say that the $35 silk tee is going to end up costing you hundreds of dollars if you pay to have it cleaned after each wear.

Last but not least: Dry cleaning is neither dry nor particularly clean, from an environmental and health-related standpoint. In dry cleaning's infancy, the solvent involved was kerosene or gasoline, but these days, the process relies on a peculiar chemical called perchloroethylene, street name "perc"—a known carcinogen that has been linked to lots of health problems. Clothes are put in a giant machine with perc, some special detergent, and perhaps a splash of water, and agitated, just as they are in a regular washing machine. Then your precious garments are dried and pressed, and the perc is separated from the dirty water so it can be reused. The solvent residue, which is a hazardous waste, must be recycled or incinerated.

You *can* avoid this toxic cycle by seeking out "green" cleaners who don't use perc (ask them what they clean with—it should be either liquid carbon dioxide or a silicone-based cleaner), but this will most likely cost even more.

Cover a Bleach Spot

Use a touch of permanent marker. They are available in a rainbow of colors, but this is an especially good technique for black clothes. No one will be the wiser.

DRY CLEANING TIPS BY MELISSA KIRSCH

The Secrets of Stain Removal

Don't replace—rejuvenate! If you're someone who can't eat a plate of spaghetti marinara without transforming your shirt into a bona fide spatter painting, you'll need to get handy with the stain removal.

To prevent stains from sticking around for good, you need to be quick and targeted. The following formulas work on clothes, furniture, and carpets, though each type of material will respond to different tricks in its own way (and the amount needed of each remedy is, of course, dependent on the size of the stain).

Antiperspirant. Combine half a teaspoon dish detergent (or castile soap), a few drops of white vinegar, and a half-cup water. Press into the stain with a rag. Flush with water and blot.

Blood. Spit on it. It's true—your own saliva is the best thing for getting your own blood out fast. Next lines of defense: Soak the stained item in cold water mixed with a handful of salt, or apply equal parts ammonia and water with a sponge. Weirdly, bleach doesn't work well on bloodstains.

Chocolate. Rinse the stain thoroughly, from the back if possible, with cold water.

Coffee. With a sponge, apply a mixture of half a teaspoon of white vinegar to 2 cups of cold water.

Gum. Freeze it by applying an ice cube to the gum. The frozen gum should break off.

Hair dye. Use a little shampoo—it gets it off your skin, and it should work on your clothes.

Ink. Gently massage some aerosol hairspray into the stain, then run it under cold water.

Makeup. Regular detergent should do the trick. First pretreat the stain with alcohol or a stain remover. (This should work on any grease.)

Red wine. Apply a little white wine if available. Then sprinkle liberally with salt (it absorbs) and rinse immediately, rubbing the stain out.

Sweat. Apply a mixture of water and baking soda or a few tablespoons of white vinegar. If this doesn't work, soak in salt water.

Vegetable oil. Use a liquid dish detergent that cuts grease.

Wax. Scrape off what you can. Put a paper towel over the wax and iron until all the wax is absorbed.

STAIN REMOVAL TIPS AND BUTTON-SEWING INSTRUCTIONS BY MELISSA KIRSCH

Sew on a Button, Save a Shirt

A lost button or unraveled seam should never lead to the retirement of your favorite garments. These minor clothing afflictions are so common and so easily repaired that you'd be a fool to let them cramp your style. Everyone should have a sewing kit of some sort. Assemble your own, with thread in the colors you favor, or buy a small ready-made kit at any supermarket, pharmacy, or convenience store.

PROJECT | Button-Sewing 101

Button-sewing is phenomenally easy, so don't be discouraged by the number of steps below—this technique is particularly good for staying power. To sew on a coat button, use extra-strong thread, or try unwaxed white dental floss. (Color the floss with a marker to match the button.)

TOOLS: Button; needle; thread; scissors

1. Thread a needle, double the thread over, and knot the end twice.

2. Starting from the underside of the fabric, make two stitches, one on top of the other, where you want to affix the button. This anchors your knot.

3. Hold the button over the "anchor" stitches and pull the threaded needle through from the underside and up through one of the button's holes. Go back down an adjacent hole. Don't pull the stitches too tightly—you want wiggle room so you can button the garment when you're done.

4. Do this three times, then repeat for the other two holes if the button has four holes.

There's no need to make crisscross stitches over the button—just a few loops through both sets of holes will do the trick.

5. Pull the button slightly away from the fabric and wind the remaining thread several times around the stitched thread, under the button and above the fabric.

6. Push the needle back through the fabric and knot on the underside, then make a few small stitches over the knot to secure the button.

7. To make your work last, put a drop of clear nail polish over the thread on top of the button.

Hem It Yourself | by Diana Rupp

The most common tailoring jobs are some of the easiest. If you have a needle and thread and a bit of patience, you should be able to shorten or lengthen your own skirts and pants. As a general rule, hems should be discreet and the stitches invisible. Keep them that way by using a thread color that matches the fabric as closely as possible. If your hems pucker or look lumpy, loosen your stitching. Pulling thread tight does not make for smooth hems.

TOOLS: Needle; thread; scissors; pins; tape measure; flexible ruler (see skirt); seam ripper; chalk; pencil; paper; iron and ironing board

Stitches for Hemming

A couple of stitching techniques will help you master the art of neat hemming. Overcast stitching will do for most; perfectionists will want to try the slip stitch.

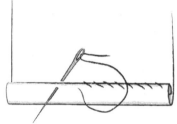

The overcast stitch (or whipstitch). The overcast stitch is the easiest and fastest way to hem or to join two finished or folded edges. Work with the hem facing you, garment inside out. Start by bringing the needle up through the inside edge of the hem (to hide the knot). Take a tiny stitch into the single layer of skirt or pants fabric that the hem is meeting. Though it's painstaking work, picking up a single thread in the fabric will make the hem nearly invisible. Then, tuck the needle behind the hem edge (about ⅛ inch from the fold) and pull the needle through. Make your stitches about ⅛ inch apart.

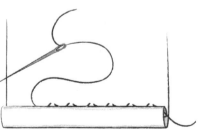

The slip stitch. The slip stitch is an almost invisible stitch formed by slipping the needle inside the fold of the hem. In addition to hemming, this stitch works particularly well for repairing torn seams.

Draw the needle out through the folded edge of the hem. Take a small stitch in the main fabric. Then slip the needle back into the fold of the fabric. Keeping the needle inside the fold, bring the needle out through the edge about ¼ inch along and pull it through. Continue in the same fashion with stitches approximately ¼ inch apart.

PROJECT | # Shorten a Skirt

For a dollar or less, a flexible ruler, also known as a sewing ruler, is a worthwhile tool if you're looking to expand your sewing repertoire. Here, it allows you to create a slightly curved hemline and avoid the pucker effect.

1. Put on the skirt and the shoes you will wear with it—high heels or flat sandals, or both—to help you decide which length looks best.

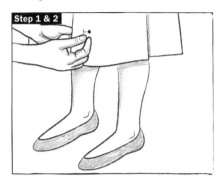

2. Place a pin in the front where you'd like the skirt to end. Err on the conservative side and leave your hem length slightly longer than you think you want it. You can always shorten the skirt more, but once you cut fabric away, there's no going back.

3. Lay the skirt flat on a table and measure down from the waistband to the pin. Add an extra $\frac{1}{2}$ inch just to be safe. Then add the width of the original hem plus $\frac{1}{4}$ inch to this number and write it down.

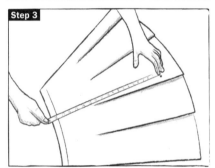

4. Measure this amount against your skirt, tearing out or cutting off the original hem if necessary.

5. Hold the tape measure from the waistline down to the pin and mark this desired length with chalk every 3 to 4 inches around the bottom of the skirt.

6. Turn your flexible ruler on its side edge and bend it into a gentle curve (with the ends of the ruler flipping up toward the waistband). Trace the curve with chalk to connect the marks.

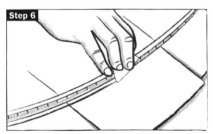

7. Turn the skirt up to the desired length, pin, and try it on again in front of a mirror. (Remember that the finished product will be shorter.) Make adjustments if necessary, then lay the skirt flat on a table and cut off the excess fabric along the chalk line.

8. Turn the skirt inside out. Tuck the raw edge under $\frac{1}{4}$ inch and press. Turn up the hem to the original hem length. Press well with an iron.

9. Pin every 2 to 3 inches at a right angle or parallel to the edge.

10. Start at a side seam (to hide your knot) and hem with a whipstitch (see facing page). Watch for puckers and lumps. Don't pull too tightly on the thread.

11. When you're done, press to set the stitches and take out any unevenness in tension.

PROJECT | # Let Down a Hem

First, check the existing hem to verify there's enough fabric to let down. Most hems on store-bought clothing are turned-and-stitched, which means the hem can be twice as long as it looks. If, for instance, you want a pair of pants to be one inch longer and the current hem is two inches wide, it's quite likely you'll have a happy ending.

1. Undo the old hem by cutting the thread with your seam ripper. Be careful not to cut the fabric.

2. Press (iron) out the crease. This is the trickiest part of lengthening because the hemline on manufactured clothing can be stubborn. Steam helps, as does dampening the cloth.

3. Redo the hem by pressing it up to the desired length, tucking under by ¼ inch, and stitching with your favorite hem stitch.

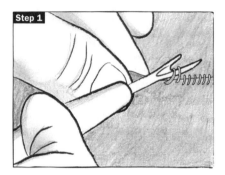

PROJECT | # Shorten Unlined Pants

Note the specification. Though it's not impossible to alter lined garments at home, it does tend to involve a more advanced technique.

1. Using the seam ripper, carefully tear out the original hem on each leg.

2. Measure the width of the original hem from bottom crease to edge and write this number down. Hem sizes vary depending on style and fabric. In general, you want the new hem to be the same width as the old hem because that first hem was calculated to match the drape and weight of the fabric.

3. Try the pants on in front of a full-length mirror. Put on shoes and a belt (if you plan to wear one) to get the correct length. Turn one pant leg under until the length looks right, and then pin it in place at each side seam. (*Note:* Standard-length pants rest on the top of the shoe, but you know what you like.)

4. Take off the pants and measure the length of the upturned cuff from the fold to the raw edge. Jot this number down as well.

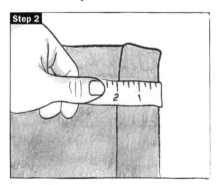

5. Turn the pants inside out and lay them flat on a table. Turn the pant legs up to the desired length (the measurement you just wrote down) and pin at sides.

6. Press (iron) the pant leg bottoms in place. Pin every few inches. Turn pants right side out.

7. Try on the pants again to double-check the new length. Adjust if necessary.

8. Turn the pants inside out again. Using chalk and a ruler, mark the measurement from step 2. For example, if the original hem was 2 inches of fabric, draw a line 2 inches above the pressed hem. Cut away excess fabric.

9. Tuck the raw edge under about $\frac{1}{4}$ inch; press and pin.

10. Choose a hemming stitch and, starting at a side seam, hem around both cuffs.

11. Press the finished hems.

Step 9

When to Consult a Professional

Don't try elaborate alterations on your own unless you're an experienced seamster or seamstress—you might pay a high price in potential agony and a destroyed garment. If you need one of the following fixes, get thee to a tailor:

- Replacing a stuck or broken zipper
- Replacing the lining of pants or coats
- Replacing the elastic in pants or skirts

- Altering a garment that is too big or too small
- Letting out or nip in the shoulders of a garment

Beauty & the Budget

The lure of the makeup and beauty aisles can be difficult to resist. Haven't you occasionally wondered if all you needed was new lip gloss or magic "time-erasing" face potion to make your life complete? And has it ever worked? The real result is often a drawer full of half-used makeup and a bout of buyer's remorse. (Alas, even the priciest lotion can't stop time, or gravity.) But you *can* be thrifty and primped—it's just a matter of knowing when to spend, and when you're better off taking matters into your own hands. Everything from aromatherapy to hair trims and manicures can be transferred to the home front. And if you get really good, you can open a pricey spa of your own. . . .

When Terminology Spells "Markup"

I n the world of beauty products, conviction trumps evidence—woe to him who challenges the efficacy of a woman's signature product—but the following terms shouldn't be used as justification for a higher price tag:

Hypoallergenic. The term is virtually meaningless, because no regulatory or even voluntary standard definition has been established. "Hypoallergenic" does not mean the product will not cause an allergic reaction. The same warning goes for terms such as "dermatologist-tested," "sensitivity-tested," "allergy-tested," and "nonirritating."

Fragrance-free. Contrary to what you might think, products with this label can still contain fragrances. A more precise term would be "smell-free" —and to achieve this effect the manufacturer probably had to add some fragrance to mask the product's original smell.

Natural. There are no standards for this term; it can mean virtually anything to anybody. "Natural" cosmetics often contain pretty much the same ingredients as any other cosmetics, including preservatives. Always read ingredients lists to see if there's anything on there you'd rather avoid. But don't take "natural" at face value.

PRODUCT DECODING BY MARK GREEN

No animal testing. Claims that products have not been tested on animals may be splitting hairs. While it's true that the product itself was "tested" only on people, the ingredients were most likely tested on animals. Both U.S. Food and Drug Administration and industry officials say that companies making these claims use well-known ingredients that have already been proven safe—most likely with animal tests, since there are almost no cosmetic ingredients for human use that weren't first tested on animals.

The Skin of Your Dreams

Next time you are confronted with a choice between a no-name $0.19-per-ounce moisturizer and a luxurious $40-per-ounce cream with a designer label, try to make an educated decision.

Don't be taken in by empty promises that a product will "lift the eyes," "firm," "nourish," "recondition," or "retrain" the skin; "relieve," "remove," or "reduce" cellulite; "target" trouble areas, "wash away" free radicals, or "prevent" aging. Cosmetics affect only the outermost layer of skin to temporarily change its appearance. The collagen molecule, for example, is too big to penetrate the outermost layer, the epidermis, to reach the dermis below, where it might rejuvenate the skin. To be blunt: A surgeon can lift sagging eyelids; a cream cannot.

Price says nothing about quality. The beneficial ingredients in beauty products are often inexpensive, varying little from one product to another. When you buy expensive products, you are usually paying for advertising, fancy packaging, free samples, perfumes, and all the other razzmatazz that contribute to the creation of the fancy image.

All you really need to maintain healthy skin is to wash with mild soap; to avoid exposure to the sun or wear a sunscreen; to eat healthy foods, drink plenty of

Drugstore Deals

When it's time to re-up at the drugstore, you can save a lot of money by comparing deals among various stores and mediums *before* setting out to make your purchases. Start with printed circulars in the newspaper or at the store, or online. National chain drugstores may offer deals specific to your area; you can find them by going to the chain's website and searching by zip code.

Drugstore loyalty cards are another good way to save money, but beware the siren song of a six-pack of soap that you'll never use because it dries your skin.

liquids, and exercise regularly; and to refrain from smoking. If you have minor skin problems, consider one of the easy homemade tonics on page 250. If you have serious skin problems, consult a dermatologist. Do not rely on salespeople or anyone else frocked in a white lab coat and standing at a cosmetics counter for a diagnosis or treatment.

When to Save, When to Splurge

As a frugal consumer, you probably don't mind spending a bit more on a beauty product if you know that it's worth it. But the question is, how do you know? Here's a brief overview of when to save on products, when to splurge, and when to toss.

SAVE ON . . .

Eye and lip pencils. In most cases, the biggest difference between a $0.99 pencil and a $15.99 pencil is $15. Feel the top of the pencil; it should feel smooth, not dry.

Shampoo and conditioner. Unless you love the smell of a particular product, you'll find that most less-expensive versions perform just as well.

Sunscreen. As long as it has both UVA and UVB coverage (titanium dioxide, zinc oxide, or Parsol 1789 listed as an "active ingredient"), one sunscreen is pretty much like another. Sunscreen loses its efficacy after a year.

Blow-dryer. With a few exceptions (such as ionic dryers, which dry hair faster) an inexpensive blow-dryer is fine. Just make sure it has a low and a cool setting.

Nail color. Unless you're drawn to a particular shade, there's no reason to splurge on nail color. Prolong its life by storing it in the refrigerator.

Mascara. Go for an inexpensive brand—mascara should be tossed every few months.

SPLURGE ON . . .

Foundation. Many pricier brands are formulated with gentler, less-occlusive ingredients that aren't as likely to clog your pores, discolor, or fade throughout the day.

Eye shadow. A great color is worth more, and cheap shadow tends to be chalky. Quality shadow—which goes on smoother and lasts longer—should feel silky and creamy, not dry and crumbly.

Powder. Pricier powders last longer, which means that you get good value. Because it sits on your face for the entire day, make sure it's the best quality you can afford.

Lipstick. There's no substitute for a great color—which is the best reason to splurge. Besides, cheap lipstick tends to act cheap by bleeding and feathering. When it comes to staying power, it's all about color and texture: Darker, matte shades last longest, though they tend to be most drying, while light, sheer, glossy shades are the most fleeting.

SAVE OR SPLURGE BY RONA BERG

The At-Home Spa

Ever noticed that the fewer ingredients a beauty treatment contains, the more it costs? And that if those ingredients are things you can buy at the supermarket, it costs even more? The truth is, natural products can do wonders for the skin, but you don't have to squeeze them out of a tube or pay a "facial consultant" to get their benefits. In fact, your home can be transformed into your very own spa—just whip up a custom skin treatment, ease into a scented bath, and leave your worries behind.

RECIPE | **Oatmeal and Honey Cleanser**

Ground oatmeal is a gentle exfoliator that removes dead surface cells and residue and helps restore the skin's moisture. It can be used as a mild cleanser in the place of soap. The combination of yogurt, which will soften the skin, and honey, a natural humectant, makes for an effective everyday cleanser.

½ cup raw rolled oats
2 tablespoons honey
¼ cup plain yogurt or buttermilk

1. Finely grind the oatmeal in a blender or food processor.

2. In a small bowl, combine the honey and yogurt, then add the ground oatmeal. Mix thoroughly until it has a paste-like consistency.

3. Smooth over the face and neck and leave on for 15 minutes. Rinse off with warm water and pat dry.

RECIPE | **Apple Cider Wash**

This formula is very effective for removing dirt and residue from oily skin.

2 tablespoons apple cider vinegar
2 tablespoons distilled water

1. Mix the water and apple cider vinegar in a small bowl and apply to the face with a cotton ball. Avoid the eye area.

2. Rinse with tepid water. Pat dry.

Painless Instant Facelift

Beat an egg white until it is frothy, apply to face, and leave on for five minutes. The mask will tighten. Rinse off thoroughly, first with warm water, then with cool. It's not Botox, but it works!

LAVENDER OIL FROM *COUNTRY WISDOM $ KNOW-HOW: OTHER FORMULAS* BY CATHERINE BARDEY

RECIPE | **Mayonnaise and Avocado Hair Pack**

The combination of eggs and oil (from the mayonnaise) and avocado creates a wonderful conditioner for dry hair. Try to buy all-natural mayo from a health-food store, or make your own from scratch (see page 161).

> 1 ripe avocado, peeled and pitted
> 1 cup mayonnaise

1. In a small bowl, mash the avocado and blend in the mayonnaise.

2. Gently massage into the scalp and hair.

3. Cover head with a shower cap or plastic wrap and leave the treatment on for 20 minutes.

4. Shampoo as usual.

RECIPE | **Molasses Hair Wrap**

This treatment is incredibly easy to apply and will add shine and moisture to your hair. One word of caution: Stay away from bees (and bears!).

> ½ cup molasses

1. Apply the molasses directly to damp hair and massage into the scalp.

2. Cover your hair with a shower cap or plastic wrap and leave in for 20 minutes. Rinse with warm water.

3. Shampoo as usual.

RECIPE | **Simple Lavender Massage Oil**

Lavender is often used for its relaxing, soothing properties, but you can use any essential oil that appeals to your senses.

> ⅔ cup grape-seed oil
> ⅓ cup wheat-germ oil
> 10 drops vitamin E oil
> 6 drops lavender essential oil

1. Pour all the ingredients into a dark bottle with a spout.

2. Shake well before each use.

3. Pour the oil into your hands to warm it before putting it on your body.

GRAPE-SEED TIP FROM RONA BERG

RECIPE | Invigorating Rosemary and Sage Bath

Herbal baths are cleansing and intensely relaxing. The herb or combination of herbs you use depends on the effect you are after: to soothe the skin, promote sleep, stimulate circulation, relieve muscle aches and pains, or merely enjoy an aromatic experience. The concept, however, remains the same: You're essentially relaxing in a giant cup of herbal tea.

There are several ways to brew an herbal bath. The easiest is to toss several storebought herbal tea bags directly into the bathwater. Another option is to fill pieces of cloth with herbs and tie them closed. The little sacks can be attached directly to the faucet so the running water goes through them, or floated in the tub. Use the latter method with this mixture.

¼ cup dried rosemary
¼ cup dried sage
2 tablespoons oatmeal

1. Spoon rosemary and sage into several tea bags or small pieces of cloth. Knot or tie closed.

2. Draw a warm bath and add the oatmeal directly to the flowing water.

3. Toss in the tea bags.

RECIPE | Citrus and Milk Bath

Cleopatra was famous for bathing in milk. Rich in protein, calcium, and vitamins, milk is easily absorbed by the skin, leaving it smooth and moisturized. The lavender and citrus peel in this bath formula stimulate the circulatory system and add a wonderful aroma.

1 cup dried milk powder (if you have oily skin, use nonfat)
¼ cup orange peels
¼ cup lemon peels
4 drops lavender essential oil

Draw a warm bath and add all ingredients while the water is flowing.

Antioxidant Eye Moisturizer

Grape-seed oil can be found in supermarkets and specialty food shops. It's an extremely light, absorbent oil that is relatively odor-free. Dab it on the undereye area. It will also remove eye makeup and soften fine lines around the lips.

The Kitchen Dermatologist

Sure, all that skin technically needs to stay healthy is proper cleansing and moisturizing. But everyone's skin occasionally rebels. Fortunately, there are some super-simple ways to get it back under control—right in your kitchen and medicine cabinets.

PROBLEM	HOMEMADE SOLUTION
Dehydrated skin	Mix 2 drops of lavender oil with baking soda and water until it becomes a paste. Put mixture on face and leave on for 5 minutes. Rinse. Moisturize. This light exfoliating mask makes skin more receptive to moisture.
Dull, tired-looking skin	Wrap grated cucumber in cheesecloth, lie down, and apply to your face for 5 minutes. Rinse with cool water.
	Refrigerate aloe vera gel for at least 1 hour. Pat it on your face, and lie down for 10 minutes. Rinse.
	Lie on your back and hang your head over the side of the bed for 5 to 10 minutes. This position feeds oxygen to your face, thereby improving your color and tone.
Flaky skin	Rub half an apple on your skin to help even out the texture.
	Place a sprinkling of sugar in your palm and dampen it with water. Gently massage it on the flaky areas. Rinse.
Inflamed, irritated, or sensitive skin	Make a pot of chamomile tea. Let cool, then pour into an ice-cube tray and freeze. Pop out a cube, wrap it in a thin cloth, and rub gently on face.
	Soak a clean cloth in a small dish of milk, squeeze, and apply the compress to the affected area for 10 minutes. Rinse off with warm water.
Oily patches	Keep a small spray bottle of rose water in the refrigerator. Give yourself a wake-up spritz in the morning, after you wash your face, or saturate a cotton ball and dab it on at night after washing.
Pimples	Make a paste with water and coarse-grained sea salt, and apply it to the blemish twice a day until healed. Do not rub.
	Dab a bit of non-gel toothpaste on your pimple(s) before bed.
	Soak a piece of bread in milk. Place it on the pimple and lie down. Leave it there for as long as 30 minutes. Rinse.
Red, blotchy spots	Put a few drops of Visine on red, blotchy spots. Because it constricts blood vessels, it will do for your skin what it does for your eyes.
Undereye puffiness	Apply damp, ice-cold tea bags (with caffeine, a diuretic) or hold a bag of frozen peas to the eyes for a few minutes to reduce swelling.
	Wrap a grated potato in two little cheesecloth sacks, lie down, and place the sacks under the eyes. Leave on for 10 minutes, then rinse.
	Place sliced cucumbers on your eyes; cover with a damp, cool cloth; and lie down for 10 minutes.

SKIN CARE SOLUTIONS AND DIY NAIL SALON BY RONA BERG

PROJECT | **The DIY Mani-Pedi**

Even if you don't consider perfectly polished nails a requirement for leaving the house, manicured hands and feet make everyone look neat and well-maintained. (And, yes, "everyone" means men, too.) But the costs of professional manicures and pedicures add up quickly, particularly if you're hooked on polish. Do your own nails and you can skip the salon—or extend the time between visits—and still put your best appendage forward.

TOOLS: Cotton balls; nail polish remover; nail clipper; nail file; cuticle oil or moisturizer; exfoliating scrub; sloughing paddle, loofah, or pumice stone; nailbrush; orangewood stick or Hindostone; base coat; nail polish; fast-drying top coat (optional)

1. Remove any old, leftover polish with cotton, the most absorbent fiber your money can buy. If you need to get into nooks and crannies to remove stubborn polish, use a Q-tip or an orangewood stick with a cotton-swathed tip soaked in nail polish remover.

2. If necessary, clip nails straight across using nail clippers. File and shape your nails in one direction only, parallel to the nail bed, and don't curve into the corner of the nail. Use a soft-grade file (240 grit or higher).

3. Massage a light cuticle oil or moisturizer into the nail and cuticle area for a minute or two.

4. Soak your hands or feet in warm, soapy water for about five minutes to soften the cuticles. (If you like, add a few drops of your favorite essential oil. It smells nice and it moisturizes.)

5. For feet, apply an exfoliating body scrub or foot sloughing cream to a sloughing paddle, loofah, or wet pumice stone and scrub rough patches on the balls and heels of the feet. Use a nailbrush to scrub around and under the toenails. Rinse.

6. Moisturize, then gently push your cuticles back with the tip of an orangewood stick. You can also use a product called Hindostone, a pumice stone shaped like an orangewood stick, which is available at most drugstores. It works beautifully and, like pumice, lasts forever. Carefully trim hangnails as needed.

7. Wipe your nails with a clean cloth to get rid of residual oils on the nail and ready them for the polish, if using. (If there is still oil or lotion on your nail, the polish can bubble.)

8. Apply a base coat to help the polish adhere. Then apply the polish. One coat is fine, but if you apply more, make sure to let each coat dry for a few minutes in between to prevent creasing.

9. If you're in a hurry, apply a fast-drying top coat. The only drawback is that the top coat makes the top layer of polish feel dry to the touch but doesn't necessarily speed the drying process underneath. If you wait until each coat is dry before you apply another, a fast-drying top coat will work like a charm.

Ask a Hairstylist

Nick Arrojo, founder, Arrojo Studio, New York

Q When do you know it's time to go to the salon?

A Look at and feel your hair. Look for split ends and general signs of wear and tear. When your hair is starting to look deflated and dull, it's time for your stylist to work some magic. A good cut lasts a minimum of six weeks, so you could also plan on heading back to the salon after six to ten weeks. If you wear your hair short and like to keep it that way, then you'll need more salon trips. If you're not too worried about your long hair growing even longer, you can put more time between salon visits.

Coloring at home. At-home color from a box uses basically the same technology that you'll find in the salon. It's okay to use if your hair has never been previously colored and is in perfect health. But most people have color, some damage, or both. If that's the case, the color needs to be modified for you, and this is where a professional salon colorist—with knowledge and expertise—comes in. A salon professional can review your hair history and determine exactly what is right for you. If you're intent on coloring from a box, be aware of the condition of your hair.

The color correction money pit. When color goes wrong, as it sometimes does, what's needed is color correction. It's often a long, expensive process that involves removing the bad hair color, restoring health and vigor, then putting in a new, bright hue. It can take repeat services over several months and should never be done at home. (And, yes, color correction services are most often required by people who were trying to be thrifty by using at-home color treatments.)

They'll do it for free. Ask your stylist to teach you how to style your hair yourself. They should definitely be willing to do that for free.

Make the Most of Your Appointments

If you're paying for a beauty service, be wily and get as much out of it as possible.

At a **day spa**, give yourself a good time cushion. If you arrive early, you can spend some time in the relaxation rooms before your treatment begins. All those little seating areas are there for you to lounge in—so put on that robe, sip that fruity water, and read a book.

If you live near a **salon within a gym,** try booking haircuts there; often they'll let you use the sauna or steam room for an hour or two before your trim.

At the **nail salon**, ask for a polish change only; your salon may offer a lower price. (Do the grunt work at home; see page 251.)

Hair Trims and Cuts

Cutting your own hair is risky: It could save you the cost of a trim, but it could also cost you a repair job. That said, bang trims are relatively klutz-proof (the key word being *relatively*), and children's and men's haircuts can be simple as well—though if you know you have shaky hands, do not venture forth! No matter your abilities, though, if you go in for the sleek look, you'll really be able to save some cash by mastering the art of the salon-style blow-out.

TOOLS: Sharp scissors or clippers—dull scissors will not cut hair well; rat-tail comb for sectioning; spray bottle of water to keep hair damp while you cut; combs (wide-tooth comb for long hair and thick hair, fine-tooth comb for short hair and fine hair); half a dozen hair clips (use jaw-style clips for long hair); two mirrors—wall and handheld; for some men's haircuts, a trimmer

The Big Bangs Theory

Cutting your own bangs can help you avoid those bang-trim charges and extends the time between salon visits. It's easy to get all sorts of shapes and styles in minutes. Here's how to decide what's best for you:

- Asymmetrical or long, wispy, or layered bangs are best for a square face.
- Blunt-cut bangs shaped along the contour of the eyebrows will minimize the width of the forehead on a heart-shape face.

- For an oblong or diamond-shape face, cut longer, textured bangs, or sweep them to the side. Have your bangs cover the narrowest part of your forehead.
- Soft and layered bangs, straight in the center of your forehead and a little longer on each side, or longer bangs combed to one side, elongate a round face.
- Any style can work for an oval face, so your priority should be your hair's texture.

PROJECT | # For a Fuss-Free Bang Trim

1. Section the amount of hair you want to cut or trim as bangs.

2. Comb the section to the front of your face.

3. Twist and hold the section in front of your nose.

4. Gauge the length you want to cut, and grasp the hair between your index and middle fingers, just above this line.

5. Hold this section in front of your nose to center it, and cut just below your fingers.

For Blunt Bangs

1. Section the amount of hair you want to cut or trim as bangs, and pin the rest of your hair out of the way.

2. Horizontally divide the section into two thinner sections, and pin the top section out of your way.

3. Comb the bottom section straight down, and hold it between your index and middle fingers.

4. Cut the section in a straight line across your forehead, directly below your fingers.

5. Unpin and comb the second section with the first, holding both sections between your fingers.

6. Cut the longer hairs to the same length as the shorter ones.

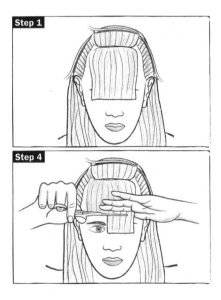

For Wispy, Textured Bangs

1. To create casual, choppy, or wispy bangs, first cut them blunt, shaped, or contoured by using the twist method.

2. Comb and hold the bangs a half-inch from the ends.

3. Holding the scissors perpendicular to the line of the cut, chop small V-shape sections.

PROJECT | ## A Salon-Style Blow-Out

No matter how sleek and shiny and flawless your tresses may turn, shelling out $40 or more to have your hair blow-dried is just not thrifty. Luckily, you can have professional-looking results at home simply by learning to use your blow-dryer properly. Some tips: It is essential that you remove excess moisture from your hair before you start, and you might want to use a smoothing product to coat the hair and minimize damage. For best results, dry curly hair with a diffuser (an attachment to your blow-dryer).

1. Comb out your hair. Section the top front of your hair and clip it out of the way.

2. Begin with the back, bottom section. Use a vent brush for drying and getting more air into your hair, or a round brush for smoothing and styling.

3. Hold the dryer at least three inches above your brush to avoid burning your hair or scalp, and lay the brush on your scalp.

4. Roll the brush under, grabbing the hair, and gently pull the brush down, from the roots to the ends.

5. When the bottom is dry, repeat the process on side sections.

6. To finish, pull up the top section, a piece at a time, and brush and blow-dry by pulling up and away from your scalp, from your roots to the ends.

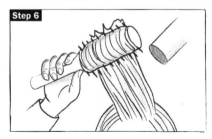

The New-Cut Splurge

When you're changing your style or color, splurge on a great stylist or colorist. Then, maintain the look with someone less expensive. Remember to take photos after the initial cut to show your next stylist exactly how you want your hair to look.

PROJECT | **A Kid's Haircut (Long, Straight Hair)**

1. Cut your child's bangs first, if necessary, as instructed on page 254.

2. Comb the child's hair, and part it down the middle, from the center of the forehead to the back of the head.

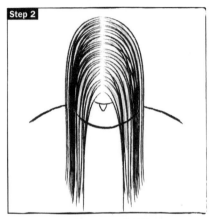
Step 2

3. Tell the child to turn his or her head all the way to the right. Comb the section straight down in front of the shoulder.

4. Grasp the hair with your index and middle fingers just above where you want to cut.

Step 5

5. Reminding the child to hold still, cut a straight line just under your fingers.

6. Repeat on the left side, matching the length to the right side.

7. Comb all the hair to the back and check that the two sections are even.

8. With one hand on the top of the child's head, snip any longer hairs to make the line straight.

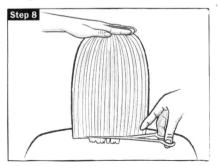
Step 8

Kids and Haircuts

To keep your child's head still while you cut, have her close her eyes. Kids will automatically turn to look at anyone who talks or anything making a sound. Give little kids their favorite toy, blanket, pacifier, finger food, or drink with a straw. Be sure to comb out the tangles with a leave-in spray conditioner before you cut. Some very young children are understandably afraid that cutting hair will hurt. Assure the child that cutting hair is not like cutting skin. Quickly snip a piece of hair and say, "See, you can't even feel that!"

PROJECT | A Kid's Haircut (Short Hair)

1. Part the child's hair down the center.

2. Comb the hair straight down on the sides.

3. Start in the front, combing and grasping a section of hair on one side of the part between your index and middle fingers.

4. Cut on an angle from the eyebrow toward the middle of the ear.

5. Repeat on the opposite side.

6. Pick up the section of hair behind the ear, and comb it from underneath.

7. Grasp the section of hair between your index and middle fingers.

8. Cut on an angle from the center of the ear to the center of the neck in back.

9. Repeat on the opposite side. You've now established the perimeter of the cut.

10. Part the hair horizontally into a section an inch wide, from the forehead toward the crown.

11. Comb the hair straight up from the scalp, grasping it between your index and middle fingers.

12. Cut this section to the length you want.

13. Make a one-inch section from the crown toward the neck, pulling the hair straight out from the scalp.

14. Cut this section of hair, matching the length to the top section.

15. Making sections parallel to the section you just cut, continue cutting around the head, matching each section to the length of the section next to it.

16. Comb the whole head of hair into place, and neatly cut around the ears.

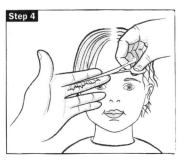

Step 4

Step 6

Step 11

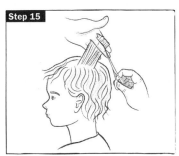

Step 15

PROJECT | **A Man's Haircut**

1. Wet the hair and comb through.

2. Cut at the bottom of the head straight across the neckline at the length you want.

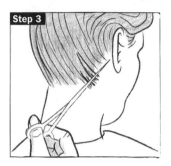

3. Comb the hair in back over to the right side, and cut on an angle toward the ear. (Ultimately, you will create a line that wraps from the nape of the neck, up one side of the head, across the front, and over the opposite side.)

4. Repeat on the other side.

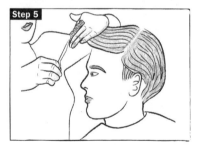

5. Next, cut the front. Comb the hair forward, and grasp it between your index and middle fingers.

6. Cut to the desired length.

7. Using this cut as your guide, comb one-inch horizontal sections and make successive cuts as you move toward the back of the head.

8. Part the hair horizontally above the ear into a one-inch section.

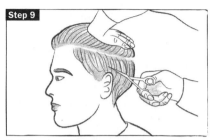

9. Cut around the ear, connecting to the guideline at the back.

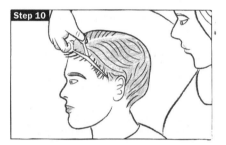

10. Move to the front of the head. Part the hair naturally, or in the middle if there is no natural part. Comb the hair at the side forward toward the temple, then cut at an angle toward the ear.

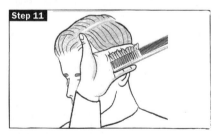

11. Comb the hair above the ear, pulling it away from the head.

12. Grasp the uncut hair with your fingers, then cut it to match the length of the section underneath.

13. Continue cutting up from the ear until you meet the top section of hair.

14. Repeat steps 9 through 14 on the opposite side.

15. Comb through the hair, sliding it between your index and middle fingers, and cut any long pieces or uneven sections to match the guideline.

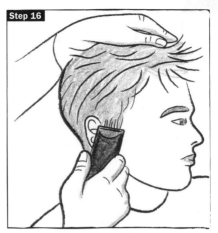

16. Clean up the ends of the sideburns and back of the neck by laying the edge of a trimmer against the skin and pulling it straight down.

Healthy Body, Happy Wallet

News flash: Health really *is* wealth. This is true on the most basic level (you cannot work if you're very ill), but also because treating illness costs money. Checkups may not be anyone's idea of a good time and, yes, healthy living takes a bit of effort, but what are all your thrifty lifestyle changes worth if you let this one thing slide? It's not just doctors, diet, and exercise, though. There are plenty of other factors that influence your well-being—from the amount of time you dedicate to spending with your friends to the quality of your sleep.

Five Ways to Improve Your Health

Diet and exercise, as we all hear over and over again, are key elements to a healthy lifestyle. Your food choices affect your health head to toe, so it's the best place to start your new healthy lifestyle. That's not to say you can never have cake or fried chicken again—life would hardly be worth living without certain foods. Eat for health and enjoyment. Here's how:

Stay Out of Debt

A study at Ohio State University suggested a connection between health and the strain of debt. Dr. Paul J. Lavraks, director of the study, says, "We found that people who are stressed about debt, particularly from credit cards, tend to be in worse physical condition than those without money worries. We've known that such folks are more likely to smoke and be overweight. What was a surprise was that we found heart attack to be the single most prominent health problem stemming from credit-card debt."

1. Avoid refined foods and sugars. Go for brown rice instead of white, whole fruits over fruit juice. Steer clear of anything that contains corn syrup, high-fructose corn syrup, or concentrated fruit juices.

2. Drink less caffeine and avoid sodas. Just knowing how much sugar is in one can of soda is enough to make your teeth fall out.

3. Limit your alcohol intake. Yes, red wine may help prevent heart disease, but only if it's consumed in moderation. That means one to two drinks a day at most, and ideally less than that for women.

4. Steer clear of trans and saturated fats. The hydrogenated (or partially hydrogenated) fats found in processed foods essentially have no nutritional value. Trans fats upset your normal bodily functions and contribute to all kinds of problems, including obesity and heart conditions. They're found in snack foods and "junk food."

5. You're exercising, right? (If not, see page 276 for some easy ways to get started.)

The Best Free Health-Booster | by Jessie Sholl

Friends can be flaky and family can be frustrating. But just the fact that you have concerned and caring people—your pals, peeps, BFFs, and phone-a-friends; your cousins, siblings, even the sister of your brother-in-law's father—in your life is a benefit in the long run: Having good relationships with friends and family reduces stress and keeps you healthy.

There's proof. In 1961, in Roseto, Pennsylvania, an offhand observation

DEBT AND HEALTH CORRELATION FROM JOSEPH C. PISCATELLA

by the town's physician launched a dramatic thirty-year study to understand the town's low incidence of heart attacks. Roseto, a town of 1,600, had half the number that were documented in 5,000-resident Bangor, Maine.

Both towns had similarly high numbers of smokers and similarly cholesterol-crammed diets. But Roseto, populated almost exclusively by Italian immigrants, boasted a cohesion that didn't exist in Bangor. As researchers discovered, many of Roseto's homes housed three generations under one roof; nearly every family ate dinner together every evening. The town's residents stopped on the streets to chat, brought each other food, and worked together in civic organizations (twenty-two of them—remarkable for such a small town). On Sundays they attended the same church.

But then things began to change. Factories closed, and kids left for college. As cohesiveness diminished, heart attack rates began to rise until they equaled the numbers in Bangor. A flurry of research proved the link.

How does the "Roseto effect" work exactly? Here's how John Cacioppo, a professor at the University of Chicago and coauthor of *Loneliness: Human Nature and the Need for Social Connection,* explains it: "When you're alone or disconnected from others, your brain is on high alert, looking to interpret dangers around you. Perhaps you've walked through the woods, enjoying the scenery, only to look down and see a curved stick in the path. Well, you weren't walking around looking for snakes, but your *brain* was walking around looking for snakes. Loneliness increases your sensitivity, so you will see a threat even when it's not there. That increases vascular resistance, and that can cause blood pressure to rise." Loneliness can also cause a rise in the level of the stress hormone cortisol—which can weaken your immune system.

Especially in the digital age, it is important to note that the depth of your relationships matters far more than their quantity. What good are six hundred Internet "friends," when not a one has your phone number?

A recent study at Brigham Young University further confirms a link between heart health and closeness: Researchers found that blood pressure was higher when participants discussed a negative event with an ambivalent friend than it was when they had the same discussion with a supportive friend. They concluded that individuals may not be able to fully relax in the presence of ambivalent friends and may not benefit from the support offered by these more casual friends during stressful times.

Ultimately, the joy and relief is based on knowing that you're not alone. "It's about the union," said Professor Cacioppo. "It's about greater than one. That's the secret of the human species, it's greater than one."

Ask a Doctor . . .

Henry S. Lodge, MD, Columbia University College of Physicians and Surgeons, New York

Q In what area of health care should one *not* cut corners?

A Some people say they can't afford a $20 co-pay for a doctor's visit, but this is your *health*. Be honest with yourself about the co-pay in terms of other things in your budget. The least cost effective thing you can do is to wait until you need to go to urgent care centers or emergency rooms. That practice is not only expensive, it's also a sign that you're letting things go until they break. Staying healthy, catching problems early, and staying on top of chronic health issues are the thriftiest things you can do. Illness can be a catastrophic expense.

Making the most of your time with the doctor. Prior to your appointment, take a moment to write down what you want to go over. Most people will forget things they want to talk about. You should also make a list of medicines you are taking. Include information about how frequently you take them and the exact dose. Note any changes. If your cardiologist adjusted your dosage of a medicine or you started taking birth control, that's important information. Your internist is supposed to coordinate the various data, but there is no easy system for keeping all the information in one place.

If you're not taking your medication, you need to say so. People are often embarrassed to admit that, but your doctor needs to know if the prescription is causing a side effect or if you're forgetting to take it. One third of prescriptions are never filled, and noncompliance is a big deal. Doctors are there to help you and can work with you if you are having trouble with your medications, or can't afford them, so let us know.

Generic drugs. The good news is that it's rare that the more expensive drugs do a better job for you than the generics. The difference is often just marketing.

Antibiotics and the common cold. The common cold is a viral infection, and antibiotics attack bacteria. They cannot cure your cold, and taking them for a cold is actually counterproductive: the bacteria in your body build resistance to antibiotics over time.

Your health insurance provider and your health. The health insurance industry is stacked against preventative care. Employers and employees are constantly switching to secure better deals. The average person switches health-insurance providers about every three to five years. So to the insurance provider, you're just passing through. You may have a stroke in 20 years, but the insurance company's concern is about your health for the three to five years that you are its customer. It is likely to put minor impediments in your way. It's up to *you* to make preventative care a priority.

. . . and a Preventative Care Specialist

Pamela Hops, MD, Continuum Center for Health and Healing, New York

Q What is a rule of thumb for preventative health care?

A I'll give you three: Be tobacco-free, be physically active, and eat a healthy diet. Try to go outside in the fresh air as often as you can. The benefits of exercise are numerous for both physical and mental health, and sunshine will give you vitamin D. (Higher levels of vitamin D have been shown to help protect against breast, ovarian, and colon cancer and heart disease; it's also good for bone health and the prevention of osteoporosis.)

Keep your brain active. Do crossword puzzles or challenging mental exercises daily.

Take advantage of free annual flu vaccines if they're offered by your employer. Take care of yourself—carve out time for yourself every day.

In the expensive and overrated category. Multivitamins and certain supplements—many people try to find "cures" in supplements. But it's better and less expensive to eat your vitamins and supplements in whole foods, especially fresh, seasonal produce.

Exercise and stress relief. Exercise may not eliminate stress, but it definitely alleviates it. Studies have found that twenty minutes a day will benefit your mental health, reduce your stress, and even increase your confidence. It also helps prevent some chronic diseases and reduces the risk of dementia (and Alzheimer's) and some cancers. And, of course, it increases your metabolic rate, decreasing your appetite and helping to reduce body fat and prevent cardiovascular disease and bone loss (osteoporosis).

The common cold. If you smoke, stop when you are ill. Smokers remain ill for an average of three additional days. When you are sick, old-fashioned advice still works best: rest, drink plenty of fluids (including chicken soup), and use a nasal saline wash; a humidifier with eucalyptus oil can be helpful as well. On the front end, moderate exercise and 500 milligrams of vitamin C each day have been shown to reduce the frequency of colds (though vitamin C hasn't shown any benefit in reducing the severity or length of a cold once it's started).

Doctor, Doctor!

No, your eyes aren't playing tricks on you; we asked two doctors for advice. That's how important we think these issues are. Dr. Henry Lodge focuses on how to get the most out of a doctor's visit, while Dr. Pamela Hops explains how to keep yourself in tip-top shape.

One for the Obvious File

Let's get this one out of the way: Responsible for more than 500,000 deaths annually, smoking is the single most preventable cause of death in the United States. According to the American Lung Association, if a person starts smoking before age twenty, each cigarette costs him or her about twenty seconds of life.

Most people assume that the greatest health risk from smoking is cancer. And while it's true that smoking leads to more than 150,000 cancer deaths each year, the impact of smoking on the risk of heart disease is much greater. Smoking contributes to about 40 percent of all cardiac deaths. Smokers are twice as likely as nonsmokers to have a heart attack and are five times more likely to die from sudden cardiac death. In one study, the mortality from coronary heart disease in people who smoked twenty-five or more cigarettes per day was nearly triple that of nonsmokers. It's the same for stroke.

Cigarettes pose the greatest health hazard, but other forms of tobacco are also harmful. Cigar and pipe smokers have a higher risk of heart disease than nonsmokers. This is probably due to the fact that cigar and pipe smokers actually do inhale, even though most of them think they don't. Snuff and chewing tobacco contain nicotine, usually in levels that are more concentrated than the amount in cigarette smoke. The body absorbs nicotine through the nasal passages and the lining of the mouth, rather than through the lungs, but the result is the same: a kick in the heart rate and blood pressure, producing strain on the cardiac muscle. Then there's the increased risk of oral cancers. . . . Smokeless tobacco is not a safe alternative.

When "Quitter" Is a Compliment

Quitting smoking is insanely difficult, for many reasons. Nicotine, a drug found naturally in tobacco (but enhanced by manufacturers), is as physically addictive as heroin. Then there are the emotional and psychological hurdles to overcome in quitting. If you always crave a cigarette when you're having a drink, or all your friends smoke, quitting may make you feel like you're excising a big part of your personality. It's tough to voluntarily do something that temporarily makes your life less fun. So go easy on yourself and be patient—it's hard, but you can do it.

To quit once and for all, the most common advice is to keep yourself

SMOKING CAUTIONARY BY JOE PISCATELLA; QUITTING ADVICE BY MELISSA KIRSCH; THRIFTONOMICS BREAKDOWN BY JULIANA BUNIM

out of situations and places where you're likely to smoke (for example, bars or outside the office where everyone takes smoke breaks); drink lots of water; and don't be afraid of gaining a little weight. You might, but this is a small price to pay when you consider the dangers of continuing to smoke— and you can lose it later. Exercise, knit, paint—anything to keep your hands busy and to distract you from smoking. Find outlets for stress relief if you've used smoking as a way to relax. When you get a craving, repeat the mantra, "In five minutes, I won't want it." And it's true—you won't.

There are nicotine replacement therapies, like gum and patches, that work wonders for some people. Some antidepressants also work well. Get advice from your doctor, who will be happy to help you quit.

THRIFTONOMICS

Your Cigarettes, or Your Retirement?

Need a financial incentive to quit smoking? In 2009, the average retail cost of a pack of cigarettes was $4.35 (much more in some cities). Assume you smoke an average of one pack a day. At $4.35 a day, that's $130.50 a month, or $1,587.75 a year (not to mention that you've smoked 7,300 cigarettes!). That's a serious hit on your disposable income and your ability to compound your savings.

If, instead of using that money to buy cigarettes, you decided to put it to good use, your savings could translate into some pretty impressive earnings. A 30-year-old who stops smoking and instead contributes that $1,587.75 annually into a 401(k) earning 9 percent a year (a probable return, except in times like the financial crisis of 2008) would have nearly $360,000 at age 65. That's without matching and starting with zero savings. If that same 30-year-old didn't touch his 401(k) until he was 70 years old, that balance would jump to more than $562,000.

You could also divert that money into an extra mortgage payment to save on interest payments. Say you have a $250,000, 30-year fixed-rate loan at 6 percent. Your monthly payment, including principal and interest, is $1,498.88. Over the life of the loan, you'll pay a whopping $289,593.34 in interest. But if you quit smoking, you could put that $1,587.75 you saved in nicotine dollars into an extra annual mortgage payment. Follow that plan, and you'll end up saving $66,535.04 off those interest payments, not to mention that you'll pay off your loan six years earlier.

35 Years of Smoking	
One Pack a Day	**Depositing that Money in Your 401(k)**
−$55,000	+$360,000

Your Pearly Whites, Your Life

I t's easy to take your teeth for granted—until a toothache strikes, when you'll wish you hadn't put off that dentist appointment and let your floss gather dust. The pain won't be the only thing that makes you unhappy—dental work is notoriously expensive, and dental insurance (if you have it) rarely covers major procedures in full. That's why when it comes to teeth, preventative care is nonnegotiable. It's extremely costly to fix your chompers, but you can prevent problems and keep them sparkling with minimal investment. Some guidelines to keep in mind:

Brush and floss. As the saying goes, "You only have to brush the teeth you want to keep." Same goes with flossing, which is the only way to clean between the teeth and beneath the gum line. If the potential loss of your teeth isn't enough to motivate you, consider the fact that many studies have found a link between gum disease and heart disease, stroke, and complications during pregnancy. (The secondary conditions are probably caused by the bacteria that normally resides in your mouth but can build up to the point where they enter the bloodstream and cause an increase in coronary plaque and system-wide inflammation.)

Get your teeth cleaned and examined every year. If you are uninsured, a teeth-cleaning will seem like an odious expense, but you'll potentially be saving yourself thousands of dollars in dental work. A stitch in time . . .

If you don't have dental insurance, talk to your dentist. Many dentists will reduce their fees in exchange for cash payment or will help you work out an incremental payment system. You might also look into buying your own dental insurance; it can be pretty cheap as an add-on to your medical coverage, and those free annual exams could save you big in the long run.

Use dental schools for the simple stuff. In many cities, dental schools offer lower cost care for everything from tooth whitening to root canals. While these clinics can be a great place for affordable cleanings and fillings, they may be a penny-wise-but-pound-foolish destination for more complicated procedures. It's probably worth investing in professional care for the complex stuff—students take much, much longer than experienced dentists to complete their work, and it can cost a fortune to repair errors. It's for life, it's in your mouth, and it's worth doing right.

Go on a dental tour. In this country, a root canal or post and crown can cost several thousand dollars—per tooth. In the rest of the world, it's much less expensive. "Dental tourism" is an increasingly popular way for folks to save themselves major money, and get a nice holiday at the same time. Places like Argentina have quality professional care for about a tenth of the price—so if you are in need of major work, it could be worth the airfare and hotel to save yourself a few grand.

Stop Stressing

Stress is any circumstance that imposes special physical or psychological demands on us or throws off our equilibrium. Positive stress, or *eustress,* is often reflected in a confident attitude and superior performance. When we're under pressure, we experience heightened energy and motivation levels that enable us to function at our best. A certain amount of stress also makes life interesting. With too little stimulation, we become bored and frustrated.

On the other hand, too much stress pushes us into overdrive, or *distress.* It's not unlike the strings on a violin: When they're too loose, the sound they make is poor; too tight, and the strings break. "Stress can be the spice of life," says Dr. Mark Ketterer, a clinical psychologist at Henry Ford Hospital in Detroit, Michigan, "or the kiss of death." It's the latter possibility that should worry us.

STRESS MANIFESTO BY JOSEPH C. PISCATELLA

The Stress-Health Correlation

The presence of distress in American society can actually be quantified:

- The Centers for Disease Control and Prevention estimates that 60 to 70 percent of all disease and illness is stress-related.
- Eighty-nine percent of adults state that they experience high stress levels.
- An estimated 75 to 90 percent of visits to physicians are stress-related.
- Job stress costs American businesses about $300 billion annually in absenteeism, compensation claims, mental-health claims, health insurance and direct medical expenses, and reduced productivity and retention.
- According to the American Medical Association, more than half of the national medical bill can be attributed to an unhealthy, stressful lifestyle.

Unfortunately, modern society tends to produce constant distress. How we respond is up to us. Anything you can do to relax your mind and body on a regular basis will enhance your ability to manage stress. Set aside time for yourself in the midst of your busy schedule. You deserve it! Then look for an activity that will help you switch off and relax. Go for a walk, read a book, listen to music, soak in a warm bath, practice yoga. Never use lack of time as an excuse to keep you from practicing relaxation techniques. Do it for yourself, because no one else will do it for you. Here are some ideas for simple ways to relax every day, no matter how hectic your schedule.

Keep a journal. Researchers have long recognized the health benefits of writing about emotions, especially those associated with significant personal experiences. Journaling is especially valuable in coping with the aftershocks of extremely stressful events, such as divorce or the death of a spouse or close relative. The same holds true for relieving daily stress—as long as you focus on feelings, not facts. You may want to start with where you were or what you were doing. But move quickly to a description of your reaction to the event and how it is affecting you. The best way to get started is simply to write every day, at the same time and in a place set aside as a sanctuary. Use a notebook or computer—there is no right or wrong way. Just let it rip. Even if words don't come easily to you, keep at it. The more you write, the quicker it will become second nature to you.

Clarify your goals and values. People who are under the greatest stress, say many psychologists, are those who drift through life without direction. They have no standard against which to measure their lives, which means that the act of living itself carries no reason and little joy. Stress-resistant people, on the other hand, have goals that concern quality of life as well as material success. They concentrate on what is worth being, not just what is worth having. Having goals of any sort can put us under some pressure, but when our goals focus on making life more meaningful, they work for us by allowing us to work toward them.

Tranquilize with exercise. People who exercise frequently experience more positive moods and less anxiety than people who exercise little or not at all. No one is certain why this is so. One reason may be that the physical act of exercising allows the body to "throw off" tension. Anyone who runs, walks, or swims regularly knows that post-exercise feeling: the body feels tired, even drained, but good and less stressed out.

Another possibility is that exercise reduces stress hormones, which is particularly important for people who suffer from chronic stress. Since these people are always geared up in a "fight-or-flight" mode, they generally have high levels of stress chemicals circulating in their bloodstream. When no physical response is necessary, the stress hormones bombard the coronary arteries, causing injury, inflammation, and, in rare instances, sudden cardiac arrest. Exercise appears to burn up excess stress hormones. With regular exercise, the body learns to metabolize these hormones more effectively, potentially reducing the likelihood of coronary injury.

A third possibility is that exercise stimulates the brain's production of endorphins, chemicals that produce a happy, satisfied feeling and thus enhance one's sense of calm and well-being. Simply put, people who exercise regularly feel better about life. The result is an enhanced ability to cope with stress.

Get enough sleep. Chronic sleep deprivation is linked to psychological distress, including depression and anxiety. Research at Pennsylvania State University suggests that blood levels of cortisol and other stress hormones are significantly higher in insomniacs than in healthy sleepers.

Meditate. Studies at UCLA and Harvard University have shown the physiological effects of meditation: When you're asleep, your oxygen consumption is decreased by 8 percent. When people meditate, however, consumption decreases by 12 percent, an indication that your body is equally if not even more deeply relaxed. These studies also illustrate that meditation can decrease blood pressure significantly. Author Deepak Chopra says, "Meditation is not a way of making your mind quiet. It's a way of entering into the quiet that's already there—buried under the 50,000 thoughts the average person thinks every day." See page 281 for tips on how to get started.

Listen to your spiritual side. Good family relationships, playing bridge with friends, belonging to the Elks or Rotary clubs—all are associated with less stress. Studies have found that having a religious faith and a sense of spirituality can also reduce stress. According to Dr. Fred Luskin of the Stanford University School of Medicine, "People who go to church, synagogue, mosque, or Buddhist monastery once a week average eighty-three years of longevity. For those who do not go at all, longevity averages seventy-five years. You do the math!"

Laugh. A good laugh—like a good workout—produces an overall sense of well-being. Laughter flexes the muscles of the chest and abdomen, including the diaphragm, and causes deep breathing to take place. By exercising the shoulders, neck, and face, it releases tension in the muscles. And humor itself can prompt a different perspective on life and its challenges. Just remember the words of the late Milton Berle: "Laughter is an instant vacation."

Take a vacation. Studies have shown that, over a nine-year period, at-risk middle-age men who didn't take an annual vacation were 21 percent more likely to die and 32 percent more likely to die of coronary heart disease than those who took time off each year. Some researchers believe that the scenic beauty encountered on many vacations can promote health; it focuses attention, helping people plan better and deflect distractions while lowering irritability. Others say that relaxation can be found in the escapism of reading on vacation (history or "trashy" novels, but not business books). Whatever it is, it works. (See page 315 for frugal vacation tips.)

Stretch. In addition to decreasing the risk of injury, helping to relieve lower back pain, and improving agility, regular stretching exercises promote a relaxation response. Stretching acts as an internal massage for the body.

Volunteer. People under chronic stress often make themselves the center of the universe. Almost everything in life—events, relationships, workload— is seen in terms of how it impacts them. As a result, they are constantly vigilant and prone to anxiety.

Changing from an inward to an outward perspective can break this cycle. A great way to do this is by becoming a volunteer. Coach a youth soccer team. Read to elderly shut-ins. Man the information desk at the hospital. Get involved in a political campaign. Find an area of interest and give something of yourself to it. You'll forget your problems, widen your perspective, and establish meaningful relationships.

MY THRIFT

Enough in Their Hearts

My father owned and ran a flower shop. Part of my job was to collect money from people who sent flowers for the deceased. A bouquet cost $2, but people paid me a quarter at a time, week by week. We didn't mind. These people didn't have $2 of their own money, but they felt enough in their hearts to send a basket of flowers when their friends passed.

—Joseph Zona, born 1925

Don't be a stranger. The MacArthur Foundation's landmark study on aging identifies meaningful social relationships as being of equal importance to diet and exercise in a healthy lifestyle. Associate with people who share common interests, make you laugh, and help you feel good about yourself. Stay in touch with friends and family. Talk things over. When tensions build up, discuss the problem with a close friend or with the people involved. Positive social connections keep you from feeling that you're going through life alone. You have help and support.

Get a pet. Emerging scientific evidence suggests that people who keep pets are likely to benefit from improvements in physical and emotional well-being. People with pets seem to handle stress better and have lower blood pressure. In addition, many behavioral scientists contend that loneliness, isolation, depression, and hostility—all powerful predictors of adverse health outcomes—may be partially alleviated by the companionship of pets. Some experts believe this change in outlook may stem from active involvement in the daily care of pets and from the unconditional love and acceptance that the animals offer their owners. Dogs in particular have a positive effect on health because of a third factor: Walking them is great exercise!

Turn off the television. America is perhaps the most information-saturated place on Earth. The morning news, the evening and late-night reports—these are staples of modern life. And if you're a real news junkie, you have access to all-day coverage on cable or the Internet.

Unfortunately, TV news presents hyped-up versions of the day's head-lines that are invariably sensationalized and negative. Instead of producing clarity, it increases anxiety. Every day we are subjected to unforgettable images of violence and destruction; the more raw the footage, the more we see it. The stories can fray the nerves and produce overwhelming uncer-tainty or worry every night. But you can always turn off your TV set and opt to get more of your news from written reporting, which tends to provide a calmer account of events. It also helps to concentrate on immediate surroundings—family, work, friends, and community. By being involved in "real life" events, you will feel less anxious and more in control.

The Nap as Free Vacation

It's free, it's nontoxic, and it has no dangerous side effects. Hard to believe, with these powerful selling points, that people have to be convinced to nap. But alas, for way too long, napping has been given a bad rap.

Employers want to keep their workers occupied with the business of business. Parents want their children to do homework when they come home from school or at least to play outside instead of "sleeping the day away." University administrators think the sight of students napping on campus sets a bad example. But as the facts pile up, the case for napping becomes too compelling to dismiss.

Napping Will:

1. Increase your alertness. For many nappers, this is the most important benefit of a nap. Whether you're on the road, observing market trends, diagnosing patients, or interacting with clients, staying alert is the most important determinant of your efficiency. NASA studies have conclusively demonstrated that alertness increases by as much as 100 percent after a brief nap, even in well-rested subjects.

2. Speed up your motor performance. All of us engage in tasks that involve coordination, whether we're typing at a keyboard, operating machinery, changing a tire, or bagging groceries. A Harvard study demonstrated that the speed of a learned motor performance is the same in nappers as in those who have had a full night of sleep.

3. Improve your accuracy. While greater speed usually involves sacrificing accuracy, napping offers a valuable exemption from this general rule. So whether you shoot baskets or firearms, play sonatas or golf, cut diamonds or hair, a nap helps you get it right.

4. Help you make better decisions. What are you going to eat for lunch? Should you ask for a raise or wait a little longer before making the request? What stock should you buy? Or should you sell? Of course, some decisions are so significant that lives can hang in the balance. Pilots who are allowed to nap in the cockpit commit fewer judgment errors on takeoff and landing than those who aren't.

5. Improve your perception. Think how much you depend on your eyes, your ears, and, to a lesser extent, your senses of taste, touch, and smell. Research shows that a nap can be as effective as a night of sleep in improving perceptual skills. Driving, cooking, appreciating music or art, reading, proofreading, quality control, and even bird-watching are all enhanced after a nap.

6. Fatten your bottom line. Fatigue-related accidents cost U.S. industry more than $150 million a year. According to the Shiftwork Practices survey issued in 2004 by Circadian Technologies, workers' comp costs are highest in locations where employees report the most fatigue, and claims at facilities that ban napping are four times higher than in workplaces that allow it. Judged by this standard, naps are a bargain.

7. Preserve your youthful looks. Nothing ages you like fatigue. Adding a nap to your regimen improves skin and tissue regeneration and keeps you looking younger longer. Napping is truly beauty sleep.

8. Improve your sex life. Sleep deprivation dampens sex drive and sexual function. Napping reverses these effects. So nap now and your partner will love you more later.

9. Help you lose weight. Studies show that sleepy people reach for high-fat, sugar-rich foods more often than rested people.

10. Reduce your risk of heart attack and stroke. Studies conclusively show that fatigue contributes to hypertension, heart attack, stroke, arrhythmia, and other cardiovascular disorders, even in otherwise physically fit subjects.

11. Reduce your risk of diabetes. Sleep deprivation increases insulin and cortisol levels, which can raise the risk for type 2 diabetes, the sixth leading cause of death in the United States.

12. Improve your stamina. Whether you're running a marathon or simply sitting through a series of meetings, a well-planned nap will keep you from fading out before the finish line. Studies have shown that a nap during or after work allows you to be alert and ready for the second part of your day.

13. Elevate your mood. While sleep deprivation causes irritability, depression, and anger, napping bathes your brain in serotonin, reversing those effects and creating a more positive outlook.

14. Boost your creativity. It's no wonder that history's great artists and inventors took naps. Napping allows your brain to create the loose associations necessary for creative insight and opens the way for a fresh burst of new ideas.

15. Reduce stress. Stress and a[ ] the result of cortisol being produc[ ] adrenal glands. By releasing the an[ ] growth hormone, a nap can reduce that stress and anxiety and make you a calmer person.

16. Help your memory. Much of your memory consolidation cannot occur in any meaningful way without sleep. Everything from learning a new language to remembering the periodic table of elements can be improved by adding a short nap between study periods.

17. Reduce dependence on drugs and/or alcohol. If you deprive yourself of needed sleep, you're more likely to abuse not only caffeine but also alcohol and other drugs. Saying yes to a nap will make you less likely to reach for stimulants to keep you awake and downers to get you to sleep.

18. Alleviate migraines, ulcers, and other problems with psychological components. In one way or another, cortisol is involved in all these ailments. By reintroducing growth hormone, napping can reduce their severity.

19. Improve the ease and quality of your nocturnal sleep. Sure, it sounds contradictory, but sleeping during the day helps you sleep better at night. Going past the warning signs of fatigue can push you into a slightly manic state in which your body revs up so much to compensate for lack of sleep that you can be too "wired" to fall asleep when you have the opportunity.

And finally . . .

20. It feels good. There's no way for science to really measure this, but millions of nappers can't be wrong.

Keep the Cash, Drop the Weight

I f you're trying to lose a significant amount of weight, you're likely to run into a world of advertisements that all tell you the same thing: The way to be thin is to spend—on meal-replacement drinks, prepackaged food, meal-delivery systems, diet plans, supplements, consultants, personal trainers, and more. But losing weight should be a money-saving proposition: Eating fewer calories should mean buying less food. Eat less, spend less. What's so hard about that?

Clearly, if it were that easy, dieting wouldn't be the $59 billion industry that it is. But there are ways to shed pounds without shedding cash, too. It takes some old-fashioned discipline and commitment, but slimming down and saving up naturally go hand in hand.

One easy first step is to stay away from anything marketed as a dieting aid. These products can be a drain on your budget. And creating your own food plans is just a matter of getting organized, reading labels, and cooking for yourself. If you don't have time or the skill to cook at home, there are premade options in the freezer aisle that are just as healthy as products branded for dieters. Nutritionist Mary Jane Detroyer recommends frozen dinners by Kashi or Amy's, perhaps supplemented by a side salad or some (heated) frozen vegetables. (You can handle that, right?)

Gym memberships can be another money pit, especially if you are not a frequent user. Before you take the plunge, think seriously about your habits. Give yourself a trial commitment. "Buy a pair of sneakers for $60 and go out and walk," Detroyer says. "That's not expensive. That's thrifty. Besides, if you're not willing to go walk five days a week, then why would you be willing to go to the gym?" Some dieters find that signing up for running clubs and races does the trick.

But if you need more help with commitment, there's one approach that turns the diet industry on its head: Instead of weight loss costing you money, *not* losing weight will cost you. The method was created

---

THRIFTONOMICS

1lb. Flesh, $100

A n investigation conducted by New York City's Department of Consumer Affairs found that one diet center in Manhattan would have charged a potential dieter $100 per pound to lose seven pounds and maintain the weight loss. "Worse, I was only one pound away from being underweight to start with," said the undercover investigator.

CASH-WEIGHT CONTINUUM BY ERICA ORDEN; INVESTIGATIVE REPORTING BY MARK GREEN; QUICK CALORIE-BURNING TIPS BY JOSEPH C. PISCATELLA

by Dean Karlan, now an economics professor at Yale University. When Karlan was in graduate school, he wanted to drop between thirty and forty pounds, but he couldn't figure out how to stick to his rudimentary, low-cost plan: exercising more and "eating fewer cookies and more salads," as he puts it.

So Karlan and a friend, who also wanted to lose weight, made a pact: If one of them failed to lose a predetermined amount of weight within six months, that person would have to pay the other an agreed-upon amount of money. Karlan and his pal were willing to risk some hefty sums: half their annual incomes. The agreement worked so well that Karlan transformed the basic concept

| How to Burn 150 Extra Calories a Day* ||
ACTIVITY	MINUTES
Washing/waxing car	45–60
Washing windows/floors	45–60
Volleyball	45
Touch football	30–45
Gardening	30–45
Walking 1¾ miles (20 minutes/mile)	35
Bicycling 5 miles	30
Dancing (fast)	30
Pushing a stroller 1½ miles	30
Raking leaves	30
Walking 2 miles (15 minutes/mile)	30
Water aerobics	30
Swimming laps	20
Basketball	15–20
Jumping rope	15
Running 1½ miles (10 minutes/mile)	15
Shoveling snow	15
Stair walking	15

*These values are estimates for a 154-pound person.

into a business, stickk.com, which helps people arrange their own commitment contracts. Users can sign up to a have a predetermined amount of money deducted from their bank account and routed either to a friend or to a charity of their choice if they don't stick to their diet and fitness plans and drop the pounds. That's, um, thrifty incentive for you.

If you just want to shed a few pounds and save a few bucks, skip the booze and beer. Even a light beer has 95 calories. By skipping three rounds, you'll save about $15 and almost 300 calories. Your social life may suffer and your bartender will miss you, but your pants will fit and your wallet will thank you.

Just Do It! (Here's How)

Exercise is a friendly trick you play on nature. Your body expects you to walk ten miles a day, with an hour or two of hunting and some sprinting and heavy labor thrown in, but fortunately it's not that smart. You can convince it that spring has come to the savanna with less than an hour of exercise a day. That means it takes less than an hour a day to be lean, fit, alert, energetic, healthy, and optimistic for decades to come!

Nature is not a treadmill at the gym. It's an ever-changing physical environment, so it should come as no surprise that a variety of different exercises and intensities do more good than a single, unvarying routine. Nature's rule is simple: Do something real every day. Ignore all that talk about exercising three or four days a week. Like our national cholesterol guidelines, it's a bare minimum, a desperate plea from the medical profession to a nation of couch potatoes. Remember, your body craves the daily chemistry of exercise. Whether the exercise is long, slow, and steady (an hour or two of vigorous walking) or shorter and more intense (running, swimming, or using the exercise machines at the gym) is a lot less important than the "dailyness" of it, six days a week. So experiment with a variety of aerobic exercise, and find an outdoor sport that you like: biking, kayaking, downhill or cross-country skiing, or stiff hiking. Keep your heart rate in the high aerobic zone at the gym and in the low aerobic zone while exercising outside, and you'll get great results.

The earlier in life you start, the bigger the payoff. It may seem exhausting to fit exercise into your crazy work schedule, but that's looking at it backward. We are not tired at the end of the day because we get too much exercise. We are tired because we do not get enough exercise. We are mentally, emotionally, and physically drained from being sedentary. Walking through the door exhausted each night is not living; it is merely surviving large stretches of the only life we have. Besides, study after study shows that the productivity gains at work outweigh the time spent exercising, and that we function better at home—with more satisfaction and on less sleep—when we're fit. If you put any value at all on your quality of life, the time you spend exercising becomes a bargain.

Gym Smarts

When it comes to exercise, "I can't afford it" is not a valid excuse. Check out some of the following ways to slash your gym bills, or ditch the fees altogether by exercising at home. (Read on for some simple exercises to get you started.)

- Try out as many gyms as you can before committing. Most facilities will happily give you a free day or week pass for a tryout. You can probably cadge a month or two of free workouts by shopping around and taking advantage of all the offers.

- Depending on where you live, your local YMCA may be your best gym option or a great, cheaper alternative to larger chains. Don't be seduced by the fancy gyms; the Y or a community fitness center may have better facilities and is usually a lot easier on the wallet.

- If you live near your alma mater, you may be able to get access to the university facilities for a comparatively small fee. Even if you didn't attend the school, if there's a university in your area, it may offer discounts to community members. Look into it.

- Because it's in a company's best interest to have healthy employees, many offer special corporate rates for memberships in a certain gym. Your health insurance plan may also give you a subsidy for a gym membership as long as you show proof that you're going regularly.

- Read the fine print on your contract. A gym contract can be as complicated and binding as a mortgage. Ask questions: Is there an initiation fee? Does the gym offer a monthly payment plan? Can you freeze your membership if you go out of town or decide to take a break? Does the membership include a free session with a personal trainer? If it doesn't, can you have one anyway? Do classes cost extra? And most important, what are you committing to when you sign? Will you owe the gym an organ if you try to get out of your contract early?

The Gym-Free Exercise Routine

It doesn't take much more than a good pair of sneakers to start in on a cardio-vascular regimen. But in order to get truly fit, you need to balance all that running, walking, and jumping with exercises that build strength and flexibility throughout your body. Sit-ups and crunches are time-honored ways to strengthen your abdominal muscles (and all you need is a floor!), but here is an assortment of exercises that will work other key muscle groups.

TOOLS: Armless chair; hand weights or cans of food; sofa

CALL TO ARMS BY HENRY LODGE AND CHRISTOPHER CROWLEY; BUDGET-SAVVY GYM TIPS BY MELISSA KIRSCH

EXERCISE | **Triceps Extension**

This exercise strengthens the muscles in the back of your upper arms. Keep supporting your arm with your hand throughout the exercise.

1. Sit in a chair. (Your back should be supported by the back of the chair.)

2. Keep your feet flat on the floor, shoulder-width apart.

3. Hold a weight in your left hand. Raise your left arm straight toward the ceiling, with your palm facing in.

4. Support your left arm, below the elbow, with your right hand.

5. Slowly bend your left arm, bringing the hand weight toward your left shoulder.

6. Slowly straighten your left arm toward the ceiling.

7. Hold this position for 1 second.

8. Slowly bend your left arm toward your shoulder again. Pause.

9. Repeat the bending and straightening until you've completed the exercise 8 to 15 times.

10. Repeat 8 to 15 times with your right arm.

11. Rest; then do another set of 8 to 15 repetitions.

EXERCISE | **Hip Flexion**

This exercise strengthens your thigh and hip muscles. Use ankle weights when you're ready for an extra challenge.

1. Stand straight behind or to the side of a chair or table, holding on for balance.

2. Slowly bend your right knee toward your chest, without bending at your waist or twisting your hips.

3. Hold this position for 1 second.

4. Slowly lower your right leg all the way down. Pause.

5. Repeat with your left leg.

6. Alternate legs until you've completed 8 to 15 repetitions with each leg.

7. Rest; then do another set of 8 to 15 alternating repetitions.

EXERCISE | **Shoulder Flexion**

This exercise will strengthen your shoulder muscles. You'll need hand weights for this, but soup cans do the trick!

1. Sit in an armless chair with your back supported by the back of the chair.

2. Keep your feet flat on the floor, shoulder-width apart.

3. Hold the hand weights straight down at your sides, with your palms facing inward.

4. Raise both arms to shoulder height in front of you, keeping them straight and rotating your wrists so your palms face up.

5. Hold this position for 1 second.

6. Slowly lower your arms to your sides. Pause.

7. Repeat 8 to 15 times.

8. Rest; then do another set of 8 to 15 repetitions.

EXERCISES BASED ON PROGRAMS BY THE NATIONAL INSTITUTES OF HEALTH (NIH)

EXERCISE | **Side Leg Raise**

This exercise works the muscles at the sides of your hips and thighs. For an extra challenge, add ankle weights.

1. Stand straight, directly behind a chair or table, with your feet slightly apart.

2. Hold on to the chair or table for balance.

3. Slowly lift your right leg 6 to 12 inches out to the side. Keep your back and both legs straight. Don't point your toes outward; position your feet so your toes face forward.

4. Hold this position for 1 second.

5. Slowly lower your right leg. Pause.

6. Repeat with your left leg.

7. Alternate legs until you've completed 8 to 15 repetitions with each leg.

8. Rest; then do another set of 8 to 15 alternating repetitions.

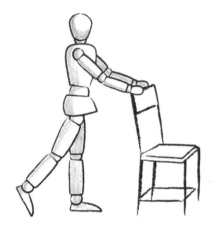

EXERCISE | **Hamstring Stretch**

This exercise stretches the muscles in the backs of your thighs.

1. Stand behind something stable, like a car or a tall sofa, holding on to the back with both hands.

2. Bend forward from your hips (not your waist), keeping your back and shoulders straight at all times.

3. When your upper body is parallel to the floor, hold the position for 10 to 30 seconds. You should feel a stretch in the backs of your thighs.

4. Repeat 3 to 5 times.

EXERCISE | **Stop, Drop, and Meditate**

Just as exercise helps your body fight disease, meditation helps you cope with the mental and emotional stresses and strains of modern life. It is proven to reduce blood pressure and curb anxiety—and it doesn't cost a dime. You just have to do it, regularly. Here's how to get started:

Create a meditation space. The space should be quiet, pleasant, clean, naturally lit, and simple—an oasis in which to meditate. Make a comfortable seat by choosing a cushion, bench, or favorite chair.

When to meditate. The best time to meditate depends upon your constitution and when you are alert and fresh—not worn out or overstimulated. Consider first thing in the morning, before bed, right after work, or during a lunch hour or coffee break, waiting periods, or other predictably idle times.

How long to meditate. Short, regular sessions are better than infrequent longer sessions. You can start slowly (five minutes) and work up to twenty to sixty minutes.

Positions for meditation. The position in which you sit or kneel should be comfortable. Your back should be straight, with the vertebrae stacked like blocks and your head being pulled up by an invisible string. Be a mountain or a tree. Your hands should be in a position that feels natural or is meaningful to you. Your eyes can be closed or half-closed.

Focusing on the breath. Focusing on the breath calms the mind and provides the stability necessary to cultivate concentration. You will be studying the nuances of your breathing and how it changes—and it will teach you awareness of the present moment.

Working with what arises. When sounds become dominant and call your attention away from breathing, focus all your awareness on the experience of the sound. Make a soft mental note of "hearing," but do not specifically name the sound "car" or "clock" or another concept. Attend to the sound, then let it go and return to the breath.

Working with sensations. When sensations in the body become dominant and call your attention away from breathing, focus all your mindfulness and attention on the sensation. Make a gentle mental note of "sensation" or "feeling" or "ache" or "pain." Attend to the sensation, then let it go and return to the breath.

Working with thoughts and images. When thoughts or images arise in the mind, as soon as you become aware of this, make a soft mental note of "thinking" or "wandering" or "seeing." Notice when you become aware of the thought or image—without judgment. Be mindful of where your mind has gone, then let the thoughts or images go and return to the breath.

Working with hindrances. When different mental states or emotions arise, especially the hindrances of desire, aversion, sleepiness, restlessness, and doubt, make note of them. As soon as you become aware of one of these, make a gentle mental note. Do not get lost in the emotion. Observe it, then let it go and return to the breath.

MEDITATION QUICK-START BY BARBARA ANN KIPFER

inside this chapter . . .

RECIPES

PROJECTS

living the life of leisure

Gatherings, Getaways & Gifts

YOU'VE TILLED YOUR SOIL, YOU'VE STRAINED YOUR BROTH, AND you've set your vinegar-whitened linens out to dry. Now it's time to let down your hair and have some fun—without tossing your newfound principles out the window. Thrifty leisure is, quite literally, simplicity itself.

You know how in almost every one of those idyllic Italian movies, there's a scene in which the (very good-looking) characters gather around for a country picnic of bread, cheese, and salad? And it looks like they just might be eating the best meal of their lives? And having the most engaging conversation ever captured on film? Simple is good.

All right, so a cramped balcony, or no balcony at all, may be no match for the fields outside a Tuscan villa. But with a modicum of effort, any setting can be gussied up to guest-worthy standards. Tight quarters can yield surprisingly intimate and satisfying dinner parties. A "cozy" deck might be the perfect backdrop for a late-afternoon cocktail—and it'll taste that much sweeter when you know how much you saved by mixing it yourself.

And what of those *vacanza,* after all? Thrift and travel aren't mutually exclusive—everyone needs a change of scene from time to time. You just have to travel smart.

Events Small & Large

Home is where the bargains are. The maître d' will never snub you, you always know what's really the special of the day, and your presence is not subsidizing anybody's rent. You don't want to turn into a housebound curmudgeon—so it's time to bring your entertaining in. Invite people to you, and odds are they'll return the favor; simple as that. But inexperienced thriftertainers will find that party bills have a way of getting out of hand. Wild salmon for two may be a palatable sometime extravagance, but when you're feeding ten, think again. The good news is that entertaining doesn't have to be expensive or lavish. It doesn't have to leave people in awe. At its best, it brings joy and levity to life. And to that aim, it doesn't take the finest champagne to get the job done.

A Welcoming Home

Before the guests arrive, you've got to get your place entertainment-ready. How to do so for less? One of the easiest ways to warm up the look of a room is by turning off the overhead light. There's a reason the candlelit dinner earned itself a spot as *the* romantic cliché: Mood lighting works. So switch on the lamps and light the candles. Aim for three light sources per room, which will create flattering pools of light without harsh shadows. Flea markets are good places to find lamps, and learning how to repair a lamp is a valuable skill (see page 54). To better control existing overhead lighting, try installing three-way bulbs or dimmer switches.

Sultry lighting has the added bonus of obscuring dust bunnies, but no amount of subterfuge can redeem a downright grimy abode. If you haven't had time to do a thorough cleaning, quickly wipe down coffee tables and countertops. If you do nothing else, give the toilet and sink a quick scrub.

If you find yourself playing host frequently, set aside one go-to room that is always guest-friendly. Tidy the space regularly so you're never faced with a day-long deep-clean. Keep a caddy under the sofa or in a nearby cabinet and stock it with an all-purpose surface cleaner, rags, and a duster or dust-cloth so that sparkling cleanliness is always at your fingertips. To

HOME AND GUEST-ROOM TRANSFORMATIONS BY SOPHIE DONELSON

get family or roommates involved, encourage a two-minute cleaning frenzy during TV commercial breaks.

As for decor: A handsome living room can be attained via smart furniture and chic accessories, but top interior designers agree that comfort is dictated more by feel than by looks. A deep-seat, loose-cushion sofa is more inviting than a firm settee. Chairs with arms say "stay a while" more than the armless variety. Fabrics like velvet, silk (or a silk blend), and linen are more pleasing to touch than pleather or vinyl. Voluminous curtains and area rugs spell comfort in a way everyone can read. If you're not in the market for furniture, you can improve the look and feel with easy-on-the-wallet accessories like a throw blanket or pillows.

Even if you happen to have a showroom's worth of fancy furnishings, a room won't feel homey unless it's arranged with finesse. The most common mistake in setting up a room is pushing all the furniture up against the walls. It's a conversation killer. Instead, create intimate seating areas that encourage interaction. For pitch-perfect furniture placement, begin with a rug or coffee table near the center of the room and position seats and sofas around it, filling in the gaps with an ottoman or side table. A table lamp and floor lamp will be the finishing touches. No matter where a guest sits in the room, she should be within arm's reach of a side table or coffee table; don't make your friends strain to reach their beverages. (You did offer a beverage, right?)

Speaking of which: The promise of food and drink is one of the reasons guests gravitate toward the kitchen, but the heart of the house holds more than just sustenance. For partygoers, especially those who don't know other guests, cocktail pouring and food-prep assistance can be welcome forms of activity.

Which is why if you arrange a snack bar in the living room, you'll see a similar comfort level develop. But be aware that another reason people congregate in the kitchen is that it's easy to stand and move around. Sitting on a sofa or chair seems like a commitment compared with leaning against a

Beyond the Sit-Down Dinner

Formal dinners have their place, but they can wind up being fairly expensive. Lunch, brunch, and breakfast call for less alcohol and less food. You can send people home stuffed after a hearty lunch of a fresh salad, egg casserole, and white wine. If you want to invite more people than you can seat, consider a potluck buffet (page 292) or a barbecue (page 295).

countertop or a high stool. If you get trapped in an awkward conversation in the kitchen, it's easy to excuse yourself, but extricating yourself from a sofa might be more involved. But with your mood lighting and comfy seating, who's going to want to get up anyway?

Prepping the Sofa

When out-of-towners come to visit, inviting them to stay overnight is a kindness that benefits all. You'll spare your guests the cost of a hotel room, and with everyone under the same roof, you get to spend more time together.

You don't need a separate guest room to create a cozy home-away-from-home. The trick is to spend time, not money—a little forethought goes further than fancy treats or lavish extras. Some inn-worthy ways to prep:

- To start, take a look around your home and anticipate your guest's needs. A traveler's first urge will be to ditch his stuff, so create a dedicated spot for his bags and coat. If your guest is staying in your living room, offer a surface—be it a table, bench, mantel, even a plastic crate—for personal items. For a longer stay, you might spare an empty drawer or some space in a closet (with extra hangers).
- When it comes to bedding, clean linens are a must. A neatly folded stack of freshly laundered towels goes the extra mile.
- If your home doesn't have a spare room, a sofa, futon, or an air mattress will have to do. A sturdy self-inflating mattress can be had for less than $50, and it's a major step up from the sofa-cushions-on-the-floor method. If the sofa is guest-friendly, remove the back cushions to create space.
- No matter where the guest is sleeping, offer a table with some niceties: a lamp, a glass for water, maybe a stack of reading material.
- If you have travel-size toiletries or samples, set out a few in a basket—even seasoned travelers are bound to forget a thing or two. Out-of-towners will be grateful for a local magazine or a map, as well as timetables for trains, buses, subways, or ferries.
- Hosts with a spare room and a stash of unused electronics can set up an alarm clock, radio, or television. And if you have an extra robe, wash and fold it, tucking in a note to the weary traveler.

The Charismatic Cocktail Party

Cocktail parties are synonymous with glamour, but their dirty secret is, they're easy and cheap! They cost less than a dinner party, and they're more forgiving to small spaces and reluctant cooks. Don't have room to seat more than six? Let them stand! Can't cook a roast? Set out some crackers and cheese! Don't want to shell out to feed a crowd? You don't have to.

The only potential big-ticket item on the cocktail party menu is the booze, but there are plenty of values to be had in that area. Cocktail parties can bring together loads of people from your life—coworkers, friends, neighbors—for just a few hours. And parties tend to breed more parties: Friends will want to reciprocate. No more ponying up at the bar weekend after weekend—you'll have a long string of fêtes to attend. Here's to mingling!

The Five Cocktail Party Commandments

1. The food should be simple, flavorful, and not too messy. (You want the memories of the party to remain in your heart, not smeared into your upholstery.)

2. Start the party early, about 6:30 or 7:00 P.M., and anticipate that it will last about two hours. Make it clear on the invitation that the guests are joining you for cocktails. This way they won't be expecting dinner. Plan to serve about six or seven appetizers, some to pass around, others to set out in baskets or on platters.

3. Pace the food. The first ten guests can wolf down all the shrimp, leaving none for those arriving fashionably late. Set out your offerings slowly, but be prepared for a rush around thirty minutes after the party starts. Hold one dish back until the second half of the party. This will keep the guests sated and the surprises coming.

4. Keep the bar simple. Better to invest in a few high-quality wines and liquors than in lots of cheaper stuff. (Read on for five classic cocktail recipes.)

5. While you don't want to skimp, don't feel you have to serve your guests mountains of food. They'll probably be going out for dinner afterward. For a rough idea of the amount of food you will need, estimate one and a half portions of each appetizer per person.

PARTY TIPS BY BOB SLOAN

The Home Mixologist

When you're out on the town, mixed drinks will drive up your tab faster than you can say, "One more round!" If you want to enjoy all the fabulousness of cocktails, minus the sticker shock, try making them at home. There are drinks you can make with fewer ingredients—a gin and tonic, for instance, is simplicity itself. But these five cocktails will draw your friends over to your house—and keep you all far away from the $12 specials. A note: When you're serving a crowd, mixed drinks *can* get complicated, and prohibitively expensive, involving everything from the right glasses to garnishes and mixers, particularly if you are trying to anticipate everyone's tastes. That's when you should class it up with a featured cocktail, one special drink that you offer alongside beer and wine. Do it with intention, and it won't come off as cheap.

RECIPE | ## The Real-Deal Martini

The world's most celebrated cocktail, the martini was originally made from gin; vodka was not widely introduced into the United States until the 1930s. A vodka martini is more subtle and cleaner tasting, while a gin martini has more pronounced aromatics and a bigger bite. A martini is not a martini without at least a drop of vermouth, but how much or how little is purely a matter of taste; the less vermouth, the drier the martini. Though some insist on shaken martinis, liquor drinks without juice should really be stirred—shaking tends to give them a fuzzy texture. The classic garnish for a martini is an olive, but try a bay leaf instead for a distinctive touch.

Makes 4 drinks

> 14 ounces gin or vodka
> 2 ounces dry vermouth
> 8 cocktail olives or 8 bay leaves for garnish

1. Place the cocktail glasses in the freezer or refrigerator to chill for 30 minutes before serving.

2. Fill a tall pitcher with ice and add the gin or vodka and vermouth.

3. Stir well (about 50 times).

4. Strain into the cocktail glasses, leaving all the ice in the pitcher, add the olives or bay leaves, and serve.

WITH THE EXCEPTION OF THE BLOODY MARY, COCKTAIL RECIPES BY NICK MAUTONE

RECIPE | **The Beachside, Poolside, Partyside Margarita**

The margarita is among the most popular drinks ever. One reason for the demand is that it goes so well with food—the margarita's balanced blend of sweet-tart earthiness and acidity cuts through the richness and spice of many dishes, particularly Mexican. Whatever the accompaniments, it certainly hits the spot on a hot summer day. . . .

Makes 4 drinks

Coarse salt, for rimming the glasses

4 ounces fresh lime juice (from about 4 limes), some lime rind reserved for rimming the glass

8 ounces tequila

6 ounces Cointreau or triple sec

4 lime rounds for garnish

1. Pour the salt onto a small plate. Cut the reserved lime rind as necessary and rub the juicy side along the outer edge of the lip of each cocktail glass—not along the inside of the rim. Holding each glass at an angle, roll the outer edge of the rim in the salt until it is fully coated.

2. Fill a cocktail shaker with ice and add the lime juice, tequila, and Cointreau or triple sec. Shake vigorously until the outside of the shaker is beaded with sweat and frosty.

3. Strain into the salted glasses, garnish with the lime rounds, and serve.

For frozen margaritas: Place the tequila, Cointreau or triple sec, and lime juice in a large pitcher without ice and stir to mix. Process in a blender in batches, using 1 cup of crushed ice and 4½ ounces of mix per serving. Blend until smooth and pour into salted glasses.

THRIFTONOMICS

Drink at Home and Save

Go out for two $6 vodka tonics per weekend, and the tab will add up over the course of a year. Assuming that you tip an additional dollar per drink, that's $14 per weekend. Multiply that by 52 weeks, and just for stepping out the door, here's what you're racking up . . .

Bar tab: $700/year

At home, a liter of decent vodka costs about $30. A liter bottle of tonic adds an extra $2 to your tab.

Following a recipe that calls for 1.5 ounces of vodka to 3 ounces of tonic, that bottle will yield 22 drinks. Cost per homemade drink? Around $1.55! Add that up for a (conservative) year of two-cocktail weekends, and you'll spend approximately $160.

Homebody discount: $500/year

RECIPE | ## The Tangy, Hip-Shaking Mojito

The cooling, thirst-quenching mojito originated as the drink of choice for the Cuban working class. The now-familiar formalized recipe was created at La Bodeguita del Medio, a hotel in Cuba and one of Hemingway's haunts. If you prefer this drink short and stronger, reduce or omit the seltzer.

Makes 4 drinks

> 12 fresh mint sprigs
> 4 ounces Simple Syrup (see page 327)
> 4 ounces fresh lime juice (from about 4 limes)
> Ice for serving
> 8 ounces white rum
> 24 ounces club soda

1. In each of four highball or collins glasses, place 2 mint sprigs, 1 ounce syrup, and 1 ounce lime juice. Lightly mash the ingredients together with the back of a spoon.

2. Add ice and 2 ounces rum to each glass and stir to blend.

3. Fill each glass with club soda, garnish with the remaining mint, and serve.

RECIPE | ## The New-Again Old-Fashioned

Some say that this genteel, bourbon-based drink was the first to be called a cocktail, at the turn of the nineteenth century in Kentucky. You can make it more or less sweet without impinging on its integrity.

Makes 2 drinks

> 1 orange round, cut in half
> 2 maraschino cherries
> 1 teaspoon sugar
> Ice for serving
> 6 ounces bourbon, rye, scotch, or brandy
> 4 ounces club soda

1. Place 1 orange half slice, 1 cherry, and ½ teaspoon sugar in each of two rocks glasses.

2. Crush the ingredients with the back of a spoon until the fruit is well mashed and mixed with the sugar.

3. Fill the glasses with ice, pour in the bourbon, and stir well. Top off with soda, stir again, and serve.

RECIPE | **The Brunchalicious Bloody Mary**

This classic hair-of-the-dog concoction was invented by an American bartender in Paris in the 1920s and transplanted to New York in 1934. (It was another favorite cocktail of Hemingway's—but what wasn't, really?) It has since become an indispensable part of any brunch menu, a fine start to a lazy weekend day.

Makes 6 servings

1 quart tomato juice
1 cup vodka
1 tablespoon Worcestershire sauce
1 tablespoon fresh lemon juice
½ teaspoon Tabasco sauce
Salt and freshly ground pepper
Celery salt (optional)
6 lemon wedges
6 celery stalks

1. Combine the tomato juice, vodka, Worcestershire sauce, lemon juice, Tabasco sauce, and salt and pepper to taste in a 2-quart pitcher; stir well.

2. Pour over ice into tall glasses. Garnish with lemon wedges and celery.

CROSTINI IDEAS BY ANNE BYRN

Ten Crostini Without a Recipe

It's easy to get stuck in the old crackers, cheese, and grapes routine. But when you're keeping it simple, every gesture counts. Crostini is a great example of how a little care can transform a slice of bread into a delicacy.

Begin with a loaf of French bread. Slice it diagonally into ¼-inch-thick slices, spread these with olive oil, and bake them at 400°F until crisp, about 15 minutes. Then top the toast rounds with any of the following:

1. A smear of soft goat cheese and a dab of fig preserves
2. A spoonful of caramelized onions and garlic and a scattering of shredded parmesan cheese
3. A rubbing of garlic and a slice of roasted red pepper
4. A slice of plum tomato and a dab of pesto
5. A slice of creamy blue cheese and a sliver of pear
6. A bit of soft goat cheese and a sliver of steamed asparagus
7. A dab of olive paste and a slice of yellow cherry tomato
8. A spoonful of tuna salad and a grinding of black pepper
9. A spoonful of hummus and a kalamata olive
10. A smear of herbed cream cheese and a rosemary leaf

The Painlessly Portable Potluck

Bring back the potluck! Not just because it's thrifty to spread around the cost, time, and effort of food preparation, but because the end result is fun, simple, and communal. The easier you make entertaining, the more often you're likely to do it. What's more, a potluck is a ready-made theme—one that lends itself to endless iterations. An around-the-world potluck, where each guest brings a dish that's representative of his heritage. A barbecue potluck, where guests bring something to put on the grill. An Iron-Chef-style potluck organized around a single ingredient. A 1950s potluck with retro delights. A finger foods potluck. And on and on and on.

Have Casserole, Will Travel

The best potluck dishes travel well. They are quick to assemble when you're on-site or require no on-site work at all. And if they involve only a handful of ingredients, that's even better.

But there is another consideration: The best dishes not only taste delicious, they look appetizing. Even the simplest food—sliced tomatoes, sliced melon, sliced ham, a few good cheeses—looks smart when arranged on a pretty platter. It's the presentation that garners those first "oohs" and "aahs."

When transit is involved, how do you keep the food looking good? Start with the right container. Have a look in your cupboards and pantry for good toting containers—glass dishes with snap-on plastic lids, plastic containers with lids, glass and ceramic casseroles, pretty trays, baskets, quart-size glass jars, and slow cookers.

Aluminum foil casserole pans with lids that lock in place are great for anything that needs to be reheated or baked on-site. For brownies, lemon bars, or tea sandwiches, save clean cardboard shirt boxes, and line them with parchment paper or waxed paper. For pasta and rice salads, try large resealable plastic bags.

Of course, the simplest way to transport food is to place it on a serving platter or in a serving bowl and cover it with plastic wrap. It's a good idea to write your name on a piece of tape and stick it on the bottom of the platter. (It's also wise to leave the heirloom dishes at home.)

POTLUCK TIPS AND RECIPE BY ANNE BYRN

The Potluck Commandments

There's always an element of surprise when it comes to potlucks. Unlike a formal dinner party, at a potluck everyone, not just the host, gets to show off a kitchen skill (or lack thereof). But there is such a thing as potluck etiquette, for guest and host alike, as well as ways to avoid ending up with three courses of green bean casserole.

TIPS FOR THE GUEST

1. Let your host know what you're bringing. And follow through and prepare the type of dish (appetizer, dessert) that you said you would.
2. Select a recipe that needs little or no on-site assembly. Let your host know if your dish will require space in the oven or refrigerator.
3. If you need to use the host's kitchen, try to stick to a small area, and clean up after yourself.
4. Check to see how many people are coming to the party so you make enough food to go around.
5. Bring a serving spoon or fork or a platter, if needed.
6. Don't abandon your dish! Replenish it if needed.
7. Offer leftovers to the host. And take your dishware with you.

TIPS FOR THE HOST

1. Plan a menu so you have all the courses covered, including an appetizer, a salad, a main dish, and a dessert. If you aren't working with a theme, at least assign types of dishes to your guests.
2. Decide how formal you want the gathering to be—china and glass, or paper and plastic?
3. Clear kitchen counters and free up refrigerator space for the food your guests will be bringing.
4. Set the serving table and decorate it, allowing space for each dish.
5. Have serving utensils ready in case your guests don't bring their own.
6. Preset the oven to low heat in order to keep food warm.
7. Empty the trash can, and have plenty of paper towels, kitchen towels, and food wrap on hand.

RECIPE | # Spinach & Mushroom Strata

A great potluck dish serves a crowd, looks impressive, and doesn't take too long to make. This *strata*—the fancy name for a bread, milk, and egg casserole— includes no pricey specialty ingredients; can serve as a main or side dish; fits in at breakfast, lunch, or dinner; is a wonderful way to use leftovers; and can linger in the refrigerator for a day before you bake it. In the oven, it puffs up golden and important-looking. This recipe calls for spinach and mushrooms, but feel free to use your imagination (and whatever's hanging out in your fridge).

Serves 8 to 12

Vegetable oil, for the baking dish

1 large (1 pound) loaf soft Italian-style white bread

2 tablespoons olive oil

4 loosely packed cups chopped or baby spinach, rinsed and drained well

2 cups (8 ounces) sliced mushrooms

2 cloves garlic, sliced

6 ounces prosciutto or ham, chopped (optional)

6 large eggs

4 cups milk

2 tablespoons Dijon mustard

3 cups (12 ounces) each shredded fontina and parmesan cheeses

1. Place a rack in the center of the oven and preheat the oven to 350°F. Lightly oil a 13 x 9-inch glass or ceramic baking dish with vegetable oil and set it aside.

2. Cut the bread into 1-inch cubes and set them aside.

3. Place the olive oil in a large skillet over medium heat. Add the vegetables and garlic and cook, stirring, until the spinach wilts and the mushrooms begin to lose some of their liquid, 3 to 4 minutes. Set the mixture aside.

4. Scatter half of the bread cubes in the prepared baking dish. Spoon the spinach mixture over the bread. Scatter the chopped prosciutto or ham, if using, over the spinach mixture. Scatter the remaining bread cubes on top.

5. Place the eggs, milk, and mustard in a small bowl and beat with a fork until the eggs are lemon colored, about 1 minute. Fold in the cheeses. Pour the cheese and egg mixture over the bread cubes, taking care to distribute the cheese evenly. Bake the strata, uncovered, until golden brown, about 45 minutes. Serve at once.

A note: Stratas are best eaten within 10 to 15 minutes of being taken out of the oven because they sink a little as they cool.

The Backyard (or Balcony) Barbecue

A h, the barbecue. What better way to take advantage of warm weather than to turn your backyard into an outdoor kitchen and dining room? And the traditional hotdogs and hamburgers route is pretty straightforward and cheap: For less than $40 you should be able to feed ten friends heartily. (Care for an economical beer with that?) Since he or she who owns the grill and has the space often ends up doing the lion's share of hosting during the summer months, have your guests bring the side dishes to cut down on prep time and cost. Assign various salads (potato, mixed greens, fruit) and dessert. If you want to take it up a notch, you can do that without breaking the bank (see recipes, following, and the guide to cheap cuts of meat, page 132).

RECIPE | **Homemade Barbecue Sauce**

Don't get suckered in by one of those pricey barbecue sauces—it's so easy to make your own, with ingredients you already have in your cupboard. (And then you'll get to brag about it.)

Peppery and piquant, this sauce is the preferred condiment of eastern North Carolina. In the western part of the state, the sauce becomes more tomatoey, while in southern parts of the Carolinas, mustard sauce reigns supreme.

RECIPES AND GRILLING COMMANDMENTS BY STEVEN RAICHLEN

Makes about 4 cups

2 cups cider vinegar
½ cup plus 2 tablespoons ketchup
¼ cup firmly packed brown sugar, or more to taste
5 teaspoons salt, or more to taste
4 teaspoons hot red pepper flakes
1 teaspoon freshly ground black pepper
1 teaspoon freshly ground white pepper

1. Combine the vinegar, ketchup, brown sugar, salt, red pepper flakes, black pepper, and white pepper with 1⅓ cups water in a nonreactive medium-size bowl and whisk until the sugar and salt dissolve.

2. Taste for seasoning, adding more brown sugar and/or salt as necessary; the sauce should be piquant but not quite sour.

RECIPE | **$2 North Carolina Pulled Pork**

Thinking of barbecuing for a crowd? Don't fear—just think big. Instead of those pricey individual-serving pork chops and steaks, go for a big, tasty pork shoulder. The meat will cost you about $2 per person. It takes four to six hours to cook, but you will be rewarded with authentic pulled pork sandwiches. Doused with vinegar sauce and eaten with coleslaw on a hamburger bun, pulled pork is one of the most delicious things on the planet, and it requires only one special ingredient: patience.

Serves 10 to 12

> 6 cups hickory chips or chunks, soaked for 1 hour in cold water
>   to cover and drained
> 1 Boston butt (bone-in pork shoulder roast; 5 to 6 pounds),
>   covered with a thick (½ inch) layer of fat
> Kosher or sea salt
> Freshly ground black pepper
> Barbecue sauce (see previous page)
> 10 to 12 hamburger buns

1. Generously season the pork with coarse salt and freshly ground pepper.

2. Set up the grill for indirect grilling and place a drip pan in the center. If using a gas grill, place all the wood chips in a smoker box and preheat the grill to high; when smoke appears, reduce the heat to medium. If using a charcoal grill, preheat the grill to medium-low and adjust the vents to obtain a temperature of 300°F.

3. When ready to cook, if using charcoal, toss 1 cup of the wood chips on the coals. Place the pork shoulder, fat side up, on the hot grate over the drip pan. Cover the grill and smoke the pork shoulder until it is fall-off-the-bone tender and the internal temperature on an instant-read thermometer reaches 195°F, 4 to 6 hours (the cooking time will depend on the size of the pork roast and the heat of the grill). You'll need to add 10 to 12 fresh coals to each side every hour and toss more wood chips on the fresh coals; add about ½ cup per side every time you replenish the coals. With gas, all you need to do is be sure that you start with a full tank of gas. If the pork begins to brown too much, drape a piece of aluminum foil loosely over it or lower the heat.

4. Transfer the pork roast to a cutting board, loosely tent it with aluminum foil, and let rest for 15 minutes.

5. Pull off and discard any skin from the meat, then pull the pork into pieces, discarding any bones or fat. Using your fingertips or a fork, pull each piece into shreds 1 to 2 inches long and ⅛- to ¼-inch wide. If patience isn't one of your virtues, finely chop the pork with a cleaver. Transfer the shredded pork to a nonreactive roasting pan. Stir in 1 to 1½ cups of the barbecue sauce, enough to keep the pork moist, then cover the pan with aluminum foil and place it on the grill for up to 30 minutes to keep warm.

6. To serve, mound the pulled pork on the hamburger buns and, for true authenticity, top with coleslaw. Serve with barbecue sauce.

Five Commandments of Perfect Grilling

No matter what's on the grill, make the most of your feast by mastering a few central tenets of the technique.

1. Be organized. Have everything you need at grillside—the food, marinade, basting sauce, seasonings, and equipment—before you start grilling.

2. Gauge your fuel. When using charcoal, light enough to form a bed of glowing coals 3" larger on all sides than the surface area of your food. When cooking on a gas grill, make sure the tank is at least ⅓ full.

3. Preheat the grill to the correct temperature. Remember: Direct grilling is a high-heat cooking method. To achieve a seared crust, distinctive flavor, and handsome grill marks, you must heat your grill to at least 600°F. When using charcoal, let it burn until it is covered with a thin coat of gray ash. Hold your hand about three inches above the grate. When the grill is hot enough to cook, after 2 to 3 seconds, the intensity of the heat should force you to snatch your hand away. If you are using a gas grill, preheat it to high (at least 600°F); this takes 10 to 15 minutes. When indirect grilling, preheat the grill to 350°F.

4. Keep it clean. Fresh food will stick to a dirty grate. Clean the grate twice: once after you've preheated the grill and again when you've finished cooking. Use the edge of a metal spatula to scrape off large bits of food and a stiff wire brush to finish scrubbing the grate.

5. Keep it lubricated. Oil the grate just before placing the food on top. Use a tightly folded paper towel soaked in oil, or rub it with a piece of fatty bacon, beef fat, or chicken skin.

RECIPE | ## Spicy Thai Beef Salad

Flank steak is one of the most inexpensive and flavorful cuts of beef. Because it's tougher than other cuts, it's generally marinated and served sliced—which makes it perfect in fajitas, or on steak salads, where a little meat goes a long way.

A note: Be sure to get the meat in the marinade two to eight hours ahead of serving time.

Serves 4

1 flank steak (1¼ to 1½ pounds)
3 tablespoons soy sauce
2 tablespoons Asian fish sauce
2 tablespoons sugar
3 cloves garlic, minced
1 tablespoon minced peeled fresh ginger

FOR THE DRESSING

3 cloves garlic, peeled
1 to 6 Thai or bird chiles or serrano or jalapeño peppers, stemmed, seeded, and thinly sliced (for a hotter dressing, leave the seeds in)
4½ teaspoons sugar
3 tablespoons Asian fish sauce
3 tablespoons fresh lemon juice

FOR THE SALAD

1 head Boston or Bibb lettuce, separated into leaves, rinsed, and spun dry
1 cucumber, peeled and thinly sliced
12 cherry tomatoes, cut in half
12 fresh mint leaves (optional)
1 small red onion, very thinly sliced
¼ cup fresh cilantro leaves
¼ cup coarsely chopped dry-roasted peanuts

1. Prepare the beef: Lightly score the flank steak in a crosshatch pattern, making the cuts ¼ inch deep. Place the meat in a glass baking dish. Combine the soy sauce, fish sauce, sugar, garlic, and ginger in a mixing bowl and whisk until the sugar dissolves. Pour this mixture over the flank steak and let marinate, covered, in the refrigerator for at least 2 hours or as long as 8 hours, turning several times.

2. Prepare the dressing: Combine the garlic, chiles, and sugar in a mortar and pound to a paste with the pestle. Work in the fish sauce and the lemon juice. If you don't have a mortar and pestle, puree the ingredients in a blender or food processor.

3. Prepare the salad: Line a platter with the lettuce leaves and arrange the cucumber, cherry tomatoes, and mint leaves (if using) on top.

4. Set up the grill for direct grilling and preheat to high.

5. When ready to cook, drain the steak. Brush the grill grate with oil, then place the steak on the hot grate and grill until cooked to taste (3 to 5 minutes per side for medium rare), turning with tongs.

6. Transfer the grilled steak to a cutting board and let cool slightly or completely (the salad can be served warm or at room temperature). Thinly slice the steak across the grain on the diagonal. Spoon the dressing over the salad and arrange the beef slices on top. Scatter the onion, cilantro, and roasted peanuts over the salad and serve.

Five More Commandments of the Grill

(Psst: Don't forget to have fun. Grilling isn't brain surgery.)

1. Turn, don't stab. The proper way to turn meat on a grill is with tongs or a spatula. Never stab the meat with a carving fork—unless you want to drain it of its flavor-rich juices.

2. Know when to baste. Sugar-based barbecue sauces should be applied toward the end of the cooking time; sugar burns easily and should not be exposed to prolonged heat. Marinades made with oil and vinegar, citrus, or yogurt can be brushed on throughout the cooking time. If you want to use a sauce as both a marinade and a baste, to avoid cross-contamination make extra and divide it into two portions. Whatever the flavorings, never reuse a marinade in which raw meat has been marinating as a sauce.

3. Keep it covered. When cooking larger cuts of meat and poultry, such as a whole chicken or the pork shoulder shown on page 133, use the indirect method of grilling or barbecuing. Keep the grill tightly covered and resist the temptation to peek. Every time you lift the lid, you add to the cooking time.

4. Give it a rest. Beef, steak, chicken—almost anything you grill—will taste better if you let it stand on a cutting board for a few minutes before serving. This allows the meat to relax, making it juicier and tastier.

5. Never desert your post. Grilling is an easy cooking method, but it demands constant attention.

The Delicately Decked-Out Dinner Party

Got something to celebrate? Itching to spend quality time with friends? Don't be afraid of a good old-fashioned dinner party. Like the cocktail party, the dinner party has an air of elegance that belies its thrift. While cooking for ten may be more expensive than splitting the bill at a restaurant, if you factor in reciprocity, the savings are (wink-wink) gastronomical!

Deciding What to Make

The traditional way of thinking about menu planning is to start with the protein, then add a complementary starch and a vegetable. That's fine, but it's not necessarily logical. Instead, you could start by thinking about what produce is in season. Meat, fish, and poultry don't tend to have a season (spring lamb and local seafood being exceptions), so from both a financial and a flavor standpoint, it doesn't pay to build a menu around that choice. In spring, you might begin with asparagus. How would you like to prepare it? And what goes with asparagus? Soon enough, you'll have devised a full meal that takes advantage of seasonal produce at its tastiest and thriftiest.

Pairing Wine with Food

People who know how to pair wine and food don't have a set of rules as much as they have good instincts. But here are some expert guidelines, as a shortcut:

- Match delicate to delicate, robust to robust. A delicate red burgundy will taste like water beside a dramatically spiced curry. Dishes with bold, piquant, spicy, and hot flavors are perfectly cut out for big-flavored wines.

- Saltiness in food is a great contrast to acidity in wine. Think about smoked salmon and champagne or parmesan cheese and Chianti. Asian dishes that include soy sauce often pair well with high-acid wines like German Rieslings.

- Saltiness is also a stunning contrast to sweetness. This is the principle behind that great old European custom of serving Stilton cheese (something salty) with port (something sweet).

- With desserts, proceed with caution. Sweet desserts can make the wine they accompany taste dull and blank. The best dessert and wine marriages are usually based on pairing a not-too-sweet dessert, such as a fruit or nut tart, with a fairly sweet dessert wine.

FOOD AND WINE PAIRING TIPS BY KAREN MACNEIL

PROJECT | **Fold a Napkin**

Should you decide to go all out and use place cards, this napkin fold provides a charming holder for the card; you can also use it to hold silverware or (if you're being really fancy) a single flower.

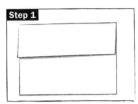

1. Begin with the napkin fully open, laid out as a square, then fold the top edge down one third of the total height of the napkin. Press.

2. Fold the bottom edge up on top of the already folded third so the top layer completely covers the bottom layer and the edges meet.

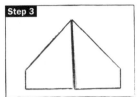

3. Fold the napkin in half and then unfold, leaving a center vertical crease to work from. Fold each top corner down so they meet at this crease.

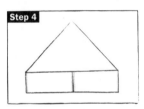

4. Flip over the napkin with the point at the top. You now have a triangle on top with two tails that extend beneath its bottom edge.

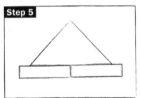

5. Roll up the left tail onto the triangle. Roll up the right tail onto the triangle. You may need to hold the first roll in place as you roll the second.

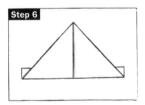

6. Holding the rolls in place, flip over the napkin.

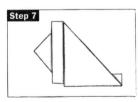

7. Fold the bottom-left rolled edge up to meet the center line.

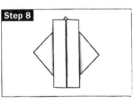

8. Fold the bottom-right rolled edge up to meet the left. Slide your place card or silverware between the folds. Please be seated.

NAPKIN GUIDANCE BY DAVID STARK

Arrange Some Flowers

A centerpiece of freshly cut flowers is one of those small touches that really makes a house feel festive and welcoming. Though buying bouquets doesn't pass the thrift test (houseplants are forever!), those who love flowers will buy them; and those whose gardens bloom should feel free to show off every once in a while. To keep those blossoms looking their freshest:

- Cut flowers first thing in the morning or late in the day.
- Choose flowers when they are almost open, or have just opened.
- When you're prospecting for blooms, take a bucket of lukewarm water to the garden with you; strip lower leaves off as you cut stems, then immediately plunge the stems into the water.
- Make clean, angled cuts, using sharp tools. For thick, tough, or woody stems, use your shears to fray the ends, taking care not to mash them.
- Immediately cauterize the cut ends of plants that bleed, such as poppies. Use a lit match or very hot water to seal in the plant's sap.
- Add a teaspoon of vinegar to the vase to make it easier for the flowers to take up water and to discourage decay-causing bacteria.
- Change the vase water every day or two. Recut stems and remove leaves to minimize decay.

Keep a Thrifty Wine Cellar

Because it generally makes economic sense to buy more than one bottle at a time, most of us will eventually be faced with the issue of wine storage. How and where should wine be stored? It doesn't matter if it's a $10,000 custom-built cellar, a damp basement, or closet, as long as three things are true:

- The environment is cool.
- The bottle is lying on its side or upside down (but not standing upright).
- There is no direct sunlight.

Temperature matters because it affects the rate at which various chemical changes will take place as the wine matures. Wines forced to mature too quickly show a sharp, exaggerated curve of development, followed by dramatic deterioration. Scientists suggest that all wines, regardless of cost, be stored at temperatures under 72°F, ideally at 55°F.

When a wine is stored upright, the cork begins to dry out and shrink. After a few months, air may begin to slip between the cork and the neck of the

FLORAL KNOW-HOW FROM BARBARA DAMROSCH; WINE STORAGE TIPS BY KAREN MACNEIL

The Cheap Wine Revolution

We didn't plan on it, but we've become advocates for cheap (and good) wine. It started with the biggest blind wine tasting ever: We poured more than 6,000 glasses of wine from bottles bagged in brown paper and ranging in price from $1.50 to $150 for more than 500 tasters of all ages and backgrounds. Not everyone was happy with the results, which we published in a book called *Wine Trials*. When the ratings were tabulated, we discovered an *inverse* correlation between price and preference. Put more simply: On the whole, people preferred cheaper wines to more expensive ones, as in the case of Domaine Ste. Michelle, a $12 sparkling wine from Washington State. Tasters preferred it to Dom Pérignon, whose price tag tips the scales at $150 a bottle.

Our tasters were a mix of wine experts and everyday wine drinkers. They ranged in age from twenty-one to ninety. They were college students and college professors, economists and artists, doctors and lawyers, writers and wine nerds, waiters and hairstylists. They swirled, sipped, and spit (well, some swallowed), all the while taking notes on each brown-bagged wine—no peeking allowed. They then ranked the wines in order of preference, and rated them as bad, okay, good, or great. And it turned out that they got just as much, or more, pleasure from cheap wine as they did from expensive wine.

These results were first revealed in a scientific article that we published in the *Journal of Wine Economics:* "Do More Expensive Wines Taste Better?" As you can imagine, the high-priced wine brands weren't very happy about our results. Neither were the wine mags that made a business of promoting the rule that great wine has to be expensive.

Many tasters were shocked to find that they had rated a wine they thought to be among their favorites as not so great. Or that they actually rated a wine from a box at the top. When you hide the label, the truth comes out.

If you want to sample some of the great wines we've tried out, see page 304.   —*Robin Goldstein and Alexis Herschkowitsch*

bottle, oxidizing the wine. A bottle is best kept on its side or upside down, so the cork, moist with wine, stays swollen against the neck of the bottle.

Sunlight is harmful because ultraviolet light in particular causes free radicals to develop in wine, resulting in rapid oxidation. (This is why the best wine stores don't display wine in the windows, unless those bottles are dummies that are not going to be sold.)

A Few Fine Wines for $10 & Under

Not all box wine is pleasant, and not all cheap wine is a good value. But follow the recommendations of the Wine Trials team and you won't be disappointed. And don't limit yourself to the list: Invite some friends over, pick a few wines in different styles, and host a blind taste yourself. It's a civilized drinking game with a thrifty end.

Don't block the box. Don't turn up your nose at box wine. Low prices aren't always indicative of bad wine. In this case, they can reflect the lower cost of packing and shipping a box as opposed to a glass bottle. Plus, because its pouch shrinks as the wine is poured, squeezing oxygen out, boxed wine keeps longer (two or three weeks) than bottled wine. A few of our boxed favorites:

- **Almaden Chardonnay:** A light-bodied white wine with lots of bright citrus flavors. Drink it outside on a warm summer day.
- **Black Box Cabernet Sauvignon:** An easy-to-drink red wine whose aromas are faint—but in a good way.
- **Franzia Chillable Red:** Warning! We're not actually recommending that you drink this as is. Rather, throw in some brandy and freshly cut apples and oranges and you've got yourself quite a nice sangria.

Brush up on your Spanish. Wine trends are changeable, but certain regions tend to be underrated—which, in thrifty terms, is a good thing. There's a lot of hype about wines from South America, but there are better values coming from Spain. Tempranillo is the dominant red grape in Spain, and it gives the wine a light and earthy flavor. The main white grape, viura, is fruity, but won't hit you over the head. A healthy dose of acidity means that you can drink the wines now or let them age a few years.

- **Campo Viejo Rioja Crianza:** This wine is old-school. With its light body and unique earthy flavors, it's good by itself or with food.
- **Marqués de Cáceres Rioja:** A versatile white rioja with tropical fruit flavors (banana in particular) and floral notes. Never fear: Some acidity swoops in to hold it all together.
- **Panarroz Jumilla:** Big and expansive in the mouth, with dark fruit flavors.
- **René Barbier Mediterranean Red:** Also not from Rioja, this light red blend hails from Catalonia. It's dominated by pepper, both green and black.

Bargains on bubbles. Spanish sparklers are great, too. Cava, as it's called, is made in a style similar to champagne, where the secondary fermentation takes place in the bottle. But the premiums on cava are much more agreeable.

- **Freixenet Brut:** Smooth bubbles mean it goes down fast. It's a little fruity, but it also has those sought-after champagne-y notes of yeast and buttered bread.
- **Freixenet Extra Dry:** In an oddity of the naming system, *extra dry* is actually less dry than *brut*. So expect those same delicate bubbles, but this time with a little more sugar and fruit.
- **Segura Viudas Brut Reserva:** This wine smells very much like it tastes, with lots of pear, breadiness, and minerality. Cheers!

- **Cristalino Brut Rosé:** A little on the sweet side, this wine can't be beat at its price point, and it's bursting with bright strawberry flavors. And the fact that it's a rosé is fun.

The other side of Iberia. Portugal produces some superb wines within its borders. Vinhos verdes, in particular, are a unique breed; they have a tiny prickle—not enough to classify them as a sparkling wine—that results from a secondary fermentation that takes place in the bottle.

- **Aveleda Vinho Verde:** Faint fruit flavors are here, but so is a hint of spiciness, especially on the finish. This wine is so refreshing you might find yourself resisting the urge to pour it over a glass of ice.
- **Casal Garcia Vinho Verde:** If you're ever looking for a wine to drink with sushi (a notoriously wine-unfriendly genre), this is your bottle. There's some good mouth-puckering acidity, and its alcohol content is low.
- **Fâmega Vinho Verde:** Vinho verde should be served cold—a maxim that's especially important in the case of the Fâmega. Its bubbles are a bit on the coarse side, but the taste is crisp and refreshing.
- **Gazela Vinho Verde:** This wine is made for outdoor sipping on a hot day, with its bright citrus effervescence, and just the right amount of acidity.

Drink like the Ancients. Greece? In the public eye, the region isn't popular or sexy enough to command the high prices of France or Italy. But remember: These guys have been doing it longer than most.

- **Kourtaki Vin de Crete:** A dry Greek red, this wine embodies rustic. It's got an austere finish that reminds us of French wines. It's best to drink this one with food.

- **Samos Muscat:** A delicious, decadent dessert wine made from the muscat grape on the island of Samos in the Aegean Sea. This wine skillfully combines honey, apricot, and sour apple flavors. It's viscous and irresistible.
- **Mavrodaphne of Patras:** There's a slight oxidation on this wine, and if you let your imagination run wild, you might even be able to trick yourself into thinking it's a port. Caramel, nuts, chocolate—what's not to like? Drink it with dessert, and philosophize.

The southern cone. South American wines get a lot of press, with Argentine and Chilean wines in particular becoming quite trendy. Some of the wines are overbearing and overconcentrated in style, but we like these two:

- **Cousino Macul Riesling:** This Chilean Riesling isn't the syrupy sweet wine you might expect when you hear the R-word. Instead, it's simple, with citrus flavors that aren't challenging but do hit all the right notes.
- **Casa Rey Malbec:** An Argentine red, this wine is not all New World plonk. Instead, its flavors are a careful mix of bright red fruit with herbs and vegetables. A big, powerful wine.

A Bulky Equation

Whatever bottle you choose, it will behoove you to buy by the case or half-case. If you do so, you'll save anywhere from 5 to 20 percent. Some wine stores grant the discount only if you buy a full case of the same wine, while others will allow you to put together a mixed case (any six or twelve bottles).

A Doable Date | by Andrew Stuttaford

Dating can be a tricky business at the best of times, but when you're on a budget, the routine fears—boredom, rejection, incompatibility, and total humiliation—risk being compounded by the worst trauma of all: expenditure. Celibacy is, undoubtedly, cheap, but there really is no need for frugal daters to resign themselves to the romantic life of monk or nun. Eros and Ebenezer can be reconciled. All it takes is careful planning, unflinching realism, and, truth to tell, the willingness to spend some money.

Who should be doing the spending? In the early stages, the one who asks out coughs up. But we're running ahead of ourselves. Frugal dating begins well before the first date, and it begins with watchful, cold-eyed, stone-hearted observation. A woman may be smart and pretty, but if she's dripping in jewels, clad in couture, or just a little too familiar with the best restaurants in town, the frugal dater knows that it's better to move on.

When it comes to the actual first date, don't be fooled by the false economy of meeting at a bar, an option often perceived as an inexpensive alternative to a restaurant. If the two of you hit it off, you'll end up in the restaurant anyway—having already paid for several rounds of drinks. As for the choice of restaurant: A sandwich counter may not do, but nor will that five-star palace where your clumsy attempts to steer your dining partner toward the omelet will appear as unattractive as they are gauche. I know. I've tried. Opt instead for a place with a broadly comfortable price range. If that means it has to be on the downscale side, make sure it is interesting. Oh, I know this tiny Serb *kafana* downtown. . . .

If all goes well, and the relationship evolves, the frugal dater should feel neither panic nor any obligation to abandon his acute sense of value. Walks in the park are free. Walks through the mall are asking for trouble. The museum is enlightenment (and cheap). The spa is idiocy (and not cheap). In the absence of a poorly protected botanical garden in your neighborhood from which you can "borrow," occasional bunches of flowers are an inevitable expense. Otherwise, the best gifts are those that show that you have been paying attention. A carefully chosen book or DVD will impress in a way that some generic, so-much-in-love gewgaw will not.

Eventually (unless you are one of those ruthless types who dumps their new fling shortly before Christmas, a birthday, or Valentine's Day, a practice I cannot endorse), you will have to buy something substantial. At those admittedly trying times, avoid ostentation (a bad precedent), wincing, or playing the cheapskate. And remember: A mountain of cubic zirconia is, ultimately, a mountain of nothing.

The same approach holds for the little romantic trips. Decide what the two of you can afford, and then do some proper research. Cost alone is not enough. There once was a frugal dater (me) who took his girlfriend to stay in a rather keenly priced Connecticut "inn." The yard was Astroturf. The view was a parking lot. The result was disaster.

Pack a Picnic

Picnics are everything summer (and dating) should be: informal, peaceful, relaxed. Here are some tips for packing the perfect outdoor spread:

- Freeze bottles of water or non-carbonated beverages before you pack them in your picnic basket. Not only will they stay nice and cool, they'll keep your food chilled as well.
- Food spoils quickly in hot weather, so if you're traveling long distances, be sure to carry anything perishable in an ice-filled cooler. If you're driving, transport your picnic basket in the air-conditioned car, not in the steamy trunk.
- Bring foods that are easy to eat and travel well. Think finger foods, hearty sandwiches, and barbecued drumsticks.
- If you're making sandwiches ahead of time, keep moist ingre-dients separate so your bread doesn't get soggy.
- As simple appetizers, consider a few wedges of good cheese, some easy-to-eat fresh fruit (like grapes, cherries, sliced apples or pears), and dried fruit and nuts.
- Use common sense: In extreme heat, discard any food that's been sitting out of the cooler for more than an hour.
- Avoid foods with mayonnaise, which can spoil quickly. German potato salad is a good substi-tute for traditional potato salad because it uses a dressing made of oil and vinegar.
- Green salads wilt easily, so substitute sliced raw vegetables with dip.
- For dessert, opt for some easy-to-handle cookies, brownies, and bars rather than pies or cakes.

A "Special Occasion" at Home

For most couples, there are occasions—New Year's Eve, Valentine's Day, anniversaries, birthdays—that seem to call for restaurants. And not just any restaurant, but Somewhere Special, where elegant food, fresh flowers, attentive staff, and an outrageously rich chocolate dessert all result in a whopper of a bill. This is especially true for New Year's Eve and Valentine's Day, when restaurateurs sharpen their knives and welcome you to your table for a dinner with fewer options, higher prices, and, sometimes, a suggestion that you not linger over coffee, as someone else has dibs on your table.

Happily, there is an alternative: Turn your home into Somewhere Special. With a few little touches, you can make your dinner stand out from the ordinary—and show just how thoughtful you are.

The first step is counterintuitive: Keep the menu delicious and familiar. You can re-create a dish from a significant dinner—your first date, the night you got engaged—but don't get in over your head with difficult foods. You may wind up exhausted (or resentful). Foods that can be prepared ahead of time or that the two of you can easily cook together are best. But do see the night as an opportunity to create a new tradition: We always have sole meunière on Valentine's Day.

Budgeting the proper amount of prep time will allow you both to enjoy the evening and focus on one another, not pots and pans and kitchen timers. Set the table in advance, so you're not scrambling at the last minute. If cooking is a challenge, order from a local restaurant or pick up a few dishes from a good gourmet shop. Even if this raises the cost, you'll save money on service and avoid the markup on wine.

Don't forget the decor. You don't have to turn your dining room into a Moroccan souk, but some subtle changes will make you feel like you're not just playing pretend. If you can, eat in a different part of the house than you usually do. Add any special silver, linens, or serving pieces that you save for important occasions. Dim the lights, and put the laptop out of sight. Turn off the phones and PDAs (and, of course, the television). Try to make sure clocks aren't visible from the table.

Of course, if you feel more celebratory going out, or if time is at a premium, go out! Just know that it *is* possible to celebrate special occasions at home—and that restaurants will typically give you better service (and possibly better food) on non–"special occasion" nights.

HOME AND ROMANCE BY SIOBHAN BURNS

A Call for Culture

No matter how strong your embrace of your newfound thriftiness, eventually you will want to talk about more than canning peaches and darning socks. But what happens if you've reduced your arts and entertainment spending to nil? Suddenly, you're out of the cultural loop—and that's no way to be a part of the ideas economy. Even on a shoestring budget, you've got to be "part of the conversation."

Lectures at libraries and museums, author readings, and walking tours are often complimentary. If you have some money to spend, establish an arts budget. Arts organizations, like most businesses, want loyal, repeat customers. If variety is what you seek, keep an eye on online ticket discounters to find out which venues sell inexpensive same-day tickets. In big cities like New York and Los Angeles, seat-filling organizations arguably offer the best deal: members pay a yearly fee of less than $100, then pay about $4 per ticket from a list of shows. In some cases, the thriftiest way to see a performance has the advantage of doubling as a kind of insider's sneak preview: an open rehearsal or staged reading. Not all companies offer them, but when they're available, they're often free. Several opera companies transmit live performances to movie theaters at a drastically reduced cost.

Many major museums offer free admission or set aside hours every week or every month for pay-what-you-wish admission. In any city, when you want to go gratis, gallery-hopping is the thing. (Experienced gallery-goers know that invitations to art openings come with the added bonus of free wine, cheese, and crackers.)

For concerts and plays, think summer arts festivals and head to the park. The hitch? Your neighbors may yammer through the performance. The fix: True aesthetes sit closer to the stage, where you'll find less banter and more serious concentration. So get there early, nab a spot up front, and text your dawdling friends to come find you.

CALL FOR CULTURE BY LAURA COLLINS-HUGHES

Use Your Local College

It's relatively easy to see art for free or at low costs in big cities, but there are deals to be found in college towns, too. Universities, conservatories, and art schools are inexpensive sources of cultural enrichment. Tickets to professional performances on campus are likely to be a good deal, and if there's a university museum, admission is probably low or free.

A Workable Wedding | by Mindy Weiss

Tying the knot? Know someone who is? (Perhaps someone whose bills you'll have to front?) Congratulations! Now get out your virtual calculator. Is the scope of the wedding you're planning in line with your budget? Is your budget inflated? Take the future view, and you'll realize that overspending on a wedding isn't a good investment. Why? Because the money you plunk down can't be leveraged against future happiness, and you don't want to start off your married life with a mountain of debt. (A word of advice: If you're going to read bridal magazines, take them with a grain of salt, and see if you can adapt high-design ideas to a low-impact budget.)

That said, everyone wants a beautiful, memorable wedding day. The key, as in all things, is knowing where to spend and where to save. Here are eight ways to keep the bills down and the quality high:

1. Trim the guest list. Your cost per head is your biggest expense.

2. Choose a gorgeous, amenities-included setting, whether it's a conservatory or a Tudor-style ballroom. You'll save a bundle on decorations.

3. Skip the off-site location and go with a reception site (a hotel, club, or restaurant) that is equipped with tables, chairs, flatware, and staff. Tents and other rentals add up to a substantial expense.

4. Schedule the wedding on a Sunday instead of a Saturday; if you need to bring down the price even more, move it to a weekday. Vendors lower their fees for days that are less in demand.

5. Eliminate the champagne toast. Most of the bubbly will be thrown out anyway. Have guests toast with whatever they're drinking at that moment.

6. Instead of a band, hire a great deejay or use an iPod.

7. Opt for an inexpensive method to print your invitations. Use design cleverly and you can get a great effect with offset printing for a fraction of the price of letterpress or engraving.

8. Skip the favors. Write a personal note instead.

The Boozy Wedding & the Budget

Booze and weddings are notorious bedfellows. Sure, they get along great, but the budgetary hitch is in not knowing exactly how many glasses of wine Aunt Edna is going to put down. Alcohol is a hefty expense, and one that can be tough to predict. Use these strategies to keep the bar bill in line without killing the fun:

- Forgo a full bar. Instead, offer a soft bar with wine, beer, and soft drinks, which can cut your bill by 50 percent. If you have the budget, you can add either champagne or a signature cocktail.

- Opt for sparkling wine, not champagne. Try a sparkling Burgundy (Crémant de Bourgogne), prosecco and sparkling moscato from Italy, and cava from Spain. Cava usually costs less than $10 a bottle at wine stores, and there are lovely proseccos for $10 to $15.

- Instruct waiters to refill wineglasses upon request instead of automatically topping off.

- Ask bartenders and the catering staff to open wine and liquor bottles only as needed. Some open everything before the reception to speed up the service, but if they overestimate, you're paying for unpoured wine and liquor.

- Schedule your wedding during the day. The earlier the wedding, the less alcohol people consume. Or schedule it on a weekday, when guests drink less than they might on weekends.

- Ask waiters to clear drinks only if they're complete, meaning the glass has been drained or is clearly abandoned. When waiters whisk away glasses the minute a guest puts one down, it increases your bar consumption.

- Serve a champagne cocktail. A sugar cube, bitters, and lemon peel can turn a mediocre sparkling wine into an elegant sip, or try classics like kir royale (champagne with crème de cassis), Bellini (champagne and white peach puree), or mimosa (champagne with orange juice). Buy a less expensive sparkling wine if you're using it as a mixer. Stick with a brut, which is dry, when you're going to add sweet ingredients.

- Consider having an off-site wedding where the caterer allows you to buy your own alcohol. You bypass the markup, paying only a setup fee and the hourly fees for bartenders; buy by the case to nab discounts of 10 to 15 percent, and shop around for a store that will allow you to return unopened bottles.

Great Music for Less | by Tom Moon

Here's a thrifty newsflash for the digital age: The humble compact disc, almost a relic these days, has become a genuine bargain. Now that music downloads have largely replaced CD sales, the business is in what might be described as a seismic upheaval. Millions of people have transferred their collections onto hard drives—and they've ditched their discs and those loathsome plastic holders. The upshot? The offloading has created a surprisingly robust secondary market, filled with not just current hits, but works that stand among the all-time greatest recordings ever made.

That means there's no reason to pay full price. Where a new disc might run between $11 and $18, a used version can be obtained for as little as $3.99. Many titles, even multidisc boxed sets, cost no more than $10.

Ten Artists to Rescue from the Bins

Below are ten established artists whose works can usually be found in decent-size used-CD stores. These recommendations, many of them featured in Tom Moon's book *1,000 Recordings to Hear Before You Die,* are intended as starting points to launch a new listener on a lifetime exploration of music.

- Miles Davis. To trace high points in the long evolution of the jazz trumpet maverick, seek out *Workin', Friday Night at the Blackhawk, Kind of Blue, Sketches of Spain, Nefertiti, Bitches Brew,* and *Decoy.* In that order.
- Willie Nelson. The troubadour responsible for some of the most plaintive songs in country music has recorded his share of astounding albums—among them *Stardust, Red Headed Stranger,* and *Teatro.*
- Bob Marley. Everything the reggae trailblazer recorded is enjoyable; *Natty Dread, Exodus,* and *Kaya* are among the top-shelf standouts.
- Public Enemy. This Long Island crew took the basic two-turntables-and-a-microphone formulation of hip-hop and exploded it, creating dizzyingly dense sound collages that remain essential listening. Seek out *It Takes a Nation of Millions to Hold Us Back* and *Fear of a Black Planet.*
- Bill Evans. *Waltz For Debby* and *Sunday at the Village Vanguard* stand as peak achievements of piano-trio jazz; the visionary *Conversations With Myself* and

To be sure, the CD buying experience has changed in recent years. Many small and independent stores have disappeared, and the mall stores and big-box retailers stock mostly big sellers rather than cult classics and obscure recordings. But there are still places where the spirit of discovery lives on: used CD shops, where, with a little patience, the thrifty aesthete can assemble a highly personalized collection. These days most decent-size cities have a few places specializing in old, vintage, and recycled music, and these temples of sound are loaded with unexpected treasures. Next to the multiple copies of Shania Twain's *Greatest Hits* (which, for some reason, seem to proliferate in such places) you might encounter a long-neglected chestnut by country singer George Jones. Or a pristine copy of Woody Guthrie's American classic *Dust Bowl Ballads.*

That's no accident: Countless gems from the back catalog of genres such as country and classical, R&B and pop, blues and jazz exist in a kind

the aptly named *Everybody Digs Bill Evans* are also thrilling.

- Emmylou Harris. Since the mid 1970s, she has blended elements of country and confessional pop in unique ways. Her astonishingly pure voice shines on such gems as *Pieces of the Sky, Wrecking Ball,* and *Roses in the Snow.*

- Antonio Carlos Jobim. A grand master of the poignant melody, bossa nova composer Antonio Carlos Jobim recorded his exquisite tunes in various settings—check out the instrumental *Wave* and *Elis & Tom,* a collection of vocal duets with Elis Regina.

- Sarah Vaughan. The most daring improvisor ever to sing jazz, Vaughan made great records for decades. Look for *In the Land of Hi-Fi,* which captures her

in 1956 at an early peak, and *Live in Japan,* a 1974 concert that is one of her most stunning mature works.

- Andras Schiff. The Hungarian pianist with a deft sense of dynamics has brought sharp clarity to the piano works of Schubert and Beethoven, among many others. Schiff's recent multidisc exploration of Beethoven Sonatas is breathtaking—particularly *Vols. VI* and *VII.*

- The Replacements. Thanks to a long-overdue 2008 catalog upgrade, the tart and trenchant songs of Paul Westerberg have never sounded better. The alt-rock band's *Let It Be* is the critic-approved must-have; the later *Don't Tell a Soul* holds up magnificently as well.

of format limbo. They were once issued on CD, but have long since gone out of print. They are, therefore, impossible to find new—and still not available from download services, at least not in original form. On iTunes, compilations are more common than the original albums. The best way to find these works is to happen upon them in the used bins.

And consider this: Unlike downloaded music files, the CD is a digital master. If it's in decent shape (and many surface imperfections can be corrected with inexpensive cleaning tools), the disc will sound as good as the day it was purchased new. Drop a CD into the computer, and you can control exactly how it will be imported. By selecting a higher "bit rate," it's possible to obtain better sound quality, a customization level not always possible in download-land.

That's not all: If you like to know the names of the musicians involved in a recording, the CD booklet offers much more information than is readily available through downloading. The printed material—which details personnel and credits, when and where a work was recorded, and often includes liner notes that describe the project and talk about the circumstances of its creation—isn't merely arcana. It can enhance both your listening experience and your understanding.

To prowl for used CDs is to be engaged in a protracted and perhaps never-ending scavenger hunt. Some people maintain extensive spreadsheets filled with titles they consider high-value acquisitions, and spend hours searching online for deals. Others go shopping with just a few artists in mind.

Being open to the unknown is key: Because price points are low, used CDs offer an ideal way to dip a toe into unknown waters, or fling yourself wholeheartedly into new worlds. Not everything you pick up will be a keeper worthy of space on the hard drive, and that's just fine: This is a low-risk endeavor.

Double the Green

Used CD shops aren't just for shopping: You can also use them to recycle the recordings you no longer care for. If you sell those titles back to the shop, you're not only recouping a bit of the initial investment, you're putting the music back into circulation—where someone else can discover it.

Have Tent, Will Travel

Being thrifty is not to be confused with being a workaholic. Everybody deserves a break, and vacationing isn't being profligate—it's taking care of yourself. Research says that those who don't take vacations, or who don't take them often enough, eventually experience a decline in productivity. Vacations don't have to be extravagant, and they don't even have to require travel. If you're a recent convert to thrift who's trying to bulk up an anemic savings portfolio, or if you just want to take a few days off minus a schlep, consider the staycation. Spend a day playing tourist to get a fresh perspective on the place you thought you knew best. Sign up for a walking tour of the historic district or visit the "tourist traps" you've always avoided.

But if you are going to travel, make the most of it.

The Frugal Traveler | by Matt Gross

Sunburned, thirsty, tired, and disoriented, I took one last look at the impossibly long, unpopulated Mediterranean beach in front of me, then turned to walk inland. It was late afternoon in July, and I needed a ride home—badly. My hotel lay twenty miles away, back down the Karpaz peninsula, here in the far northeastern corner of Cyprus, and I had no choice but to hitchhike. In fact, I'd been sticking my thumb out for days along dusty highways, putting my faith in the island's drivers—and so far I'd been rewarded, not just with transportation but with iced coffee, fresh plums, smiles, advice, and companionship.

But as anyone who's thumbed it knows, you never know when your luck will run out. I was wary.

Coming up from the beach, I burst through a line of bushes into a compound of rental bungalows, where a man about my age stood staring at me from an open doorway. I explained the situation, in English, and Rifat offered to drive me to the highway.

"But," he added, "my friends and I are about to have a cookout on the beach. You're welcome to join us."

It's at times like this, when stupendous, unearned generosity erupts

Long-Distance Travel Cheat-Sheet

Whether it's to far-off lands or nearby mountains, travel is one of life's great pleasures. Of course, it can cost, especially if you're traveling abroad. With the plethora of online trip-planning resources out there these days, deals on airfare and lodging are a cinch to find. That takes care of your fixed costs, but you'll still need to keep an eye on those spontaneous in-the-moments splurges. Here's how:

- Establish priorities. You may decide to save on lodgings but splurge on the local cuisine. In some cases, lodging may be paramount—to be right on the beach or downtown in a city.
- Think in the local currency. A handful of currency may be worth a fraction of a dollar, but it may also be the average day's wage in the country you're visiting.
- Look for the best exchange rate—local banks and ATMs usually offer good values. Be careful about changing money at your hotel or in shops; an exorbitant fee is sometimes added.
- Keep your gifts cheap. Focus on inexpensive local specialties: a CD of regional music, inexpensive handmade jewelry. Grocery stores are often a gold mine of inexpensive food gifts (no fresh produce, meat, or dairy products, though—that'll get you stuck in customs).
- Research the specialties of your destination before you leave for

into my life, that I marvel at the power of thrift. Few human endeavors are as costly as travel. Plane tickets, hotels, meals, and gear hack into a checking account without mercy, making the prospect of leaving home for any length of time a potentially bankrupting endeavor.

Yet with frugality as a guiding philosophy, travel is entirely possible. It's not just a matter of hitchhiking (a dicey proposition), backpacking, or sleeping at youth hostels. It's about making smart choices and connecting with people—regardless of your budget.

Couchsurfing.com, for example, has created a network of over half a million travelers who welcome each other into their living rooms, bedrooms, barns, and backyards free of charge. WWOOF—World Wide Opportunities on Organic Farms—offers outdoors-minded wanderers room and board everywhere from Argentina to New Zealand in exchange for the sweat of their brows.

LONG-DISTANCE TIPS BY DEBORAH BURNS

your trip. Then check out the prices of the same items in your stomping grounds. Travelers often complain that they thought they found a great deal while on a trip, only to come home and find the same item selling for less!

- Ask around for deals. Are there any craft fairs? Street markets? Seasonal sales? Talk to other tourists and locals to learn about any special shops, areas, good deals, or interesting items they've discovered.

- Be aware of duty charges, but never assume *duty-free* means "best buy."

- Pay attention to how credit card charges incurred while abroad are billed. You'll be billed at the exchange rate in effect on the day the charge clears in the United States, not the rate on the day you made the purchase. And you will generally be charged a not-unsubstantial conversion fee.

- In many countries you must pay a Value Added Tax (the VAT has different names in different countries), a sales tax that residents of the country also pay.

  You can get reimbursed for the VAT (it can be as much as 30 percent of the cost of an item) if you spend a minimum amount and obtain a special form from the merchant. When you leave the country, give the form to a customs officer, who will sign it and send it to the Customs Office. Your refund is then mailed to you, or sometimes can be picked up at the airport.

What these organizations essentially teach is that travel can be less about the size of your wallet and more about human connection. Through Couchsurfing, I've met a Montenegrin restaurateur, a Romanian software engineer, and a stay-at-home dad in Indiana. While WWOOFing, I've befriended a yoga-loving Turkish farmer and a French couple seeking to escape city life. To me, their faces and personalities represent something deeper than any fancy meal I've bought or museum I've visited; more than any historic site or magnificent landscape, *they* are their nations, their towns, their homes. They are the reason I travel. And I could not have met them had I been staying in five-star hotels.

It's important to be aware that extreme thrift does pose risks. For some travelers, saving money becomes not the means but the end. The backpacker who boasts of a $3 hovel, the hitchhiking Dumpster-diver, the obsessively penny-pinching motel-hopper—all are missing the point. Travel can cost a lot of money, but it's occasionally money well spent. Nice meals and comfortable beds are not the sole province of luxury travelers; we all deserve foie gras and air-conditioning once in a while.

The trick is deciding when to spend, when to splurge, and when to simply skip. Truly frugal travelers will face this dilemma many times, but they understand the choices. Faced with a big charge to visit, say, the Coliseum, they ask not "Can I afford it?" but "Do I really want to see it? What is its appeal? Why have I come to Rome anyway?" The answers to those questions may send them running in the other direction, to the working-class neighborhood of San Lorenzo or the nightclubs of Testaccio—or perhaps into the Coliseum's 2,000-year-old maw to ponder the glories and tragedies of a long-dead empire. Some experiences are, in the end, worth the expense. What matters is the choice.

Which is why, after dining on grilled-beef pitas with Rifat and his friends, I was not all that worried when they dropped me on the side of the highway just as night was falling and traffic was thinning. After all, if no ride showed up, I could easily rent a nearby beach bungalow for the evening and try again come morning—I had the money. But what did I actually want? I wanted to persevere—to prove to myself and to the world that, relying on nothing but my faith in humanity and some weird inner strength, I could make it from point A to point B and back. And so I waited, swatting away the mosquitoes as darkness fell. I didn't have to wait long.

Ready, Set, Camp!

Ah, the great outdoors. Sleeping under the stars. Camping is all-natural, inexpensive, and active. And it can be enjoyed at every level, from pup tents and hotdogs to elaborate gear and campfire espresso. Whatever your style, be sure to obey the campground rules and share in the spirit of making do, helping others, and cleaning up.

According to the U.S. Census, camping is the fourth most popular sport in America. (S'mores might have something to do with that.) As a result, with millions of people hauling gear and pitching tents all over the country, some places are bound to be crowded. If you're going to a national or state park or campground, you may need to make reservations months in advance, so plan ahead.

CAMPING KNOW-HOW BY LYNN BRUNNELLE

Camper's Survival Kit

If you're not going into the arctic tundra, you don't need to spend a lot of cash on high-performance, all-weather gear. Keep your costs low by focusing on items that are durable, necessary, and, when applicable, serve multiple functions. Here's a general list of camping essentials:

- Backpack
- Tent (waterproof, bug-proof, and big enough for you, your family, and your stuff)
- Tarp(s)
- Sleeping bag (synthetic bags are usually the best, because they will warm you even if they get wet)
- Sleeping pad
- Day pack (a smaller backpack for short hikes and excursions)
- Toilet paper (a necessity if you're camping in the backwoods, but pack a roll no matter where you're headed)
- Trowel
- Flashlight or headlamp with batteries
- Small plastic bags (for keeping clothes dry and packing out garbage)
- Several large heavy-duty garbage bags (for spur-of-the-moment rain ponchos, for covering your stuff in a sudden downpour—and for garbage)
- Lantern/candles
- Duct tape (to patch a tear in the tent, fix a hole in an air mattress, hang a lantern, lash together a broken tent pole, mend rips in clothes or boots—the possibilities are endless)
- Superglue
- Dental floss and a heavy-duty sewing needle (for repairing tears in clothing, webbed straps, backpacks, tents—and for your teeth)
- A multipurpose tool (similar to a Swiss Army knife, and sometimes including scissors, pliers, screwdrivers, a can opener, and tweezers)
- A first-aid kit: Band-Aids, antibacterial spray or cream, antibacterial hand cleanser, gauze pads and adhesive tape, small scissors, tweezers (for pulling out thorns or splinters), instant cold pack, elastic bandage, safety pins, moleskin (for blisters), alcohol wipes, pain relief/fever-reducing medicine, anti-itch cream, antidiarrheal medicine, baking soda (combine about one tablespoon with water to make a paste for treating bee stings), and antihistamines (for allergic reactions).

PROJECT | Build a Campfire

The campfire can be the best part of a camping excursion (assuming that it's legal where you are—make sure to check). While you sit around it at night telling stories, it provides light and warmth—and it's a necessary element for s'mores. So don't get stuck in the cold not knowing how to get one started.

TOOLS & MATERIALS: Kindling (sticks, small logs from fallen branches, dry leaves, paper) and logs; bucket of water or water source; shovel; small- to medium-size rocks and stones (for optional fire ring)

Step 1

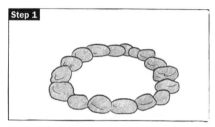

Step 2

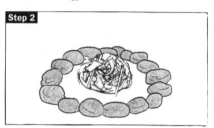

1. Build your fire at least ten feet away from tents, trees, roots, and other flammable items. A fire ring is simple to make with stones and rocks and helps contain the flames. If you can't build one, just clear a space 24 to 32 inches across.

2. Gather dry firewood and kindling, using only fallen branches, then build a small, loose pile of twigs, dry leaves, paper, and kindling, allowing space for air to flow through and feed the fire.

Step 3

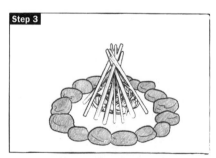

Step 4

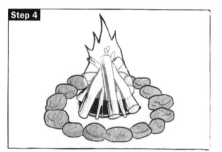

3. Build a pyramid of dry twigs and small sticks around and above the pile of kindling, allowing space for the air to flow through and feed the fire. Light the kindling with a match.

4. As the fire grows in strength, add increasingly larger sticks, then logs, making sure to always leave enough space between them for the fire to breathe.

CAMPFIRE INSTRUCTIONS BY SUZANNE BROWN

The Camp Kitchen

Camp cooking is half the fun, but it does take a little doing. Some meals can be prepared at home ahead of time, wrapped in foil and ziplock bags, and kept in a cooler. Plan to get these on the fire within a day or two. Other meals you'll need to assemble right before you eat. Whatever's on the menu, the essential camp kitchen includes:

- A stove (sometimes cooking over a campfire isn't practical, or legal)
- Fuel for the stove (make sure you have enough to last you for the entire trip)
- A grill rack (for fire-pit grilling)
- A cooler
- Pots and pans (two pots with lids, one big and one medium, plus a griddle or skillet)
- Dishes and utensils (a metal or heavy-duty plastic plate, bowl, and cup for each camper, plus a fork, knife, and spoon)
- Cooking utensils (measuring cup and spoons, wooden spoon, pocketknife, small cutting board, tongs, spatula, strainer, oven mitt, and fast-drying kitchen towel)
- Matches
- A water bottle
- A roll of aluminum foil
- Water and water purifiers (not necessary if you're staying at a campsite that has bathrooms and potable water)

Campfire Safety Tips

- Build a fire that's only as big as you need.
- Never build a fire near tents or other flammable items.
- Never use flammable fluids to start a fire.
- Never leave a fire unattended.
- Keep a bucket of water and a shovel nearby just in case.
- Completely extinguish the fire when you're done.
- Scatter the ashes or embers inside the ring, then sprinkle with water. Stir with a stick. Repeat.
- Drench the charred logs.
- Repeat until everything is cold.

Giving a Thrifty Gift

Holidays have become too materialistic! Kids' birthdays are overly feted! Baby showers, weddings, bachelorette parties, graduations, sweet sixteens, bar and bat mitzvahs—will it ever end?

The answer is no. And though it's true that in some cases expectations may have gotten out of hand, gift-giving is one of those human things that is important precisely *because* it lacks rhyme or reason. In the best of all possible worlds, you give someone a gift as an expression of emotion or in heartfelt celebration of a milestone. You can't put a price on that.

Yet when you're trying to spend less money, it's natural to wonder why you should spend fifty dollars on a gift for Larry when you haven't spent that kind of discretionary income on yourself in a good long while. Well, you don't have to—but that doesn't mean you should skip the gift altogether. Don't go giving thrift a bad name.

Luckily, gift-giving is a great example of an area in which thoughtfulness and a little bit of effort can supplant dollars spent. Too often, gifts are given as a rote gesture. Pull out the wallet, dole out the amount deemed appropriate by the conventions of the occasion, sign the card. Mission accomplished.

A handmade or truly personal gift, no matter how unpolished or inexpensive, will carry more meaning for most givers and recipients than any bit of impersonal frippery. And it's a great solution to the problem of what to give the person who has everything—the phrase "I made it myself" covers a lot of ground.

Using Your Time | by Julia Levy

When my sister Isabelle got engaged, I knew that the best possible wedding gift I could give her would be a homemade wedding cake.

Until I launched what would be a ten-month cake initiative, I'd baked mostly cookies, brownies, and the occasional birthday cake. I'd never heard of ganache or gum paste. I'd never tried piping royal icing, rolling fondant, or creating sugar flowers. I'd certainly never constructed a four-tier cake for two hundred and thirty people.

When I asked a professional pastry chef about my idea, she told me I was crazy. It would take years of practice and failure before I could execute a project like this successfully, she said, urging me not to take this kind of risk on my sister's wedding day.

Advice disregarded. I wanted to give my sister (who adores sweets) a very special gift, and I wasn't going to let a little thing like common sense stand in my way.

I looked into cake classes, but my busy work schedule left no time for formal instruction. My next stop was a bookstore, where I picked up a few cake decoration books. I started reading them before bed as if they were novels. Early on, I felt like I was learning a new language, but after a few weeks of research and grocery store reconnaissance, everything started making more sense.

Next, I turned my tiny kitchen into a cake lab. Late at night, after I got home from work, I experimented with techniques and ingredients. I became a master of leveling so cakes wouldn't lean. I created smooth crumb coats. I tested recipes. I crafted sugar and chocolate flowers—and realized that playing with clay as a child had practical grownup applications. I lugged my practice cakes to the office and sought feedback from colleagues. I also used family and friends as guinea pigs. As the months passed, I got more and more comfortable with the methods (and everyone in my orbit grew a bit plumper).

We went with a white cake with alternating layers of chocolate and caramel filling, bedecked by a simple pink buttercream icing and adorned with handmade white chocolate roses.

This final, ultimate cake took three days. It was summer. I blasted the air-conditioning as I baked layer after layer, concocted fillings, shaped roses, and assembled. I emptied out all the shelves and food from my refrigerator to hold the four-tier confection.

On the morning of the wedding, my dad and I carefully carried the cake from my apartment to his SUV and slid it in through the rear door. I sat in the back with the cake as he drove carefully—avoiding bumps—to the wedding site.

The reviews were glowing. One guest was convinced that the cake came from a well-known cake baker and designer. My sister and her husband took a big wedge along on their honeymoon. I had spent a year learning to bake a cake. And yes, I would do it all over again.

Giftable Nibbles, Artisanal Spirits

Handmade edibles are a pleasure to make and receive. And they often trump those expensive boutique food gifts you used to snap up at the specialty store. Same goes for the drinks featured here. You can easily steep fruits, nuts, and other flavorings in vodka and other spirits to make decadent liqueurs of the type favored by hoity-toity mixologists. To package your gourmet moonshine, use glass liquor, water, or soda bottles that have been thoroughly cleaned and dried. Beer bottles with latches and reusable caps are ideal. Or seek out unique glass bottles or lidded decanters at flea markets and garage sales.

RECIPE | **Peanut Brittle**

Making candy is easier than it seems—and nut brittle is perhaps the easiest, with only two ingredients. But don't tell your friends, who will be super impressed by a gift of boardwalk-quality peanut brittle! You can use whatever nuts you want for the peanuts in this recipe. Salted nuts make the best-tasting brittles, and chopped cashews are particularly good. Brittles should be made only when the weather is dry, but they will keep indefinitely in airtight tins.

Makes ¾ cup

> Butter, to grease one cookie sheet
> 1⅓ cups granulated sugar
> One 6½-ounce can cocktail peanuts

1. Before you start, butter a cookie sheet very thoroughly.

2. Cook the sugar in a frying pan over low heat until it has melted and turned a light brown. Stir in the peanuts, then pour the mixture onto the baking sheet.

3. Immediately start stretching the candy by pressing it out with the backs of two spoons. Don't touch it with your hands, as it will be very hot. Keep this up, working quickly, until the brittle is no more than 1 peanut deep.

4. When the candy is completely cool, break it into pieces. Keep it in an airtight tin.

BRITTLE FROM *COUNTRY WISDOM & KNOW-HOW*

RECIPE | ## Cinnamon & Sugar Pecans

These sweet, crisp pecans have a hint of cinnamon. They are a perfect gift for the holidays, but they also make a perfect gift for a host.

Makes 4 cups

> Vegetable oil, for greasing the pan
> ⅔ cup sugar
> 1 teaspoon salt
> 1 teaspoon ground cinnamon
> 1 large egg white
> 1 tablespoon water
> 1 pound pecan halves

1. Preheat the oven to 250°F. Lightly oil a baking sheet.

2. Toss together the sugar, salt, and cinnamon in a medium-size bowl.

3. In a large nonreactive bowl, beat the egg white and water together until frothy. Toss the pecans in the egg white mixture to coat. Add the sugar mixture, one third at a time, to the pecan mixture, tossing gently after each sugar addition, to coat the pecans.

4. Spread the coated nuts on the baking sheet and bake for 45 minutes, stirring carefully every 15 minutes. Put the nuts on wax paper to cool, separating them while still hot. Store in an airtight container for up to 1 week.

Herbal Tea Blends

The elaborate packaging of store-bought teas might lead you to believe that tea-making is some kind of unattainable science. But herbal tea (literally) boils down to dried herbs steeped in water. Supplement your own harvest with bulk-bought herbs from the store as needed. Blend equal parts of each ingredient; then adjust to taste. Present your gift in a small jar with a gift tag and an inexpensive tea ball. Experiment with your own blends (remember, it's not a science!), or try one of the following combinations:

• Rosemary and lavender
• Dried citrus zest and aniseed
• Hibiscus petals, rose hips, and lemon verbena
• Fennel, anise, coriander, and caraway seeds
• Birch leaves, peppermint, savory, and bee balm
• Lavender flowers, rosemary, lemon balm, spearmint, and cloves

PECAN RECIPE BY DEEDEE STOVEL AND PAMELA WAKEFIELD; TEA BLENDS BY BETTY OPPENHEIMER

RECIPE | ## Herbal & Spicy Vinegars

Those high-priced vinegars you see on the shelves of gourmet stores seem to have been invented for gift-giving. (What reasonably thrifty home cook would spend all that money on a bottle of vinegar for themselves?) Treat the foodie in your life by making some fancy vinegar of your own.

Makes 1 quart

FOR HERB VINEGAR
> ¼ cup fresh basil
> ¼ cup fresh oregano
> 6 cloves garlic
> 1 teaspoon black peppercorns
> 2 cups red wine vinegar

FOR SPICE VINEGAR
> 1 teaspoon black peppercorns
> 1 teaspoon whole cloves
> 1 hot red chile pepper
> 1 quarter-size piece of fresh ginger root
> 2 cups balsamic vinegar

1. For herb vinegar, combine all ingredients in a quart jar. For spice vinegar, combine all ingredients in a nonreactive metal or enamel pan and heat on the stove to 110°F. (Or use a glass bowl and heat to the same temperature in the microwave.) Pour into a quart jar.

2. Line the metal lid with plastic wrap and seal the jar.

3. Store the jar in a dark place to steep. Shake every few days for 1 week to 1 month. The longer you steep the herbs, the stronger your vinegar will be. If you feel that your vinegar is not flavorful enough, strain out the first steeped batch of herbs and replace them with a fresh batch.

4. Sterilize vinegar bottles by washing in hot, soapy water with a bottle brush. Rinse well. Pour boiling water into each bottle, allow it to sit for 10 minutes. Pour out the water and invert the bottles until ready to use. (Sterilize just before you are ready to use the bottles.)

5. Strain the vinegar and herb mixture through cheesecloth or a coffee filter placed in a strainer. Using a funnel, decant into sterilized bottles.

6. Seal the bottle with a cork or with its original cap. Label or tag the vinegar with the date. Vinegars are best used within 6 months, and should be stored in a dark place.

VINEGARS BY BETTY OPPENHEIMER; SPIRITS BY MIMI FREID

RECIPE | **Pear Liqueur**

The Bartlett pear is the best to use for liqueur-making. Avoid fruits with cuts, bruises, dark spots, or decay. This recipe also works well with apples.

Makes 1½ pints

½ pound pears (see headnote)
1½ cups vodka, rum, or brandy
½ cup sugar syrup (see box)
Pinch of cinnamon, 1 clove nutmeg

1. Slice the pears and add to the other ingredients in a large bowl, adding sugar syrup last. Stir gently and steep for 3 weeks in a wide-mouth glass jar.

2. Strain and filter through cheesecloth or a coffee filter. Taste and adjust flavor by adding fresh fruit or sugar syrup if needed.

3. Age 3 to 4 more weeks, then strain again (if necessary) and bottle the liqueur.

RECIPE | **Hazelnut Liqueur**

For a variation on this recipe, try using pistachios. This liqueur is excellent over ice cream and as an aperitif.

Makes 1 pint

6 ounces hazelnuts
1 vanilla bean
Pinch of allspice
1½ cups vodka
⅓ cup sugar syrup (optional; see box)

1. Chop the hazelnuts (this releases the flavor of the nut) and add to the vodka with the vanilla bean and allspice. Steep for 2 weeks in a glass jar, lightly shaking occasionally.

2. Strain and filter through cheesecloth or a coffee filter until clear.

3. Add sugar syrup, if desired, and age for 3 additional weeks before bottling.

Simple Syrup

Sugar syrup, also known as simple syrup, is easy to make and good to have on hand. Not only is it a key ingredient in homemade liqueurs, it is often used as a sweetener in cocktails, such as gimlets and mojitos (see page 290). If you love mixed drinks, make a large batch and store it in a glass bottle for quick use as needed. It keeps in the refrigerator for several weeks.

To make a simple syrup, combine 1 cup sugar and ½ cup water in a saucepan. Bring to a boil, stirring to dissolve the sugar. Remove the syrup from the heat and allow it to cool entirely before using. If the syrup is not cool before being added to an alcohol mixture, the heat will evaporate the alcohol. (And where's the fun in that?)

Gifts for New Parents

When new babies arrive, the tiny presents are quick to follow. What's a wise gift to give? It's the thought that counts, but some thoughts are more useful (and more welcome) than others. (Yes, a new mother *can* have too many organic cotton onesies.)

As you spend time and money picking out a present, consider the ultimate value—not just the cost—of what you want to give. Will the gift be useful or helpful to the parent? Will it entertain or educate the child? Will it offer financial support for both? Whatever you choose, avoid the irrelevant or impractical. And when in doubt, ask.

What to Give

Babysitting. The best gift is one that costs nothing but time: an offer to babysit. A mom whose six-week-old baby is still nursing every few hours probably isn't yearning for a night on the town just yet, but she might need a nap. The offer of a few hours of child care will earn her eternal gratitude.

Clothing in large sizes. Babies grow fast. Beware the cuteness of tiny outfits that a child may be able to wear only once. New parents appreciate gifts their little one can grow into. Consider buying items in the 6- to 12-month (or larger) sizes.

Registry items. Parents create registries because they want or need specific items. So while a bottle sterilizer or cloth diapers may strike you as boring, the parents-to-be will be grateful to cross something off the to-buy list.

The big stuff. With trendy strollers topping $800, new parents are on the hook for a number of pricey must-haves. Help them out by pooling your resources with a few friends who'll contribute to big-ticket items—or give them a gift card that they can use toward those purchases.

Experiences. Something like a music-for-babies class will be enriching for baby, and a regular trip out of the house for mom. It may not feel as fun as giving a big, shiny toy, but indoor playground passes, children's museum memberships, and even gift certificates to kid-friendly restaurants go a long way for parent and child.

Financial gifts. The gift of cash is always helpful, but there are lots of ways to make sure your generosity goes toward the long term. Custodial stock

GIFT GUIDE BY ERIKA RASMUSSON JANES

accounts and savings bonds can be purchased through brokers or local banks. Cash contributions to a college savings plan—a 529 plan—will take some coordination with the parents. Either way, rest assured that you're making baby's future brighter.

Hand-me-downs. Be it a changing table, a baby carrier, or a bundle of gently used baby clothes, most new parents will be grateful for what you have to share. Just make sure the items you're passing on are in near-new condition and haven't been subject to any recalls. Handing down is also ecofriendly: Why toss it if someone else can use it?

What Not to Give

Blankets. If you think there's nothing wrong with giving a baby blanket, you're in good company—and that's the problem. One new mom received thirty-one blankets when her first child was born. "Some I boxed up and saved because they were special," she said, "but for the most part, they're all over the house and just seem to collect dog hair." Unless you've knitted it by hand (see page 335), or it's on the registry, you can put your gift dollars to better use.

Items with a million little pieces. Toys with tiny parts make a mom's life harder. They get lost under the couch and chewed on by the pets—and they are a choking hazard for babies and toddlers. Make sure your gift is age-appropriate and, preferably, includes just a few pieces.

Stuffed animals. They're cute and cuddly, but they wind up as clutter. A child needs only so many. Some lucky bunny and bear will attain most-favored status, but the rest will gather dust. If you really want to buy an object, make it a book instead.

Baby shoes. Tiny designer sneakers are fun to coo over, but the truth is, babies don't need shoes until they can walk. (And baby shoes are expensive.)

MY THRIFT

Popcorn on a String

During Christmas, we made homemade taffy and decorations out of popcorn on a string. My grandpa used to make wreaths out of princess pine, which grows low to the ground. We cut down our own Christmas tree. Lots of people had hard tack candy from Sears, Roebuck. The tin would be used for various purposes—it was never thrown away.

—Bob Conrad, born 1932

How Thrifty Is Your Knitting? | by Ruth Graham

Traditionally, knitting has been one of those unglamorous but revered domestic arts—like baking bread or canning. But at some point, a funny thing happened: Knitting became cool. The handicraft became hugely popular among the young people and celebrities who reclaimed the aesthetics of the homemade. And still, it's touted as a way to save money; after all, what could be more thrifty than buying raw materials and making the finished product yourself? But knitting has a dirty little secret: It can be expensive.

A plain pullover sweater in a size medium requires about 1,200 yards of yarn, which means the knitter needs at least eleven balls of basic yarn, at about $5 each—for a total of $55. Higher quality yarns cost more: the same sweater in a wool, silk, or bamboo blend would cost at least $80. Top-of-the-line materials like vicuña wool can run $300 for a single ball. A pullover from the Gap or H&M often costs much less than even the cheapest calculation

---

Buy the Best Yarn for Less

If you look for yarn in traditional retail outlets, knitting anything bigger than baby booties in nice, quality yarn will cost you. But with a few tricks up your angora-silk-blend sleeve, you can get the very best yarn at bargain-basement prices. Here are some places to look:

- **Bargain bins.** Every local yarn store will have a bargain bin containing yarns that are out of season, overstock left over from a larger dye lot, or styles that have been discontinued. Check this bin frequently as its contents will turn over quickly.
- **EBay.** Although you can't rely on online auctions to find a particular brand of yarn in a specific color or quantity, searching for "yarn" on eBay will bring up hundreds of choices at low prices. You'll get the best results if you are familiar with the brand and make of yarn—otherwise, you might be disappointed when that fluffy hot pink ball turns out to be as rough as steel wool. And if you're buying from individual sellers, find out if the yarn has been kept in a smoke-free environment.
- **Online stores.** Many online stores specialize in discounted yarn, and a simple Internet search for "discount yarn" will bring up the most current listings. Be sure to factor in the price of shipping and handling before placing your order to know if you are actually saving money.

YARN-FINDING TIPS BY DEBBIE STOLLER; YARN RECYCLING TIPS BY MIRANDA HASSETT (VIA DEBBIE STOLLER)

here. Another example: a normal pair of solid colored socks—a standard early knitting project—requires two balls of yarn that cost at minimum $6 apiece. A bag of a dozen pairs of athletic socks at a drugstore costs about a dollar, and even nicer dress socks can be had for far less than $12 a pair. Even if you're knitting as a gift, you might end up spending much more to make a scarf than you would if you were to buy one.

And don't forget a pattern. They cost about $10 apiece, or up to $50 for a book of them. Then there are the labor "costs"—the knitter's hours of hard work. On top of that, the results will still tend to look, well, homemade.

These are the approximate costs in individual projects, but most knitters have far more yarn on hand than projects in mind. My mother, a devoted knitter, has a home filled with more yarn than she could use in three lifetimes. She whips out a few beautiful sweaters a year.

None of this should discourage ardent knitters, of course. The point is that knitting is a hobby. And just like golfers or painters, knitters pay for their pleasure. There are circumstances in which knitting can truly save you money. Buy a sweater at the thrift store, unravel it, and reuse the yarn. Or take a page from my sister, also an accomplished knitter. She often buys deeply discounted knitwear and alters it herself. The fix is fast, the materials are minimal, and the result is (almost) like new.

Knit Lingo

These abbreviations, frequently used in knitting patterns, appear in the four projects that follow:

- Beg: beginning
- BO: bind off
- CC: contrasting color
- CO: cast on
- cont: continue
- dpn: double-pointed needle
- foll: follow
- k: knit
- MC: main color
- meas: measures
- p: purl
- patt: pattern
- pm: place marker
- pu: pick up
- rem: remaining
- rep: repeat
- rnd: round
- RS: right side
- sl: slip
- ssk: slip next stitch knitwise twice, knit stitches together through back loop
- st: stitch
- St st: stockinette stitch
- tbl: through back loop
- tog: together
- WS: wrong side
- [*]: An asterisk indicates that a pattern should be repeated. For example, "*K1, p1; rep from * across" translates to "Knit one, purl one. Repeat to end of row."

PROJECT | **Turn a Thrift-Store Sweater Back Into Yarn**

Scavenge for super-cheap yarn by visiting your favorite thrift store and looking through the sweater rack for something made in a yarn you like. But before you lay down your $3, check the seams. Some cheap sweaters are made by cutting pieces out of machine-knit cloth; these pieces are then serged together with what looks like a zigzag stitch. If you took apart a sweater like that, you'd just have lots of little lengths of yarn. So make sure that the inside seams of the sweater look like knit edges, sewn together. This means that each piece of the sweater was individually knit (by hand or machine) and should come apart into one or two lengths of yarn.

TOOLS AND MATERIALS: Sweater; small pair of scissors; knitting needle

1. Take apart the sweater. Most sweaters come apart into four pieces: front, back, and two sleeves. Some have a collar or other elements. You're going to reduce the sweater to these component parts by undoing all the seams. Turn the sweater inside out and start with a side seam (because it's the easiest).

2. Find the thread that's holding the seam together. It will be a different type of thread from the yarn (a bit like embroidery floss, but thinner) and will show up on one side of the seam as a row of little V shapes. Follow the tops of those Vs to one end of the seam. Then use small, pointed scissors to cut through one side of one of the Vs, as close to the end of the seam as you can.

3. With the scissors' point or a knitting needle, pull up on the same side of the next V down; that should pull up the end of the thread you just cut. Grab that loose end with your fingers and pull. It should undo all of the Vs (which turn out to be little loops) down the entire seam. If it catches and stops, just pull the two sides of the seam apart with a sharp but gentle tug, and things should loosen up. If you get really stuck, you can always pick another V and start again with a new loose end.

4. Repeat this process with all the seams until you have four (or more) flat pieces of knit fabric. (Note: Sometimes a shoulder or neck-edge seam will be bound with some other kind of stitching or be especially difficult to undo. You can, in a pinch, cut along the top of a knit piece and take that seam off; you'll only lose a few yards of the yarn that way. But never, ever cut along a side seam!)

5. Pick one piece and start unraveling. If you can, find the loose end at one top corner of the piece and undo it; otherwise you can just cut into the top row somewhere and start pulling it apart. If the yarn catches a bit at the end of a row, a gentle tug should loosen it.

6. As you unravel, wind the yarn into a ball. The yarn will be kinky, but this won't affect the process of knitting with it or the way it looks once it's reknit. Now you've got yourself three or four or five balls of some really cool yarn for the price of one skein of cheap acrylic!

PROJECT | **Keyhole Scarf**

This keyhole scarf, perfect for windy winters because it won't blow away, is quick to make and doesn't call for a mountain of yarn. *A note:* This and the following projects assume a rudimentary familiarity with knitting techniques and terminology. For further instruction, check out some of the source books listed on page 365.

SIZE: About 4½" x 40"

MATERIALS: Four skeins heavy worsted wool (50 grams/65 yards) in two contrasting or complementary colors (A & B); US 9 (5.5 mm) knitting needles, or size needed to obtain gauge

GAUGE: 30 sts and 20 rows = 4" in k1, p1 rib

Stitch Pattern

K1, P1 Rib (over even number of sts)

All rows: *K1, p1; rep from * across.

Directions

With A, CO 30 sts. Work 45 rows in k1, p1 rib.

Divide in half for opening: Rib 15 sts, attach second skein of A, and rib rem 15 sts. Rib 10 rows, knitting both sides at the same time.

Rejoin two sides by working across the next row with one skein only. Cont until 100 rows total have been worked with A.

Change to B and cont in rib for 100 rows. BO. Weave in yarn ends.

PROJECT | **Tube Socks**

If the man in your life is an athletic-sock kind of guy, this is a great pattern for him. While they look like your average, everyday jock socks, knit in a silky soft hand-dyed merino, they add up to a luxury handmade item for a very special guy. You can knit the stripes in any colors you like.

SIZE: Men's US 11

FOOT CIRCUMFERENCE: 9"

CUFF TO HEEL: 7½"

FOOT LENGTH: Approximately 10¾"

MATERIALS: Four skeins finely spun wool (50 grams/185 yards)

- MC: 2 skeins
- CC1: 1 skein
- CC2: 1 skein

US 0 (2 mm) double-pointed needles (set of 4), or size needed to obtain gauge

GAUGE: 32 sts and 44 rows = 4" in St st

Stripe Pattern

2 rnds MC, 5 rnds CC1, 3 rnds MC, 10 rnds CC2, 3 rnds MC, 5 rnds CC1, 3 rnds MC.

Directions

Note: The 3-st garter ridge border on the heel is a nice way to end the heel rows and creates an easy edge to later pick up the stitches for the gusset.

CUFF

With MC, CO 72 sts. Divide sts over 3 dpns as foll: 18 (Needle 1), 18 (Needle 2), 36 (Needle 3). Pm and join. Work 31-rnd Stripe patt in k2, p2 rib as foll: K1, *p2, k2; rep from * to last st, k1.

LEG

Work remainder of sock in MC only.

Rnd 1: K1, p2, k30, p2, k2, p2, k30, p2, k1. Rep rnd 1 until leg meas 7½" from beg or to desired length, turn.

HEEL

The heel is worked over 36 sts of Needle 3, beginning with a WS row and ending with a RS row.

FLAP

Row 1: (WS) K3, p to last 3 sts, k3.

Row 2: K3, *sl 1, k1; rep from * to last 3 sts, k3.

Rep rows 1 and 2 until there are 36 rows in heel flap, ending with a RS row.

TURN HEEL

Row 1: (WS) Sl 1, p18, p2 tog, p1, turn.

Row 2: Sl 1, k3, ssk, k1, turn.

There will be a small gap between sts of heel turn and unworked sts.

Row 3: Sl 1, p to 1 st before gap, p2tog, p1, turn.

Row 4: Sl 1, k to 1 st before gap, ssk, k1, turn.

Rep rows 3 and 4 until all sts have been worked, ending with a RS row—20 sts. Heel flap measures approx 2⅜".

GUSSETS

Renumber needles and rearrange sts as foll: 20 heel sts on Needle 1. With Needle 1 with RS facing, PU and k18 sts along side of heel flap plus 2 sts between heel and instep; Needle 2, k36 across instep; Needle 3, PU and k 2 sts between instep and heel plus 18 along side of heel flap and k10 from Needle 1—96 sts. Pm for new beg of rnd. K 1 rnd.

SOCK PATTERN BY CLAUDIA LANG; BLANKET BY LISA SHOBHANA MASON (VIA DEBBIE STOLLER)

SHAPE GUSSETS

Rnd 1: Needle 1, k to last 2 sts, ssk; Needle 2, knit; Needle 3, k2tog, k to end.

Rnd 2: Needle 1, k to last 3 sts, ssk, k1; Needle 2, knit; Needle 3, k1, k2tog, k to end.

Rnd 3: Knit.
Rep rnds 2 and 3 until there are 72 sts.

FOOT

Work even in St st until foot meas 8¾" from back of heel or 2" less than desired finished length.

TOE

Rnd 1: Needle 1, k to last 3 sts, k2tog, k1; Needle 2, k1, ssk, k to last 3 sts, k2tog, k1; Needle 3, k1, ssk, k to end.

Rnd 2: Knit.
Rep rnds 1 and 2 until there are 36 sts.

Rep rnd 1 until there are 20 sts.

Cont with Needle 3, k5 from Needle 1.

Graft toe sts using kitchener st.

Finishing: Weave in ends, and block to shape.

PROJECT | # Baby Blanket

Don't skimp on quality when it comes to selecting a yarn for your baby blanket. (See if you can scrounge some merino.) The elegant yet easy-to-knit results will garner rave reviews for generations!

SIZE: 28" x 28" unblocked; 31" x 31" blocked

MATERIALS: Eight skeins finely spun wool (50 grams/175 yards); US 9 (5.5 mm) 29- to 40-inch circular needle, or size needed to obtain gauge; rust-proof pins for blocking

GAUGE: 18 sts = 4" in St st with 2 strands of yarn held tog

Stitch Pattern

Seed Stitch (even number of Sts)

Row 1: *K1, p1; rep from * to end of row.

Row 2: *P1, k1; rep from * to end of row.

Rep rows 1–2 for patt.

Note: You will be working with 2 strands of yarn held tog throughout.

Directions

With 2 strands of yarn held tog, CO 126 sts.
Work 20 rows in seed st.

Row 1 (RS): *K1, p1; rep from * 5 times, k53, p53, *k1, p1; rep from * 5 times.

Row 2 (WS): *P1, k1; rep from * 5 times, k53, p53, *p1, k1; rep from * 5 times.

Rep these 2 rows until entire piece measures approx 14" (or until you have finished your 3rd and 4th skeins of yarn). End with a WS row.

Next row (RS): *K1, p1; rep from * 5 times, p53, k53, *k1, p1; rep from * 5 times.

Next row (WS): *P1, k1; rep from * 5 times, p53, k53, *p1, k1; rep from * 5 times.

Rep these 2 rows until entire piece measures approx 25½" (or same number of St st rows as lower half). End with a WS row.
Work 20 rows in seed st.
BO.

Finishing: Immerse blanket in cool water. Very gently squeeze, then roll the blanket in a towel to absorb excess water. Lay flat on a dry towel. Gently stretch until it measures 31 x 31". Pin with rust-proof pins. Let dry.

thrift &
your wallet

All Systems Go

I T MIGHT SEEM LIKE MONEY IS A STRANGE TOPIC WITH WHICH TO
end. Why not start there? Well, as you've probably picked up on by now,
the funny thing about thrift is that it's not really a matter of finance.
"Finance" sounds scientific, perhaps a bit intimidating; intangibles figure
prominently, along with images of trading floors and zigzagging charts.
Thrift is more concrete, far less lofty; you're likely to picture a gardener
with dirt under his fingernails, a cook in a quaintly frayed apron stirring
a long-simmering stew. But thrift *is* about money—skipping the lattes or
growing your own tomatoes won't do you much good if you're ignoring your
mounting credit card debt. Your thrifty house needs a solid foundation.

Awareness is key. Many of us are so afraid of losing or not having
enough money that we do everything we can to avoid thinking about it. But
that's how debts are swept under the rug. Fear is not a good organizing principle. So if you haven't done so yet, get ready to sweep away those cobwebs.
With a clear eye and an ordered wallet, you'll be able to make the smart
choices that will engender and sustain your financial health. It's not too
terribly complicated, and it's within reach—no matter what your profile.
Thrift can benefit millionaire and scrappy student alike.

The Nuts & Bolts

Financial stability isn't the result of complicated mathematical equations, a CEO-level salary, or innate money smarts. (After all, fuzzy math is to blame for some pretty major screwups in the financial industry.) Some people with huge salaries go into debt, and some people with not a lot of money manage to hold on to it. What's the central difference? Frugality and forethought (aka planning), two qualities that anyone can cultivate. Whatever the size of your bank account, the twelve simple rules that follow will help you maintain, or improve, your financial well-being.

1. Budget

Budgeting means balancing what you earn against what you owe (and spend) and making sure that your credit (assets, income, bank balance) exceeds your debit (living expenses, credit card debts, loans, health insurance, car payments, and so on).

The best way to build a budget is to compare your monthly expenditures to your income. First gather together all your receipts, bank statements, bills, and invoices. On a blank sheet of paper draw up two columns for the month: income and expenses. Divide the expenses into fixed and discretionary. (Fixed expenses are recurring charges, such as rent or utilities, with little or no change. Discretionary costs change or vary from month to month, such as entertainment or food.)

When you have listed all your expenses and all your income, add up both columns and subtract primary expenses from your income. If expenses exceed income (and they usually do), you need to develop a plan to reduce your debt. To meet expenses you must either find a way to earn more or, more likely, devise a strategy to spend less.

Impose your first budget by setting aside the exact amount needed to pay for rent, food, transportation, and utilities. If you can, have your paycheck deposited electronically into your bank account, and then arrange for your bank to pay as many of your bills as possible—loan payments, utility bills, and savings for retirement can often be paid electronically. These automatic deductions are a great help in maintaining a budget, because they preempt the illusion of available cash.

TWELVE RULES (THROUGHOUT) BY ANNA JOHNSON

Your Digital "Checkbook"

In the old days, people balanced their checkbooks every month—or tried to. Most months, it was an exercise in frustration, with bills and checks spread across kitchen tables and lots of arguments about missing receipts. In some ways, the digital age has made it easier to track your finances: If you bank online and pay with debit, your receipts live online.

But in other ways, the process has become more complicated. Did you remember to update your credit card's expiration date on the phone company's website so your payment would go through? Did you remember to call such and such number and say yes at the tone in order to authorize payment?

It's great to automate your bill paying, but it's not great to forget about your expenses. And when you have a mix of bills and payment options across various media and systems, things can get confusing. (Some bills come in via snail mail, some via e-mail; some you have to remember to pay, and some are automatically deducted—it's a whirlwind.)

Even though it may seem like the world's great virtual network is somehow taking care of tracking your spending, there's no escaping the fact that *you* must take responsibility for doing the tracking. The first step is to get in the habit of organizing your bills and receipts. You might have a drawer or a box specifically for financial documents. Just toss them in, and process later. But make a commitment to sort, record, and file once a week so that it doesn't become overwhelming. In the digital realm, organize a receipts bookmark for purchases made online, or print out all receipts and file them; if you pay your bills electronically, file your proof of payment in a virtual "expenses" folder on your desktop or in your e-mail.

Some people make an appointment with themselves for Saturday morning to take care of the household bookkeeping. Some use personal finance software—online or on their computers. Others simply use a spreadsheet. If you're comfortable with technology, learn how to import transactions from your bank and credit card accounts.

As you track your spending, beware of "stealth" transactions. It can be difficult, for example, to remember where you spent your cash. (If this is a problem for you, carry a pen and notebook in your pocket or purse.) Don't forget to merge online and real-world transactions when you add things up.

Whatever your method (and there's no one right way), balancing your checkbook is at the heart of financial awareness.

2. Set Up a Home Office

A home office can live in an accordion folder or a large hatbox, if you so fancy, but it does need to be concentrated in one place. Find a bookkeeping method that works for you. You need a space and a system to track your receipts, your bank statements, your income, and your bills.

3. Pay Yourself First

Pay yourself first and you may be surprised at how quickly you gather together an emergency fund (living expenses in case you get fired or fall ill), a slush fund for a nice vacation, or, perhaps more important, a retirement nest egg that you barely notice yourself building.

To start a savings plan, if you don't already have one in place, try to bank a minimum of 10 percent of your salary every time you get paid. If this seems like too much, give yourself a smaller goal, say $100 every month. If you have trouble putting aside even the smallest amount, establish a savings account and ask if your employer will channel funds straight into it. What you don't see, you won't miss, and there's nothing worse than working twelve-hour days and having nothing to show for it by year's end—or, worse, career's end.

4. Be Retirement Savvy

Retirement—the very word summons images of golf slacks and canasta, or in the worst-case scenario, of having to live on cat food. Planning for your retirement is a responsibility, but it's also one of the easiest ways to learn the basic principles of investment. And you are never too young to start doing either one.

In the old days Social Security and pensions provided retirement security. Today, not many companies pay for pension plans. Social Security was intended as a supplement to retirement plans and matches only a portion of your income upon retirement. Your retirement program will be shaped by your work status (full time or freelance) and by your employer. Many employers offer a 401(k) plan, which allows you to save a portion of your salary directly from your paycheck. (See page 353 for more on the subject.) Some employers will add to your funds by matching a percentage of your contribution. The self-employed should look into setting up an IRA.

When you put money into a retirement plan you save in two ways: You set money aside and you pay less in taxes. Because your contribution is deducted from your paycheck before taxes are calculated, your taxable

Six Common Mistakes in Retirement Planning

1. The Scarlett O'Hara mentality: I'll worry about it tomorrow. This usually translates to putting off planning until age 45 or later.

2. Trusting in government. Overestimating how much Social Security and an employer's pension will contribute to retirement income. In a survey of 400 people aged 45 to 64, about 59 percent said they expect to rely primarily on Social Security or pension benefits when they retire. However, according to the U.S. Department of Treasury, these two sources combined will account for just 35 percent of the average retiree's income.

3. What? Me? Retire? Believing you'll work until you drop. Healthy 40- and 50-year-olds often declare they'll never retire completely, but statistics show that most people don't work much beyond age 65.

4. Impatience. Not giving savings and investments time to grow, and instead moving money around seeking higher, and riskier, returns.

5. Neglecting personal decisions. Shoving aside questions about what you'll do, where you'll live, and with whom. It's not all about money—a healthy retirement also requires having a purpose to your day, something to look forward to, and someone to share it with.

6. Assuming living expenses will drop. Depending on your lifestyle, where you plan to live, and what you plan to do, retirement may easily cost as much as your working life.

income is reduced. You'll eventually have to pay taxes on the money you're setting aside, but not until you actually withdraw funds. And then, because your taxation rate will be based on your income as a retiree, your taxes will most likely be much lower.

5. Get Out of Debt

Most everyone lives with some level of debt, but the degree of debt we're shouldering has spiraled out of control in recent years. We are maxing out not just one card but several at a time, and we have little to show for it—a few dinners here, a vacation there—and we're still paying years after the initial buzz of the purchase.

RETIREMENT DON'TS BY LISA BERGER

The first step in getting out of debt is to face exactly how much you owe, and to whom. If you phone everyone you owe and arrange for even a minimal repayment plan, you've already made a giant leap. In just a few minutes you've bought yourself time to tackle the next step: deciding your strategy for increasing your income, lowering your overhead, or both. Here are some ideas:

Increase your income. If you can find the work, a weekend job or an additional freelance project is sometimes the best way to attack a problem debt. But extra income must be channeled straight into your debt and not frittered away on feel-good pick-me-ups.

Consolidate your debt. By putting all your debts in one basket, you can often save money and cut down the hassle factor. Instead of sending payments to several creditors, you pay only one. Your interest rate may be lower, there's a lot less paperwork, and your credit report looks cleaner immediately.

If you have several credit cards, you can transfer the balances to just one card. To do this you need a clean repayment record and you must research to find the card that's offering the best interest rates. Of course, keep in mind that the whole point of consolidation is reduction, which means no new debts on any other plastic.

Borrow against your retirement fund. It is possible to borrow up to 50 percent of the money you have in your employer's 401(k) plan. The loan is usually low-interest; you have five years to pay it off and the interest you pay goes back into your fund. (That's right, it goes into your account, but don't be fooled into thinking it's a can't-lose proposition—the amount of interest you pay yourself seldom makes up for revenue lost when you pull chunks of cash out of your investing pool.)

Think twice before borrowing this way. If you leave your job (whatever the circumstances), the sum you've borrowed is due in full; if you can't pay it back, you'll have to pay ordinary income taxes on that money; and if you're under age 59½, you'll pay a 10 percent penalty as well. But if you're drowning in credit card interest, it may be advantageous to give yourself a clean slate with a much lower interest rate for your repayments.

Sell your assets. When things get really dire you might be tempted to sell off treasured possessions—Grandma's ruby ring, bonds, or investments. Conventional wisdom says to never dispense with an investment whose interest rate is greater than that of your debt. Meaning, if you are earning

15 percent on an investment, and your credit card interest stands at 12 percent, hang on to your nest egg. This rule is fine until your debt becomes unmanageable. If you have to liquidate, start with the least sacrifice first, and hold what breaks your heart till last.

Seek professional help. Because there are so many people in money trouble, a whole industry has sprung up to help folks deal with bad credit ratings and unmanageable debt. Some companies that claim to "repair" your credit history or help shift your debt can simply add to your problems by demanding an upfront payment and delivering very little. Nonprofit organizations are safer, and through them you will find moral support as well as solid repayment strategies. If you want to join a twelve-step program to help overcome your debt, contact Debtors Anonymous to see where you can find a meeting in your area. Your city's public advocate office will be able to help you find nonprofit credit counseling services, as will the National Foundation for Consumer Credit. Another useful organization is Consumer Credit Counseling Services.

Declare bankruptcy. When debt exceeds income by 50 percent, bankruptcy is an option, but it should be your absolute last choice. Once you've declared bankruptcy it will be difficult for you to get any kind of credit in the future, and you are still not absolved from paying alimony, child support, student loans, and taxes.

6. Learn How Credit Cards Work

The word *credit* implies money paid. However, what a credit card offers is money extended and then money owed. Credit cards put you in debt, sometimes very quickly. A credit card debt over $500 needs to be viewed as a loan from the bank, and the interest rates charged on this money are often much higher than those of a conventional loan (usually twice the rate of a home loan). Initially a card seems like a very good idea. You have surplus funds plus some superficial benefits (like frequent flier miles or a high balance), and the card provides a method of establishing a credit rating. But miss just a few payments and you blemish your credit rating immediately. The best way to build a credit history and not a debt is to acquire a secured credit card. This operates like any other card except that it's secured by a bank deposit. The balance available is the balance you have in your bank account, so essentially you work on a debit rather than a credit system. Another option is to take out a small bank loan and repay it on time.

SOME TIMELESS INVESTMENT ADVICE

When the stock market is in a state of upheaval, investing may not seem like a calculable (or desirable) risk. But smart investors have been known to thrive in the direst circumstances. Though there are entire books and industries devoted to gaming the system, at its core, thrifty investing boils down to some good old-fashioned wisdom. As proof, we submit the remarks of two very learned fellows—one of whom *Fortune* magazine called an "Investment Giant" of the 20th century, the other of whom is arguably the father of thrift. In this excerpt from a longer speech, Vanguard Group founder John C. Bogle reinterprets aphorisms from Benjamin Franklin's seminal book *The Way to Wealth,* for the modern investor.

	BENJAMIN FRANKLIN	JOHN C. BOGLE
On saving for the future	If you would be wealthy, think of Saving as well as Getting. Remember that time is money. Lost time is never found again.	Not investing is a surefire way to fail to accumulate the wealth necessary to ensure a sound financial future. Compound interest is a miracle. Time is your friend.
On taking risks	There are no Gains, without Pains. He that would catch Fish, must venture his Bait.	Invest you must. The biggest risk is the long-term risk of not putting your money to work at a generous return, not the short-term—but nonetheless real—risk of market volatility.
On understanding what's important	An investment in knowledge always pays the best interest. Learning is to the Studious, and Riches to the Careful. If a man empties his purse into his head, no man can take it away from him.	To be a successful mutual fund investor, *you need information.* If information about the past returns earned by funds—especially short-term returns—is close to meaningless, information about risks and costs is priceless.
On the markets	One man may be more cunning than another, but not more cunning than everybody else.	Don't think you know more than the market, nor act on insights that you think are your own but are in fact shared by millions of others.
On looking after your own interests	If you would have a faithful Servant, serve yourself.	Investors must not ignore their own economic interests.
And finally, on steadfastness	Industry, Perseverance, and Frugality make Fortune yield.	Stay the course. Patience and consistency are the most valuable assets for the intelligent investor.

CHART FROM REMARKS GIVEN BY JOHN C. BOGLE TO THE GREATER PHILADELPHIA VENTURE GROUP, JANUARY 25, 2006

As songwriter Tom Waits puts it: "The large print giveth and the small print taketh away." With credit cards, details are everything. Special offers to lure new customers can conceal hidden pitfalls in their small print—an inviting grace period or waiver of finance charges might be followed a few months later by a huge hike in interest rates. The meter is also running in other areas of your account. Annual fees, late payment fees, cash advance fees, and over-the-credit-limit fees all conspire to cost you more. So you can't afford to keep yourself in the dark. For more on credit cards, see page 348.

7. Spend Only What You Have

Don't carry money in your wallet that you can't afford to spend. This applies to an evening out, a stroll to the supermarket, or a trip out of state. Try using a bank debit card in place of a credit card—it functions the same way, but the funds you spend are deducted out of your bank balance. Whatever is left after utility bills, debts, and rent is yours, and when it's gone it's gone. Brutal but fair.

8. Have a Goal and Stick to It

Financial plans can have a life span of a month, six months, a year, or much longer, depending upon your goals. Formulate a plan and remind yourself of it as you chart your own progress. If you need an incentive, keep a photo of a tropical island or a house on your money file. At the end of all your hard work, there's a reward you have earned by yourself, for yourself.

9. Bank Well

What is your bank doing for you? Before you open an account, investigate the interest rates, the fees, any limits placed on fee-free transactions—along with the service and general helpfulness of the organization. Banks provide a service, and you shouldn't lose money getting it. To keep updated, investigate www.bankrate.com, and for goodness' sake read your bank statements to make sure you have a handle on what's going on.

FIVE MARKETING TACTICS BANKS USE TO TRICK YOU

While you're shopping around for the best place to keep your money, beware of some of the following sales tactics:

- Teaser rates ("6 percent for the first two months!"). What happens in the first two months doesn't matter. You want to pick a bank that you can stick with for years—one that offers overall great service, not a promo rate that will earn you only $25 (or, more likely, $3). Banks that offer teaser rates are, by definition, to be avoided.

- Requiring minimum balances to "avoid paying fees for services like checking and bill paying."

- Up-sells to expensive accounts ("Expedited customer service! Wow!"). Most of these "value-added" accounts are designed to charge you for worthless services.

- Holding out by telling you that the no-fee, no-minimum accounts aren't available anymore. They are. Banks will resist giving you a no-fee, no-minimum account at first, but if you're firm, they'll give you the account you want. If they don't, threaten to go to another bank. If they still don't, walk out and find one that will.

- Bundling a credit card with your bank account. If you didn't walk in specifically wanting the bank credit card, don't accept one.

If Your Partner Spends Too Much . . .

How to get your financial other-half on the thrift bandwagon? Keep telling your partner not to spend money on something, and he or she will resent it and ignore you. More than anything, people hate to be judged for their spending, so if you make it personal ("You can't spend that much on shoes each month!"), you'll get nowhere.

Instead, keep it simple and tactical. Look into how much it costs to save for common purchases like vacations, Christmas gifts, or a new car. Then have a conversation about what your savings goals are and how much you need to save to reach them—and come to a savings plan that you both agree on.

If you do this, the next time you have an argument about spending, you can steer it away from you and your partner and instead make it about the plan. Nobody can get defensive when you're pointing to a piece of paper (rather than pointing at the other person). Say, "Hey, cool sweater. Are we still on track to hit our savings goal?" This is hard to argue with if you say it in an innocent voice. In fact, your partner definitely can't get defensive, because he or she agreed to the plan!

By focusing on the plan, not the person, you sidestep the perception of being judgmental and work on bringing spending in line with your shared goals. This is the way handling money is supposed to work.

10. Invest Well

Investment is a word that intimidates many otherwise competent people. But it shouldn't, because at the most basic level, an investment is simply anything that puts your money to work. The rationale behind investing is that money grows over time. The initial sum you start with isn't important. Starting is.

You can put your money into a savings account with your bank—a safe choice, but your money won't earn its keep after taxes and inflation take their toll. You don't have to take terrifying risks when you invest. A good retirement fund is a sound investment that's within the reach of anyone who contributes regularly.

11. Reward Yourself

If you have counted your pennies until they are smooth with wear, then indulge in a little splurge. Small pleasures feel like extravagances when you've been living frugally. But don't overcompensate. Saving $600 in order to spend $1,000 is a wildly false economy.

12. Give Some Back

Once you have attended to bills, security, savings, and insurance, you might still have a little extra money kicking around. An inheritance may land in your lap, or you may sell your diary of poems to a big record company and find yourself with a stack of royalties. Sudden affluence or even a little extra can feel like a responsibility, and can create even more anxiety than being broke. Relax and do something creative and beautiful with your money. Tithing a portion of your income to a charity or a cause you believe in is tax-free and good for the soul. Giving even a tiny amount creates positive feelings—feelings of abundance, of having enough, and of making a constructive contribution.

Get a Handle on Your Credit

Some people handle credit cards sensibly, paying their balance each month to avoid interest fees and staying below their credit limit to avoid a penalty. But many more people use credit cards for things they cannot afford to buy with cash. "I'll charge it," they say grandly at the cash register, ignoring the reality of their monthly statement.

The Long-Term Cost of Overdue Credit Card Bills

One of the biggest problems with credit cards is the hidden cost of using them if you don't pay your bills on time. Take, for instance, an iPod. It looks like it costs $250, but if you buy it using a credit card with a 14 percent annual percentage rate (APR) and a 4 percent minimum payment, and then pay only the minimum each month, you'll be out almost 20 percent more in total.

Let's say you buy this . . .	Making minimum payments, it will take this long to pay it off . . .	On top of the cost of the item, you'll pay this much in interest . . .
$250 iPod	2 years, 6 months	$47
$1,500 computer	7 years, 9 months	$562
$10,000 in furniture	13 years, 3 months	$4,062

Credit Survival

If you make only the minimum payment on your card each month, you will deepen your debt very quickly and spend years paying it off. Here's an example: If you have an average balance of $1,100 on a credit card that charges an 18.5 percent interest rate, and you pay the minimum of 1.7 percent, it will take you twelve years and six months to pay the debt and $2,480.94 in interest. Pay just $10 per month more on your minimum, and you could cut the repayment time in half and the interest by $676.37.

The minute you get a bill or statement from your credit card company, open it and attend to it straight away. Pay just a day late and you will be penalized by late fees and an interest rate that can roll over and double. Until you get control over your cards, keep a desk calendar to monitor your due dates.

If you have been turned down for credit, the lender is legally required to tell you the reason credit was denied, and give you the name and address of the credit bureau that supplied derogatory information.

To find out your credit rating, contact the three national credit-reporting bureaus:

1. Equifax (800-685-1111, www.equifax.com)
2. Experian (800-682-7654, www.experian.com)
3. Trans Union Consumer Disclosure Center (216-779-7200, www.transunion.com)

IMPULSE-MANAGEMENT ADVICE BY DONNA SMALLIN

How Risky Are You? Your Credit Score

Your credit *report* gives potential lenders—the people who are considering lending you money for a car or home—basic information about you, your accounts, and your payment history. In general, it tracks all credit-related activities, although recent activities are given greater weight.

For a minimal fee, you can also find out your credit *score* or *rating* (often called your FICO score because it was created by the Fair Isaac Corporation), a single, easy-to-read number between 300 and 850 that represents your credit risk to lenders. It's like Cliff's Notes for the credit industry. The lenders take this number (higher is better) and, with a few other pieces of information, such as your salary and age, decide if they'll lend you money for a credit card, a mortgage, or a car loan. They'll charge you more or less for the loan, depending on the score, which signifies how much of a risk you are as a borrower. Check out the box below to see just how damaging a poor credit score can be.

The Long-Term Cost of a Poor Credit Score		
On a $200,000 30-year mortgage, if your FICO score is . . .	your APR* (interest rate) will be . . .	with interest, you'll pay a total of . . .
760–850 (best range)	4.384%	$359,867
700–759	4.606%	$369,364
680–699	4.783%	$377,021
660–679	4.997%	$386,381
640–659	5.427%	$405,515
620–639 (worst range)	5.973%	$430,427

*Annual Percentage Rate calculated in January 2009

Know Your Credit Personality

Take a look at the way you use your card. Do you use it to splurge? Are you more liable to spend using a card than cash? Are you now in credit card debt over $2,000? Can you recall how you spent the money? If the answers to these questions disturb you and you are haunted by debt, cut yourself free. Literally cut your cards diagonally in half and don't replace until the card balances are all paid off.

Impulse Management

Buying on credit can be a slippery slope, but these three simple points can help you keep tabs on where your money is going:

- Consider the real cost of your purchases. Think in terms of how many hours you need to work to pay for each item you want to buy.
- Before purchasing something, think about where you will put it when you get it home. If you have nowhere to put it, don't buy it.
- Shop with cash. To minimize impulse buying, leave your credit card at home.

Work Smarter

If you think the starting point for a personal budget is your take-home pay, think again. Are you leveraging every budget-boosting benefit that your employer offers? The savings are clear when the boss foots the bill for major costs like adoption (generally tax-free up to $12,150) or education (up to $5,250). But not everyone is headed for school or looking to expand the family. For a surefire way to increase your take-home pay, take advantage of benefits that allow you to spend your pretax dollars. Of course, the best way to make sure you're getting the most out of your employer is by advocating for yourself from the start. That's when a little negotiation know-how comes into play.

Negotiation Know-How

Job-hunting is the pits. Landing a job? Divine. But don't just accept the first offer—negotiate. Now's the best time to improve your financial well-being by making sure you'll be paid fairly. Some people are natural negotiators; others dread the very idea. Mind-set is key. You need to understand and express confidence in your own worth and value. The company has already shown it wants you—what could be more confidence building than that?

No matter what your personality, you can stack the odds in your favor by understanding five key points:

1. The salary you accept is the starting point for future raises and the salary at your next job.

2. The lowest number you state during a negotiation may be your salary. If you can't live with it or on it, don't put it out there, secretly hoping to make yourself an attractive candidate by looking inexpensive at first and then convincing the employer you're worth more.

3. The low end of your range should be higher than the lowest salary you would actually accept. That way, you leave yourself room to negotiate. (But don't overdo it at the top of your range; you don't want to appear uninformed or arrogant.)

4. The employer's job is to lowball you and pay you as little as possible; your job is to try to get as much as you can. This holds true especially for entry-level positions, as employers are apt to take advantage of your inexperience. It's not evil, it's just business. Companies are always looking for ways to cut costs.

5. Your lifestyle choices, debt, or financial issues are not the employer's concern. Never discuss your needs during negotiation; couch the discussion in terms of industry standards and what your skills and experience are worth, and you'll make a much more convincing case.

Negotiation Don'ts

Sometimes what you don't say is as important as the information you do volunteer. Be especially on your guard while you're negotiating the terms of a job offer, and take heed of the following "don'ts":

- Don't get specific until the time is right. Only at second interviews or when the offer is presented should you inquire about benefits, vacation, and the review process.
- Don't confuse a perk and a benefit, and don't bring up perks during the negotiations. A perk is something like a health club membership; it's not considered a negotiable benefit, but rather an extra bonus offered to all employees. Wait until you're on the job to look into it.
- Don't price yourself out of a job. Be realistic and do your homework so you're familiar with industry and regional standards.

- Be positive, not adversarial. You don't want to warp a relationship with a potential employer during the negotiation.
- Don't lie about a previous salary in the hopes of making yourself look expensive. The information is easily verifiable. Don't volunteer your previous salary, but be honest if asked; be sure to factor in any bonuses and benefits.
- Don't undersell yourself. The biggest regrets you'll hear are from candidates who simply accept an offer on the spot without negotiating and later find out others hired at the same time and level have higher salaries or better benefits—because they negotiated.

Same Job, More Dough

Go to your company's intranet site or human resources manual, and you may be happily surprised to find a windfall awaiting you. Review your employer's "cafeteria" plan (also known as a "section 125 plan"). By cutting out the taxman, you can save 30 cents of every dollar you spend on eligible expenses. Your employer's plan may allow you to put pretax dollars toward:

- Health- or dependent-care flexible spending accounts
  (FSAs or flex accounts)
- Commuter costs
- Life or disability insurance
- A 401(k) retirement plan
- Health savings accounts
  (at small companies with high-deductible coverage)

Flexible Spending Accounts

Flex accounts allow you to set aside a lump sum of money before it's taxed to cover certain health care costs every year. (If you're buying certain things anyway, you may as well buy them and reduce your tax burden at the same time, no?) You can use pretax dollars to pay for:

- Health insurance premiums and deductibles
- Copays
- Dental care and orthodontics (although there are limits, and work that's considered cosmetic may not be covered)
- Eyeglasses
- Contact lenses
- Laser eye surgery
- Chiropractic care
- Prescription drugs
- Pregnancy test kits
- Band-Aids and over-the-counter medicines like Tylenol and Claritin
- And more . . .

The catch? With flex accounts, you have to decide up front how much you think you'll spend. Every year, you determine the total you'd like to set aside (it must fall within your plan's minimum-to-maximum range). Then you must use it up or forfeit the remainder to your employer by the end of the year (or by March 15, if your employer allows for the optional grace period). This dreaded "use-it-or-lose-it" provision scares people off, but it doesn't take a rocket scientist to tally a conservative estimate of your expected expenses (see box, following page). To give yourself some wiggle room, schedule your annual physical or dental checkup toward year-end; that way you can squeeze in additional appointments (root canal, anyone?) to deplete your account as necessary; if it's already empty, you can shift the appointment to January.

> **THRIFTONOMICS**
>
> # The Cost of Not Participating in Pretax Options
>
> Let's say your commute involves an $80 monthly train pass. If you enroll in your employer's commuter benefit program, you can buy the monthly pass before your salary is taxed. The cost: $80. Don't participate, and your pass costs you $104—that's $80 plus the $24 in income and payroll taxes that you pay on that sum. Why pay more?

Dependent care flex accounts can be used to pay for day care, a babysitter, or a home-care attendant for an elderly parent. By planning ahead, you can purchase $1,000 worth of health care that would cost you roughly $1,300 out of pocket.

A note: A child care FSA limits the amount you can claim as a dependent care credit on your tax return. According to Mackey McNeill, a CPA/PFS (personal financial specialist) and president of Mackey Advisors, when it comes to child care, flexible spending accounts are almost always a better deal, but you do have to review the numbers.

Your 401(k)

If your company offers a 401(k) retirement plan, you should definitely contribute; Uncle Sam will kick in for it, and your company may, too. Your contributions defer federal and state income taxes, until you begin to withdraw the funds—upon retirement, when, presumably, your taxable income will be much lower than it is while you're working.

Contributing to a 401(k) can expand your savings by 21 percent at the low end, according to McNeill. "You'd have $100 in your 401(k) instead of $79 after taxes," she says.

Many companies offer what are called matching contributions;

You and Your FSA

Wondering how much to allot to your FSA? Online calculators can crunch the numbers for you.

Healthzone.com prompts you with usually eligible health-care items and services, then spits out your yearly expenses and—ka-ching!— your savings if you contribute to a flex spending account. Bankrate.com/calculators.aspx (under "tax" and "retirement") lets you compare your take-home pay with and without cafeteria plan or 401(k) deductions.

in essence, they're rewarding you for saving, and for sticking around. If that same $100 contribution is matched by 50 percent, you'll have $150 in your retirement account. "*Never* put in less than what the employer matches," McNeill advises. "That's free money." Check out the long-term payoff for you (that is, gray-haired you) at the American Institute of Certified Public Accountants' website, 360financialliteracy.org (search "calculators"). You can adjust your contribution and age of retirement to see the various outcomes down the road.

When You Get a Raise | by Trent Hamm

Every year, many Americans receive a welcome addition to their paycheck: a cost-of-living raise. This raise is a small percentage (usually between 3 and 4 percent) of salary that is added to keep pace with inflation. Some employees get even luckier and receive a performance-based raise or a promotion.

I know the joys of receiving a raise—and I also know how tempting it can be to spend the extra money. When I received my first significant raise as a working adult (a 10 percent increase in my salary), I celebrated. I bought an iPod and a pile of video games, and then later I "invested" the rest of that raise in some vintage baseball cards.

To a small degree, that kind of behavior is fine. It's great to celebrate our successes. As with many things in life, however, true success comes from a healthy balance. So when you receive a raise, don't feel bad about celebrating—but do it modestly. Go out for a dinner date with your partner, or buy a DVD. And then stop. A mere increase in your income is not a call to change your standard of living.

Instead, use your raise to put yourself in a better financial position.

Start by calculating how much your take-home pay will increase each month after your raise. Plan on setting aside most of that extra money. Automatically transfer that amount from your checking account to your savings account each time you're paid, so you're never tempted to check your account balance and spend more than you should.

What do you do with that saved amount? Use it to eliminate your personal debt. Let it build up in your savings account as an emergency fund. Invest it toward a long-term goal.

Storing away your extra income also has a secondary benefit: It keeps you from growing your standard of living in step with the growth of your paycheck. Look at Warren Buffett. His abilities as a businessman and investor have made him the richest man in America, yet he still lives in the same modest house that he's lived in for much of his adult life. Buffett realized long ago that having money doesn't require you to spend it and that the money you don't spend can be invested. His $50 billion net worth certainly attests to that.

about the editors

Pia Catton is a journalist and the coauthor of *The Comfort Diner Cookbook*. Her work has appeared in the *Wall Street Journal,* the *Weekly Standard, ArtNews, ArtInfo.com,* the *New York Post* and the *New York Sun.* She's handy with a hot-glue gun and a bag of sequins and aspires to turn even the harshest skeptic into a fan of broth-making and bean-soaking. She lives in Washington, D.C., where she happily makes pasta from scratch.

Califia Suntree runs the food blog Spooningmag.com. She has worked as a magazine editor, cookbook editor, restaurant manager, and recipe writer. Though her sewing machine, knitting needles, and garden shears have been known to gather dust, she continually renews her vows to make more of her own stuff. She lives in Los Angeles, where she recently refurbished a bicycle she has owned since 1992—de-rusted with nothing more than a two-liter bottle of Coca-Cola.

our thrifty contributors

Gardeners, knitters, cooks, scientists, linguists, vets, doctors, oenophiles—oh my! The following journalists, writers, and experts either contributed original material or graciously permitted us to reprint selections from their previously published books:

Jay Akasie has been a reporter for *Forbes, Grant's Interest Rate Observer,* and *Worth,* and was the business editor of the *New York Sun.* He is currently the managing editor of *Trends*, the Middle East's leading business magazine.

Kelly Bare is an editor at newyorker.com and the author of *The F Word* and *The DIY Wedding,* along with three years of Workman's *Living Green Page-A-Day* calendar. Her writing has appeared in publications including *Modern Bride, Cosmopolitan*, and *The New Yorker.*

Ame Mahler Beanland is an award-winning editor and art director, and coauthor of *Nesting: It's a Chick Thing* and *Postcards from the Bump.*

Rona Berg is the editor-in-chief of *Organic Beauty* magazine and the author of *Beauty* and *Fast Beauty*. The former beauty editor for *The New York Times Magazine*, she writes for numerous national publications, including *Vogue, InStyle, Cosmopolitan, Mirabella, Self,* and *Mademoiselle.* She lives in New York City.

Lisa Berger is the author of *Feathering Your Nest: The Retirement Planner.* Her articles have appeared in the *Atlantic Monthly, Savvy, Working Woman,* and other magazines and journals.

Betsy Brevitz, D.V.M., is the author of *The Complete*

Healthy Dog Handbook. Prior to becoming a veterinarian, she had a ten-year career as a magazine writer and editor. She graduated from Tufts University School of Veterinary Medicine and now lives and practices in northern New Jersey.

Suzanne Brown is the author of *Summer.* An award-winning graphic designer, she is the owner of Suzanne Brown Design, a design and image consulting firm in Chappaqua, New York.

Lynn Brunelle, a four-time Emmy Award–winning writer for *Bill Nye the Science Guy,* is the author of *Pop Bottle Science* and *Camp Out!.* She lives on Bainbridge Island, Washington, with her husband and two children.

Juliana Bunim is the local news editor at the *San Francisco Examiner.* Her coverage of personal finance, art and culture has appeared in publications including TheStreet.com, *Time Out New York*, *People* magazine and *Radar.*

Deborah Burns is the author of *Tips for the Savvy Traveler.* She's lived and worked around the globe, from the West Indies to South America, India, and Ireland, where she helped start a still-thriving newspaper. .

Peggy Burns is the associate publisher of Drawn & Quarterly, a graphic novel and fine arts book publishing house in Montreal.

Siobhan Burns, a New York–based writer and consultant, is a restaurant junkie, chef groupie, and die-hard foodie.

Anne Byrn is known to millions of fans through her *Cake Mix Doctor* baking books and *What Can I Bring* and *Dinner Doctor* cookbooks, which she has promoted in more than 200 television appearances on *Good Morning America*, *Roker on the Road*, QVC, and local stations. She lives with her family in Nashville, Tennessee.

Grant Catton is a novelist and freelance journalist. He has lived and worked in New York City, Buenos Aires, Montreal, and northern Italy, and currently resides in Indianapolis, Indiana.

Laura Collins-Hughes is a journalist in New York. Her writing on arts and culture has appeared in publications including *The Los Angeles Times*, *The New York Times*, *Newsday*, *American Theatre*, *Tablet Magazine* and the *New York Sun.*

Bobbi Conner is the author of *Unplugged Play* and

Everyday Opportunities for Extraordinary Parenting. She is the creator and host of the award-winning national radio program *The Parent's Journal* and a mother of three.

Sean Connolly is the author of *The Book of Totally Irresponsible Science.* He has written more than 50 books for children and adults.

Michael Covarrubias is pursuing a Ph.D. in linguistics at Purdue University. Since 2006 he has maintained a blog about language called *Wishydig.*

Cynthia L. Copeland is the bestselling author/ illustrator of more than 25 books for adults and children, including *The Diaper Diaries, Really Important Stuff My Kids Have Taught Me,* and *Fun on the Run.* Her books have been recommended by Oprah, Regis Philbin, Ann Landers, and the hosts of *Good Morning America.* She lives in a New Hampshire farmhouse where she is a mom to three kids, and a stepmom to three more.

Carol Costenbader is the author of *The Big Book of Preserving the Harvest* and Storey's *Well-Stocked Pantry Series: Mustards, Ketchups & Vinegars*, and *Preserving Fruits & Vegetables.*

Rena Coyle, mother and former professional pastry

chef, develops recipes for Go Soup to Nuts creative campaigns and is the author of *Baby, Let's Eat, My First Cookbook* and *My First Baking Book.*

Catherine Crawford is the editor of the book *If You Really Want to Hear About It: Writers on J. D. Salinger and His Work.* A regular blogger for Babble.com, she divides her time (unequally) between her family, her freelance writing, and her work at a literary agency.

Chris Crowley, coauthor of the *Younger Next Year* series, is a former litigator at Davis Polk & Wardwell. When he's not writing, he enjoys skiing, sailing, biking, playing tennis, and cooking.

Barbara Damrosch is the author of *The Garden Primer.* She writes a weekly column for *The Washington Post* called "A Cook's Garden," and she appeared as a regular correspondent on the PBS series *The Victory Garden,* and on The Learning Channel as cohost of the series *Gardening Naturally.* She is the co-owner, with her husband, of Four Season Farm, an experimental market garden in Harborside, Maine, nationally recognized as a model of small-scale sustainable agriculture.

Sophie Donelson has written for magazines including *Elle Decor, Interior Design,* and *Martha Stewart Living.* Photos of her thrifty home design projects can be found at sophiedonelson.com.

Joseph Epstein is an essayist, short story writer, and editor best known as a former editor of the Phi Beta Kappa Society's *The American Scholar* magazine, and his recent essay collection, *Snobbery: The American Version.* He is the author of *The Love Song of A. Jerome Minkoff and Other Short Stories.*

Cathy Erway is the author of *The Art of Eating In,* a book based on her blog, "Not Eating Out in New York," which chronicled a two-year mission to eat in. She writes about sustainable food and living at *The Huffington Post* and Saveur.com, and hosts the show *Cheap Date* on the Heritage Radio Network.

Barbara Flanagan is the author of *Flanagan's Smart Home* and *The Houseboat Book.* A writer and designer who trained as an architect at Yale, she has written extensively for *The New York Times, The New York Times Magazine, Elle Décor, Metropolis,* and *I.D.,* where she is a contributing editor. She has designed products for the MoMA Design Stores,

and also designed her own tiny, high-tech house in Bethlehem, Pennsylvania.

Isabel Forgang is a writer whose work on food and home has appeared in a variety of publications including *Martha Stewart Living, Ladies Home Journal* and *Woman's Day.* She has been a feature writer at the *New York Daily News* for more than 25 years.

Ruth Graham is an editor and writer in Brooklyn, New York.

Mark J. Green is the president of Air America Radio and the author of many books, including *The Consumer Bible.* He has served as New York City's consumer affairs commissioner and as the City's first public advocate.

Matt Gross writes the "Frugal Traveler" column for *The New York Times.* He lives in Brooklyn with his wife, Jean, and daughter, Sasha.

Robin Goldstein is coauthor of *The Wine Trials,* the world's bestselling guide to inexpensive wine, currently in its second edition. He is founder and editor-in-chief of the Fearless Critic restaurant guide series, and has written for more than 30 Fodor's travel guides, from Italy to Thailand, Argentina to Hong Kong.

Robin is a graduate of Harvard University and the Yale Law School. He has a certificate in cooking from the French Culinary Institute in New York and a WSET advanced wine and spirits certificate.

Kathleen Hackett, coauthor of *The Salvage Sisters' Guide to Finding Style in the Street and Inspiration in the Attic,* is the former executive book editor for Martha Stewart Living Omnimedia. She has written for both the *Pottery Barn Style* series and *Budget Living* books, as well as various other publications, including *Elle Décor.* She lives in Brooklyn, New York, with her husband and son.

Jane Hammerslough is the author of 30 books for young readers and adults, including *Dematerializing: Taming the Power of Possessions.* A former parenting columnist for the *New York Post* and other publications, she writes frequently for national magazines.

Kathleen Cannata Hanna is an architect and public speaker who has also run a successful baking and catering business. She is the mother of two busy teenagers who were enthusiastic testers for *The Good-to-Go Cookbook.*

Lyn Herrick is the author

of *The Woman's Hands-on Home Repair Guide.*

Alexis Herschkowitsch is coauthor of *The Wine Trials.* She has written and edited for five Fearless Critic restaurant guides, and for the Fodor's travel guides to Mexico, Central America, and Thailand. She is a graduate of the University of Texas at Austin, and has a WSET advanced wine and spirits certificate.

Peter Hyman is the media and politics correspondent at TheFasterTimes.com and the author of *The Reluctant Metrosexual: Dispatches from an Almost Hip Life.* His work has appeared in *The New York Times, The Wall Street Journal, New York* magazine, Slate.com, *McSweeney's* and on NPR.

Erika Rasmusson Janes is a New York–based freelance writer whose work has appeared in publications including *Fortune Small Business,* the *New York Sun, Modern Bride,* and *Redbook.*

Steve Jenkins is the author of *The Cheese Primer,* which received a prestigious James Beard Award. The first American to be awarded France's prestigious Chevalier du Taste Fromage award, Jenkins has written for *Food Arts, Food & Wine,*

and the *Gourmet Retailer* and has been a regular commentator on NPR's *The Splendid Table.*

Anna Johnson is the author of *The Yummy Mommy Manifesto, Three Black Skirts,* and *Handbags.* She has written for *Vogue Australia, Vogue UK, Condé Nast Traveler, Vanity Fair,* and *Elle.*

Emma Johnson is a New York–based freelance writer specializing in business, finance, and the culture of money. Her articles have appeared in *The New York Times, The Wall Street Journal, MSN Money, Entrepreneur,* and *Forbes.*

Bridget Kachur, author of *Every Woman's Quick & Easy Car Care* and a self-confessed grease monkey, found her calling as a child when she tinkered with car engines alongside her father, a backyard mechanic. Now she teaches automotive courses for women, writes regular newspaper features on car-related topics, and has fixed more cars than she can remember. She lives in Calgary, Alberta, Canada.

Judy Bart Kancigor is the author of *Cooking Jewish,* which she wrote to preserve her family's recipes. She is a food columnist for the *Orange County Register* and a popular teacher of Jewish cooking and family life. She lives with her husband in Fullerton, California.

Barbara Ann Kipfer is the author of more than 45 books, ranging from *The Order of Things* and *14,000 Things to Be Happy About* to *Roget's International Thesaurus, 6th Edition.* She is the lexicographer for Wolfram|Alpha and holds numerous degrees, including a Ph.D. and M.Phil. in linguistics, a Ph.D. in archaeology, and an M.A. and Ph.D. in Buddhist studies. She lives in Connecticut.

Melissa Kirsch is the author of *The Girl's Guide to Absolutely Everything.* She is a former senior producer at Oxygen Media, where she wrote the "Ask Princess" column, and has written for *National Geographic Traveler, Ladies' Home Journal, Nerve, New York* magazine, and *Scientific American.* She lives in New York City.

Julia Levy served in the New York City Department of Education under Mayor Michael Bloomberg after reporting on politics and education for the *New York Sun.* She is a devoted amateur baker.

Henry S. Lodge, M.D., coauthor of *Younger Next Year* and a board-certified internist, is listed variously as "One of the Best Doctors in New York/America/the World." He heads a 23-doctor practice in Manhattan and is a member of the clinical faculty at Columbia Medical School. He is a contributing expert to HealthCentral.com and lives in New York City.

Sharon Lovejoy is the author of *Toad Cottages & Shooting Stars: A Grandma's Bag of Tricks, Trowel & Error,* and *Roots, Shoots, Buckets, & Boots,* among other books. An illustrator, lecturer, and teacher, she has been a guest on *Today,* PBS's *The Victory Garden,* and the Discovery Channel. She divides her time between San Luis Obispo, California, and South Brunswick, Maine.

Sheila Lukins, author of *Ten,* was the cofounder of the legendary Silver Palate takeout shop. Her celebrated *Silver Palate* and *New Basics* cookbooks, written with Julee Rosso, helped change the way America eats. She was the food editor of *Parade Magazine* for 23 years.

Gail MacColl is the author of *The Book of Cards for Kids.*

Karen MacNeil is the author of the award-winning *The Wine Bible.* She was named "Outstanding Wine and Spirits Professional of the Year" by the James Beard Foundation in 2004, and the "2005 Wine Educator of the Year" by the European Wine Council. Her articles on wine and food have been published in more than 50 United States magazines and newspapers, including *The New York Times, Food & Wine, Saveur,* and *Town & Country.*

Carleen Madigan is an avid gardener and homesteading enthusiast who lives in rural western Massachusetts. She previously lived on an organic farm outside Boston, where she learned many of the skills covered in *The Backyard Homestead,* and worked as managing editor of *Horticulture* magazine.

Nick Mautone is the owner of a food management and consulting company and the author of *Raising the Bar.* He has managed a series of restaurants including New York's Gotham Bar and Grill and Gramercy Tavern, and he has been featured in *The New York Times, Food & Wine,* and on CBS's *The Early Show.*

Rose Marie Nichols McGee is the coauthor of *McGee & Stuckey's Bountiful Container.* She is the president and owner of Nichols Garden Nursery, a venerable family-owned seed company in the heart of Oregon's Willamette Valley.

James W. McKenzie is the author of *Antiques on the Cheap.*

Sara Mednick, Ph.D., author of *Take a Nap!,* is an Assistant Professor of psychiatry at the University of California, San Diego. Her napping research has been covered by CNN, Reuters, NPR, *The Economist, The Wall Street Journal, The New York Times, Real Simple,* and *Men's Journal.*

Beverly Mills is the coauthor of *Cheap. Fast, Good!, Desperation Dinners,* and *Desperation Entertaining.* She and her writing partner, Alicia Ross, have been working and cooking together for over ten years.

Tom Moon is a saxophonist, an award-winning music journalist, and the author of *1,000 Recordings to Hear Before You Die.* He is a regular contributor to National Public Radio's *All Things Considered* as well as *Rolling Stone, Blender,* and other publications. During his 20-year tenure as a music critic at the *Philadelphia Inquirer,* his writings appeared in hundreds of daily newspapers and magazines. He lives with his wife, daughter, two

dogs, and thousands of CDs in Haddonfield, New Jersey.

Arden Moore is the author of 20 books on cats and dogs, including *The Cat Behavior Answer Book, The Dog Behavior Answer Book,* and *Real Food for Dogs.* She is the editor of *Fido Friendly* magazine and *Catnip,* an animal behavior consultant, and host of the *Oh Behave!* weekly radio show on PetLifeRadio.com. She is known as "America's Pet Edu-Tainer" and gives pet talks throughout North America. She shares her Oceanside, California home with two dogs, Chipper and Cleo, and two cats, Callie and Murphy.

Betty Oppenheimer is the author of *Sew & Stow, The Candlemaker's Companion,* and *Growing Lavender and Community on the Sequim Prairie.* An experienced crafter and seamstress, she studied textile science at the Fashion Institute of Technology and has worked as a textile quality assurance manager and engineer for several sportswear companies.

Erica Orden is a freelance writer in New York. Her work has appeared in *The New York Times, New York* magazine, *Time Out New York,* and the *New York Sun,* among other publications.

Vibhuti Patel is a contributing editor at

Newsweek International. Her work has also appeared in *The New York Times, Ms.* magazine, Bloomberg News, *Travel + Leisure,* and several major English-language publications in India. She wrote the text for a book of paintings, *Mrs. Kennedy Goes Abroad,* about the First Lady's foreign trips.

Deborah Peterson is the coauthor of *Don't Throw it, Grow it.* A founder of the Rare Pit & Plant Council, she is the proprietor of Landmark Landscaping and has landscaped and designed many gardens and private parks in New York and Massachusetts.

James Peterson is the author of nine award-winning and short-listed cookbooks, including the James Beard Cookbook of the Year *Sauces: Classical and Contemporary Sauce Making,* as well as *Essentials of Cooking, Glorious French Food,* and *What's a Cook to Do?* He teaches, writes about, photographs, lives, breathes, and cooks fine food.

Joseph C. Piscatella, author of *Positive Mind, Healthy Heart* and *Road to a Healthy Heart,* became an active proponent of healthy lifestyle changes after undergoing open-heart surgery. As president of the Institute for Fitness and Health, Inc.

in Tacoma, Washington, he lectures extensively to medical organizations, corporations, and professional associations, and is a consultant on major wellness projects for Fortune 500 companies and the U.S. Army, Navy, and Air Force.

Carol Prisant is the American editor of the British magazine *The World of Interiors*. She is the author of *Antiques Roadshow Collectibles* and *Antiques Roadshow Primer*. She writes about antiques and collectibles for *Martha Stewart Living*, *House Beautiful*, *New York*, and other magazines. A former antiques dealer, she is also an appraiser of fine and decorative arts and a member of the Appraisers Association of America.

Steven Raichlen, America's "master griller" (*Esquire*) is author of the bestselling, award-winning *Barbecue! Bible* cookbooks and star of the popular PBS TV show *Primal Grill*. His articles appear regularly in *Food & Wine, Bon Appetit*, and other magazines and newspapers.

Ellen Gordon Reeves, who holds an Ed.M. from the Harvard Graduate School of Education, is the author of *Can I Wear My Nose Ring to the Interview?*. She divides her time between Boston, Providence, and New York City, where she serves as

the résumé and job-hunting expert at the Columbia Publishing Course.

Gail Reichlin is the coauthor of the bestselling book *The Pocket Parent,* which was the recipient of a 2007 iParenting award. A former teacher with 30 years of experience, she is the founder and executive director of the Parents Resource Network.

Steven Rinella is the author of *American Buffalo: In Search of a Lost Icon* and *The Scavenger's Guide to Haute Cuisine*. His writing has appeared in many outlets, including *Outside*, *Men's Journal*, *Field & Stream*, *The New Yorker*, *The New York Times*, and *Glamour*.

Elizabeth Roberts is a freelance writer and editor based in Brooklyn. She has written for *Budget Living*, *Martha Stewart Living*, and the *New York Post*.

Alicia Ross is the coauthor of *Cheap. Fast, Good!, Desperation Dinners,* and *Desperation Entertaining*. She and her writing partner, Beverly Mills, have been working and cooking together for over ten years.

Julee Rosso cofounded The Silver Palate with Sheila Lukins and cowrote the *Silver Palate* cookbooks and *The New Basics Cookbook*. She is

the author of *Great Good Food* and *Fresh Start*, and runs the Wickwood Inn in Saugatuck, Michigan.

Genevieve Roth is a magazine editor living in New York.

J. D. Roth runs "Get Rich Slowly," a personal-finance blog and community where thousands of readers a month share ideas on how to improve their finances. He lives with his wife and four cats in a hundred-year-old house in Portland, Oregon.

Diana Rupp, author of *Sew Everything Workshop*, founded and runs Make Workshop in New York City. The Lower East Side craft school teaches everything from how to use a sewing machine to spinning your own yarn. She lives in Brooklyn.

Bernadette Serton is a writer and editor living in New York City.

Ramit Sethi is the author of *I Will Teach You to Be Rich* and the cofounder of PBwiki, a company that provides online tools and services. A graduate of Stanford, he lives in San Francisco, California.

Jessie Sholl is a freelance writer and editor whose essays and stories have appeared in *The New York Times*, EverydayHealth.com,

Other Voices, and *Fiction*. She is the coeditor of *Travelers' Tales: Prague and the Czech Republic*.

Karyn Siegel-Maier is a health writer, mother of three, and the author of *The Naturally Clean Home*. She contributes articles about herbal health and alternative medicine to magazines including *Natural Living Today* and *Mother Earth News*.

Bob Sloan is a professional chef and teacher, and the author of *Dad's Own Cookbook* and *Dad's Awesome Grilling Book*, among others.

Donna Smallin is a nationally recognized organizing expert and bestselling author of books including *One-Minute Cleaner* and *One-Minute Organizer*. Her tips have appeared in publications such as *Reader's Digest, Woman's Day, Real Simple,* and *Better Homes & Gardens*.

David Stark is the author of *Napkins with a Twist* and coauthor of *To Have and to Hold* and *Wild Flowers*. He is the president and creative director of the event-planning firm David Stark Design & Production. His innovative ideas have been featured in magazines such as *InStyle Home, House Beautiful,* and *Elle Décor*, and he has appeared on national

television shows including *Martha Stewart Living, Today*, and *The View*.

Debbie Stoller is the bestselling author of the *Stitch 'N Bitch* series of knitting and crochet books. She comes from a long line of Dutch knitters, has a Ph.D. from Yale in the psychology of women, and is the editor-in-chief of *Bust* magazine. She lives in Brooklyn, New York.

DeeDee Stovel is an experienced caterer, the coauthor of *Let's Get Together,* and the author of *Picnic* and *Pumpkin*. She lives in San Carlos, California.

Maggie Stuckey is the coauthor of *McGee & Stuckey's Bountiful Container* and the author of *The Complete Herb Book* and other books on gardening. She lives in Portland, Oregon.

Andrew Stuttaford, who works by day in the financial markets, has written frequently on political and cultural topics for publications including *National Review, National Review Online*, the *New Criterion*, the *New York Sun,* and the *Weekly Standard*.

Julia Szabo is the author of *The Underdog* and writer of the weekly "Pets" column for the *New York Post*. She has written for *Country*

Living, The New Yorker, Travel + Leisure, Departures, Interview, and *The Bark*. She lives in New York.

David Tanis, author of *A Platter of Figs,* is a chef, cook, teacher, and author whose career has spanned three decades. When he is not cooking in restaurants, he cooks for his friends at home or travels the world's open-air markets. He has been featured in *The New York Times, Gourmet*, and *Saveur*.

Emily Miles Terry, coauthor of *Nesting: It's a Chick Thing* and *Postcards from the Bump*, is a partner in the book publicity firm Open Book Publicity.

Rebecca Thomas is a freelance journalist living in New York City.

Michele Urvater is the former host of the Television Food Network series, *Cooking Monday-to-Friday*. Her books include the award-winning *Monday-to-Friday Cookbook* and *Monday-to-Friday Chicken*.

Heather Wagner is the author of *Happiness on $10 a Day* and *Friend or Faux*. Her work has been published in *Vanity Fair, Travel + Leisure, Dwell,* and *Domino*. She lives in New York City.

Pamela Wakefield is the coauthor of *Let's Get*

Together. She lives in Princeton, New Jersey, where she often hosts large dinner parties.

Mindy Weiss is a highly sought-after wedding planner and the author of *The Wedding Book.* She is regularly featured in *Modern Bride* and *InStyle Weddings, The New York Times, The Wall Street Journal,* and *The Los Angeles Times.* She lives in Los Angeles.

Caroline Winkler is the coauthor of the bestselling book *The Pocket Parent,* which was the recipient of a 2007 iParenting award.

Victoria Wise, alumnus of the Chez Panisse restaurant and cofounder of Oakland's Good & Plenty Café, is the author and compiler of *The Gardener's Community Cookbook,* the author of *The Pressure Cooker Gourmet,* and the coauthor of *The Well-Filled Tortilla.* She lives in Oakland, California.

Mary Ann Young is the coauthor of *The Salvage Sisters' Guide to Finding Style in the Street and Inspiration in the Attic.* She is the author of *The Complete Idiot's Guide to Decorating Your Home* and *The Complete Idiot's Guide to Needlework,* and she has contributed to *Martha Stewart Living, Better Homes and Gardens,* and *Country Living* magazines. She and her husband are founders of Camden Harbor Company, a design/build firm in Rockport, Maine.

our thrifty library

In making this book, we had the very good fortune of being granted access to the libraries of Workman Publishing, Storey Publishing, Artisan Books, and Black Dog & Leventhal. Over the years, Workman and its affiliates have put out a rich trove of practical, informative books on subjects ranging from health and fashion to parenting and gardening. We gratefully acknowledge permission to reprint material from the following titles:

STOREY PUBLISHING

TIPS FOR THE SAVVY TRAVELER
by Deborah Burns

THE STAIN AND SPOT REMOVER HANDBOOK: *How to Clean Your Home and Everything in It* by Jean Cooper

THE BIG BOOK OF PRESERVING THE HARVEST: *150 Recipes for Freezing, Canning, Drying and Pickling Fruits and Vegetables* by Carol W. Costenbader

MAKING LIQUEURS FOR GIFTS
by Mimi Freid

THE GOOD-TO-GO COOKBOOK: *Take-along Food, Quick Suppers, and Satisfying Snacks for On-the-Go Families* by Kathleen Cannata Hanna

THE WOMAN'S HANDS-ON HOME REPAIR GUIDE
by Lyn Herrick

EVERY WOMAN'S QUICK & EASY CAR CARE: *A Worry-Free Guide to Car Troubles, Trials & Travels* by Bridget Kachur

THE BACKYARD HOMESTEAD: *Produce All the Food You Need on Just a Quarter Acre* Edited by Carleen Madigan

HAPPY BABY, HAPPY YOU: *500 Ways to Nurture the Bond with Your Baby* by Karyn Siegel-Maier

THE ONE-MINUTE CLEANER PLAIN & SIMPLE: *500 Tips for Cleaning Smarter, not Harder* by Donna Smallin

LET'S GET TOGETHER: *Simple Recipes for Gatherings With Friends* by DeeDee Stovel and Pamela Wakefield

HAPPY CAT, HAPPY YOU: *Quick Tips for Building a Bond with Your Feline Friend* by Arden Moore

GIFTS FOR HERB LOVERS: *Over 50 Projects to Make and Give* by Betty Oppenheimer

ARTISAN BOOKS

SUMMER: *A User's Guide*
by Suzanne Brown

THE SALVAGE SISTERS' GUIDE TO FINDING STYLE IN THE STREET AND INSPIRATION IN THE ATTIC by Kathleen Hackett and Mary Ann Young

RAISING THE BAR: *Better Drinks, Better Entertaining* by Nick Mautone

WHAT'S A COOK TO DO?: *An Illustrated Guide to 484 Essential Tips, Techniques, and Tricks* by James Peterson

NAPKINS WITH A TWIST: *Fabulous Folds with Flair for Every Occasion* by David Stark

A PLATTER OF FIGS AND OTHER RECIPES
by David Tanis

BLACK DOG & LEVENTHAL

SECRETS OF THE SPAS: *Pamper and Vitalize Yourself at Home* by Catherine Bardey

HOW TO GET RED WINE OUT OF A WHITE CARPET: *And Over 2,000 Other Household Hints* by Erik Bruun

COUNTRY WISDOM & KNOW-HOW: *A Practical Guide to Living off the Land* by the Editors of Storey Publishing's *Country Wisdom Bulletins*

HOW TO CUT YOUR OWN HAIR (OR ANYONE ELSE'S!): *15 Haircuts with Variations* by Marsha Heckman

WORKMAN PUBLISHING

NESTING: *It's a Chick Thing* by Ame Mahler Beanland and Emily Miles Terry

BEAUTY: *The New Basics* by Rona Berg

FAST BEAUTY: *1,000 Quick Fixes* by Rona Berg

UP YOUR SCORE: *The Underground Guide to the SAT 2009–2010 Edition* by Larry Berger, Michael Colton, Manek Mistry and Paul Rossi

FEATHERING YOUR NEST: *The Retirement Planner* by Lisa Berger

DAD'S OWN HOUSEKEEPING BOOK: *137 Bright Ideas* by David Bowers

THE COMPLETE HEALTHY DOG HANDBOOK: *The Definitive Guide to Keeping Your Pet Happy, Healthy, and Active* by Betsy Brevitz, D.V.M.

CAMP OUT! *The Ultimate Kids' Guide* by Lynn Brunelle

WHAT CAN I BRING? by Anne Byrn

UNPLUGGED PLAY: *No Batteries. No Plugs. Pure Fun* by Bobbi Conner

THE BOOK OF TOTALLY IRRESPONSIBLE SCIENCE: *64 Daring Experiments for Young Scientists* by Sean Connolly

BABY LET'S EAT! by Rena Coyle, with Patricia Messing

YOUNGER NEXT YEAR: *A Guide to Living Like 50 Until You're 80 and Beyond* by Chris Crowley and Henry S. Lodge, M.D.

THE GARDEN PRIMER by Barbara Damrosch

FLANAGAN'S SMART HOME: *The 98 Essentials for Starting Out, Starting Over, Scaling Back* by Barbara Flanagan

THE CONSUMER BIBLE: *1,001 Ways to Shop Smart* by Mark Green and Nancy Youman

THE STEP DIET: *Count Steps, Not Calories to Lose Weight and Keep It Off Forever* by James O. Hill, John C. Peters and Bonnie T. Jortberg

THE CHEESE PRIMER by Steve Jenkins

THREE BLACK SKIRTS: *All You Need to Survive* by Anna Johnson

COOKING JEWISH by Judy Bart Kancigor

THE MENOPAUSE BOOK by Barbara Kantrowitz and Pat Wingert Kelly

SELF-MEDITATION: *3,299 Mantras, Tips, Quotes, and Koans for Peace and Serenity* by Barbara Ann Kipfer

THE GIRL'S GUIDE TO ABSOLUTELY EVERYTHING by Melissa Kirsch

1,000 GARDENING QUESTIONS AND ANSWERS by *The New York Times*

TROWEL & ERROR: *Over 700 Tips, Remedies, and Shortcuts for the Gardener* by Sharon Lovejoy

TEN: *All the Foods We Love and Ten Perfect Recipes for Each* by Sheila Lukins

THE BOOK OF CARDS FOR KIDS by Gail MacColl

THE WINE BIBLE by Karen MacNeil

MCGEE & STUCKEY'S
BOUNTIFUL CONTAINER:
*A Container Garden of
Vegetables, Herbs, Fruits,
and Edible Flowers*
by Rose Marie Nichols
McGee and Maggie Stuckey

ANTIQUES ON THE CHEAP:
A Savvy Dealer's Tips
by James W. McKenzie

TAKE A NAP!
CHANGE YOUR LIFE
by Sara Mednick and
Mark Ehrman

CHEAP. FAST. GOOD!
by Beverly Mills and
Alicia Ross

DESPERATION DINNERS
by Beverly Mills and
Alicia Ross

CRAFTY MAMA: *Makes 49 Fast,
Fabulous, Foolproof (Baby
& Toddler) Projects*
by Abby Pecoriello

DON'T THROW IT, GROW
IT! *68 Windowsill Plants
from Kitchen Scraps*
by Deborah Peterson
and Millicent Selsam

TAKE A LOAD OFF YOUR HEART:
*109 Things You Can Actually
Do to Prevent, Halt and
Reverse Heart Disease*
by Joseph C. Piscatella and
Barry Franklin

ANTIQUES ROADSHOW PRIMER:
*The Introductory Guide to
Antiques and Collectibles
from the Most-Watched
Series on PBS*
by Carol Prisant

THE BARBECUE! BIBLE
by Steven Raichlen

CAN I WEAR MY NOSE RING
TO THE INTERVIEW? *Finding,
Landing, and Keeping Your
First Real Job*
by Ellen Gordon Reeves

THE POCKET PARENT
by Gail Reichlin and
Caroline Winkler

THE NEW BASICS COOKBOOK
by Julee Rosso and
Sheila Lukins

SEW EVERYTHING WORKSHOP
by Diana Rupp

I WILL TEACH YOU TO BE RICH
by Ramit Sethi

DAD'S OWN COOKBOOK
by Bob Sloan

DREAM IT. LIST IT. DO IT!
*How to Live a Bigger &
Bolder Life*
by Lia Steakley and the
Editors of 43 Things

SON OF STITCH 'N BITCH:
*45 Projects to Knit and
Crochet for Men*
by Debbie Stoller

STITCH 'N BITCH: *The Knitter's
Handbook*
by Debbie Stoller

THE UNDERDOG:
A Celebration of Mutts
by Julia Szabo

MONDAY-TO-FRIDAY COOKBOOK
by Michele Urvater

THE WEDDING BOOK: *The Big
Book for Your Big Day*
by Mindy Weiss with
Lisbeth Levine

Smith & Hawken:
THE GARDENERS' COMMUNITY
COOKBOOK
by Victoria Wise

acknowledgments

Be Thrifty has many contributors, and we are grateful to them all for their hard work and patience. Many thanks go to the individuals who shared their personal stories of making it through hard times. We'd also like to thank the experts answered our toughest questions about thrift: hairstylist Nick Arrojo; *This Old House* editor Alex Bandon; veterinarian Bernadine Cruz; State Farm spokesman Kip Diggs; Dr. Pamela Hops; Dr. Harry Lodge; college counselor Bill McClintick; and author Amity Shlaes. John C. Bogle generously gave us permission to reprint experts from his speech to the Greater Philadelphia Venture Group.

We are fortunate to have many frugal friends who became constant sources of inspiration. Our families, each in their own way, instilled in us a sense of thrift that made writing about it come naturally.

This project could not have happened without the creativity, guidance, and good humor of Savannah Ashour, an excellent editor. Our sincere appreciation goes to Susan Bolotin for her faith in us. *Be Thrifty* draws on many impressive books from the Workman library, all of which ultimately owe their existence to the vision of Peter Workman.

Also at Workman, Ian Gross was particularly helpful in guiding us through the morass of official paperwork. Beth Levy calmly steered the project through to its conclusion, and her grace under fire (along with her trove of thrifty instincts) was a true gift. In typesetting, Jarrod Dyer brought an impressive level of detail and care to a very complex layout. In the art department, David Matt and Janet Vicario directed the visuals, and Julie Duquet translated a design into a real, live, and very good-looking book. Thanks as well to Oleg Lyubner and Kristin Matthews for their efforts in promoting *Be Thrifty*.

The staff at Storey Publishing welcomed us in their offices and provided an enormous amount of help; thanks in particular go to Maribeth Casey. At Black Dog & Leventhal, Nathaniel Marunas graciously helped things along.

index

Note: Page numbers in *italic* refer to illustrations; page numbers in **bold** refer to charts.